Also by Ben Zion Bokser

PHARISAIC JUDAISM IN TRANSITION

THE LEGACY OF MAIMONIDES

THE WISDOM OF THE TALMUD

FROM THE WORLD OF THE CABBALAH

JUDAISM AND MODERN MAN

THE GIFT OF LIFE

JUDAISM: PROFILE OF A FAITH

edited and translated

THE WEEKDAY SABBATH AND FESTIVAL PRAYERBOOK

THE HIGH HOLY DAY PRAYERBOOK

Judaism and the Christian Predicament

Judaism and the Christian Predicament

by Ben Zion Bokser

with a Foreword by FREDERICK C. GRANT

ALFRED·A·KNOPF

1967 *New York*

THIS IS A BORZOI BOOK

PUBLISHED BY ALFRED A. KNOPF, INC.

First Edition

 Distributed by Random House, Inc. Published simultaneously in Toronto, Canada, by Random House of Canada Limited.

Library of Congress Catalog Card Number: 66-19370

Manufactured in the United States of America

Portions of Chapter iii originally appeared in slightly different form in *The Wisdom of the Talmud* by Ben Zion Bokser, and portions of Chapters vii and xiv originally appeared in *From the World of the Cabbalah* by Ben Zion Bokser. This material is reprinted here by permission of the Philosophical Library, Inc.

Foreword

This is a book that had to be written—it is fortunate that it was written by a capable scholar with sufficient breadth of mind and understanding to grasp the whole problem of Jewish-Christian relations. For Jews and Christians ought, surely, to be closely related in friendship and sympathy: Christianity is a revised and modified Judaism, not a rival, antagonistic religion. The popular idea, on the Christian side, that the "Jews" crucified Christ and persecuted his disciples, and were solely responsible for the tensions that developed in the early days and have lasted through the centuries—this widespread idea is mistaken, and has been responsible for endless hatred and crime. Dr. Bokser examines the evidence and, with careful documentation, shows how flimsy the charges against the Jews really are. He cites both ancient authorities and modern, and as many Christian scholars as Jewish.

These evidences have been cited here and there in journals and magazines and in sundry books. What Rabbi Bokser does is gather them all together, under a title whose challenge demands that they be read and weighed. Something must be done with these refutations of ancient lies. The difficulty in both Protestantism and Catholicism is that the idea of an authoritative, divinely inspired, infallible Scripture involves the acceptance of statements that seem to justify anti-Judaism; even the Old Testament is warped into agreement with far later theological views. In the best theological schools in America these facts have been known and recognized for two generations or more, but they have not reached the laity. The reason for this lag is that most clergymen and teachers consider it hopeless to stem a tide that has been running high for sixteen centuries: they are unwilling to question publicly the traditional biblicism of the churches, including the traditional interpretation of both Old Testament and New. Even the more liberal and better educated Christian leaders incline to accept the advice, "Take the Bible 'as is,' and do not get entangled in the endless problems of exegesis, not to say the negative views of 'higher criticism.' " Modern society lays a huge penalty on nonconformists and champions of minority views. In business, politics, education, even in religion, the young are not rewarded for their independence but for their acceptance of tradition and of recognized "organization" policies. The young man who wishes to get ahead must not challenge accepted views —or prejudices.

The recognition of strong traces of prejudice and misinterpretation in the text of the New Testament involves a degree of historical and literary criticism which to the orthodox and conservative seems dangerous; it also involves a familiar knowledge of ancient Jewish religious literature totally beyond the grasp of the average clergyman, let alone the average Bible reader or teacher. Moreover, for most Christians religion is not derived directly from the Bible as a whole, but from a system of theological ideas (the systems vary) which are independent of first-hand exegesis. If necessary, these are simply forced upon the scriptures in the effort to secure consistency or to safeguard major theological doctrines. The *natural* interpretation of many a New Testament text is set aside in favor of one more consistent with dogma—as Dr. Bokser points out in the case of the gospel narratives of Jesus' ancestry and birth. The impossible account of the "Jewish" trial of Jesus, and the legendary tale of the "curse" invoked upon themselves by the Jews in Matthew, are further instances. Coming across these narratives anywhere else in ancient literature, one would not hesitate to criticize and reject them. But the Christian who has pledged his loyalty to a theological system (understood as his "faith") can do no other than support the interpretation that has hitherto claimed to be consistent with the dogma. It is no wonder that most theologians are suspected of being "retained attorneys," as Emerson called them, whenever questions of exegesis arise. But the exegesis, the historical and literary criticism, should come *first*, and not the system of theology. It is strange but true: Christianity inherited its idea of a divinely inspired book from Judaism. But no one knew how far it would lead!

At long last the churches are awakening to another fact, namely that the young are more radical than they suspected—despite the ambitious conformists among them—and that the laity are not any longer charmed into silence by "vain repetition." The outstanding position taken by the Vatican Council, cribbed, cabined, and confined as its *language* of necessity had to be, under pressure from the conservatives (who demanded verbal agreement with the New Testament texts)—this remarkable avowal has gone out into all lands. The Church is at last awaking to the centuries of injustice which it has dealt the Jews, and it has mumbled a kind of confession, not very articulate but nevertheless a confession, of its responsibility, that is to say, its guilt. The Council, as Cardinal Cushing has said, is not over: it has "just begun." The mighty reversal of views, destined to carry the rest of Christendom with it, will in time, we trust, involve more than just a formal repudiation of anti-Semitism. It will also include a repudiation of impossible literalism and legalism in the interpretation of the Bible, or the refusal to interpret it at all. It will include the recognition that the early Christians were not historical scholars or profound exegetes or exact theologians, but very simple men and women who handed on, at first, a vivid tradition, much supplemented and revised as it was transmitted, and influenced by a variety of human motivations and prejudices—like all literature that ever existed. Someday the Bible will be loosed from its chains and will be understood in a natural and intelligent way. Then its real treasure, hitherto in "earthen vessels," will begin to be apparent—as the poet Coleridge said long ago. That treasure is its purely religious teachings. These must be separated from human prejudices and antagonisms and bigotries. Combined with these religious treasures are the moral teachings that underlie its whole structure, in both the Jewish and the Christian scriptures.

Among the books with a high and holy mission to fulfill these days, a mission of enlightenment, information, and awakening to the truth, is this noble work, *Judaism and the Christian Predicament*. Its author is a calm and careful scholar who marshals the evidence without beating drums; one who is as understanding of Christian views as of those cherished in his own Jewish faith; and who tells the age-old story with deliberation and persuasion. If only the right people will read it! Let us hope it may find a wide circulation, and then a careful weighing of its contents. Speaking as a Christian, I believe we simply cannot go on any longer without challenging the lies and rejecting the misinterpretations that have clung to our views of the Bible and to our unchanging religious tradition for many centuries. A radical pruning and cleansing is long overdue in our Christian vineyard.

FREDERICK C. GRANT

New York
Union Theological Seminary

Acknowledgments

The perceptive reader will recognize the views of many scholars, quoted and unquoted, which underlie my own thinking on the larger theme of Jewish-Christian relations. I wish it were possible for me to thank them by name for all that I have learnt from their work. It is a matter of deep regret to me especially that I cannot mention the names of all the scholars who commented on various aspects of this study, thereby helping me to gain a better perspective on the issues involved. I am indebted to each of them and this study owes much to their assistance, although I alone must bear responsibility for the views expressed in it.

I am grateful to Dr. Frederick C. Grant for contributing the foreword that is included in this study.

Rabbi Marvin S. Wiener, Director of the National Academy for Jewish Studies of the United Synagogue of America read the manuscript and gave me valuable advice on the treatment of the subject matter and on planning the scope of this work. Rabbi Solomon S. Bernards, National Director of the Department of Interreligious Cooperation of the Anti-Defamation League of B'nai B'rith placed at my disposal his erudition in the Jewish and the Christian traditions and his knowledge of the literature in these fields. His copious criticisms and suggestions were helpful in bringing this work to its final fruition.

Dr. Norman Schanin offered a number of criticisms which proved helpful in the organization of the material. Mr. A. G. Kraus read the manuscript and gave me numerous suggestions toward making the presentation more comprehensible and free of needless obfuscation. Mrs. Shirley Tendler typed the manuscript and rendered me various other technical assistance, and I feel a great sense of indebtedness for her kindness.

Dr. Abraham Berger of the New York Public Library and Mr. Angus Cameron and his associate Mrs. Ellen Fertig extended to me many kindnesses for which I am most grateful.

I am indebted to members of my family who shared in some of the burdens which this study involved. My wife extended to me continued encouragement to pursue this study and she counseled me on a number of problems in research and in the organization of the material. My daughter Miriam Ruth originally posed to me some of the questions to which this study is addressed. My son Baruch Micah assisted me with research, and his critical comments sharpened my perception of the issues under discussion.

Much of this work was done during a period of illness, and I feel grateful to Almighty God who kept me in life and sustained me in strength and enabled me to reach the completion of this work which has engaged my mind and my hands for a number of years.

To the memory of six million Jews and their fellow martyrs of other faiths who perished in the blaze lit by Nazism.

"And all the elders of the city nearest to the victim shall wash their hands . . . and they shall declare, 'Our hands did not shed this blood, nor did our eyes see it done. . . .' And you shall remove the stain of innocent blood from your midst, when you will do what is upright in the eyes of the Lord" (*Deuteronomy* 21:6, 7, 9).

Rabbi Meir was wont to say, How do we know that even a pagan, if he pursue the spiritual and ethical precepts of the Torah, is as precious in the sight of God as a High Priest in Israel? Because it is written (Leviticus 18:5): And you shall keep My statutes and Mine ordinances, which if a man do, he shall live by them. It does not say "which if Priests, Levites, Israelites," but rather "if a man *do, he shall live by them." From this it may be inferred that* any man, *even a pagan, if he pursue the spiritual and ethical precepts of the Torah, is as precious in the sight of God as a High Priest in Israel.*

THE TALMUD

Contents

Judaism and the Christian Predicament

Introduction

The problem of effecting a viable pattern of co-existence between Judaism and Christianity is only another instance of the need to establish a ground of freedom for multiple ideologies within the same society. The claim to a monopoly of truth ultimately inspires an attempt to suppress dissident thought as heresy. This in turn breeds tension, which often erupts into open conflict. Whatever truth there be in a given ideology is moreover corrupted when it becomes the center of a power struggle.

The adherents of an ideology, religious or political, will serve their own cause best by renouncing the claim to a monopoly of truth and entering fully into the ferment of ideas in a climate of freedom. For truth thrives in freedom and is stimulated by the challenge of competing truth. And there is no one household of faith on which God has limited the graces of His revelation. His light shines on all men, and every household of faith can become a shrine for His service.

The tensions which have existed between Judaism and Christianity through the long centuries of their confrontation have derived ultimately from Christianity's claim to be the only true religion, and its insistence that only through Christianity can man attain salvation. This claim implies a challenge to all non-Christian religions. But the Christian claim has been directed with special aggressiveness toward Jews. For Christianity has presented itself to the world as the heir of the Jewish people, the completion of ancient Judaism and its final perfection. The image which the Church has drawn of itself is that of the new Israel, the replacement of the Israel of old as God's chosen vehicle for the spiritualization of the human race. Christianity has claimed that the Jewish Scriptures, when properly understood, lead directly and inevitably to Christianity.

By the logic of this Christian doctrine the Jewish people should have disappeared as a distinct community; they should have been the first people to embrace the new revelation of Christianity. The refusal of Jews to act out the part assigned to them by Christianity, their insistence that Judaism remained alive and of undiminished validity became an exasperation to the Church and a source of continued irritation, which has been responsible for much of the bitterness that has characterized Jewish-Christian relations.

Christianity sought to deal with the challenge of Jewish survival through a threefold strategy. The Jewish refusal to accept Christianity was blamed on diabolical forces which had gained control over Jews and blinded them to the Christian truth. In addition the Jewish community was subjected to discriminatory legislation and persecution so that their lowly condition might be demonstrated as an expression of divine judgment, and thus a proof of their error and, by implication, proof of Christian truth. A third strategy, evangelization, was the attempt to missionize Jews away from their own faith and to induce them to enter the Church.

The present endeavor to build bridges of better understanding between Jews and Christians, which the Church has embraced with impressive earnestness, has much too often only limited goals; it seeks to counteract the hostility toward Jews as a social community. It has been much less concerned with cultivating respect for Judaism as a faith. Among the proponents of goodwill for Jews there are active advocates of missionizing the Jews toward the embracing of Christianity. A posture of goodwill toward the Jewish people is felt to offer more promise for success to the missionary. A true fraternity between the different religions of mankind depends on the recognition of the legitimacy of diverse paths to God. The tensions between Judaism and Christianity—and all other interreligious tensions—will dissolve when the validity of pluralism is accepted in the religious realm as it is in all other realms within a democratic society.

While the present effort to effect better understanding between Jews and Christians has by no means broken down the basic causes of tension between them, there has been on the part of many Christian leaders a confrontation of the problem which promises greater progress in the future. Those who believe in the ultimate emergence of a world order based on respect for the individual—the individual person and the individual community—will rejoice in this progress and turn it into the ground for a new advance.

The Jewish-Christian dialogue is not a modern invention. It has a long history behind it. There is a considerable literature of Jewish-Christian confrontation in the period of the early Church. Sometimes, as in the religious disputations of the Middle Ages, it was forced on Jews. Sometimes it was conducted through the printed word. Jews and Christians explored the issues between them in an extensive literature. It is the direct confrontation of Jewish and Christian leaders in a free discussion of their respective faiths which is characteristic of the most recent phase of Jewish-Christian relations.

The Jewish-Christian dialogue in its full ramification has involved three primary themes: the nature of the Jewish Scriptures, the nature of the rabbinic tradition, and the nature of the Christian experience. We shall enter into a detailed discussion of each of these themes in order to see the issues between the two faiths in their true context.

The Jewish Scriptures are shared ground between Judaism and Christianity. For Jews these Scriptures have a completeness which makes them the foundation on which Judaism rests. For Christians on the other hand the Jewish Scriptures are incomplete and presuppose a completion in the writings of the New Testament. The incompleteness of the Jewish Scriptures is asserted generally in one of two ways. Some Christian writers have maintained that the Jewish Scriptures teach an inferior religion, and that biblical faith does not reach its perfection until the writings of the New Testament.

Many Christians who have studied the contents of the two bodies of writings, especially under the influence of modern biblical scholarship, have acknowledged that this is false. Theodor Filthaut decried the tendency of preachers and catechists to praise the New Testament at the expense of the Old: "The Old Testament is more often presented as a religion of fear and trembling, whereas the New Testament is contrasted as the religion of love and joy. The same kind of misrepresentation and simplification occurs when the God of justice is contrasted with the God of grace, or the fear-inspiring king contrasted with the loving father. As a parallel to such contrasting concepts there is the confrontation of the Jews' outward and legalistic piety (to the letter) and the Christians' inner and 'truly heartfelt' piety. . . .There seems to be but one remedy for the dangerous effects of misrepresentations: unbiased reading of the scriptures of both the Old and the New Testaments." [1]

The incompleteness of the Jewish Scriptures has also been argued in another direction. It has been maintained that the Jewish Scriptures as written contain veiled truths and that when the veil is removed from these truths we find them proclaiming the doctrines of Christianity. The final logic of this position has been to deny that the Jewish Scriptures are really "Jewish" Scriptures. Christianity has claimed them for itself, as its Old Testament. As R. Travers Herford observed: "The Church solved this problem [of reconciling Christian teachings with the Jewish Scriptures] by . . . boldly declaring that Christians and no longer Jews were the true Israel, that the Scriptures belonged of right to the Christians and not to the Jews, and that Christians alone were competent to interpret them, that the real meaning of those Scriptures was a foreshadowing of Christ and the Church, while the Jewish

[1] "The Jews in Christian Religious Education," in Theodor Filthaut (ed.): *Israel in Christian Religious Instruction* (Notre Dame: University of Notre Dame Press; 1965), p. 14.

dispensation had been only a temporary order now definitely overthrown." [2]

Our study will indicate that the Hebrew Bible speaks with a distorted voice when it is constrained to conform to a sectarian blueprint. Its true literary eloquence and the cogency of its doctrine are impressively revealed when we allow it to speak without prior suppositions, when the sages, poets, and prophets who composed its documents are given a hearing for what they have to say in their own terms. The moral and spiritual riches of the Hebrew Bible can be possessed by those who are willing to listen to what it has to say. They are missed by those who approach it with a prejudgment as to its place in a dogmatic scheme which is extrinsic to itself.

Sister Alexa Suelzer, in her recent study *The Pentateuch*, a work which is published with the imprimatur of the Roman Catholic ecclesiastical authorities, has called attention to the hazards of turning the Hebrew Bible into a source of citations for religious apologetics: "Polemic needs of a later day (a day not yet ended) made of the Old Testament a rich quarry for the hewing of citations to fill dogmatic or apologetic needs. The use of Scripture in the formulation of theological theses can limit or distort a text if there is no regard for its context. . . . Utilizing the Old Testament solely as a repertory of proofs does not contribute to an understanding of the word of God. Therefore, the Christian approach to the Bible should be determined not by the needs of apologetics or dialectics but by a desire to enter into the vital, personal relationship God has established between man and himself, a record of which he has given us in the Bible." [3] This of course should also be the Jewish approach to the Bible. There is no other if we wish to confront the biblical word for what it has to teach us concerning man and his destiny.

The second theme to which the Jewish-Christian dialogue has historically addressed itself is the nature of the rabbinic tradition.

[2] *The Pharisees* (New York: The Macmillan Company; 1924), p. 222.

[3] Sr. Alexa Suelzer: *The Pentateuch* (New York: Herder and Herder; 1964), p. 14.

The rabbinic tradition is more accurately described as the Oral Torah, in contradistinction to the written Torah, which designates the writings of the Hebrew Bible. The nature of the Oral Torah is that of a supplement to the Hebrew Bible; it arose in Judaism to implement its understanding of biblical life and thought. Its creative epoch began prior to the appearance of Jesus and continued during the centuries when Christian doctrine was moving toward crystallization. The Oral Torah is thus by its very being a denial that the Hebrew Bible moved naturally and inevitably toward one fulfillment, that of Christianity. It exemplifies another path of development—the Jewish path. The presence of another path, especially since this path depends on the open rather than the veiled meaning of the Hebrew Bible, constitutes a challenge to Christianity.

The Oral Torah is set forth in a vast literature embracing commentaries on the Bible known as the Midrashim, a compendium of law known as the Mishnah, and a supplement to this compendium known as the Tosefta. Copious discussions of the material in the above sources, enriched by original subject matter, appear in a work known as the Gemara. The Gemara is presented in a form of a commentary on the Mishnah, and together with the Mishnah comprises what is called the Talmud.

The Oral Torah which constitutes the rabbinic tradition is a rich treasury of ethics, law, theology, and folk wisdom interspersed with historical and scientific notes, personal anecdotes, homilies, and parables. Many of the problems of social ethics with which modern man is struggling are brilliantly illuminated by rabbinic discussions. The Oral Torah offers cogent precedent for those struggling to reconcile the claims of religious authority and personal freedom. Some of the most intimate questions concerning the meaning of the human odyssey find suggestive and pertinent answers in various teachings of the Oral Torah. But this literature has in effect been a closed book for the non-Jewish world.

The conventional attitude of Christian teachers toward the Oral Torah was to ignore it. They recognized only one source of Judaism, the Bible, and this was designated by them as the Old Testament, a prelude, in other words, to Christianity. When they did concern themselves with it they generally sought to belittle it. The most common charge leveled against rabbinic literature is that it is narrow and unduly centered on the externals of the religious life; the over-all term of denigration one generally finds in Christian sources concerning this literature is the epithet of "legalism."

As we have noted, the charge of legalism has sometimes been leveled at the Hebrew Bible itself. But if Christians were inhibited in the disparagement of the Hebrew Bible because it was after all part of the Christian canon of Scriptures, no such inhibition existed to deter the disparagement of the Oral Torah, which was the distinctive doctrinal source of Judaism. And Christian writings often abound in all kinds of derogatory characterization of rabbinic Judaism, all of it generally deriving from the one over-all complaint that the Rabbis taught a religion which was narrow and centered on the externalities of rules and precepts, that it was a system of legalism rather than a faith which speaks to the heart of man. As Adolf Exeler observed: "A mere glance at the commentaries used in Bible instruction reveals the tendency to describe Judaism in the darkest possible background as a most effective contrast for the radiant figure of Jesus. For the sake of accentuating Jesus, the temptation is to attribute all kinds of evils to the Jews . . . as if most Jews had been superficial formalists or malevolent hypocrites." [4]

More recently a number of Christian scholars have recognized the importance of rabbinic literature and their studies have helped Christians as well as Jews to appreciate the great spiritual riches of the Oral Torah. They have helped to dispel the charges of "legalism" and narrowness leveled against the Judaism of the post-biblical period.

Here is the testimony of a noted Christian student of rabbinic literature, R. Travers Herford: "As to this alleged hardening and sterilizing of religion, under the tyranny of the 'Law' (Christian writers insist on rendering 'Torah' by 'Law'; this single mistranslation of the Hebrew word meaning 'teaching' is actually the source of the innumerable condemnations of Judaism as a 'legalistic' religion): if the effect of the 'Law' was to kill religion how

[4] "Our Bible Instruction and Judaism," in T. Filthaut (ed.): *Israel in Christian Religious Instruction*, p. 57.

explain the full vigor of the synagogue in the time of Jesus? . . . How explain that it was the custom of Jesus himself to go there on the Sabbath? . . . If the men of the synagogue were cold legalists would they have included the Psalms in their services to be a standing rebuke to their hollow pretensions of piety? The truth is that the men of the synagogue and the Pharisees who directed its activities included the Psalms because they loved them and felt . . . their incomparable power as devotional song. But admitting this, is it still not true that the Pharisaic system included the Halachah, and was this not a rigid law binding the entire community to precise, prescribed and mechanical observance? On the contrary, it can be stated categorically, the Halachah always emphasized the *intention* behind the act, which was to perform the will of God, and never its merely perfunctory performance."[5]

Herford's summation is a good characterization of rabbinic Judaism. But it will remain only assertion unless one examines the actual pronouncements of the Rabbis and recognizes their bent of mind and the goals toward which they directed their efforts. There is ultimately no way to answer the distortions of the Oral Torah which abound in Christian writings except to engage in a detailed study of the nature of the Oral Torah and its vast literary sources. This remains a vital necessity for those who want to understand Judaism. It was the Judaism of the Rabbis which formed the faith into which Jesus and his disciples were born. A better understanding of rabbinic Judaism should thus also be of great significance for those seeking to understand Christianity.

The Jewish-Christian dialogue also involves a discussion of what we may call the Christian experience. The claims concerning the passion of Jesus, of his divine nature, of the atoning efficacy of his death on the cross, and of the indispensability of faith in his messiahship as a means of salvation are elements in the cleavage between the Jewish and Christian ideologies. Insofar as Christianity insists that these doctrines are compatible with, nay, are an inescapable inference from, the teachings of the Jewish Scriptures, Judaism is under the necessity of entering its dissenting position. The Christian experience, too, at least as conventionally

[5] R. T. Herford: *The Truth About the Pharisees* (New York: The Menorah Press; 1925), pp. 30–1.

articulated, has turned the Jew into an ally of the Satanic forces which conspired to destroy Jesus and continue to obstruct the full triumph of the Gospel in the world. This is expressed in the conventional Christian imputation of guilt to the Jews for the crucifixion of Jesus, from which have proliferated various corollary teachings in disparagement of Jews and Judaism. Here the Jew is involved in an appeal to history which has established the various accusations against Jews as slander and malignity.

An examination of the ground which has been at issue between Judaism and Christianity makes melancholy reading. But the scene shifts as we move toward the modern period. For while the old battle lines remain in many instances intact, there has occurred a perceptible change. The most significant indication of this change is that the defense of Judaism against derogation finds some of its most eloquent spokesmen in the Christian community itself. Scholars of the Old and New Testament, theologians, and historians have broken with the conventional dogmatic system to study the history of these two faiths without sectarian prejudgment. The views of these men have not always effected a change in the official thought of their respective church bodies, but their voices are being heard in every Christian denomination and we have reason to expect that the future will be better than what the past has been.

One of the most moving pleas for a new approach in interfaith relations was recently made by the Father General of the Society of Jesus, the Very Rev. Pedro Arrupe. Speaking before an ecumenical gathering which included Protestant as well as Jewish leaders, Father Arrupe acknowledged contritely the part played by members of the Jesuit order in the past in escalating religious tensions to "formidable proportions." He invited Jewish participation in a continuing interfaith dialogue, blaming the religious tensions of the past on a narrow religiosity: "An exaggerated sense of loyalty to one's own Church or confession at the expense of charity; a too rigid concept of the truth, where personal opinions were sometimes easily confused with divine revelation; a misguided zeal for propagating the Gospel, which sometimes made use of means not always in accord with that Gospel; an ignorance of the true thought of others or a facile misjudging of motives; a too easy yielding to nationalistic or partisan prejudices—these are the common burdens we all must bear from the past." [6]

He added that Jesuits would now be encouraged to play a leading part in the ecumenical movement, to foster better understanding in interfaith relations.

Father Arrupe's pronouncement is a timely reminder to men of goodwill in every faith community to re-examine their convictions. Religion offers itself to the world as the solution to man's moral problem, as the answer to the evils which flow from hate and malice. But is not religion itself part of man's problem, if it turns out that piety is the breeding ground of prejudice, that religion is a force for hate rather than of love in human relations? Those who dispense the therapy of religion for the healing of our sick world must make sure that the medicine they offer will indeed help the patient and not aggravate his ailment.

Father Arrupe's mission will not be an easy one, because the weight of tradition will resist the call for change. The extent of this resistance is well illustrated in the reported failure of a recent effort to modify the portrayal of the Jews in the Oberammergau Passion Play.[7] This play is a great artistic spectacle re-enacting the events of the crucifixion, whose viewers are led to a reverent reaffirmation of Christian piety. Its portrayal of the Jews, however, is wholly negative, depicting them as "a fiendish, bloodthirsty people, who avidly seek the death of Jesus." The director of this play, troubled because this portrayal of the Jews contradicts the spirit of the Vatican II declaration which decries anti-Semitism as an offense to truth and to Christian morality, proposed that this text be modified. His proposal was at first accepted but eventually the decision was reached to continue the old text of the play unchanged, whereupon he resigned in protest. The incident illustrates the difficulty the Church will have in re-educating the Christian public to eliminate these distortions. Long after the truth has become known people will be content to ignore it, and prefer clinging to old myths which are deeply rooted in their folk traditions.

[6] *The New York Times*, April 19, 1966, p. 84.
[7] *The New York Times*, October 16, 1966, p. 52.

Our opening chapter describes the effort in contemporary Christendom to disavow anti-Semitism and to foster friendship for the Jewish people, but it notes the limited results obtained because of a failure to deal with the doctrinal aspects of Jewish-Christian tensions. Since the Hebrew Bible is the source from which Judaism as well as Christianity trace their development, our study continues with the endeavor to delineate the literary and historical context within which the biblical records must be understood and interpreted. From this we proceed to describe the line of development from biblical Judaism to classic Judaism. This involves an understanding of what is technically known as the Oral Torah, and the literary documents in which it is set forth: the Midrash, the Mishnah and the Tosefta, and the Gemara. This section of our work is summed up in a chapter entitled "The Bible in Judaism."

The study of the development from the Hebrew Bible to Christianity begins with an attempt to sketch what the meager historical sources permit us to know about Jesus in the setting of his own time, and about the crucifixion. This is followed by a study of the theology evolved in Christianity to account for the life and death of Jesus, and the interpretive bridge fashioned by Christian teachers to reconcile this theology with the teachings of the Hebrew Bible. This section of our work is summed up in the chapter entitled "The Bible in Christianity." The historical and contemporary interrelations of Judaism and Christianity are discussed in a final chapter, "Between Judaism and Christianity."

Chapter I
The Christian Predicament

An American Protestant scholar recently declared: "The Church in the past has misused and continues to misuse the seemingly hard statements of the New Testament concerning the Jews. Anti-Semitism has very deeply entered into the life and teaching of Christianity. In view of the hundreds of years of persecution and suffering culminating in the horror of two decades ago, we can only deplore and disavow whatever might have been done in the past that has promoted, contributed to, and prolonged the hatred of the Jews."[1]

Like all human aberrations, anti-Semitism has been with us for a long time. It is paradoxical that one of the components in its unholy brew is Christian teaching. The primary offense of the Jews to Christianity was their refusal to acknowledge Jesus as the messiah who offered the one and only door to human salvation. The Christian retort to this offense, first formulated in the New Testament, was a proliferating invective of mounting bitterness. Jews were accused of being blind, unspiritual, hypocritical, and under the spell of the devil. Because of the involvement of some Jews in the events of the crucifixion, the entire Jewish people as a

[1] James J. Michael: "Jesus in Jewish-Lutheran Dialogue," *The American Lutheran*, XLVIII: 7 (July 1965), 13.

corporate and historical entity was charged with the crime of "deicide" (literally the murder of the deity and here referring to Jesus). These charges and accusations became a vital component in the anti-Semitic virus which has continued to afflict the world throughout the centuries.

Modern Christianity has witnessed a change in the conventional Christian image of the Jew. In Protestant and Catholic circles there have been marked efforts to renounce anti-Semitism and to call for good relations with the Jewish commnuity. Numerous pronouncements toward these ends have been made by various Christian bodies, and various projects have been launched in the fields of education and community relations to build bridges of understanding between Jews and Christians. In part these developments have been an influence of the democratic process in this country. But they received fresh impetus from the Nazi holocaust, which exposed Christianity's failure to save man from lapsing into bestiality. Indeed, the tragic reality is that the antipathy toward Jews long fostered by Christian teaching had in fact helped to create a climate that was receptive to the Nazi campaign against Jewry.

The most dramatic of these actions within Protestantism was the convocation of the Lutheran World Federation's International Consultation on the Church and the Jewish People at Lagumkloster, Denmark, April 26 to May 2, 1964. The statement which issued from this conference abounds with reiterations of friendship for the Jewish people. Among other things this statement declares:

> Anti-Semitism is an estrangement of man from his fellow-men. As such it stems from human prejudice and is a denial of the dignity and equality of men. But anti-Semitism is principally a denial of the image of God in the Jew; it represents a demonic form of rebellion against the God of Abraham, Isaac, and Jacob; and a rejection of Jesus the Jew, directed upon his people. Christian anti-Semitism is spiritual suicide. This phenomenon presents a unique question to the Christian church, especially in the light of the long terrible history of Christian culpability for anti-Semitism. No Christian can exempt himself

from involvment in this guilt. As Lutherans, we confess our own peculiar guilt, and we lament with shame the responsibility which our Church and her people bear for this sin. We can only ask God's pardon and that of the Jewish people. . . . At the same time, we must pledge ourselves to work in concert with others at practical measures for overcoming manifestations of this evil within and without the Church and for reconciling Christians with Jews."[2]

The action of the Catholic Church, speaking through the Vatican Ecumenical Council, in denunciation of anti-Semitism, the removal of the charge of deicide against Jews, and the call for the cultivation of good human relations between the Jewish-Christian communities was one of the dramatic moments in the eventful proceedings of this august body of Roman Catholicism. The Vatican statement that was originally adopted by the Ecumenical Council, declared in part:

> This synod, in her rejection of injustice of whatever kind and wherever inflicted upon men . . . deplores, indeed condemns, hatred and persecution of Jews, whether they arose in former or in our own days. May, then, all see to it that in their catechetical work or in their preaching of the word of God they do not teach anything that could give rise to hatred or contempt of Jews in the hearts of Christians. May they never present the Jewish people as one rejected, cursed, or guilty of deicide. All that happened to Christ in His passion cannot be attributed to the whole people then alive, much less to those of today. Besides the Church held and holds that Christ underwent His passion and death freely, because of the sins of all men and out of infinite love. . . . Thus, any theory or practice that . . . discriminates between man and man or people and people . . . is shown to be without foundation. All men, therefore, but especially Christians, must refrain from discrimination against, or harassment of others because of their race, color, creed or walk of life. . . .

The statement adopted by the Council was revised administra-

[2] *The National Lutheran* (November 1964), p. 19.

tively by the Church authorities and the new version was ratified by the Council at its session on October 15, 1965, and then promulgated by the Pope on October 28, 1865. The new version was diluted in spirit and verbiage, but the substance remained generally the same. It deleted the condemnation of hatred of the Jews, using instead the milder term "decries": "Furthermore in her rejection of every persecution against any man, the Church, mindful of the patrimony she shares with the Jews, and moved not by political reasons but by the Gospel's spiritual love, decries hatred, persecutions, displays of anti-Semitism directed against Jews at any time and by anyone." It deleted the renunciation of the charge that the Jews were "deicides." The original draft read: "May they never present the Jewish people as one rejected, cursed, or guilty of deicide." The final version reads: "Although the Church is the new people of God, the Jews should not be presented as rejected or accursed by God, as if this followed from the Holy Scriptures." It restates the charge that "the Jewish authorities and those who followed their lead pressed for the death of Christ," but then concludes, "still, what happened in His passion cannot be charged against all Jews, without distinction, then alive, nor against the Jews of today."

How widely has the new development pervaded the Church and to what extent do its sponsors recognize that the historic roots of Christian anti-Semitism go back to basic teachings of the New Testament? How resolute are Church leaders in really trying to uproot anti-Semitic elements in the teachings of Christianity?

Religion is a world where tradition holds great sway. The change in the attitude of the Church toward Jews faces grave obstacles that cannot be readily overcome. Christian conservatives are sensitive to the far-reaching doctrinal implications which any move to revise the conventional Christian attitude toward the Jews would involve. And they are vocally resisting the revision in defense of doctrinal orthodoxy. After the Ecumenical Council adopted the original draft of its document calling for a revision in attitude toward Jews, a conservative minority continued to agitate for a rejection or at least a dilution of the pronouncement. A spokesman of the conservative faction, Biship Luigi Mario Carli of Segni, Italy, wrote a ringing reaffirmation of the old position: "I consider it legitimate to affirm that the entire Jewish people at the time of Christ was responsible for deicide, although only their leaders and a portion of their followers materially committed the crime. . . . In this sense, and according to biblical mentality, Judaism after the time of Jesus is objectively participating in the responsibility for deicide by the measure in which this Judaism constitutes the free and voluntary continuation of the Judaism of those times." [3]

James Daane represents a like reaction in Protestantism. In an essay entitled "The Anatomy of Anti-Semitism," which appeared originally in *Christianity Today*, he declared: "According to the New Testament records, Jews desired, plotted, and promoted the execution of Jesus (Matthew 27:1). No rewriting of history by those interested in freeing the Jews from responsibility for the crucifixion . . . dispels these claims of the New Testament historical record"; and it is the entire Jewish people, as a corporate and historical entity, according to Daane, who bear the responsibility for the crucifixion. The "degenerate character of the Jews' spirituality is revealed precisely by their rejection and crucifixion of Christ"; as a result of their offense in the rejection of "the crucified and living Christ" and by their general rejection of the Gospel, the Jews are rejected and live under a curse, and their election has been transferred to Gentiles. And "the Christian Church believes that Scripture affords sufficient grounds for regarding the destruction of Jerusalem as an act of divine judgment." Jewish destiny follows the divine pattern of rejection and retribution, and a change in Jewish destiny "can only occur in the Church where both Jew and Gentile find their unity in Christ." [4] At the same time Daane denounces anti-Jewish feelings on the part of Christians with the statement: "Christians are not God. God may curse; they may not. . . . God alone may punish the Jews for their rejection of the crucified and resurrected Christ; the Church may not. God may punish his enemies; the Church

[3] Quoted in *The Christian Century* (May 5, 1965), p. 571.

[4] James Daane: *The Anatomy of Anti-Semitism and Other Essays on Religion and Race* (Grand Rapids, Mich.: Wm. B. Erdman Publishing Co., 1965), pp. 21, 22, 25, 31, 32, 35, 36.

may only love its enemies and pray for them."[5] Daane regards himself as a foe of anti-Semitism because he believes that the degradation of the Jewish people is not irretrievable. He cherishes the faith that someday they will regain their exalted position by joining the Church!

Another force agitating against the original declaration of the Ecumenical Council on the Jews were the churches in Arab countries. The Arab hostility to the State of Israel has spilled over into a hostility against Jews. Spurred on by this hostility Arab churchmen, Catholic and non-Catholic alike, have opposed any action that would reduce anti-Jewish prejudice, even if such action be dictated by truth and morality. The Council of the Greek Orthodox community in Damascus issued a manifesto condemning "the decision taken by the Vatican Council to delcare the Jews innocent of the blood of Christ, because it is contrary to the sacred Scriptures in which Christians have always believed." The Jacobite Patriarch Ignatius III Yacub expressed amazement that Pope Paul VI should lend himself to clearing Jews of guilt for the crucifixion, declaring: "It is a dogma of the church that the guilt of the crucifixion of Christ must fall upon the Jewish people until the end of the world."[6]

Even Christian liberals who advocate revision often reveal various levels of insensitivity to the issues involved. The very idiom of the Church is saturated with anti-Jewish allusions. The word "Pharisee" remains a linguistic symbol of all that is narrow and unspiritual. The very effort to present Jesus as an advocate of moral values invites painting his adversaries as corrupt and decadent. Jesus is often made relevant to our day by equating the evils of our time with the civilization against which he rebelled, and for the sake of concreteness that civilization is identified with the Jewish people.

This is well illustrated by Lloyd C. Douglas who, after twenty-five years in the ministry, became the author of such popular novels as *Magnificent Obsession*, *Green Light*, *The Robe*, and *The Big Fisherman*. Douglas is an adherent of Christian liberalism and has openly disclaimed the belief in the Christian doctrine that

[5] Ibid., p. 30.
[6] Cited in *Herder Correspondence* (March 1965), p. 81.

Jesus is the son of God or that his death was a necessary sacrifice to atone for the sins of humanity. He is sensitive to the issues of social and racial justice and he has fought the Ku Klux Klan; yet this is how he recapitulated the story of the crucifixion: "When Jesus of Nazareth went to his death, it was at the instance of and the indictment of the established, proud and haughty, ivy-covered, smug and self-sufficient, walled and moated religion of the most religious people on the earth." [7] Douglas was not writing as a historian but as a preacher, and his primary concern was to attack the smugness of the contemporary Christian establishment. His allusion to the Jews were rhetorical, intended only to produce an effect. But beyond the effect of shaking the complacency of those whom he addressed such rhetoric was also bound to have as its side effect the subtle confirmation of prejudice, the degradation of the Jewish religion in the time of Jesus and, by implication, the degradation of those who have persisted in remaining faithful to that religion.

Recent development in Christian theology whose most radical position is summed up in the "death of God" concept reveals the same insensitivity. Jesus is presented as a spiritual reformer who fought against the religious decadence of Judaism in his time. The rejection of Jesus as the messiah by his own people is attributed to their pride, which made them insensitive to God. One cannot accuse these men of wanting to foster hostility for Jews, but their writings continue and thereby confirm and reinforce the conventional Christian image of the Jew as the adherent of a faith which lacks inwardness and which demands rigid conformity to a narrow legalism. There are various evils in conventional Christianity against which this school of radical churchmen are in rebellion, but the defamation of Jews and Judaism is not one of them.[8]

The events of the first century cannot with any justice be made to imply culpability for those who had no share in them.

[7] Lloyd C. Douglas: *The Living Faith* (Boston: Houghton Mifflin; 1955), pp. 86, 90, 65.

[8] See John A. T. Robinson: *Honest to God* (Philadelphia: The Westminster Press; 1963), pp. 116 ff.; David L. Edwards (ed.): *Honest to God Debate* (Philadelphia: The Westminster Press; 1963), p. 210; Harvey Cox: *The Secular City* (New York: The Macmillan Company; 1966), pp. 47, 112, 153, 154, 216.

The vast numbers of Jews in Palestine and those in the Diaspora were in no way involved in the crucifixion. Certainly the generations yet unborn while the crucifixion was enacted cannot be implicated. Responsibility for an act rests solely on those who share in its performance. The doctrines of corporate or inherited guilt are repugnant to our sense of justice. But when soberly examined, the facts show unmistakably that the primary responsibility for the crucifixion lay with the Roman authorities, not with the Jews.

The Jews in the time of Jesus were a subject people, enslaved by Roman power, as we shall have occasion to note later on. The Roman occupation was maintained ruthlessly and every unrest that seemed to threaten the established order was suppressed mercilessly, usually by crucifixion. One Roman procurator, Florus (64–66), crucified some thirty-six hundred people, including women and children, in one outburst of fury. The procurator who presided over the Roman administration in the time of Jesus, Pontius Pilate, was one of the most cruel and cynical to govern the Judean province. The Jewish High Priest was a Roman appointee whose major responsibility was to collaborate with the Romans in maintaining law and order. Even the robes of his office were kept in Roman custody and were given him only when he officiated at Temple ceremonies, as a reminder that the ultimate center of power was with the Roman authorities. The Jewish people at that time enjoyed no independent juridical initiative. When a Jewish official was allowed a zone of autonomous action he remained no more than a front for the Roman power structure. The sign attached to the body of the crucified Jesus, "King of the Jews," indicated he was crucified for a political offense, as were thousands of other Jews in those troubled times. The Jews were not supposed to have any other king but Caesar.

The Gospels were written after the Church had resigned itself to the Jewish rejection of Christianity and had turned to seek its converts among the Roman pagans. It seemed awkward to missionize the Romans to a faith whose central figure was executed by a Roman procurator. The story was therefore subtly reshaped to minimize the Roman involvement and center the blame on the Jews. Indeed, ever since Constantine the Church was part of the Roman establishment. It could not have achieved this status if at its heart there were a judgment of censure against Roman power. As Kristar Stendahl has summed it up: "There is increasing evidence that the role of Pontius Pilate was considerably greater in the execution of Jesus than the tradition and even the gospels lead us to think. The precise role of the Jewish leaders we cannot assess. . . . The crucifixion—a Roman execution—speaks its clear language, indicating that Jesus must have appeared sufficiently messianic, not only in a purely spiritual sense, to constitute a threat to the political order according to Roman standards. At this very point we can discern . . . how tensions between Judaism and Christianity have affected the writings of history. Already in the gospels two tendencies are at work. The role of the Roman official, Pilate, is minimized—it was not easy in the Empire to have a founder who was crucified by a Roman procurator; and the 'no' of the Jews was the theological basis on which Paul and other missionaries claimed the right to bring the Gospel to the gentiles. . . . Under the pressure of these two tendencies, one political and one theological, the exact events of history have been lost as to the interplay between the members of the Sanhedrin and Pontius Pilate. But it is reasonable to see the latter as the key figure. . . ."[9]

Alfred Loisy has written categorically: "The crucifixion of Jesus is explicable on one ground only: he was sentenced to death and executed by the Roman authority as a sower of sedition against itself, and simply so. The efforts of the traditional legend have been concentrated on transferring responsibility for his death to the Jews, and on doing this in such a way as to make it appear that the death sentence was extorted from Pilate, or imposed upon him, while he, for his part, acknowledged the perfect innocence of the accused. . . . Historically the case of Jesus is intelligible only if we admit from the outset that he was sentenced to death by Pilate alone, acting as representative of Roman authority. Need we repeat once more that our texts are in no way concerned with history in the strict sense of the term? Their object is catechetical, and, in a minor degree, apologetic . . ."[1]

[9] "Judaism and Christianity: Then and Now," in *The Harvard Divinity Bulletin* (October 1963), pp. 4 ff.

[1] A. Loisy: *The Origins of the New Testament* (London: George Allen and Unwin; 1950), pp. 103 ff.

The persecution of the disciples of Jesus, which has likewise been blamed on the Jews, when analyzed critically shows the same pattern. The instigator in every instance is the priestly oligarchy which shared power with the Roman occupation authorities. When Stephen was arrested, it was the High Priest who conducted the interrogation (Acts 7:1). James the brother of Jesus was tried and executed by the instigation of the Sadducean High Priest Ananus. The action aroused "those who seemed the most equitable and such as were most uneasy at the breach of the laws," as Josephus describes them, and they protested to the Roman procurator Albinus. The High Priest received a reprimand and eventually was removed from his office. Josephus does not identify those who protested the action of the High Priest, but his characterization best fits the Pharisees (*Antiquities* XX 9:1). Paul's trial was also before the "chief priests and all their council," at which we are told "the chief captain and soldiers were present" (Acts 22:30, 23:10). The trial of Peter and John is especially helpful in placing these events in proper perspective. Those pressing for action against the two apostles are the High Priest and the Sadducees (Acts 4:1, 5:17). Their release was secured by "a Pharisee in the council named Gamaliel, a teacher of the law, held in honor by all the people" (Acts 6:34). As we shall have occasion to see later on, the council (Greek *synedrion* from which derives the word *sanhedrin*) that acted with the High Priest was a political body distinct from the religious Sanhedrin which remained under the control of the Pharisees.

The charges levelled against these men are not clearly political. In some instances they are accused of subverting the laws and customs of their people, or of agitating against the Temple and the cult of Temple worship. But there was no sharp delineation between the purely religious and the political in a social structure such as the Romans fashioned in Judea. The Temple, for instance, was the apex of the existing order and it was under the protection of the Roman authorities. Any disturbance to the status quo was a threat to civil peace and it was put down mercilessly by the Romans and those who collaborated with them in the administration of the country.

The large meaning of the crucifixion has been well characterized by the noted historian of this period, Professor Solomon Zeitlin: "No fair-minded student of contemporaneous affairs would hold the Norwegian people responsible for the murder of patriots by Quisling who rules under the protection of his German overlord. No impartially minded judge today would blame the Czech nation for the killing of their own patriots by the Germans with the help of the puppet government of Hacha, so-called president of the Czech Protectorate. So, the facts and realities of history exculpate the Jewish people from the burden of guilt for the crucifixion of Jesus, for they were bowed beneath the yoke of Rome, ruled by evil procurators who held power of life and death over them, and gave protection to Jewish Quislings—the High Priests—who served their and Rome's purposes.

"Indeed, even upon Pilate alone the entire blame for the crucifixion of Jesus cannot be set. Men are oft-times the victims of their own systems. Inherent in the very nature of imperialism are evil forces that distort men's natures, that give rise to cruelties and terrorisms, that compel men to degrade and use other men to nefarious ends. The system of Roman imperialism and the destruction of small nations inevitably brought about their Pilates, their Quislings, and their crucified victims. As long as imperialism exists, there are bound to be traitors and betrayers who will help the conqueror to destroy those men who are working and sacrificing for the liberty of their countries. The death of Jesus at the hands of Pontius Pilate was but another example of how victim and oppressor were equally the resultants and creatures of a universal evil, imperialism." [2]

If Rome were presented as the adversary responsible for the death of Jesus, the logic of Christian rhetoric would have won sympathy for the Jews who bore the oppression, of which the crucifixion of Jesus was only one episode among many. In a larger sense, the logic of that rhetoric would have directed itself against imperialism, against the oppression of small nations by the big powers, against the tyranny of the state. The Church has not been ready for this. It has therefore been easier to make Jews the target, utilizing old prejudices, confirming those prejudices through

[2] *Who Crucified Jesus?* (New York and London: Harper & Brothers, 1947), p. 211.

reiteration, and thereby intensifying them with fresh emotional momentum.

This trap of Christian rhetoric has affected even Pope Paul VI. The present pontiff is no friend of bigotry. One remembers his 1964 trip, as a person of goodwill, to Israel, where he spoke warmly of the Jewish people. The declaration of the Ecumenical Council on the Jews enjoyed his sponsorship and it would not have been adopted without his blessing. The final draft of this declaration states explicitly that "what happened to Christ in His passion cannot be attributed to all Jews, then alive, nor to the Jews of to-day." Nevertheless, Pope Paul, speaking at a Passion Sunday Lenten service was quoted as having said the following: "A grave and sad page [is the Gospel account of the crucifixion] because it narrates the conflict between Jesus and the Hebrew People, a people predestined to await the messiah but who, just at the right moment, not only did not recognize Him but fought Him, abused Him and finally killed Him." [3] The dismay caused by the Pope's words brought reassurance from Vatican sources that Pope Paul VI had intended no offense to the Jewish people, that his words were merely "a pastoral reference to scriptural texts, without any significance for the declaration." [4] He spoke to a lay public and he used a familiar idiom rather than a language of doctrinal precision. Words long on the lips of people often continue to flow even when the basic assumptions on which they rest have been abandoned. But words effect evil as well as good, whether or not they are uttered with conscious and deliberate motivation. The road to heaven cannot be built with good intentions alone. If the Church really is to free itself of centuries of anti-Jewish expressions, it will have to wage an earnest and relentless struggle to coin a new idiom to use when speaking of the Jews and of their relations to the events on which basic Christian doctrine is founded.

If the Jews were not to be blamed for the offense of deicide, then the blame continued over the centuries was a grave offense that resulted in incalculable harm. It fed the hatred of Jews, which erupted finally in violence, whose climax was reached in

[3] *The New York Times,* April 5, 1965, p. 33.
[4] *The New York Times,* April 25, 1965, p. 16.

"the final solution" of the Jewish question by the Nazis. By the lurid light of Auschwitz, it is distressing to see how lightly many Christians deal with the question.

One looks in vain for any contrition in the statement on the Jews adopted by the Ecumenical Council. There is no indication of it. If the charge of deicide was wrongly made, then those who made it were guilty of a grievous slander. One cannot bring back to life those who died in the crematoria of Europe and in all the pogroms throughout the centuries that were a rehearsal for those crematoria. But it is possible to express remorse, and one is shocked at its absence. As A. Roy Eckardt phrased it: "In vain does one search the draft of Vatican II for even the slightest sign of Christian contrition, for even a single word of recognition that the Church of Jesus Christ has been a knowing and willing participant in the centuries-long nightmare of anti-Semitism. Could there be a more damning judgment upon the church of our century than this one—that not until after the day of Auschwitz did Christians see fit to fabricate a correction of the record?" [5]

Contemporary Christian leaders have made many impressive gestures of friendship toward the Jewish people, but on closer examination they often remain evangelical in motivation. Christian leaders have revived Luther's theory that harshness had repelled Jews and a kindly approach might win them over. The evil of anti-Semitism is generally dealt with by the missionary arm of the Church, not by its commissions which deal with the problems of the social order. Gabriel Herbert of the Society of Sacred Mission, Kelham, England, a well-known writer on Catholic doctrine, says: "The tragedy is that centuries of persecution of Jews by Christians and the anti-Semitism which is still alive today have made it impossible for any but a tiny minority of Jews to accept the Christian answer, that the Old Testament found its fulfillment in Jesus the Messiah. Here is one of the major sins of the Christian Church." [6]

Philip A. Johnson of the National Lutheran Council expresses essentially the same position: "Why aren't Jews interested in

[5] *The Journal of Bible and Religion*, XXXIII:2 (April 1965), 122.

[6] Gabriel Herbert: *The Old Testament from Within* (London: Oxford University Press; 1962), p. 123.

Christian churches? This a question which has puzzled many sincere Christians whose well-intentioned efforts to approach Jews in the interest of Christian faith or membership in the Church have been notably unsuccessful. . . . The truth is that when a Christian and a Jew approach each other in religious matters, 2000 years of history, most of it unpleasant and all too much of it barbaric, are looking over their shoulders. . . . Is it any wonder in the light of this history that it is somewhat difficult to convince Jews of the moral superiority of Christianity or the good faith of Christians, both of which we so uncritically assume?" [7]

Writing in the same issue of *The National Lutheran*, Thomas Basich defines the goals which as a Christian he seeks to accomplish through the dialogue with Jews: "The Christian brings to the dialogue with the Jew the hope that all men should acknowledge Jesus Christ as God, Savior, Lord. . . . Implicit in what we have been saying is the fact that the Christian is bound to obey the missionary command of his Lord. Witness is not optional. To fail either to love in the name of Christ or to speak in the name of Christ is to betray Christ." [8]

The statement which issued from the Logumkloster conference of the Lutheran World Federation calls for a relentless struggle to purge every phase of Church life of anti-Semitism, professing abiding friendship for the Jewish people. But it also declares: "Thus the Church testifies that, by the fulfillment of the promises in Jesus the Messiah and by His acceptance of but a part of the Jews, a division has arisen which has placed the 'old' Israel outside the 'new.' This division will be healed when 'all Israel' (Romans 11:26) recognizes Jesus of Nazareth as its Messiah." A section in this declaration captioned "Mission and Dialogue" includes the following: "The witness to the Jewish people is inherent in the content of the Gospel, and from the commission received from Christ, the Head of the Church. The mission will most effectively reflect the glory of Christ in His Gospel when it is pursued in the normal activity of the Christian congregation, which reflects itself in the Christian witness of the individual

[7] Philip A. Johnson: "Prelude to Understanding," *The National Lutheran* (November 1964), p. 4.

[8] *The National Lutheran* (November 1964), p. 12.

members. Where Jewish communities in the world cannot normally be reached by Christian congregations, mission organizations must provide for the proclamation of the Gospel to these people."[9]

The evangelical motivation also conditions the Vatican's profession of friendship to the Jews. One of the preliminary drafts of the Vatican declaration on the Jews had stated explicitly that the conversion of the Jews is part of the Christian hope and that the Church "expects the entrance of the Jews" in Catholicism. The draft that was finally adopted is more subtle in expressing this evangelical motivation but it is there and it casts a shadow on the document. The Vatican document expresses the hope for a reconciliation between Jews and Christians and for the triumph of unity among men in a common service to God. But it bases this hope on passages cited from the writings of the Apostle Paul (Ephesians 2:14–16, Romans 11:11–32). An examination of these passages discloses that for Paul this reconciliation was to occur through the surrender by Jews of their distinctive laws and practices, and that the unity for which he hoped involved the Church's absorption of other faiths, particularly that of Judaism.

The present Pope, Paul VI, in his Encyclical Letter of August 6, 1964, asserted explicitly the Church's claim to exclusive truth. According to him, the Catholic Church alone represents the true religion and any real "dialogue" with the world is but another form of endeavor to convert it.

It will be instructive to cite in Pope Paul's own words: "Obviously we cannot remain indifferent to the fact that each of them [the non-Christian religions, with a specific reference to Judaism] . . . should authorize its followers not to seek to discover whether God has revealed the perfect and definitive form [of religion] free from all error, in which He wishes to be known, loved and served. Indeed, honesty compels us to declare openly our conviction that there is but one true religion, the religion of Christianity. It is our hope that all who seek God and adore Him may come to acknowledge its truth."[1] In defining the goal of the

[9] Ibid., p. 18.
[1] *The New York Times*, August 11, 1964, p. 21.

dialogue in which he urged Catholics to engage with non-Catholics, the Pope declared: "Even before converting the world, nay, in order to convert it, we must meet the world and talk with it." [2]

The evangelical goals of the Roman Catholic Church are more directly expressed in the new prayer for the Jews recently promulgated by Pope Paul. It is a prayer recited on Good Friday. Its original title was "Prayer for the Conversion of the Jews." On March 31, 1965, the Pope announced a revision in the text of this prayer and a change of its title to "Prayer for the Jews." A comparison of the text of the two prayers reflects a continuing concern on the part of the Church to correct ancient wrongs against the Jews, but it reflects also a persistence of evangelical goals, and by implication a belief that the Jewish people have been displaced by the Church as the carrier of God's covenant. The new prayer speaks of the Jews as having "once" been God's chosen. Presumably their old prerogatives have been transferred to the Church. In order to attain "fullness of grace in the redemption," this prayer asks that the Jews be guided to accept Christianity.

We cite the two prayers as quoted in a report that appeared in *The New York Times* on April 1, 1965:

> OLD PRAYER
>
> *Prayer for the conversion of the Jews.*
>
> Let us also pray for the Jews: That our God and Lord would withdraw the veil from their hearts: That they also may acknowledge our Lord Jesus Christ.
>
> Let us pray. Almighty and eternal God who drives not away from his memory even the Jews; hear our prayers which we offer for the blindness of that people; that acknowledging the light of your truth, which is Christ, they may be delivered from their darkness.

[2] *The New York Times*, August 11, 1964, p. 20.

NEW PRAYER

Prayer for the Jews.

Let us pray for the Jews: Our Lord God deign to let your face shine upon them, so that even they may recognize the redeemer of all, our Lord Jesus Christ. O almighty and eternal God who has made his promises to the people of Abraham beloved by God, heed with kindness the prayer of your Church, that those who once were your chosen people will be able to attain to the fullness of grace in the redemption.

The new prayer is more refined in language than the old, but it has not advanced appreciably beyond the old in substantive thought. It persists in the claim that all truth abides in Christianity, and that only through faith in Jesus can men attain salvation.

Christian missionary propaganda takes many forms. One line of argument accuses Jews who remain loyal to Judaism of being unfaithful to the Hebrew Bible. As we shall have occasion to note, Christian exegetes developed a method of figurative and allegorical interpretation which helped them read the basic doctrines of the Church into the writings of the Old Testament. This type of interpretation, as many contemporary Christian scholars readily acknowledge, often does violence to the obvious meaning of the original Hebrew text. But it enabled the missionary-minded Christian to claim that Jews who did not follow the new truth were unfaithful to their own Scriptures.

The endeavor to place the roots of Christianity in the Hebrew Bible goes back to the earliest beginnings of the Church. It was inspired by several considerations. The early Christians were Jews who added to their Judaism the belief in the messiahship of Jesus. Before they had a scripture of their own, a Christian scripture, they continued to draw on the Jewish Scriptures. It fortified their faith if they could reconcile it with the sacred writings of Judaism to which they still owed their allegiance. There was an additional consideration, as S. G. F. Brandon has shown: "The ancient world esteemed, particularly in religion, all that had the aura of antiquity. It added to the prestige of Christianity to be linked with the ancient writings of the Jews. But this endeavor to turn the Hebrew Bible into a stepping stone to Christianity has created various problems for Jewish-Christian relations."[3]

The Protestant Commission on the Witness to Israel of the Protestant Federation of France, in a paper submitted to the World Council of Churches for its First Assembly held in Amsterdam from August 22 to September 5, 1948, declares: "The Church must say that their [the Jews] sufferings are not God's vengeance for the death of Jesus, but an appeal to conversion and to turn from their unfaithfulness. It is obviously very hard to use this language to the survivors of the Nazi massacres. But Christians cannot proclaim the Gospel to the Jews unless they begin by affirming that Jesus really is the Christ, the son of God, and that their unfaithfulness consists in their refusal to recognize Him as the Messiah foretold by the prophets."[4]

A contemporary Jesuit scholar has in a recent study repeated the classic Christian indictment of Judaism. Joseph Bonsirven has written thus: "We cannot really accuse Judaism of not having been enlightened by the Christian revelation which it had rejected. But do we not have a right to blame Judaism for having rejected Christ and his message? We Christians believe that the Old Testament intended to pave the way for Christianity. Therefore, when the physical heirs of ancient Israel did not recognize the one who was the expected and intended blossoming of their religion, this means that they were disloyal to the mission which God had entrusted to them. The statement of this basic infidelity encourages us to investigate whether it is not the consequence of another more secret and prolonged infidelity, an infidelity to the spirit, or even to the letter of the revelation of which Israel was

[3] S. G. F. Brandon: *History, Time and Deity* (New York: Barnes & Noble; 1965), p. 190.

[4] *Bulletin on the Relationship of the Church to the Jewish People* (Geneva: World Council of Churches; 1964), p. 5.

the trustee and missionary." [5] And what is the nature of this "infidelity"?

His strictures are extended, but prominently placed among them is the preoccupation of Jews with the perfection of the existential world. In the words of Bonsirven: "The absolute confidence in the value of human liberty was an obstacle to divine grace and a prelude to certain heresies. . . . Because of tendencies we have mentioned, exaggerating man's dignity and rights, eliminating the sense of mystery and man's spiritual dimensions, many Jews have forsaken traditional beliefs and practices. . . ." [6]

The preoccupation of Christian bodies with missionizing among Jews, to encourage them to desert their own faith in favor of Christianity, is an affront to Jews. One cannot show genuine respect, not to speak of friendship for Jews, while showing contempt for the faith by which they live. As Professor A. J. Heschel recently stated: "The idea that Judaism is a passing phenomenon and the hope of [their] conversion on the part of many Christians makes a genuine contact between Jews and Christians an impossibility. To put it bluntly, if we dedicate our lives to the preservation of Judaism, how can we take seriously a friendship that is conditioned ultimately on the hope and expectation that the Jew will disappear? How would a Christian feel if we Jews were engaged in an effort to bring about the liquidation of Christianity?" [7]

The pursuit by Christian bodies of friendly relations with Jews in the expectation that they will thereby make Christianity more palatable to Jews is bound to be frustrating. For Jews have rejected Christianity not out of blindness but out of sight—they have understood the nature of the two faiths, and they prefer to remain Jews. Out of this frustration may come impatience and new anger. The immediate result of these evangelical efforts is to irritate Jews, while their long-range results may well be a resurgence of anti-Jewish feelings.

[5] Joseph Bonsirven: *Palestinian Judaism in the Time of Jesus Christ* (New York: Holt, Rinehart and Winston; 1964), p. 253.

[6] Ibid., pp. 253, 257, 259.

[7] Quoted in *The Jerusalem Post*, July 9, 1965, p. 6.

We already have evidence of this impatience among at least some Christian "ecumenists." Commenting on an article by Rabbi Reuben Siegel on "The Ecumenical Movement and the Jews,"[8] Rev. Ludvic Nemec of Rosemont College complains that Rabbi Siegel "fails to reveal what Christians have long hoped to find, namely, some evidence that the Jews have undertaken to bridge the chasm between their failure in the past to recognize the Messiah and an acceptance of Him in the future, thereby giving concrete evidence of greater mutuality in the bond of the Judeo-Christian heritage."[9] For the Reverend Mr. Nemec, the goal of the ecumenical dialogue is "unity in Christ's church."[1] We live in a mobile society and some Jews will undoubtedly cross the boundary into Christianity as some Christians continue to cross the boundary into Judaism. But it is naïve of the Reverend Mr. Nemec and others like him to expect that Jews as a people who have been faithful to their heritage in the face of persecution will betray it because Christian ecumenists have now smiled upon them. It is difficult to know in what sense the Reverend Mr. Nemec employs the term "Judeo-Christian heritage." There is a Jewish heritage and there is a Christian heritage, and it should be understandable that just as Christians want to be faithful to their heritage, Jews want to be faithful to theirs. But if Christian friendship is indeed contingent on the expectation that it will purchase the Jewish betrayal of Judaism in favor of Christianity, then we are justified in grave apprehensions for the future of Jewish-Christian relations.

The movement within Christianity for a reconciliation with Judaism represents a phenemenon of great significance. Perhaps its greatest service has been to place the issue before the Christian conscience. But it is clear that the issues run deep and involve basic doctrinal confrontations.

The basic source of the Christian predicament rests on the insistence that the roots of its legitimacy are in Judaism, and that

[8] Charles O'Neill (ed.): *Ecumenism and Vatican II* (Milwaukee: Bruce Publishing Co.; 1964).

[9] *Theological Studies,* 26: 2 (June 1965), 327.

[1] Ibid., p. 328.

the Hebrew Bible, when properly interpreted, is "pregnant with Christ," as Gaetano Cardinal Stefanescki put it.[2] A contemporary Christian scholar, W. D. Davies, expressed it similarly: "Christianity, so Christians believe, stands in relation to Judaism as the final event does to the preparatory, as the complete to the incomplete. . . . To us Christians it [Judaism] is . . . a partial or unfulfilled religion whose completion is found in Christianity. . . . Thus, the Old Covenant wrought at Sinai finds its fulfillment in the New Covenant wrought by Christ in his death; the Old Israel, its fulfillment in the New Israel, the church; the old Law its fulfillment in the life and words of Jesus. . . . Christianity is not so much the annulling of Judaism as its completion. Christ is the end of Judaism, not in an iconoclastic sense, but in a teleological or Aristotelian one; in the sense that it is the outcome and full flowering of Judaism, so that for us Christianity is Judaism 'come of age.' "[3]

By the logic of this position Christianity is truer to Judaism than Judaism itself, for is not the ripened fruit more of a fruit than the unripe one? According to this position, too, Jews who resist embracing Christianity are a fossil people living by a fossil faith. However this is contradicted by a living Jewish people whose Judaism refuses to behave like a fossil but instead exhibits great moral and spiritual dynamism and has had many flowerings through the centuries. Every living faith is like a tree which bears continued fruit, as its moral and spiritual momentum inspires men to see new visions and dream new dreams. A religion that is truly alive—Judaism as well as Christianity—may never be spoken of as "completed," since the characteristic of all life is the capacity for growth.

The endeavor of Christianity to appropriate Judaism as a stage in its own development is challenged by the abiding loyalty of Jews to Judaism, while the eagerness of Christianity to convert Jews derives from the necessity to substantiate the basic claim of Christian doctrine. The resistance of Jews to the missionary activities of the Church thus becomes a basic Christian frustration,

[2] *The Bridge* (New York: Pantheon Books; 1961), IV, 278.

[3] "Christianity and Judaism," in Lily Edelman (ed.): *The Jewish Heritage Reader* (New York: Taplinger Publishing Co.; 1965), pp. 190–1.

an affront and a threat to the Christian image of itself. Those who are frustrated are always tempted to translate their frustration into hostility toward those responsible for their predicament.

There is another phase of Christian missionary activity among Jews that is fraught with grave danger for the future of Jewish-Christian relations. In some Christian circles it is taught that the Christian hope of final triumph in the world, the hope for the inauguration of God's kingdom, the hope for "the second coming of Christ"—all these remain contingent on the conversion of the Jews to Christianity. Typical of this view is the following statement taken from the report of the Consultation of the Joint Committee of the World Council of Churches and the International Missionary Council's Committee on the Christian Approach to the Jews, held at Bossey, Switzerland, in September 1956: "In the teaching of the New Testament (especially Romans 9–11) a 'remnant' from the Jews accept Christ. A hardening has appeared to other Jews, but God still holds out His promise for them, and their conversion is closely associated with the hope of the Second Coming. . . . Christ is a 'light to lighten the Gentiles, and the glory of thy people Israel' (Luke 2:32). His own light in the world will not be fully visible and His Church will remain incomplete until in the providence of God the fullness of the Jewish people is brought in." [4]

A bulletin of the World Council of Churches entitled *Study Encounter*, restates the same position and actually grounds it in the prophecies of the Hebrew Bible: "Our thinking on the relations between Israel and the Church seems to be entering upon a new phase, with anti-Semitism put in the pillory and true dialogue desired. It would appear, at least to some theologians—and their number will increase—that the participation of Israel is itself necessary for the progress of the ecumenical movement. This is not only because there are for us today interesting lessons to be learned from the way in which Jewish Scriptures speak of the schism between the northern and southern tribes subsequent to Solomon's reign, or in which the prophets (Jeremiah and Ezekiel in particular) announce the reunion of God's people after their

[4] *Bulletin on the Relationship of the Church to the Jewish People*, pp. 25–6.

dispersion in the Exile—and there is a collection of data here of which the ecumenical specialists should take account—but it is also, and above all, because some of these theologians are not hesitating to say that the unity of the Church will not come to pass without the Jewish people. The family of God cannot be fully reunited unless the elder son also has his seat at the common table." [5]

The vision of the Hebrew prophets of the reunion of the fragmented parts of the Jewish people here becomes a basis for the Christian hope of the entry of the Jews into the Church! It is significant, too, that in this conception the Jewish people represent the prodigal son who left the family table. It is all part of the idea that the line of growth from the Hebrew Bible leads to the Church and that the Jews who persist in remaining Jews are therefore rebels against their own divinely appointed destiny.

It is in the light of this conception that one can understand the concluding paragraph in a resolution on Jewish-Christian relations adopted by the National Council of the Churches of Christ in the United States of America on June 5, 1964: "The General Board urges that the members of its constituent communions seek that true dialogue with the religious bodies of the Jewish community through which differences in faith can be explored within the mutual life of the one family of God—*separated, but seeking from God the gift of renewed unity. . . .*" [italics mine] "The gift of renewed unity" is presumambly a reference to the hoped-for conversion of the Jews to Christianity, which is conceived of as the return of the prodigal son to the fellowship of God's people, represented by the Church. One recalls the statement of the Logumkloster conference of the Lutheran World Federation quoted earlier: "Thus the Church testifies that, by the fulfillment of the promises in Jesus the Messiah and by His acceptance of but a part of the Jews, a division has arisen which has placed the 'old' Israel outside the 'new.' This division will be healed when 'all Israel' recognizes Jesus of Nazareth as its Messiah." [6]

Dr. R. J. Z. Werblowsky, lecturer in comparative religion at the Hebrew University in Jerusalem, underscored the basic as-

[5] (Geneva: World Council of Churches; Autumn 1964), p. 30.
[6] *Relationship of the Church to the Jewish People*, p. 87.

sumption which leads Christians to this conception of Jews and of Judaism: "A Christian is forced to seek the Jew from the moment that he confronts his own Christianity. After all, he considers the New Testament the fulfillment and continuation of the Hebrew Bible; he considers the Church to be the prolongation of ancient Israel; he is a Christian by virtue of his faith in the man whom, he believes, the Law and the Prophets announce as the Messiah. The presence of the Jews, i.e., the 'old' Israel, presents the Christian with a problem—or to put it in the language of Christian theology, not with a problem but with a 'mystery.'" [7]

What is perilous in this position is that it turns Jews into villains in the drama of history. It is they who created a breach in the original oneness of God's people by refusing to continue on the main course of their destined development. It is they who obstruct the Christian hope for healing the breach; it is they who impede the consummation of world redemption. As the hope of Christendom for the "second coming" of Christ continues to fail in materializing will not Christians be tempted to turn in anger against those responsible for impeding it?

The tension between Judaism and Christianity will remain essentially unresolved until there is adopted a policy of religious coexistence and Christians desist from the preoccupation with converting Jews, even as Jews desist from the effort to convert Christians. The philosophy of religious coexistence was well expounded by Martin Buber. He based his thought on a well-known rabbinic text (Sifra on Leviticus 18:5) which makes acceptability to God dependent on the moral and spiritual quality of a person's life, and that Jew or pagan alike are to be judged by this standard. The Rabbis base their homily on a number of biblical passages, among them Isaiah 26:2: "Open ye the gates that the righteous nation (*goy zaddik*) which keepeth faithfulness may enter in." The rabbinic homily continues thus: "It does not say 'that the priests may enter in, that Levites may enter in, that Israelites may enter in.' Rather it says 'that the righteous nation which keepeth faithfulness may enter in.'" This rabbinic text, Buber points out, speaks of all mankind, and it imposes only one

[7] "The Dialogue Challenge," *The London Jewish Chronicle* (November 6, 1964), p. 9.

criterion for being acceptable to God—the pursuit of righteousness, rather than a formal religious profession. Summing up the meaning of this text, Buber declares: "The gates of God are open to all. The Christian need not go via Judaism, nor the Jew via Christianity in order to enter into God." [8]

One cannot attain the ends of a vital spiritual life by the mere profession of one faith or the other. John Calvin was a dedicated Christian, but the blood of Michael Servetus was on his hands, for he had him burned at the stake as a heretic because he refused to believe in the trinity. Many good men have stood outside both faiths, pursuing some pagan creed or perhaps none at all, preferring a secular interpretation of culture and life. If it be true that life's highest goal is the sanctity of life, the pursuit of righteousness, then such men have met the basic human obligation, even though there remain other obligations toward which they yet need to grow if they are to meet fully God's claim on their lives. Not the label we wear, or the creed we profess, but the moral content of our conduct determines our worth before God. The great Jewish teacher Hillel, when he defined the essence of the religious life in terms of love for a neighbor, added: "The rest is commentary, go and explore it." There is more than ethics in a man's total response to life. But the ethical deed, and the moral passion which sustains it, is basic.

Some Christian scholars have sought to blame post-New Testament writers for the development of Christian bias against Jews. Thus Gregory Baum maintains that "if we look to the New Testament to find what our attitude should be toward the Jewish people, we shall find the answer: It is love." The hostility to Jews he ascribes to the influence of later Church Fathers, citing specifically the violently anti-Jewish pronouncements of St. John Chrysostom and St. Ambrose. But it is not altogether fair to make these men bear the primary responsibility for Christian anti-Semitism. St. John Chrysostom, whose sermons are most vitriolic in their anti-Jewish incitements, hewed close to precedents he found in the New Testament, as the passages quoted by Baum

[8] "Church, State, Nation, Jewry," in David W. McKain (ed.): *Christianity: Some Non-Christian Appraisals* (New York: McGraw-Hill, Inc.; 1964), p. 188.

himself indicate. His quotations in support of his hate are Scriptural texts. He followed the New Testament in turning the criticism of the Hebrew prophets of their peoples' shortcomings into evidence that the prophets had branded their people intrinsically depraved. And the climax of his textual documentation is from the Gospel of John: "None of the Jews, not one of them is a worshipper of God. It was the Son of God who told them: 'If you knew the Father, you would know me also, but, you neither know me nor my Father (cf. John 8:19). Since they have disowned the Father, crucified the Son, and rejected the Spirit's help, who would dare to assert that the synagogue is not a home of demons! God is not worshipped there; it is simply a house of idolatry." [9]

Baum himself acknowledges that when as a young priest he had occasion to lecture on the relationship of the Catholic Church and the Jews, with the New Testament as his primary source of inspiration, he spoke of the Jews as a rejected people, a people under a curse: "The Jews, I then thought—and said in the talks which I gave—are in the likeness of Cain, a people condemned for murder." He changed his image of the Jew after reading the work by the French Jewish historian Jules Isaac, *Jesus et Israel.*[1]

The predicament which faces Christianity in trying to purge itself of anti-Semitism while retaining its basic theology was well described by A. Roy Eckardt in his recent article in *The Christian Century:*

"The anti-Semitic virus is a chronically nagging presence in the Christian corpus. . . . The real stumbling block is that the Christian church has never found a way to reconcile its view (inspired by the church's own origin from within Judaism) that Torah contains the Word of God with the allegation that 'the Jews' have said No to their salvation and repudiated their inheritance by 'rejecting' Jesus as messiah. As Reinhold Niebuhr showed in his Gifford lectures over two decades ago, Jesus 'disappointed' the biblical messianic expectations much more than he fulfilled them.

"Christian thought has been driven almost to distraction by

[9] Gregory Baum: *Is the New Testament Anti-Semitic?* (New York: The Macmillan Company; 1965), pp. 9, 18.

[1] Ibid., pp. 11 ff.

the effort to affirm the divine authenticity of one constituent part of its canon in the face of the truth that its lord, the acclaimed guarantor of its own election, cannot be readily fitted into the canonical promises. Were the church not held captive by its peculiar ideology as 'custodian' of divine truth, it would know and proclaim that the Israel which lives on Torah not only bears no moral liability for the 'rejection' of Jesus but is to be praised for fealty to its recognition of the divine promises, for its objective obedience to the Word of God in an unredeemed world.

"The church's ambivalence and its persistent theological embarrassment are further compounded by the fact that the New Testament, the most 'inspired' canon of all, contains the beginnings of anti-Semitic hostility.

"Why must so many Christians refuse to acknowledge the inexorable link with immorality of so many of the recorded sentiments of New Testament writers? Just what or whom are we trying to protect? . . . Because we are unprepared spiritually to live with the elements of anti-Semitism in our own Scriptures, we have to try to tell ourselves that they are somehow not there. The result is moral illusion, moral entrapment. Anti-Semitism remains the bloody brother of anti-Judaism. We stay caught in a terrible conflict between the demands of ordinary human decency and an oppressive dogma respecting the nature and place of Scripture." [2]

[2] "End of the Christian-Jewish Dialogue," *The Christian Century* (March 23, 1966), pp. 361–2.

Chapter II

The Hebrew Bible

SPEAKING to a conference on Christian missions to the Jews, Martin Buber declared in 1930: "What have you and we in common? If we take the question literally, a book and an expectation. To you, the book is a forecourt; to us it is the sanctuary. But in this place we can dwell together, and together listen to the voice that speaks here. That means that we can work together to evoke the buried speech of that voice; together we can redeem the imprisoned living word." [1]

Buber spoke about the Hebrew Bible, known to Christians as the Old Testament. It is the common Scripture of the Jewish as well as the Christian tradition. But Buber was over-optimistic in assuming that because both traditions acknowledge the sanctity of the same book this becomes a place where they can readily "dwell together and together listen to the voice that speaks" through it.

The voice that speaks in the Bible needs to be interpreted before we can comprehend its meaning. And what divergent meanings men have found in the Bible! Some have found in it a mandate to kill witches and heretics; to forbid blood transfusions and surgery; to authorize segregation of races and even to sanction slavery; to permit and to forbid divorce and birth control. Almost

[1] *The Writings of Martin Buber*, Will Herberg (ed.) (New York: Meridian Books; 1956), p. 275.

any doctrine can be, and indeed has been, supported by proof texts from Scripture, by people ingenious enough in textual analysis.

The Hebrew Bible, or as Christians call it, the Old Testament, is not only the ground of unity between Judaism and Christianity; it is also the ground of their differences. It is a divergence in biblical interpretation that underlies the cleavage between the two faiths. Judaism and Christianity differ widely in their teachings concerning God and man. But each tradition supports its claims on the same foundation, on the writings of the Hebrew Bible, through a distinctive method of interpretation.

One of the most significant chapters in the cultural history of mankind was written by the respective schools of Jewish and Christian commentators who sought and found in the Hebrew Bible the basis for their diverse doctrinal positions. The earliest and most important works in these two schools of interpretation are represented for us by the Talmud in the case of Judaism and the New Testament in the case of Christianity. These two major works of biblical interpretation define the distinctiveness of each faith and from them have grown the mighty barriers which lie between them.

The word *Bible* goes back to Byblos, a Phoenician town where the Greeks purchased Egyptian-made papyrus, on which they wrote their books. The Greeks coined the word *biblion* meaning "a book," which yielded a plural form *biblia*, "books." Latin readers mistook the word *biblia* for a singular feminine form, and it is to this that we owe the English singular noun *bible*. The Bible is in truth a collection of many books, rather than a single work of literature. We have no exact Hebrew equivalent for the term Bible. The nearest equivalent is *Kisve ha-Kodesh*, literally "Writings of Holiness," or the Holy Scriptures, a term that preserves the sense of the plurality of books that make up the Bible. The core of the Hebrew Bible is the Pentateuch, or the Five Books of Moses, and extending from this there grew up the various other books of the Bible, a supplementary literature of vast dimensions.

The Bible presents its teachings as the word of God. But even those who do indeed see in the Bible a depository of teachings which are divine in origin will generally agree that the biblical books were given their final form by human authors. The divine and the human are two dimensions in which historical events have their being. A power beyond man directs the turn of his thoughts and the passion behind his deeds and his words, but a zone where man exercises his own initiative remains. Apart from its divine origin, the Bible must also be considered in terms of its human origin. The study of the human origin of the Bible unites those who are interested in biblical literature, regardless of the religious significance they may attach to the biblical word.

The human origins of the Bible have been an object of study by Bible scholars through the generations. The Pentateuch, or the Five Books of Moses, has been subjected to critical inquiry and widely divergent theories have been propounded as to the time and circumstance of its authorship.

The most radical view was elaborated by a group of nineteenth-century German scholars whose most renowned representative was Julius Wellhausen. They regarded the Pentateuch as a late work, placing it in the epoch after the settlement in Canaan. They held moreover that the Pentateuch is not a unitary work but rather a composite of several documents, each representing an author with different religious interests. This hypothesis, too, tended to deny the originality of the Pentateuch, pointing to various parallels in contemporary cultures of other Near Eastern countries as the source from which the biblical writers drew their materials. The most recent trend in biblical scholarship has been to challenge the Wellhausen school of criticism. Some, like M. D. Cassuto of the Hebrew University in Jerusalem, and I. Engnell of the Upsala School in Sweden, have rejected the documentary theory altogether. Yehezkel Kaufmann has shown that the heart of biblical religion is so unique as to preclude any serious borrowing from neighboring cultures. Others, while not rejecting the Wellhausen hypothesis altogether, are however in agreement that his views are much too radical and stand unsupported by the facts as revealed; for example, by the evidence of archeology and comparative linguistics, which have made great strides in recent years.

The Pentateuch is not interested in the historical records as such. Its primary goal is to teach a religious and an ethical doctrine. But it refers to various historical events and to personalities who were the central characters in those events. The trend among modern scholars of the ancient Near East is to accept the credibility of these accounts in the Pentateuch. As the noted archeologist Dr. W. F. Albright expressed it: "As a whole the picture in Genesis is historical, and there is no reason to doubt the general accuracy of the biographical details and the sketches of personality which make the Patriarchs come alive with a vividness unknown to a single extra-Biblical character in the whole vast literature of the ancient Near East." [2]

The Pentateuch includes in its prefatory portions stories concerning the origin of the universe, the creation of man, the beginnings of civilization, the experience of human guilt, suffering, and retribution. These are clearly not meant to be read literally, as a record of what really transpired in the existential world. One Rabbi declared that there never was a historical figure like Job, that the entire book which deals with his predicament is only a parable to explore the mystery of human suffering. The stories in Genesis may be deemed to have a similar objective. In substance they may go back to ancient sagas preserved as hallowed tradition from the remotest antiquity or to the invention of an inspired writer. Their use in the Bible is to convey a religious or a moral truth. They seek to teach us that the world is God's creation, that man is responsible to God for what he makes of his life. They teach us the importance of the Sabbath, the unity of mankind, the duty for man to marry, raise a family, and engage in the struggle to tame Nature and subdue her to human purposes.

The Wellhausen school of Bible criticism has also been discredited in its treatment of the other books of the Bible. This school of criticism assumed that the early prophets were incapable of sublime thought or utterance, that their religion had not reached universal scope. Whenever these critics encountered passages in the writings of the early prophets that contradicted this assumption, they branded them later additions and therefore not trustworthy. They were most rash in dealing with the Book of

[2] *The Biblical Period from Abraham to Ezra* (New York: Harper & Row; 1963), p. 5.

Psalms. This book often reaches great depths of feeling. It disdains religious externality and sings of the soul's longing for God, for moral innocence, and for human fellowship. The assumption with which these critics operated did not allow for a religion of such moral and spiritual intensity in the pre-exilic period (586–538 B.C.E.). Ignoring the testimony of the book itself, those critics tended therefore to date the Psalms after the period of exile, with some even being placed in the time of the Maccabees.

Modern biblical scholarship has reversed all this, and there is today a far greater respect for the authenticity and historical character of the prophetic books. "The fashion of regarding the Psalms as largely post-exilic has all but vanished; to date any of them in the Maccabean period seems little short of impossible. The bulk of them are of pre-exilic origin, and some of them are very archaic indeed. So understood the Psalms now assume capital importance for understanding the cult and religion of Israel under the monarchy." [3]

The Five Books of Moses are designated in Hebrew as *Torah*, literally "Teaching." This term is sometimes used more broadly to cover the totality of Jewish religious knowledge, but its original usage is more restricted and denotes the five basic books. The supplementary literature which grew up subsequent to the five basic books is sometimes divided into two categories described in Hebrew as *Nevi'im* and *Ketuvim*. *Nevi'im*, or "prophets," embraces the writings of the prophets as well as the historical books of the Bible which portray the life and times during the early settlement of the Hebrews in Palestine and during the monarchy under the kings of Judah and Israel. These historical books are written from the point of view of the prophetic interpretation of history and they are, therefore, included among the writings of the prophets. The prophetic writings include eight books: Joshua, Judges, I and II Samuel, I and II Kings, Isaiah, Jeremiah, Ezekiel, and the twelve minor prophets. The latter consists of Hosea, Joel, Amos, Obadiah, Jonah, Micah, Nahum, Habakkuk, Zephaniah, Haggai, Zechariah, and Malachi. The latter twelve are called mi-

[3] John Bright: "Modern Study of Old Testament Literature," *The Bible and the Ancient Near East* (Garden City, N.Y.: Doubleday & Company; 1961), p. 27.

nor prophets because they are short works in comparison with the other prophetic writings. In terms of sublimity of thought and depth of inspiration, some of the books included in these twelve are unsurpassed in all biblical literature.

The third section, *Ketuvim*, means "writings," and this division of the Bible embraces a miscellany of books, including Psalms, Proverbs, Job, the Song of Songs, Ruth, Lamentations, Ecclesiastes, Esther, Daniel, Ezra, Nehemiah, and I and II Chronicles. The order of the books within each division of the Bible as here given follows the earliest printed editions of the Hebrew text. Manuscript copies which antedate the age of printing vary the order. But the order in the original printed edition has become standard and is followed universally in all Jewish communities.

Christians refer to the Hebrew Bible as the "Old Testament," and they acknowledge an additional supplementary literature, the books which comprise the "New Testament." The distinction between an "old" and a "new" Testament does not exist in Judaism. For Judaism there is only the Hebrew Bible, a collection of thirty-nine books divided into Torah, *Nevi'im* and *Ketuvim*, sometimes abbreviated to the term *TaNaKh*.

The Hebrew Bible has been translated into close to three hundred languages and dialects. The earliest translation of the Bible was into Greek, and it was undertaken in the second century B.C.E. It is generally referred to as the Septuagint, Latin for "seventy." Legend has it that this translation was prepared by seventy-two elders sent by Eleazar the High Priest from Jerusalem at the request of the Emperor Ptolemy, who wanted to enrich the culture of Alexandria with a Greek version of this great classic. This translation was at first limited to the Pentateuch and was later extended to include other biblical books. The Jews of Alexandria used this as their official translation but it was eventually repudiated by the Rabbis as inaccurate. A more authentic Greek translation was prepared by a Greek proselyte to Judaism, Aquila of Pontus, who worked under the guidance of Rabbi Eliezer, Rabbi Joshua, and their renowned disciple, Rabbi Akiba. The preparation of this translation was an incident in the Jewish cultural renewal, which was stimulated by the destruction of the Temple in Jerusalem in 70 C.E.

The Septuagint translation of the Bible is an important source for the study of Scripture. It was based on a Hebrew text that antedated the *masorah*, the version of the biblical text which became official in Judaism. On the basis of the Greek translation we can sometimes gain precious information on the readings of the text in the Bible prior to its standardization. In some instances the meanings of Hebrew words are uncertain and the translation by competent scholars becomes an important contribution to biblical interpretation.

The Septuagint played a crucial role in disseminating the Bible in the pagan world. It was this translation which the early Christian churches adopted as their Bible. From this source they took the translation of *Torah* as "law" (Greek *nomos*), a conception which was to aid in the later disparagement of Judaism as narrow and legalistic. The Septuagint became the basis for a series of secondary translations of the Bible prepared for use by the early churches in Europe and the Near East. These include the Coptic, Ethiopic, Armenian, Slavonic, Gothic, and Old Latin.

An Aramaic translation was made during the same period and it became the official translation of the Aramaic-speaking Jewish community in Babylonia. This translation eventually won a following throughout the Jewish world, as is attested by its inclusion as a supplement to almost all printed editions of the Hebrew Bible. It is usually called *Targum Onkelos*, "the translation of Onkelos," which is the Aramaic pronunciation of Aquila. This can only mean that it was a translation in the spirit of the work of Aquila. The translator of the Aramaic work remains unknown.

The earliest Christian translation of the Bible is known as the Vulgate, from the Latin term *vulgus*, and it was so called because it was soon adopted as the "vulgar," or common, edition of the Bible. The Vulgate was completed in 404, the work of the Church Father Jerome.

There were several English versions of the Bible before the King James Version, which was completed in 1611 and which became the great religious and literary classic of the English-speaking world. The first complete translation was made from the Vulgate by John Wycliffe (1324–84), who was assisted by Nicholas of Hereford. They completed their labors about 1383. Wycliffe, who was a celebrated religious reformer, aroused the opposition of the Church for rendering the Bible into the vernacular and in 1428, by an edict of the Synod of Constance, his remains were exhumed, burned, and cast into the river Swift. It was the same Council which ordered John Huss to be burned at the stake. The first English version made by direct translation from the Hebrew and Greek, and the first to be printed, was the work of William Tyndale in 1525. He, too, aroused bitter opposition, and in 1536 he was publicly executed and burned at the stake. Tyndale's work became the basis of later English versions. The King James Version (or the Authorized Version, as it is sometimes called) was prepared by a commission of scholars in England under the sponsorship of King James I; they labored on it from 1604 to 1611. The Douay is the name given to a popular English translation by Roman Catholic scholars; the Old Testament was published at Douay in 1609–10 (then part of the Spanish Netherlands and conquered by the French in 1667), the New Testament in Rheims, Germany, in 1582. A revision of the King James Version, called the English Revised Version, appeared in 1881–5, and an American variant of this, known as the American Standard Version, was published in 1901.

The style of the King James Version was followed by the editors of the American Jewish version, which was published by the Jewish Publication Society in 1917. A basic revision of the King James Version, including a modernization of the English idiom, was undertaken by a panel of Christian scholars who produced the Revised Standard Version, which was published by Thomas Nelson & Sons in 1952. This version is a pioneering work in many respects: it is officially sponsored by the National Council of the Churches of Christ in the United States; it seeks to steer clear of sectarian renderings, following the results of objective Hebraic scholarship even when it collides with hallowed Christian interpretations. It is noteworthy, too, that a Jewish Bible scholar, Professor Harry Orlinsky, was invited to sit on the committee which prepared this work. In recent years there have appeared a number of unofficial translations—the work of individual scholars —of portions or of the entire Bible. The latest English translation under Jewish auspices, thus far limited to the Pentateuch, is *The Torah,* issued by the Jewish Publication Society in 1962.

The Confraternity edition of the Bible is the latest Roman Catholic version, prepared by scholars under the patronage of the Bishop's Committee of the Confraternity of Christian Doctrine. The Old Testament is a new translation from the original Hebrew into a modern English idiom, and it is available with introductions and commentary by Rev. Joseph A. Grispino. But the books of Kings to Esther and I and II Maccabees were not translated anew, and were instead taken from the Douay Version. It was published by Guild Press, New York, in 1965, with the imprimatur of Catholic ecclesiastical authorities, granted in January 1964. In translation this edition is of great interest as it generally (but not in all cases) follows the conclusions of modern biblical scholarship, often ignoring conventional translations which read Christian doctrine into Old Testament texts.

The most ambitious of the independent translations is *The Anchor Bible*, being published in individual volumes by Doubleday & Company, under the general editorship of William Foxwell Albright and David Noel Freedman. It is a cooperative venture in which leading Bible scholars, Protestant, Catholic, and Jewish, are participating in their individual capacity, without denominational sponsorship. Its effort is to render an exact translation, supplemented by an extended introduction and commentary, which utilize the latest knowledge in the vast fields of Bible study. Its goal is to reach the general reader without reference to his denominational affiliation.

The Christian arrangement of the books in the Hebrew Bible follows the arrangement of the first Greek translation, the Septuagint, which placed the prophetic books last. This was more suitable for the Christian view that prophecy led directly to Jesus, in whom it found its climactic expression.

The Catholic version of the Old Testament includes a number of apocryphal works that are omitted from the Hebrew Bible. These include I and II Esdras, Tobit, Judith, Additions to the Book of Esther, The Wisdom of Solomon, Ecclesiasticus, Baruch,

Additions to Daniel, Prayer of Manasses, and I and II Maccabees. The Alexandrian Jewish community included these books in its Greek translation of the Bible, the Septuagint, and the early Church followed their example. The term *apocryphal* means "outside"; these books were extant at the time of the formation of the authoritative anthology of Jewish biblical writings, but for one reason or another the Jewish authorities in Palestine deemed them unworthy of inclusion; excluding them became normative for Judaism. The Protestant version of the Old Testament follows the Jewish version in omitting them. Some of the apocryphal books are important from a literary or historical point of view. *Ecclesiasticus*, or *The Wisdom of Ben Sirach*, is a choice collection of meditations concerning man's life on earth, and the Rabbis of the Talmud judged it a significant treasury of wisdom from which they quoted freely. The I and II Maccabees are our principal sources for the events of the Maccabean war against the Syrian-Greeks for the freedom of the Jewish people in the second century B.C.E.

Another body of writings was rejected from the canon of Jewish Scriptures, the so-called Pseudepigrapha. These works, including such books as the Book of Enoch, the Testaments of the Twelve Patriarchs, the Ascension of Isaiah, the Fourth Book of Ezra, the Fourth Book of Maccabees, are all attributed to the authorship of patriarchs, prophets, or other wise men of the Hebrew Bible. Hiding their identity under the cloak of revered names, the true authors of these works were able more freely to expound their ideas centering on otherworldliness and eschatological visions, which were frowned upon in official circles in Judaism. These books are also outside the Christian canon of Scripture. The books excluded from the Hebrew Bible remind us that the Bible is a selection from a much larger literature. The excluded material is of interest to the historian and it may be studied for its own literary merits. This material, however, may not be cited as Jewish teaching in the usual sense of the term.

The selection of the books that make up the Hebrew Bible was a slow process which continued for about five hundred years. In each age the authorities of Judaism chose certain works from a large number extant at the time. They were vested with authority and were entered in the official collection we call the *canon*, literally the "measure." The canon was finally closed in the early part of the second century C.E.

The selection of books for the canon of the Hebrew Bible did not take place without some struggle. The Rabbis have preserved some of the arguments that were propounded during those momentous sessions when the selections were made. Some objected to the inclusion of the Song of Songs, the Book of Esther, and Ecclesiastes. The last was challenged as a work which appeared to teach a hedonistic view of life, more in consonance with Greek wisdom than with Judaism. We are told (Shabbat 30b) that the work was saved because of the conclusion, which falls in line with traditional piety: "The end of the matter, all having been heard, fear God and keep His commandments, for this is the whole man." Likewise there were objections to the inclusion of the Book of Ezekiel because some of its teachings seemed to contradict provisions of the Pentateuch (Shabbat 13b), but the defenders of the book were able to ward off the attacks against it and this great classic of prophecy was saved for the Bible.

From earliest times men have attempted to create aids for the study of the Bible. The text of the Hebrew Bible consisted originally of unvoweled consonants, as the Torah scrolls used in the synagogue have remained to this day. The vowels were not fully developed until the tenth century. This means that the same Hebrew word could be read in several ways, with radically different meanings. *HRB* could be read *HOREB*, which is the name of a mountain, or *HEREB*, which means a sword. A tradition, called *masorah*, was therefore developed to preserve the correct reading of each word in the Hebrew Bible. The official text of the Bible as finally punctuated and vocalized is called the masoretic text.

In the original text of the Hebrew Bible there were no divisions into chapters and verses. The text flowed along without any breaks as is still the case with the text of the Pentateuch as inscribed on the scroll used in the synagogue service. This vital aid for the reading of the Bible was not introduced until the thirteenth century. Another aid which was to help in the interpretation of the Bible was the early development of a system of musical notes to which the entire text of the Hebrew Bible was set. All printed copies of the Bible carry these notes as an accompaniment to the text. Called "trop," these notes have proven helpful in accentuation and in the grouping of words and phrases, and in conveying intonation and emphasis.

Even with these important aids, the problem of how one reads the Bible still remains. The question may appear to border on the self-evident. We assume that anyone who is literate can read any book, including the Bible. The truth is that various branches of culture tend to become differentiated, and gradually develop a unique idiom. The racing sheet and the stock market page of the newspaper are printed in English, but only the initiated will find them intelligible. The article written by a physicist or a mathematician proceeds in a specialized vocabulary, with special symbols and a jargon of technical terms that the general reader will find baffling. Not everyone can read a poem or an accountant's report. Within a general language we have specialized idioms suited to the subject of communication. The Bible is highly sophisticated in style as well as content. Its narrative portions often have been retold to children, but those stories are parables with subtle meanings which are beyond the grasp of children, or untrained readers. Parts of the Bible are poetry, which can be grasped only by those sensitive to the poetic idiom. There is a subtle art in reading the Bible and it needs to be cultivated if our Bible reading is to yield us the great treasures of beauty and truth which these books have to offer.

The study of the Hebrew text is a work for the specialist. Those who read the Bible in English bypass many of the problems posed by the original, which had to be coped with by the translator. He had to commit himself on the definition of each Hebrew word. He had to resolve the many obscurities of language which beset the original text, the ambiguities of phraseology, the unfamiliar allusions and idiomatic expressions. In many cases he had to consider the date to be ascribed to particular biblical books or portions of books, to give the allusions relevance. All literature presents such problems to one probing its meaning in depth, especially a literature written in an ancient language. Some three thousand years separate us from the earliest record of the Hebrew Bible and it becomes a formidable task of scholarship to master its meaning. All the aids of linguistic science, including comparative philology and archeology, have to be invoked in this process. The translator has at his disposal a formidable body of commentaries which have wrestled with the study of the original Hebrew text. But once the translator has done his work and given us the fruit of his labor we can read without stumbling, unaware of the rough road by which he reached his destination.

Consider, for example, the opening sentence of the Bible: *Bereshit bara Elohim.* The very opening word, *bereshit*, is beset with problems. We usually take it to mean "in the beginning." This may be taken to introduce the order of Creation, that in the beginning God created heaven and earth. But it may also be taken as a declaration of great antiquity, that "in the beginning," in the dim past, in the long, long ago, the events about to be narrated had their occurrence. On the other hand, the prefix *be* in Hebrew also means "with" and *bereshit* may be taken to mean "with the beginning." The Rabbis showed that the Torah is sometimes described as *reshit*, "the beginning." A design, a plan, indeed precedes all creation. The Torah is the blueprint of existence, and the opening sentence may therefore be taken to declare: "With the Torah [the beginning] God created heaven and earth."

Let us remain with the conventional translation of this verse: "In the beginning God created heaven and earth." But the juxtaposition of words in the Hebrew allows for an altogether different interpretation. The word for God, *Elohim*, may be the object as well as the subject of the sentence. In the pagan world where the Bible originally took form, the notion was current that the deity was born or created from a pre-existent eternal substance. One of the common themes in pagan mythologies is the genealogy of the gods, who are sexually differentiated and who procreate. Is there perhaps an echo of this notion in the opening sentence of the Bible? As far as the grammatical structure of this sentence goes, it may conceivably be rendered thus: "In the beginning he created God together with the heaven and the earth." This would certainly involve a doctrinal revolution in our understanding of biblical religion. The text needed interpretation to yield the traditional meaning which we have generally given to it.

We have a further problem with the word *Elohim*. The form is plural. The belief in one God is basic in Judaism, the notion of a plurality of gods anathema in the Jewish conception of the deity. Why does our text then use a plural form *Elohim?* Does this perhaps carry directly or indirectly an allusion to a more primitive conception of the deity? It is interesting that Christian commentators have occasionally cited this usage as a support for their trinitarian conceptions. Here, for example, is a statement by Rev. Robert Jamieson in his commentary on Genesis: "By its use here in the *plural* form, it is obscurely taught at the opening of the Bible, a doctrine clearly revealed in other parts of it, that though God is one, there is plurality of persons in the Godhead-Father, son and spirit, who were engaged in the creative work." [4]

The several interpretations discussed above assume that the opening verse is a complete sentence. There is however a school of commentators who take this verse as an opening clause introducing the principal declaration which is in verse two, an interpretation which is perfectly compatible with the original Hebrew. Indeed the new translation of the Bible being published by the Jewish Publication Society of America adopted this interpretation, rendering the verse thus: "When God began to create the heaven and the earth—the earth was unformed and void. . . ."

We have a problem of comparable importance in Genesis 1:26 which describes the creation of man. Rendered literally, this verse reads: "And God said, 'Let us make man in our image, after our likeness.' " In what sense was man created in God's "image" and after His "likeness"? Does this imply that God is endowed with a particular shape or form? And with whom did God consult when He resolved to fashion man? We have many different interpretations of this verse. The image of God in which man was created has generally been applied to his moral and spiritual sense, which differentiate him from other creatures in the scale of life and make man truly human. The plural "Let *us* make man," has been interpreted by some commentators, Rabbi Abraham ibn Ezra among them, as a plural of majesty, which idiomatically takes a plural construction, but is really singular in substantive

[4] *A Commentary on the Old and New Testament* (New York: S. S. Scranton and Company; 1874).

meaning. E. A. Speiser, who translated the book of Genesis for the *Anchor Bible*, renders this verse in the singular: "Then God said I will make man in my image, after my likeness." The new Jewish Publication Society translation of the Pentateuch, *The Torah*, also renders this verse in the singular: "And God said, I will make man in My image, after My likeness." The latter is followed by a clarifying footnote that the translators took "the Hebrew plural forms as plurals of majesty."

It is clear that a proper interpretation of this verse is fraught with great doctrinal significance. But it is equally clear that such an interpretation can be arrived at only through deliberate and careful study of the biblical text.

The ambiguity of the biblical text sometimes invites sectarian interpretations, which seek to bolster later doctrines by reading them into the earlier writings of Scripture. Some Christian commentators, for example, interpreted the first person plural in "Let us make man" as referring to the three persons of the Trinity.[5] Modern Christian exegetes admit that this is untenable. In the words of Herbert E. Ryle: "Until recently the traditional Christian interpretation has seen in the first person plural reference to the three Persons of the Blessed Trinity. The requirements of sound historical exegesis render this view untenable; for it would read into the Book of Genesis the religious teaching which is based upon the Revelation of the New Testament." [6]

As we shall have occasion to note later on, it was characteristic of early Christian commentators to read the doctrines of their faith into texts of the Old Testament. They took their cue from the writings of the New Testament which abound in such interpretations. The "discovery" of Christian dogmas in the writings of the Hebrew Bible was intended to bolster their truth and to prove their legitimacy from the point of view of the earlier biblical revelation. Modern Christian scholars approach biblical study in a more scientific spirit and they have tended to repudiate such interpretations as artificial and false to the Hebrew text.

[5] Thomas Williams: Commentary in *The Cottage Bible* (Hartford; 1850).

[6] Commentary on the Book of Genesis in the *Cambridge Bible for Schools and Colleges* (Cambridge, Eng.; 1914).

Here are the concluding eight sentences of the Book of Deuteronomy (34:5–12): "So Moses the servant of the Lord died there in the land of Moab, according to the word of the Lord. And he was buried in a valley in the land of Moab over against Beth-peor; and no man knoweth of his sepulchre unto this day. And Moses was a hundred and twenty years old when he died: his eye was not dim, nor his natural force abated. And the children of Israel wept for Moses in the plains of Moab thirty days; so the days of weeping in the mourning for Moses were ended. And Joshua the son of Nun was full of the spirit of wisdom; for Moses had laid his hands upon him; and the children of Israel hearkened unto him, and did as the Lord commanded Moses. And there hath not arisen a prophet since in Israel like unto Moses, whom the Lord knew face to face; in all the signs and the wonders, which the Lord sent him to do in the land of Egypt to Pharaoh, and to all his servants, and to all his land; and in all the mighty hand, and in all the great terror, which Moses wrought in the sight of all Israel."

How can this passage be reconciled with the tradition that Moses himself wrote the first five books of the Bible? How could he have described the events which followed upon his death? To meet the difficulty, we have a suggestion in the Talmud (Baba Batra 15a) that these last verses in the Bible were written by Joshua, who succeeded Moses as leader of the Israelite community. The biblical text has no intimation of this answer. It is an interpretive conjecture, created by the imaginative intuition of the talmudic commentator. Here, as in many other instances, the text itself poses too many problems. We must go beyond it to make it intelligible.

Endless other questions face us as we proceed in our study of the biblical text. The Bible remained alive for mankind through the centuries because its teachings were continually clarified through generations of teachers who were sensitive to its underlying ideas and to the peculiarities of its literary style, as well as to the spiritual problems of the people who were to live by it.

The study of the biblical text reached impressive heights in the Medieval period. The commentaries of Saadia, Rashi, Abraham ibn Ezra, David Kimhi, Obadiah Seforno, among a host of others, continue to be invaluable for the reading of the Bible as a fluent and intelligent text. The writings of these medievalists have been supplemented by a number of great commentators in modern times. These include Moses Mendelssohn, David Hoffman, M. D. Cassuto, Yehezkel Kaufman, and A. S. Hartum. Among contemporaries who have contributed to Bible scholarship are Ephraim Speiser (died 1965), Moses Buttenweiser, H. L. Ginsberg, Robert Gordis, and Harry Orlinsky. The world of Christendom also produced a host of biblical commentators. A good collection of modern Protestant commentaries is to be found in the twelve-volume work *The Interpreter's Bible*, recently published by Abingdon Press under the general editorship of George A. Buttrick. A good illustration of modern Catholic Bible scholarship is afforded us by the Reverend Grispino, in his introductions and commentaries to the Confraternity edition of the Old Testament.

The writing of biblical commentaries is an endless process and many new works in the field continue to appear, reflecting an unceasing endeavor to understand the Bible.

The Bible required clarification, too, because for its adherents it was more than literature. It was a document which set forth the beliefs and practices of their faith. Its prescriptions needed minute analysis because they were deemed authoritative and were invested with the mandate to regulate and direct life. A document speaks for itself, but when such a document seeks to model life by its provisions, then it becomes essential to examine it with the greatest care, to analyze it in detail, and to delineate the over-all goals which are immanent in it. Out of this endeavor has grown a vast tradition setting forth a variety of interpretations of the Bible.

In Judaism as well as Christianity there have been movements which sought to extricate the Bible from the complexities of interpretive tradition. But they only ended by creating an interpretive tradition of their own. Such is the nature of a classic text: no matter how sublime its contents, the "naked" text is beset by incompleteness. Paralleling the articulated word is a treasury of unarticulated words required to complement its meaning. Wherever the Bible has been cherished it has inspired a secondary literature of interpretation and elaboration by the light of which the teachings of the Bible take on cogency and relevance and become the eloquent directives for man's life on earth.

In the beginning was the biblical word, and this word was pregnant with many new words. These new words were brought to birth by the masters of interpretation, whose works abound in the Jewish as well as the Christian tradition.

The diverse interpretations one finds in Jewish and Christian studies do not always follow sectarian lines. They are often diverse without being divergent; their variation corresponds in many cases to the varying plays of mind and temperament of the individual interpreters. They reflect the uniqueness which spells the mystery of individuality and makes for the otherness of persons in their response to life. But in any cases these interpretations also reflect the divergent religious commitments of the interpreters. The Jewish interpretations flow through what is called the *Oral Torah* to become classic Judaism. The Christian interpretations flow through the New Testament and help to fashion classic Christianity.

Chapter III
The Oral Torah

Pope Paul VI, in his Encyclical "Ecclesiam Suam," pleaded for friendly relations between the Church and other faiths. Speaking of the Jews he said: "Then we see another circle around us. This too is vast in its extent, yet it is not so far away from us. It is made up of the men who above all adore the one, supreme God whom we too adore. We refer to the children, worthy of our affection and respect, of the Hebrew people, faithful to the religion we call that of the Old Testament." [1]

This is not an uncommon impression and one finds it sometimes among Jews as well as Christians—that Judaism is the religion of the Hebrew Bible. It is of course a fallacious impression. Much of the Bible does indeed live on in Judaism, but whoever would seek to compare the classic Jewish tradition with the biblical world of faith and life would find some startling contrasts. The Bible conceives of all Jewish worship as centered in one sanctuary in Jerusalem, where the service is to consist of animal sacrifices presided over by an order of hereditary functionaries, priests, and Levites. The Bible knows nothing of the synagogue, of prayer service, of the office of the rabbi, of a festival like Hanukkah. Much of what exists in Judaism is absent in the Bible, and much of what is in the Bible cannot be found in Judaism.

[1] *The New York Times*, August 11, 1964, p. 21.

What is the cause of this disparity? How did Judaism break away from biblical prescription, by what authority, and for what reasons? The answer to these questions lies in the eventful role that interpretation played in the Jewish conception of Scripture.

The *Ethics of the Fathers* begins with this brief statement: "Moses received the Torah at Sinai, and transmitted it to Joshua, Joshua transmitted it to the elders, the elders to the prophets, and the prophets to the men of the Great Assembly." Having been promulgated at Sinai, the Torah did not become a finished body of literature that the people could then make their own, to study it and guide their life accordingly. Duly designated authorities had a continuing role to play in the further development of the Torah, to interpret its teachings and to probe into its underlying principles as the standard by which to direct the ongoing life of their people.

All literature requires some supplementary labor of clarification. We cannot include in one utterance all that is relevant to the subject under discussion. Every statement we make presupposes an almost endless body of other statements which we may not express but which we must assume to make our statement intelligible. We must know the definition of the terms employed, the idiomatic turns of our phrases, the allusions to contemporary or historical events. This is why every text of literature, as indeed every art, is surrounded by a commentary through which the reader, listener, or viewer seeks to explain and to appraise the work of art before him.

The Bible is in some respects a work of literature and as such requires an effort of interpretation to clarify its meaning. In the case of the Bible, however, the need is more basic, for the Bible is more than literature that addresses itself to the private individual for his edification and pleasure. The Bible is an authoritative work, presenting itself as the embodiment of divine revelation. It charts the way for the Jewish people to order its life. Its nature parallels the constitution and basic laws by which any nation decides to govern itself. Such documents can never function by themselves; they require authoritative interpretation. The constitutional structure of any people, ancient or modern, always includes a judiciary, which is charged with giving authoritative interpretation of the basic constitutional document, of the meaning of its provisions, and with applying those provisions to the flux of events in the world about them.

The reference to Joshua, the elders, and the prophets indicates that the work of interpreting the Torah began almost simultaneously with the time of its promulgation. The men of the Great Assembly did their work toward the close of the biblical canon, and with them the talmudic age may be said to begin. The men of the Great Assembly were followed by other teachers who functioned in the academies of Palestine and Babylonia for almost seven hundred years. In due time the office of rabbi was created, and ordination as rabbi became the mark of authorization for a man to interpret the Torah. The Rabbis did their work in their home communities where they served as judges and teachers of the law, and they also met in concert for deliberation, study, and teaching in their headquarters, the academy. The labor in which they engaged is directed toward the same goal, to interpret the Bible as the charter of their people's way of life, to direct events toward the principles and disciplines of the Torah. A summary of their deliberations has been preserved for us in various midrashic and talmudic writings, which constitute the principal literary legacy left by those academies to the Judaism of the future.

Let us consider an instance of this process of biblical clarification. In Genesis 1:28 we are told: "And God blessed them and said to them, 'Be fruitful and multiply and fill the earth and subdue it.' " The setting for this statement is the creation of Adam and his helpmate Eve. Having ushered them into the world which was to be their home and the scene of their life and work, God is described in this sentence as greeting them and bestowing on them His blessing. But the statement is unclear. "Be fruitful and multiply," the Hebrew *peru urevu* may be understood in the imperative sense, as conveying a command. These words may also be understood as expressing a hope, in the sense of "may you be fruitful and multiply."

If these words are to be taken in the imperative sense as prescribing a commandment, then the question arises as to whether the obligation rests on the male as well as the female. On the face of it, it should be obvious that both sexes are to be included in the obligation since they are partners in the process of creating life.

On the other hand, it is a fact of social usage that the male is the pursuer, the wooer; he holds the initiative in courtship, in establishing a marriage, and in the act of conjugal union. The woman certainly fulfills a divinely intended role in her marital life, but in the light of her relatively more passive role, would it not show greater sensitivity to rest the commandment on the male and hold him in violation of the law if he failed to live up to it? Assuming that this sentence prescribes a commandment, other questions arise: How many children must a family bring into the world in order to satisfy the commandment? May husband and wife maintain marital relations when no children can issue from their union? Are there circumstances when they may deliberately frustrate any possible conception? What if conception has occurred and it becomes clear that the pregnancy may prove fatal for the life of the mother—is it permissible to abort the unborn child?

The Golden Rule of Leviticus 19:18, which has often been cited as an illustration of the eloquent simplicity of the original text of the Bible, when carefully examined, reveals the same need of interpretation. Who, for example, is the neighbor whom we are to love as ourself? Does it include a person of another religious faith, of another race? And how can we be asked by fiat to love a person with whom we have not shared the intimacies of life? Is not love an emotion which either exists or does not exist, but which cannot be assumed at will, in obedience to an external demand? And what if there be a clash between a neighbor's interest and our own, and we must make a choice? Whose interest shall we give priority?

Other branches of biblical law illustrate the same need to supplement the biblical text with new pronouncements so as to make the written word efficacious in dealing with life. The Bible provides that on the first day of the seventh month we are to celebrate a festival to be marked by abstention from "servile work" and by "the blowing of the horn" (Numbers 29:1). We are given no indication as to how the horn, the *shofar*, is to be blown. An elaborate ritual of sounds differentiated into *tekiah*, *shevarim*, and *teruah* has been created in fulfillment of this command. And the sounding of these notes represents the most stirring moments in the festival which is celebrated as Rosh Hashanah, the Jewish

New Year. Once again the Bible does not give us specific directions as to how the commandment is to be carried out.

A festival of even greater solemnity follows Rosh Hashanah on the tenth day of the seventh month, Yom Kippur, the Day of Atonement. This holy day is equally vague in its biblical prescription. All we are told is that this day is to be marked by avoiding all work and by "afflicting" our souls (Numbers 29:7). But how is this "affliction" to take place? We express this principally through fasting, but the Bible makes no mention of fasting.

During the festival of Sukkot we are commanded to "dwell in booths" for seven days (Leviticus 23:42). But what is a booth, what are its prescribed dimensions if any, and of what materials is it to be constructed? We have elaborate instructions in Jewish ritual law as to how the booth is to be built, but not a word of it is given us explicitly in the biblical text. All these questions are answered by later authorities. And what does it mean to *dwell* in booths for seven days? Does this mean that we are to stay indoors and spend the festival in the confined setting of the booth? And what if a person is on a journey and he cannot arrange to dwell in a booth for seven days or if he is ill and the exposure to the elements in the frail booth might prove injurious to his health?

We have a like vagueness in the prescription of the Sabbath. We are requested (Exodus 20:8, 10) to "remember the Sabbath day and keep it holy." We are cautioned against "doing any manner of work" on that day. But we are given no definition of what constitutes work. Nor are we given any indication that there might be circumstances when it is vital for the preservation of life to disregard this prohibition. In times of emergency, in the case of sickness, or war, in the face of enemy attack, how can we desist from working on measures to ward off the threat to life?

The Bible does not deal with these questions directly, but the Rabbis do, and they find an answer by reference to common sense and by inference from general principles taught in the Bible. Here is the talmudic statement on this subject: "One must remove debris to save a life on the Sabbath, and the more zealous one is in doing so the more praiseworthy he is; and one need not seek permission from religious authorities. How so? If one saw a child . . . fall into a pit, he breaks loose one segment [of the entrenchment] and pulls it up—the faster the better; and he need not obtain permission from religious authorities. . . . If he saw a door closing upon an infant thereby frightening or endangering the infant, he may break it so as to get the child out—the faster the better; and he need not obtain permission from religious authorities. . . One may extinguish or isolate the flames in the case of a fire—the sooner the better; and he need not obtain permission from the religious authorities. . . .

"Rabbi Ishmael, Rabbi Akiba and Rabbi Eleazar the son of Azariah were once on a journey, with Levi ha-Saddar and Rabbi Ishmael the son of Rabbi Eleazar following them. This question was asked them: Whence do we know that in the event of danger to human life all laws of the Sabbath are superseded? Rabbi Ishmael answered and said: 'If a thief be found breaking in [Exodus 22:1], it is permissible to kill him in self-defense though the shedding of blood pollutes the land and causes the divine spirit to depart from Israel. If the defense of life takes precedence over another life—that of the burglar—it certainly takes precedence over the Sabbath. . . .' Rabbi Simeon the son of Menasya said, 'And the children of Israel shall keep the Sabbath [Exodus 31:16]. The Torah obviously implied that we suspend for an endangered person's sake, one Sabbath, so that he may live to keep many Sabbaths.' Rabbi Judah said in the name of Samuel: 'If I had been there, I should have suggested a more convincing explanation. The Torah asks a person to keep the commandments so that *he shall live by them* [Leviticus 18:5], implying clearly that one must not thwart life because of them.' Raba said: 'The other explanations may be refuted but that of Samuel is irrefutable' " (Mishnah Yoma 8:7, Yoma 85a, 85b).

Some of the details vital for the implementation of biblical law might have been common knowledge and they were omitted because it was taken for granted that the necessary additional information could readily be supplied by the student. It may be, too, that the biblical legislator was content to prescribe the general formula, leaving it to future generations to create the structure of supplementary detail by which to implement the general rule. We have a parallel in the American Constitution, in the "due process" clause. The Fifth Amendment of the Constitution provides that no one shall be deprived of life, liberty, or property without "due process of law." But what constitutes "due process of law"? The authors of the Constitution did not define this, leaving it to later jurists to use their discretion in meeting the demand of the general provision. All law abounds in general pronouncements that require the action of subsequent jurists or legislators to define the details for their implementation.

The discussion of these subjects take us beyond the simple exposition of a biblical text. They take us into a realm where the interpreter becomes a creator, where he must go beyond the text before him, leaning in some cases, on his conception of the social good. In certain instances he must proceed beyond the clear mandate of precedent because life knocks at his door and demands an answer, and inaction would surrender life to anarchy. This is offensive to our conviction that life ought to be disciplined by a scale of value judgments.

Why did not the Bible speak clearly on these subjects? The teachers of the Talmud knew that it was impossible to itemize all the qualifications that pertain to a general directive. If a law were to be promulgated together with all its conceivable applications and qualifications, we would be unable to proceed, for the details of application and qualification are as endless as the play of circumstances conspire to make them. Theoretically, a judge only interprets the law, but actually he is often called on to step outside the confines of strict interpretation, to assume the role of a maker of law as well.

There were circumstances of a more drastic nature that occasionally thwarted the efficacy of the Bible. In the course of the centuries Jewish life was subjected to many vast historic changes. The structure of law had to reflect these changes or the law was doomed. It might linger on to impede life, inhibiting its free development and stultifying it by anachronistic demands, or life might simply shed the discipline of law altogether and break out into a completely spontaneous movement without reference to the scale of values by which Judaism sought to direct its growth.

Thus the Bible centered all religious expression in the Temple in Jerusalem, at the heart of which was the sacrificial system, presided over by the Priests and assisted by the Levites. Local places of worship were discouraged. Every Israelite was expected to go on a pilgrimage to the Temple in Jerusalem for the three festivals, Pesah, Shavuot, and Sukkot. The inspiration gained during these solemn services was to nourish his religious needs. All this became a dead letter when the Temple was destroyed and the greater part of the Jewish people dispersed among the nations. The very survival of the Jewish people depended on the development of the synagogue with its distinctive way of worshipping God—the liturgy of the prayer service. But to effect this, the authorities who confronted the crisis had to go beyond the Bible. They found in the Bible much that continued to inspire them and that gave moral and religious momentum to their labors. But a new layer of juridical legislation was required to evolve new institutions that would serve in place of the old, so that the Jewish people could maintain its abiding concern: that of bending its life to the service of God under the new conditions wrought by changed circumstances.

The readiness of the Rabbis to go beyond the Bible in order to fashion appropriate legal measures to deal with life is well expressed in the following *mishnah* (Hagigah 1:8): "The laws concerning the dissolution of vows hover in the air and are devoid of biblical support. The laws concerning the Sabbath, festive-offerings, acts of trespass are mountains hanging by a hair; they have scant biblical support, but they constitute many laws. The laws concerning civil cases and the Temple service, Levitical purity and impurity, and blood relations forbidden to intermarry have what to support them. Both these and those are the essentials of the Torah."

The Oral Torah, we are here informed, consists of the laws that are well supported by biblical provision, laws that are only partially supported by biblical provision, and laws, such as those concerning vows, which are without biblical support whatever. The Bible (Deuteronomy 23:22–24) recognizes the binding character of a vow. The Rabbis, however, were impressed with the calamitous consequences which may follow a rash utterance. There was before them the rash vow taken by Jephthah (Judges 11:30–40) that he would dedicate to God whatever came forth from his house to greet him, if he returned victorious over the

Ammonites. He proceeded to carry out this vow against his daughter, who was unfortunate enough to be the first to greet her returning father. The Rabbis sought to discourage the ancient practice of vowing, and they created a technique for dissolving vows. The votary could explain to a sage that his vow had been made without due premeditation and did not anticipate the conditions confronting him. His vow would then be declared as having been assumed under error, and thus devoid of binding authority.

The legislative enactments of post-biblical leaders of Judaism were not confined to ritual. There were many enactments in the field of civil law as well, such as the extension of poor relief to needy pagans, the provision that only the least desirable parcel of real estate be taken from orphans in payment of debts, and the institution of universal elementary education in the first century B.C.E.

The legislative adjustment of law was described as a *takannah*, an enactment, or a *gezerah*, a decree. These decrees and enactments were promulgated by individuals or corporate bodies that exercised authority at a particular time. Such legislation has been attributed to Moses, Joshua, David, Solomon, Ezra, as well as to the various subsequent heads of the Sanhedrin, which combined both the supreme judicial as well as the legislative powers of the Jewish people.

The supplementation of the Bible, its rich flowering in the literature of the Talmud, was a daring process. It was conceived as a means of fulfilling the law, but it often proceeded in bold new channels. It was in a sense a confession that God's "word" is in some respect not final, and that man must step in to adapt it to the world. Adaptation is akin to change. Is it not presumptuous for man to supplement a work through which God has spoken? The Bible itself seems to warn against it. Deuteronomy 4:2 speaks out against any tampering with the word of God: "Ye shall not add unto the word which I command you, nor shall ye take aught from it."

The seeming presumption in supplementing the word of God was destined to be an issue on which conservative and progressive schools of thought debated in Judaism. This was one of the issues between the Pharisees and the Sadducees. As the populist party, the Pharisees were responsive to the needs for change, and pioneered in the labor of supplementing the Torah. At least as the spokesmen for supplementation saw it, there was ample justification for their labors in the Bible itself.

The Sadducees were the champions of the old order and resisted this supplementation as a violation of clear provision in the Bible. As characterized by Josephus (*Antiquities* XIII 10:6): "The Pharisees have delivered to the people a great many observances by succession from their fathers, which are not written in the law of Moses; and for that reason it is that the Sadducees reject them, and say that we are to esteem those observances which are in the written word, but are not to observe what are derived from the tradition of our forefathers."

Progressives and conservatives often clash on the issue of faithfulness to the constitution. The progressives favor a flexible approach which allows supplementation, while the conservatives regard such measures as a violation of the constitution. The spokesmen for supplementation found ample justification for their labor in the hallowed texts of the Bible itself. For the Bible apparently sensed the need of supplementation, and even projected an institution to accomplish it.

An elaborate system of higher and lower courts was established by Moses while the Israelites were still in the desert, upon the recommendation of his father-in-law, Jethro; a supreme court was projected as well, to resolve all legal problems that the other courts could not pass upon. The establishment of a judiciary is called for in Deuteronomy 17:8–12: "If there arise a matter too hard for thee in judgment . . . then shalt thou arise and come unto the Priests and Levites, and unto the judge that shall be in those days; and thou shalt inquire and they shall declare unto thee the sentence of judgment. According to the law which they shall teach thee . . . thou shalt do. . . ." In other words, every branch of doctrine and law seemed to be included in the sphere of authority granted to judicial bodies for clarification and adjustment.

Moses, through whom the Torah had been promulgated, himself soon discovered that there were problems which its precepts had not anticipated. The provision that the land of Canaan be parceled out equally among the male heads of each family of the tribes of Israel brought a petition from the daughters of Zelophehad in whose family there was no male issue. They asked for a ruling to decide whether in this case the women might be awarded a share in the land. Moses asked for time to consult the Almighty before replying. The decision finally announced was that in all instances where there is no male issue the daughter takes the place of the son in acquiring the inheritance of the father (Numbers 27:1–8).

A careful analysis of the historical books of the Bible indicated that Jewish authorities in the past had under certain circumstances suspended the procedures of biblical law. Thus the Bible (Deuteronomy 17:6) requires two witnesses to establish the fact of culpable crime; no one was to be found guilty of crime on the basis of his own confession without corroborating evidence. But Joshua (Joshua 7:24–5) executed a soldier by the name of Achan when the soldier confessed violating the orders of the commanding general not to loot the city of Jericho after its capture by the Israelites. What can explain the conduct of Joshua, except that it was a time of war, and martial law superseded the normal judicial procedure? The prophet Elijah, too, seems to have allowed himself to modify traditional law. He offered sacrifices on Mount Carmel (I Kings 18) when, according to biblical legislation, all sacrifices were confined to the central sanctuary in Jerusalem. Apparently the opportunity to discredit the priesthood of Baal seemed to him sufficient reason to modify the traditional procedure of worship. And, as the Rabbis interpreted the record (Moed Katan 9a), did not King Solomon suspend the fast on a Day of Atonement in order to hold the dedication of the Temple which he had built in Jerusalem?

It is thus clear that in an emergency traditional law could be suspended for specified or unspecified periods of time. What was justified in the past constituted precedent for the future. Even Deuteronomy 4:2, "Ye shall not add unto the word which I command you, nor shall ye take aught from it," was transmuted into a sanction for the adjustment of tradition. "The word which I command you," was not taken as a reference to the Bible, but to the final formulation of tradition by later authorities. Comtemporary authorities in every age, acting in their best judgment on whether to reaffirm or to revise traditional law, represent the ultimate source of guidance in life; the general public is not to "add" or "take aught" from their decisions.

All these considerations crystallized into the realization that the ultimate authority to guide life cannot be a written text, but rather the living interpreters of those texts, the custodians of religious leadership in every generation. In the words of the famous Talmudist Rabbi Jannai (Yerushalmi Sanhedrin 4:2): "If the Torah had been given in fixed and immutable formulations, it could not have endured. Thus, Moses pleaded with the Lord, 'Master of the Universe, reveal unto me how the law is to be decided.' To which the Lord replied, 'Incline after a majority [Exodus 23:2]. If a majority declare the accused innocent he is innocent, if a majority declare him guilty, he is guilty. . . .' " The law is not enshrined in some pre-existent oracular authority, but is established by the considered judgment of authoritative interpreters in every generation.

The legal powers of a generation's duly authorized interpreters of tradition were looked upon as a function of their office, regardless of their individual merits in piety or scholarship. As a well-known talmudic homily expounded it (Rosh Hashanah 25b): "When the most insignificant person is appointed leader over the community, he is to be treated as the most eminent of persons. It is said, 'Thou shalt come unto the Priests, the Levites, and unto the judge that shall be in those days' [Deuteronomy 17:9]." Could it possibly occur that a person would go to a judge who was not in his days? The meaning is that one is to be guided by a contemporary authority, whoever he be. As Scripture put it [Ecclesiastes 7:10]: "Say not, 'Why were the former days better than these?' "

There is a beautiful rabbinic parable (Baba Metzia 59b) which dramatizes man's complete sovereignty in the development of what we may call the supplementary Torah. On one occasion a fierce debate ensued between Rabbi Eliezer and his colleagues on a complicated problem of law. Rabbi Eliezer cited a variety of arguments but his colleagues remained unconvinced. Finally he invoked divine intervention to corroborate his opinion. " 'If the law is in accordance with my view,' he exclaimed, 'may this carob tree offer testimony' [by a divine miracle]. The carob tree moved a hundred (or, as others related, 400) cubits from its place. They replied to him: 'No proof can be cited from a carob tree.' Thereupon he exclaimed, 'If the law is in accordance with my views, may this stream of water offer testimony.' The stream moved backward from its normal course. They replied to him: 'No proof can be cited from water-channels.' Then he exclaimed, 'If the law is in accordance with my views, may the walls of this Academy offer testimony.' The walls of the Academy began caving in and were already on the point of collapsing when Rabbi Joshua rebuked them, 'If the students of the Torah contend with one another what concern is it of yours?' Out of respect for Rabbi Joshua they did not collapse, but out of respect for Rabbi Eliezer they remained aslope. Finally Rabbi Eliezer pleaded, 'If the law is in accordance with my views, may testimony be offered from the heavens above.' Whereupon a heavenly voice announced, 'What have you against Rabbi Eliezer? The law is in accord with his views.' Rabbi Joshua at once rose to his feet and announced, 'It is not in heaven' [Deuteronomy 30:12]. What did he mean by this? Said Rabbi Jeremiah: 'That the Torah had already been given at Mt. Sinai; we pay no attention to heavenly voices, because long ago it was declared at Sinai [Exodus 23:2] that one must follow the majority.' Rabbi Nathan met Elijah and asked him: 'What did the Holy One praised be He do in that hour?' He replied: 'He laughed with joy, saying, "My sons have defeated Me, My sons have defeated Me." ' " The Torah was given to men, and human minds interpreting the Torah in accordance with their best judgments alone define what is or what is not law.

For Judaism the most important portion of the Bible was law, and one branch of the talmudic supplement to the Bible accordingly deals with law. This is called *halakah*, a term possibly derived from a word which means "to walk," and therefore appropriately designates law, which charts a way of life. The Bible also includes vast elements of non-legal material, and the talmudic supplement reflects this as well. It includes vast portions of non-legal discussions which are crucial for our knowledge of the doctrines and values of Judaism. This is called *haggadah*, which means "general utterances."

But only *halakah* was authoritative, and once adopted by the majority of jurists it became binding on the people. *Haggadah*, on the other hand, remained open to interpretation in Judaism, and individuals could agree or disagree or propose alternative interpretations. *Haggadic* statements are all part of the rabbinic tradition, but the Rabbis never formalized their teachings into a creed which had to be followed as a criterion of orthodoxy. They strove for uniformity in practice, but belief and opinion, which involved the interpretation of the basic concepts in Judaism, was a zone in which individuals were left free to follow the inclinations of their own mind and conscience.

As there was innovation in the field of *halakah*, there was also innovation in the field of *haggadah*. Life in its varied sweep of time and circumstance continued to disclose to sensitive men many precious new insights concerning the mystery of God and His way with the world, and they sought to voice their discoveries through the spoken word. Often enough the biblical text is the stimulus which stirs their minds and hearts to the creative act of speaking. It is the utterance of a biblical teacher which becomes the occasion for igniting their imagination to see the new visions and to try and articulate them in expressive figures, in homilies and parables as well as in more formal pronouncements.

It is indeed a mark of the very power of the Bible that it could serve as a fructifying element, stimulating new cultural achievements. We treasure the Bible for what it is and also for what it has done throughout the generations to elicit in the minds and hearts of people new creative energies for the continued enrichment of Jewish tradition.

The scene where the discussions supplementing the Bible occurred were the academies of Palestine and Babylonia. The teachers who were active in these discussions spanned a period of some seven centuries beginning with the last century B.C.E. and concluding in the sixth century C.E.

In these academies there was created a vast literature called the "Oral Torah"; the Bible is called the "Written Torah." The discussions and interpretations of the biblical text were necessarily an oral activity. Individuals might have kept notes to help them present their views, and others undoubtedly kept minutes of the discussions as an aid to memory, but a work of discussion is in its nature oral rather than written. And it is primarily in its oral character that this endeavor retains its fluidity and remains free from the formalism and rigidity that is the fate of any written text. The necessity of preserving this vast tradition, however, eventually led to its organization in a systematic body of records, the most important of which are the biblical commentaries we call *Midrashim* and the formidable collection of volumes we call the Talmud. It was by the sixth century that the academies of Palestine as well as Babylonia had reduced the "Oral Torah" to writing, leaving us a precious literary monument to a great epoch in the history of Judaism.

Chapter IV
The Midrash

On June 20, 1239, Pope Gregory IX wrote to the Bishop and Prior of the Dominicans and to the Minister of the Franciscan Friars of Paris: "Wherefore, since this [the Talmud] is said to be the most important reason why the Jews remain obstinate in their perfidy, we, through apostolic letters, order your discretion to have the Jews who live in the kingdom of France, England, Aragon, Navarre, Castile, Leon and Portugal, forced by the secular arm to give up their books. Those books, in which you will find errors of this sort, you shall cause to be burned at the stake. By apostolic power, and through use of ecclesiastical censure, you will silence all opponents. You will also report to us faithfully what you have done in the matter. . . ." [1]

In due time the report came back to the Pope: "A careful examination having afterwards been made, it was discovered that the said books were full of errors, and that the veil covers the heart of these people to such degree, that these books turn the Jews away not only from an understanding of the spirit, but even of the letter, and incline them to fables and lies. From this it is clear that the Jewish teachers of the kingdom of France uttered a falsehood to your Holiness, and to the sacred fathers, the lords

[1] Jacob R. Marcus: *The Jew in the Medieval World* (New York: Meridian Books, 1961), p. 147.

cardinals, when they said that without these books, which in Hebrew are called 'Talmud,' they cannot understand the Bible and the other precepts of their laws, in accordance with their faith. After said examination had been made, and the advice of all the teachers of theology and canon law, and of many others, had been taken, all the said books which could be gotten hold of, were consigned to the flames in accordance with the apostolic decree." [2]

We shall be unable to understand the Jewish-Christian confrontation without studying the nature of talmudic literature. The reasoning of the Talmud is sometimes technical, its idiom related to an age that has vanished, and the problems on which it centers remote to the modern reader. But there is no alternative to the dictum of Goethe: *Wer den Dichter will verstehen, müs im Dichters Lande gehen* ("If you will the poet know, to the poet's world then go"). The Talmud is truly the world of Judaism, and whoever seeks to know Judaism must journey to the world of the Talmud.

The world of the Talmud consists of four major branches of literature, the Midrashim, the Mishnah, the Tosefta, and the Gemara.

The basic method by which the Oral Torah was developed in Judaism was the *midrash*. The word derives from the Hebrew *darosh*, which means "to probe" or "to search." *Midrash* was a process of probing into the written text of the Bible to deal with the various problems suggested by it. These problems varied from the obscurities of linguistics to ideology. They ranged from the quest for the simple elucidation of a text to the quest for underlying principles of theology, ethics, or law that might be applicable to new situations in need of guidance, when explicit direction was missing in the biblical text.

The masters of the *Midrash* in some cases are clearly innovators, but their probing is an attempt to find some clue, even if indirect, in the biblical text so as to establish continuity between the old and the new. The *midrash* that concerns itself with law is called *midrash halakah*, the term *halakah* referring to law. The non-legal *midrash* is called *midrash haggadah*, the term *haggadah* conveying the sense of a general utterance in any realm of

[2] Ibid., pp. 147 ff.

thought except law. The dialectic of the Talmud is an exemplification of the midrashic method, and to understand this method is to grasp the process by which the Talmud moves from the confrontation of a problem toward its solution.

Midrash forms a major part of the contents of the Talmud. But as we shall see later on, there are other elements in the Talmud besides *midrash*. There is, for example, the pronouncement of law or doctrine, without reference to the chain of reasoning by which these are related to the biblical source. The primary source of *midrash* is not in the Talmud but in a number of special midrashic works called *Midrashim*. We shall quote from a number of these works to illustrate the basic method by which the Oral Torah was developed and to introduce the climate of ideas in which the literature of the Oral Torah was created.

We shall first quote from Sifre and Tanhuma. Sifre is one of the oldest Midrashim, dating back to the second century C.E. Its title means "books," and it is an abbreviation from Sifre de-be Rav, or "The Books of the School." Its form is that of a running commentary on the biblical books of Numbers and Deuteronomy. The Tanhuma, so called after a teacher who directs the discussion in this volume, has been traced to the second half of the ninth century. It is a running commentary on each of the Five Books of Moses. The material covered in the two Midrashim is often the same, but there is a variation in treatment. The material itself is of course often much older, and the sources from which the compilers drew their material are also older than the date of compilation.

Let us consider a passage, Deuteronomy 16:18–20, and examine a number of comments from the two midrashic compilations. The original passage in the Bible states: "Judges and officers shalt thou make thee in all thy gates, which the Lord thy God giveth thee, tribe by tribe; and they shall judge the people with righteous judgment. Thou shalt not wrest judgment; thou shalt not respect persons; neither shalt thou take a gift: for a gift doth blind the eyes of the wise and pervert the words of the righteous. Justice, justice shalt thou follow, that thou mayest live, and inherit the land which the Lord thy God giveth thee."

The Midrash Tanhuma, in commenting on this passage, seeks,

in the first place, a definition of the terms used. Here is the text of the Midrash: "*Judges* and *officers—judges* refers to *dayanim*, interpreters of the law; *officers* refers to *parnasim*, executives who lead the people. Rabbi Elazar said, 'If there is no executive there is no judiciary. Thus if a person has been ruled liable to pay his neighbor any sum, unless there is someone who can exact payment, the judge is powerless to do anything'. . . . Rabbi Elazar ben Pedat declared similarly, 'Had it not been for the force commanded by Joab, David would have been unable to concern himself with rendering judgment.' Thus it is written [I Chronicles 18:14], 'And David reigned over all Israel; and he executed justice and righteousness unto all his people. And Joab the son of Zeruiah was over the army.' Whoever failed to heed the law was turned over to Joab, who exacted payment from him by force. And similarly did Job declare [Job 29:16–17], 'I was a father to the needy; and the cause of him that I knew not I searched out. And I broke the jaws of the unrighteous, and I plucked the prey out of his teeth.' " (Tanhuma, Shoftim 2).

The above passage differentiates between the judge and the executive officer who commands police power. But it is characteristic of this Midrash that it is not content with a formal definition. The definition given enters into a functional description of how each official operates. There was no need to define the role of the judge and to justify his place in society, but there was need to justify the role of the executive officer who had force at his disposal to carry out the judgment rendered. The references to David and Job are precedents reinforcing the proposition established by the Midrash that the availability of an enforcement agency is the basis of law and order in society. It was the fact that David had an army presided over by the faithful and efficient Joab that made it possible for the law as laid down by the judicial authority to prevail in the land. Job, too, as he testifies in his own account of his stewardship as tribal chief, depended on the ultimate sanction of force in his effort to protect the needy against a miscarriage of justice.

But is the force needed to assure efficacious justice only the force of coercive power? The Midrash Tanhuma continues with a second homily (Shoftim 3), pointing to another realm of force needed to win compliance with the law. It is the force emanating from the moral character of the judge. The Midrash derives this from the juxtaposition of the words "*judges* and *officers*": the judge himself is in some ways his own executive officer, whose word commands respect, provided his hands are universally acknowledged as clean and his motives honorable.

But let the Midrash expound this interesting thought in its own words: "*Judges* and *officers*—there is need that the judges be men who wield power by dint of their good deeds. This is what guided Moses in selecting judges, as we are told [Exodus 18:25], 'And Moses chose able men out of all Israel,' 'able men' being generally understood as applying to their knowledge of the Torah, their good deeds and their courage. Truly the judges themselves must be free of all claims of acting against the law, so that no one should be able to impugn their character. They must be like Moses who was able to face the Israelites and say to them [Numbers 16:15], 'I have not taken one ass from them, neither have I hurt one of them,' or like Samuel who said [I Samuel 12:3], 'Here I am; witness against me before the Lord and before His anointed: whose ox have I taken? or whose ass have I taken? or whom have I defrauded? or whom have I oppressed? or of whose hand have I taken a ransom to blind my eyes therewith?' We are then to understand as implied in the phrase *judges and officers* that the judges be of unblemished character."

The Midrash continues the above homily with a contemporary illustration. A learned and honorable judge, Rabbi Hanina, was unwittingly involved in an offense similar to one which a litigant had brought to him for adjudication. He sensed at once that he could not render a decision which would demand of the accused a higher standard of equity than he practiced himself. It was only after he corrected his own situation that he felt free to judge.

Here is the text of the Midrash: "This is well illustrated by the case of Rabbi Hanina ben Elazar who was the owner of a tree whose branches reached over into another person's field. Once a litigant came to him and charged: 'So and so's tree reaches over into my field.' He said to him: 'Leave now and return tomorrow.' This litigant murmured in objection: 'All cases which come before you, you resolve at once, but my case you put over for another time!' What did Rabbi Hanina do? He sent his workmen and they cut down his own tree which reached over into the other person's field. The next day, when the litigant returned, he informed the defendant that he must cut down the offending tree. But the latter protested: 'Why do you allow your tree to reach over into another person's field?' Then said Rabbi Hanina: 'Go and see for yourself; as you see what I have done with my tree, you do with your tree.' The latter proceeded and did so. Thus it is written: 'Judges and officers,' that there be no blemish in the judge."

The above homily of the Tanhuma is of course a bold expansion on the text. The principle enunciated is true enough. The need of an enforcement agency to render the law efficacious is satisfied through the police power of the community. By a flash of association the Rabbis glimpsed the profound truth that physical force alone is not enough. The judge by his own character helps to weaken the law or to render it potent. The juxtaposition of "*judges and officers*" did not create the homily. It only served as the stimulus which occasioned its formulation. The Midrash does not hew to a strict literal version of the text. It permits itself to expand on the text with new perceptions which have arisen through the process of association.

Let us continue with a comment from the Midrash Sifre on the same sentence: "*Judges and officers shalt thou make thee in all thy gates . . . tribe by tribe*—How do we know that we appoint a court of law over all the people? Because it is written, '*Judges . . . shalt thou make thee*' ["thee" refers to the people as a whole]: And how do we know that we appoint executive officers over all the people? Because it is written, '*And officers shalt thou make thee.*' And how do we know that we appoint a court of law for each city? Because it is written, '*in all thy gates*' [ancient cities were walled and were entered by gates]. And how do we know that we appoint executive officers for each city? Because it is written, '*and officers shalt thou make . . . in all thy gates.*' And how do we know that we appoint a court for each tribe? Because it is written, '*Judges shalt thou make . . . tribe by tribe.*'

And how do we know that we appoint executive officers for each tribe? Because it is written, '*and officers . . . tribe by tribe*'" (Sifre on Deuteronomy 16:8).

The midrashic comment in this instance appears to suggest the existing practice which the author wanted to read into the provision of the biblical commandment. According to II Chronicles 19:5–11, it was the Judean king Jehoshaphat (ninth century B.C.E.), who established a judicial system that included a supreme court in Jerusalem and a separate tribunal for each city. Josephus, who wrote toward the end of the first century C.E., reports (*Antiquities* IV 8, 14) that each city had a court of seven judicial officers. The chief court in Jerusalem is of course referred to often by Josephus. Many historical notes in the Talmud bear the same testimony. The system of courts established by Moses was slightly different. He was to adjudicate difficult cases while a group of judges serving under him were to deal with simpler cases. The people in his time lived as a compact community and there was no need for judges to function along regional lines. The geographical dispersion of the Israelites after entering Canaan apparently necessitated the reorganization of courts on a regional basis. The teachers of the Midrash sensed that our passage was apparently the basis for the prevalent system of courts, and they found each conveyed in a separate phrase which they proceeded to define. The tribal lines had of course lapsed during this period, but the Rabbis must have deemed it quite proper that the text had also provided a separate judicial jurisdiction for each tribe, to cover the tribal requirements of an earlier historic period.

The effort to clarify the simple meaning of the text remains the concern of Sifre in the comments on the biblical passage, which continue: "*And they shall judge the people with righteous judgment—and they shall judge the people*, this means even against their will; *with righteous judgment*, this refers to the criteria to be used in appointing the judges. For the judges themselves are admonished subsequently, *Thou shalt not wrest judgment.* What are we to make then of the admonition, *and they shall judge the people with righteous judgment*? This must, therefore, deal with the appointment of the judges."

We have already noted a tendency in the Midrash (evidenced

especially in the Tanhuma) to take liberties with the text, to allow itself figurative interpretations which convey a deeply felt truth though the words themselves do not really express it. A striking illustration of this is afforded us in the Tanhuma's comment on *and they shall judge the people with righteous judgment.* If detached from its context this clause may be understood to mean that they (the judges) pronounce upon the people a verdict or a judgment which declares them (the people) righteous. The instruction given is, in other words, that those selected as judges be the kind of men who can see their people as basically virtuous, who can see their merits as outweighing their faults and thus retain faith in them.

Let us cite the words of the Midrash (Tanhuma, Shoftim 4): "*And they shall judge the people with a righteous judgment*—this means that they turn the people toward righteousness. Rabbi Judah the son of Shalom said, 'It means that they find merit in the people and speak in their defense before the Holy One praised be He.' From whose example may we infer this? From Gideon the son of Joash. In his time Israel was afflicted and the Holy One praised be He sought someone who would speak on their behalf and He could not find him, because that generation was indeed deficient in the performance of commandments and good deeds. When Gideon defended his people and cried out against God's seeming indifference to their plight, the Lord at once revealed Himself to him, and asked him to lead Israel against the Midianites, telling him [Judges 6:14], 'Go with this thy strength,' the strength that has come to thee in having spoken of the merits of My children. And this is how we are to understand *and they shall judge the people with a righteous judgment*, that they espouse the merits of their generation."

The interpretation that the Midrash gives of Gideon is noteworthy. The biblical text recounts how an angel had appeared to Gideon and had encouraged him to act for his people with the statement (Judges 6:12): "The Lord is with thee, thou mighty man of valor." On hearing this Gideon is described as having retorted (Judges 6:13): "O my lord, if the Lord be with us, why then has all this befallen us? And where are all His wondrous deeds which our fathers told us of, saying, 'Did not the Lord bring us out of Egypt?' But now the Lord has cast us off, and delivered us into the hand of Midian." It was then we are told that the Lord turned toward Gideon and said: "Go with this thy strength, and save Israel from the hand of Midian." The Midrash takes the protest of Gideon as proof of his merit. As this Midrash saw it, God does not want a servile mind. He welcomes people with an independent spirit, who dare challenge an inequity even when they find it in God Himself. For it was Gideon's independent spirit which was the mark of his worth in God's eyes and confirmed his selection as a judge.

The endeavor to clarify a biblical passage leads the Midrash in many instances to add illustrative particulars to the generalized statement in the biblical text. This is well represented in the comments on the verse which follows. Once again we shall quote from the Sifre: "*thou shalt not wrest judgment*—this means that thou shalt not say to yourself, 'So and so is of distinguished appearance, so and so is my kinsman.' *Thou shalt not respect persons*—this means that thou shalt not say, 'So and so is rich, so and so is poor.' *Neither shalt thou take a gift*—surely not for the purpose of clearing the guilty and condemning the innocent, but not even to clear the innocent and condemn the guilty. *For a gift doth blind the eyes of the wise*—and obviously the eyes of the foolish; *and perverts the words of the righteous*—and obviously the words of the wicked. . . . Another interpretation: *thou shalt not wrest judgment*—this refers to decisions involving claims of money; *thou shalt not respect persons*—this refers to the procedure in the courtroom."

The Sifre is one of our oldest Midrashim and its tendency is to be terse in its comments. The Tanhuma, as we have noted, often covers the same material but presents it more profusely, with incidents and parables and other biblical episodes to reinforce its point.

This characteristic of the Tanhuma is again in evidence in the discussion of the verse under consideration (Tanhuma, Shoftim 7–8). The caution not to "respect persons" becomes the occasion in the Tanhuma for recalling Rabbi Simeon ben Shetah's refusal to be intimidated in the memorable case when the Hasmonean King Alexander Yannai was brought to trial. Yannai's slave had murdered a man and as the slave's legal owner it was the king who was held responsible for the action. The statement that "a gift doth blind the eyes of the wise," occasions the telling of an incident in which Rabbi Ishmael the son of Jose recalled how he had become partial to a person because the latter had awarded him, as a priest, a share in the shearings of his flock (which the Bible had in fact assigned as a levy due to the priests). This man was involved in a litigation and Rabbi Ishmael recalled how he had hoped for his success: "My heart felt drawn to him whenever I saw him . . . and I kept on wondering whether he had won or not, which goes to show to what degree a gift blinds the eyes. In my case what he gave me was legally due me and I did not really take a gift from him. Nevertheless, I became concerned that he win the case. How much more so does this occur, even in much graver measure, in the case of one who really accepts a gift!"

The Midrash seeks to clarify the biblical text, but sometimes it is impossible to achieve complete clarity. There are ambiguities in the language of the Bible which do not permit precise resolution. More than one interpretation is consistent with the biblical text. This is well recognized by the Midrash. After offering one interpretation, the Midrash often continues with a *davar aher*, an alternative interpretation. An instance of this is afforded us in the comment on Deuteronomy 16:20: "Justice, justice shalt thou follow." The Hebrew term for justice, *zedek*, is also the term used for mercy. We are, in other words, asked to pursue a justice, which by the connotation of the term employed is understood to be suffused with mercy. This leads the Midrash to stress on the one hand the need of compassion in judgment, and on the other hand the importance of taking one's case before a tribunal renowned for its integrity.

In the words of the Sifre: "*Justice, justice shalt thou follow*—How do we know that once the accused has been declared innocent his verdict cannot be changed to guilty? Because the text says '*Zedek* shalt thou follow' [and *zedek* means mercy as well as justice]. If he has been found guilty, how do we know that his verdict can be changed to innocent? Because the text says '*Zedek* shalt thou follow' [and *zedek* means mercy as well as justice]. Another interpretation: '*Justice, justice shalt thou follow*'—seek out a court renowned for its integrity, a court like that presided over by Rabban Johanan ben Zaccai, a court like that presided over by Rabbi Eliezer."

We shall now quote from two other Midrashim, Mekilta and Sifra. Mekilta is a commentary on Exodus, and Sifra is a commentary on Leviticus. The term *Mekilta* means "norm" or "measure," and the term *Sifra* is an abbreviation from *Sifra-de-be Rav*, which means "The Book of the School." Both these names are Aramaic. Both works were compiled some time during the second century C.E., and they represent the oldest layer of the Oral Torah. Their comments are terse and calculated to clarify the biblical text by offering definitions of terms, by citing illustrative particulars to make more concrete the general statement of the biblical text, and by assigning reasons for actions commanded or reported in the text. But we have here, too, the tendency to go beyond simple exposition, to use the text as the occasion for expanded comments concerning aspects of religion and life deemed vital by the author.

The following passage is taken from the Mekilta and is based on the commandment against stealing which is part of the Decalogue (Exodus 20:13): "*Thou shalt not steal*—why was this stated? Because elsewhere [Exodus 21:16] it is written, 'And he who stealeth a person . . . shall be put to death.' We are thus given the penalty for the abduction of a person but not a general admonition against it; therefore, it is stated here, 'Thou shalt not steal.' The commandment here is then an admonition against the stealing of persons. We take it as an admonition against stealing persons, but perhaps it is an admonition against stealing property? Since it is written elsewhere [Leviticus 19:11], 'Ye shall not steal,' we already have been admonished against stealing property. What then must be the object of the commandment here, 'Thou shalt not steal?' It must be to admonish us against stealing persons. But may not the commandment here be directed against stealing property and the other commandment [in Leviticus] be directed against stealing persons? We must reason by applying the thirteen principles by which the Torah is interpreted. Moreover, in the Decalogue the admonition against theft is one of three commandments mentioned consecutively, two being specific and the one [against theft], general. Since the two which are specified are punishable by a court of law as capital offenses, the unspecified one must deal similarly with an action punishable by a court of law as a capital offense. We must, therefore, interpret the commandment in accordance with the original suggestion and not in accordance with the latter suggestion. The commandment here must, then, be taken as an admonition against stealing persons, while the commandment in Leviticus must be assumed to deal with stealing property."

The problem to which the Mekilta directed itself was to define the commandment, "Thou shalt not steal." The Hebrew does not have a separate word for the abduction of persons. The theft of property, as well as the theft of persons, is covered by the same word *ganov*, "to steal." The commandment is, therefore, ambiguous. The Rabbis decided that the commandment in the Decalogue must be directed against the crime of kidnapping, the theft of persons. They were led to this interpretation by several considerations. Scripture elsewhere discusses theft. One of the discussions must deal with property, and the other with persons. The Decalogue in its various provisions deals with capital offenses, offenses against God, and offenses against man. The context therefore creates a presumption that the category of theft indicated in the Decalogue is an offense against a person rather than property.

The Mekilta does not elucidate how we draw the inference from the context. It merely invites us to apply the thirteen principles by which the Torah is interpreted. The author of these thirteen principles was the sage Rabbi Ishmael, and they are well-known rules of hermeneutics by which the text of the Torah was studied. The twelfth of these rules and the one obviously alluded to here reads: "Obscurities in Biblical texts may be cleared up from the immediate context or from subsequently occurring passages."

The Mekilta adds another consideration to the inference that the Decalogue was concerned with the theft of persons. Three commandments are mentioned consecutively: "Thou shalt not murder, Thou shalt not commit adultery, Thou shalt not steal." Since the first two are capital offenses, it is plausible to assume that the third also deals with a capital offense.

Another methodological principle in biblical interpretation, assumed in the Mekilta passage, is the separation of the admonition from the specification of penalty. Thus it was expected that the text would first state a general admonition, and only later prescribe the penalty.

It is of interest to note that the interpretation of the Mekilta did not go unchallenged in the Rabbinic tradition. The Palestinian Talmud (Sanhedrin 8:3) interprets "Thou shalt not steal" as applying to the theft of property. Medieval Jewish exegetes offer an eclectic interpretation including every manner of theft in the prohibition. Obadiah Seforno (sixteenth century, Italy) puts it thus: "*Thou shalt not steal*—included in the term theft is the theft of persons, the theft of property, and deception, although the primary admonition is against the theft of persons . . ." (Commentary on Exodus 20:13).

And now we shall quote from the Sifra. The comment chosen is based on Leviticus 19:17–18: "Thou shalt not hate thy brother in thy heart, thou shalt surely rebuke thy neighbor and not bear sin because of him." The Sifra comments on this verse as follows: "*Thou shalt not hate thy brother*—I might have assumed that we are forbidden to curse him, to strike him or to lay hands on him; the text, therefore, declares *in thy heart*, which includes specifically hatred in the heart. And how do we know that if one rebuked him four or five times, one must rebuke him yet another time? Because it is written, *Thou shalt surely rebuke*. It might be assumed that one must continue to rebuke a person even when seeing his face change color; the text therefore adds, *and not bear sin because of him*. Said Rabbi Tarfon, By the Temple service, if there is one in our generation who is worthy of administering rebuke! Said Rabbi Elazar ben Azariah, By the Temple service, if there is one in our generation who is ready to accept rebuke! Said Rabbi Akiba, By the Temple service, if there is one in our generation who knows how one administers rebuke! Said Rabbi Yohanan ben Nuri, I call heaven and earth as my witnesses, that four or five times was Akiba disciplined through me, because I complained against him to Rabban Gamaliel. But all the more was I certain that his affection for me continued to increase" (Sifra, Kedoshim 4).

The comment of the Sifra here cited reflects several aspects which are vital in the method of the Midrash. The Midrash presupposes a strict economy in the language of the Bible, whereby each word in a sentence is charged with a specific mission in communication. On the face of it, *Thou shalt not hate thy brother* would have been an ample expression, the final addition of *in thy heart* seems superfluous. The Midrash deemed the additional phrase as needed to establish that the hatred forbidden here includes a purely inner feeling and not necessarily overt action. Overt action against a neighbor is of course forbidden too, but the hostile act is only an overflow of hostile emotions, and the Midrash takes our text as proscribing the emotion of hostility even before it overflows into the deed of aggression.

The homily on rebuke is significant because here the Rabbis go beyond the strict exposition of the text. The Rabbis must have been deeply aware of the hazards in the administration of rebuke. They must have been deeply concerned with the perils of bringing embarrassment to a person through injudicious rebuke. Their interpretation of *and [thou shalt] not bear sin because of him* as applying to a rebuke which causes embarrassment is a figurative use of the text. The obvious meaning is the one suggested by most commentators who seek the literal sense of the text, that the failure to offer rebuke is sinful because it conceals resentment and does not permit a confrontation of grievance.

The Midrash supplements its interpretation of the text by citing several scholars who commented on the difficulties involved in rebuking people. The person to administer rebuke must be without blemish; the person rebuked must be of sufficient maturity to welcome criticism; and if the act of rebuke is actually to be performed, it must be done with delicacy and tact, for it is truly a great art, if it is to be efficacious in its purpose. A Rabbi Akiba profited from criticism but how many Akibas are there? The Rabbis did not nullify the biblical injunction but they hedged it with grave reservations.

Let us continue with the Sifra in its discussion of the sentence which follows (Leviticus 19:18): "*Thou shalt not take vengeance*—How far does vengeance extend? If A said to B, Lend me your sickle, and he refused, and the next day B said to A, Lend me your axe, and he replied, I will not lend it to you, as you did not lend me your sickle—this is revenge. *Nor bear any grudge*—How far does bearing a grudge extend? If A said to B, Lend me your axe, and he refused, and the next day B said to A, Lend me your sickle, and he replied to him, Here it is, I am not like you who refused to lend me your axe—this is bearing a grudge. . . .

"*Thou shalt love thy neighbor as thyself*—Said Rabbi Akiba, This is the most inclusive principle of the entire Torah. Ben Azzai said, *This is the book of the generations of man* [Genesis 5:1], a greater principle than this."

The comment on vengeance and bearing a grudge illustrates a familiar phase of the Midrash, the citation of illustrative particulars to explain a general statement. The comment on the love of neighbor is significant in introducnig us to the more daring side of the Midrash. Here the two sages undertake to pass a value judgment on a biblical statement. Rabbi Akiba regards the duty to love a neighbor as a summation of the entire Torah. All the Torah's teachings are best generalized in this one pronouncement. Ben Azzai did not agree, for as an ethical ideal the so-called Golden Rule is not without its drawbacks. It summons us to love a neighbor as ourself. But the term "neighbor" may be interpreted in a narrow sense, and it would shrink unduly our ethical obligation. Ben Azzai quoted Genesis 5:1, whose full provision reads thus: "This is the book of the generations of man, when God created man, He made him in the image of God." This is the more inclusive statement because it declares every man as bearing God's image on himself and as such endowed with infinite worth.

The midrashic passages we have thus far cited have all dealt with law. We shall now consider an instance of midrashic comment on the narrative portions of the Bible. We shall quote from the Midrash Rabbah. The word *rabbah* means "great" and the term *Midrash Rabbah* means, therefore, "The Great Midrash." The Midrash Rabbah is a collection of separate Midrashim on the Five Books of Moses and the five "scrolls"—Song of Songs, Ruth, Lamentations, Ecclesiastes, and Esther. Genesis Rabbah and Leviticus Rabbah were compiled about the beginning of the sixth century C.E., Exodus Rabbah about the end of the seventh century,

Deuteronomy Rabbah about the tenth century, and Numbers Rabbah in the beginning of the twelfth century. The dates of compilation, as we have already noted, do not determine the age of the contents of these works. In all instances early material, reflective of the Oral Torah in all its characteristics, was drawn by the editor from earlier collections that he had at his disposal. But the editor's special interests guided him in the selection of his materials. The Rabbah Midrashim are closer to the Tanhuma than to the Sifra, Sifre, or Mekilta; they are expansive in presentation, and favor anecdotes, parables, and historical incidents to reinforce a point made, and they take greater liberties with the text in order to convey moralistic or doctrinal lessons, even if these be only remotely suggested by the biblical text itself.

The episode we have chosen is the account of the Binding of Isaac (Genesis 22). The problem which challenged the Midrash was the baffling fact that God saw fit to impose so grave a test on his faithful Abraham. The answer suggested by the Midrash is part of the classic Jewish effort to unravel the mystery of the suffering endured by the righteous.

But let the Midrash (Genesis Rabbah 55:1) speak in its own words: "*And it came to pass after these things that God did prove* [*nisah*] *Abraham.* It is written [Psalms 60:6], 'Thou hast given a banner [*nes*] to those who fear Thee to be displayed, because of the truth, Selah.' This suggests trial upon trial, exaltation upon exaltation—in order to try them in the world, in order to raise them in the world, as the flag of a ship. And why is all this? *Because of the truth*, so as to vindicate the way of God's justice in the world. If anyone should ever complain that God is arbitrary: He makes rich whomever He wants to make rich, He makes poor whomever He wants to make poor, He makes a king whomever He wants to make a king; when He wanted, He made Abraham king, when He wanted, He made him rich. You have the means of answering him by saying, 'Can you do what Abraham did?' And when he asks, 'What did he do?' Tell him this: Abraham was a hundred years old when his son was born to him. And after all the grief of childlessness it was said to him [Genesis 22:2]: *Take now thy son, thine only son*, and he did not decline. This is what is meant by 'Thou hast given those that fear Thee a banner to display!' "

The comment of the Midrash is elicited by the word *nisah*, "He proved" or "He tested," referring to God's call that Abraham sacrifice his son Isaac. *Nisah* suggested to the Rabbis the word *nes* in Psalms 60:6, "a banner." Through the similarity of these two terms, the author spun a homily whose truth stands of course on its own feet: the tests to which righteous men like Abraham are subject are not a means to reveal their righteousness before God, but a means by which God reveals their righteousness to the world. Their ability to maintain their faith despite trials is the free affirmation of character. It accounts for the distinction bestowed on Abraham, to be the source of blessing to all the families of the earth. God's call to Abraham was not an arbitrary selection of one man over other men. Abraham earned his distinction because his readiness to serve God and to heed His will was total and without reservation. The statement, "And God tested [*nisah*] Abraham" is really tantamount to saying, "And God gave Abraham a banner [*nes*] to lift by which all might recognize his true merit." The binding of Isaac was the visible authentication of Abraham's true greatness in God's service, which earned for him the call to assume God's ministry.

The Midrash (Genesis Rabbah 55:2) continues to deal with this theme of the sufferings of the righteous. Here is the midrashic text: "*The Lord trieth the righteous but the wicked and those who love violence His soul despiseth* [Psalms 11:5]—Rabbi Jonathan said: A farmer does not beat inferior flax because it will split, but when the flax is of good quality he beats it all the more because it thereby improves. Similarly the Lord does not try the wicked because they cannot withstand it, as it is written [Isaiah 57:20], 'The wicked are as the restless sea.' He tries the righteous, as it is written, 'The Lord trieth the righteous . . .'

"Said Rabbi Johanan, When a potter examines the vessels baked in his kiln, he does not examine the defective vessels, because as soon as he will knock on them, they will split. He examines the perfect vessels, for he will not break them even with many knocks. Similarly the Lord does not try the wicked but only the righteous, as it is written, 'The Lord trieth the righteous . . .'

"Said Rabbi Elazar, It is comparable to a man who has two cows, one strong and the other feeble. Upon which one does he place the yoke? Is it not on the strong one? Similarly the Lord tries only the righteous, as it is written, 'The Lord trieth the righteous . . .'

"Another interpretation: *The Lord trieth the righteous* is fittingly exemplified by Abraham of whom it is written, 'And it came to pass after these things that God did prove Abraham.' "

The continuing exposition of the Midrash places the testing of Abraham in a general context of God's treatment of the righteous. The trials visited on them are a token not of displeasure with them but, on the contrary, of His special confidence in them. The Midrash cites illustrations from common experience to serve as analogies for this observation, that the seemingly harsher fate is reserved for those of a higher quality.

These observations of the Rabbis cited in the Midrash are not a total answer to the mystery of suffering but they are a contribution to the answer. The linking of a text with another biblical passage that expresses more forcefully the interpretation chosen, and the citation of illustration from common experience, are all characteristic of the endeavor of midrashic writing to illuminate a text under discussion. In the process the discussion seems to wander far afield, but the underlying ideas gain in depth and relevance for helping to meet the ongoing perplexities of life.

The Midrash has as its objective the clarification of the Bible, but sometimes it creates obscurities of its own. Many a midrashic passage baffles us because its idiom is unclear. All the problems that beset a biblical text often beset the midrashic text as well. Here is a passage taken from Genesis Rabbah (39:1) on the theme of Abraham's call. The Bible tells us (Genesis 12:1): "And the Lord said to Abraham, 'Get thee out of thy country, from thy kindred and from thy father's house unto the land which I will show thee.' " Commenting on this verse, Rabbi Isaac is quoted as saying: "Abraham was like a man travelling from place to place and he continued to see a palace illuminated within. He said to himself, 'Can it be that the palace is without a master?' Then did the master of the palace look out and say to him, 'I am the master of the palace.' Similarly did Abraham look out upon the world and say, 'Can it be that the world is without a master to guide it?' Then did the Holy One, praised be He, look out upon Abraham and say to him, 'I am the Master of the world.'"

The point of Rabbi Isaac's comment as here interpreted is that Abraham was sensitive to the teleolgy, or purposefulness, in the world. There was design, order, and purpose in all things in nature and this ruled out for him the absence of a guiding intelligence. The universe required a master to account for itself, as the palace surely had a master to direct its purposeful operation. It was because Abraham revealed this sensitivity that God saw him as a fitting emissary, and called on him to undertake his ministry to the world, which commenced with his departure from his birthplace.

The key word in this interpretation is the Hebrew *doleket*. We have translated it as "illuminated." However, another translation for *doleket* is possible, one that is descriptive of both the palace and the world—"afire." The analogy invoked would then be to a person who beheld a palace afire and wondered whether there was no one who cared that such a stately edifice was being consumed by fire. Similarly Abraham saw that the world was being consumed by injustice and falsehood, and he wondered whether anyone really cared that the world was being destroyed. It was then that God revealed Himself to Abraham, and made it clear to him that He is the Sovereign of the world and that He indeed cares. And it was because He saw in Abraham a sensitivity to the evils of his world that He deemed him a fitting emissary to reform the world. God therefore charged Abraham to leave his birthplace and journey to a new land where he was to commence a ministry of service to "all the families of the earth."

Which of these two interpretations is correct? It is difficult to resolve the question. Some commentators on the Midrash follow the one interpretation, others the second. The ambiguity of language gives each an element of legitimacy. The biblical text itself is silent on the subject. The Bible begins with Abraham's call.

Rabbi Isaac projected imaginatively, as the authors of the Midrash often do, a plausible setting for this call.

Rabbi Isaac's exposition is not necessarily to be taken as a factual statement of what really transpired. The past has come down to us in meager records and we are ever engaged in a labor of imaginative reconstruction to make the past intelligible. In this labor of reconstruction the past is seen in the light of the present. We employ contemporary experience as a clue to the past, but this is an inescapable procedure. We can only look with the tools we have, and the tools are the mind and the heart, which acquire their predispositions from the existing world. Rabbi Isaac's statement is clearly an imaginative reading into the past of what was in his own mind and heart. Its value is partly in the light it sheds on the biblical world. Its value is also in the insights it conveys independently of the biblical text which evoked it.

This principle is vital to our appreciation of the Midrash. Its expositions are frequently not meant as factual characterizations. They are often a kind of poetry. They are a work of creative imagination, which begins with a perception of the world and its condition, and of the values by which it may be redeemed and perfected. This perception is sometimes projected forward into the unborn future and sometimes backward into the past. These imaginative flights are precious to us in themselves, because the perceptions in which they are rooted enrich mightily the treasury of our wisdom and our faith.

The midrashic collections from which we have quoted follow the running text of the Bible. We also have a group of midrashic works in which the order of biblical passages discussed follows the Torah readings on the Festivals and special Sabbaths. There are, in addition, a number of other special collections based on various books of the Bible or on special themes, which expound their lessons regardless of the order of biblical sources where these themes are dealt with. But all these works follow the method of the Midrashim from which we have quoted. The most comprehensive of all the midrashic collections is the Yalkut Shimeoni, compiled by Simon Karo, of the thirteenth century. His sources are usually the Talmud and the earlier midrashic works, but some of them clearly suggest that he had access to earlier works, a number of which have been lost to us. The Yalkut is a summation of the entire treasury of midrashic literature and it covers almost all books of the Bible. It is the richest single work in this vast literature that sums up more than a thousand years of Jewish thought and experience.

Chapter V

The Mishnah and Tosefta

THE method of *midrash,* which we have examined in detail, yielded a rich harvest to the development of Jewish tradition. Its chief asset was that it expressed the central position of the biblical text in the literary expansion which was inspired by it. The biblical text stood out like a jewel in the center. All around it was woven the rich tapestry of comment and elaboration that was characteristic of the Oral Torah.

The Midrash was ideally suited to serve the longings of the Jewish people for a literature of edification and inspiration. It has long been customary for Jews to study the Pentateuch in weekly installments. These were supplemented with selections from other books of the Bible. But instead of studying the bare biblical text, it came to be studied with the enriching embroidery of *midrash.*

There was another need, however, that the Midrash could not meet. The Bible was not only meant for edification. One of its principal elements is law, and here a more rigorous approach is necessary. The legislation of the Bible is scattered in many different sections of the Pentateuch. Through the method of *midrash* the biblical law was expanded and became a vehicle for disciplining life, but the new legal elaborations created by the masters of the Midrash were also scattered. Moreover, each legal statement—as evolved in the school of *midrash*—was formulated in an elaborate and involved exposition. The process by which the new developments were inferred from the old provisions was preserved, with the arguments and proof texts and the give-and-take of academic dialectics.

Those interested in law felt the need for a work of simplification and systematization. They felt the need for a work that would state the legal formula succinctly without reference to the manner of its derivation, one that would organize the different provisions of the law along thematic lines without reference to the order in which the subject was treated in Scripture. Such a work was eventually created, and it has come down to us as the Mishnah.

The term *mishnah* derives from the Hebrew word *shanah*, which means "to repeat" or "to study." The Mishnah as we have it is a source book of Jewish law, as it evolved from its biblical beginnings. It was edited by Rabbi Judah the Prince and his disciples who were active in Palestine in the third century C.E. Rabbi Judah utilized earlier collections of law, but he also engaged in original research. Its objective was to encompass all the legal opinions that had been pronounced by jurists in the preceding centuries. It is written in a fine Hebrew style and is subdivided into six main subjects.

The six main subjects of the Mishnah, each a principal section of the larger work, are called *sedarim*, which means "orders." They are so called because each section is an orderly arrangement of the laws on a given subject. The six sedarim are *Zeraim*, or "Seeds," which deals with laws bearing on agriculture; *Moed*, or "Seasons," which deals with the Sabbath, the festivals, the fasts, and the feasts of the Jewish calendar; *Nashim*, or "Women," which deals with marriage, divorce, and other aspects of family life; *Nezikin*, or "Damages," which deals with civil and criminal law; *Kodoshim*, or "Holy Things," which deals with the Temple and the cult of sacrifices; *Taharot*, or "Clean Things," which deals with various questions of ritual purity.

Each of these orders is further subdivided into a number of

tractates, called *massektot* (singular, *masseket*). There are sixty-three such tractates. Each tractate is in turn subdivided into chapters, or *perakim* (singular, *perek*), and the chapters into individual paragraphs called *mishnayot* (singular, *mishnah*, like the name of the work as a whole). Some of the subject matter included in these orders seems extraneous to the main theme under discussion, but there is usually a rationale to justify the inclusion. Thus the subject of prayer is treated in the order *Zeraim*, "Seeds," because one of the major divisions of prayer concerns blessings to be recited over food; and the ethical treatise Avot or the *Ethics of the Fathers* is included in the order *Nezikin*, "Damages," because civil and criminal law involves the application of principles in the ethical life.

We shall cite selections from various tractates in each of the six orders of the Mishnah to gain a clear understanding of the Mishnah and its contribution to our knowledge of the Oral Torah.

The following *mishnah* is taken from the opening of the tractate *Berakot*, "Blessings," in the *seder* of *Zeraim*, "Seeds":

"From what time in the evening may the *Shema* be recited? From the time when the priests enter [the Temple] to eat of their Heave-offering. But the Sages say, Until midnight. Rabban Gamaliel says, Until dawn. His sons once returned from a feast and said to him, We have not yet recited the *Shema*. He replied to them, If it is before dawn, you are still obligated to recite it. Moreover, he added, whenever the Sages prescribed an act to be completed by midnight, the duty to complete it continues until dawn. . . . Why then did the Sages prescribe midnight? To deter a person from transgression" (Mishnah Berakot 1:1).

We have here the first characteristic of rabbinic law. Its scope is not limited to the relations between man and man. It also includes the relations between man and God. Man's goal is to cultivate God-consciousness and the law is the chief aid available to him in this process. It aids him through the formulation of disciplines of piety by which his life can be continually interpenetrated with reminders of God and His providence. The worship of God is thus subject to direction and regulation through the provision of the law.

The inclusion of piety within the directing function of law eliminates, of course, another characteristic usually associated with law: the dependence on sanctions to secure obedience. The conventional authority behind law is the power of enforcement, invested in some agency of government. As noted previously, rabbinic law, when dealing with civil and criminal cases, likewise depended on the police power of the state to secure obedience. But a vast realm of the law operates without any consideration of an enforcement agency. It operates on the assumption that men are eager to do what is right, and the law aids them by defining what is right. The will to obey the law, in a voluntary expression of the conscience in action, is recognized as a potent enough factor to inspire obedience.

The background of this *mishnah* is the admonition in Deuteronomy 6:7: "And thou shalt teach them diligently unto thy children, and shalt talk of them when thou sittest in thy house, and when thou walkest by the way, and when thou liest down, and when thou risest up." As understood by the Rabbis, this verse directed itself specifically to the passage that begins with Deuteronomy 6:4 and concludes with Deuteronomy 6:9. These six verses affirm the belief in the unity of God and continue with the exhortation to love God with heart and soul and might. This is the basic passage of what is known as the *Shema* and constitutes the core of Jewish faith. At an undetermined period in Jewish history the Rabbis ordained that to fulfill the admonition in verse seven this entire passage must be recited daily, morning and evening. The *Shema* beginning with the call, "Hear, O Israel, the Lord is our God, the Lord is one," has clearly remained the most celebrated testimony to the faith of the Jew, at all times and under all circumstances, throughout life and when facing death.

The discussion of the Mishnah is an attempt to remove the ambiguities of the biblical text, which does not clearly define all the terms used.

In this instance the Mishnah seeks to define the term "when thou liest down." This involves a *terminus a quo* and a *terminus ad quem*, an initial as well as a final hour to delimit the time of "lying down," or the time of retiring for the night. There is a consensus as to when this period begins. It is here defined as "the time when the priests enter to eat of their Heave-offering." We note that the Mishnah prefers to define a period of time by reference to a well-known event associated with Jewish piety. The event here cited is an incident in the life which centered in the Temple in Jerusalem. According to Scripture (Numbers 18:8–20), the priests were assigned, as perquisites of their Temple office, certain offerings from the field and from the flocks. But these were to be eaten by the priests only when they were in a state of ritual purity. If they became "unclean" by contact with a dead body, for example, they lost their right to those perquisites until after a process of purification. This involved waiting a prescribed number of days, which technically terminated at sunset of the last day of waiting (Leviticus 22:4–7). The time of sunset, when the priests regained their state of purity and their right to resume Temple functions and to enjoy the perquisites of their office, must have been made impressive for the people. Instead of citing time in the abstract, the Mishnah is less direct but achieves a link with a major aspect in the life of piety. This is indeed one of the characteristics of the Mishnah. Its language is profuse with allusions to various aspects of Jewish religious faith and life, whereby a most minute detail, in any subject under discussion, can be made to evoke associations with treasured institutions in Jewish life.

Another subject of interest to be noted is the juxtaposition of the names of the participants in the discussion of the Mishnah. They are Rabbi Eliezer, the Sages, and Rabban Gamaliel. Rabbi Eliezer and Rabban Gamaliel are readily identified. They were among the first generation of scholars who were active after the fall of the Temple in 70 C.E. Rabbi Eliezer began his career prior to the destruction of the Temple. He was a disciple of Rabban Johanan ben Zaccai and participated with a group of fellow disciples in smuggling their master Johanan out of the besieged city of Jerusalem and into the camp of the Romans. Johanan won the authorization from the Romans to establish a center of Judaism in Jabneh, and when Jerusalem fell Jabneh became the new seat of the Sanhedrin and of Jewish reconstruction after the Jewish forces surrendered to Roman power. For a short time Johanan headed the Sanhedrin, and in that role his title was changed from

"Rabbi" to "Rabban," but his place was eventually taken by Gamaliel. The latter in due time was invested by the Romans with the title of Patriarch, and he exercised limited political authority under their jurisdiction. At the same time, he was the head of the Sanhedrin, the Supreme Court for the interpretation of the Torah, the written as well as the oral law, thus serving as the religious and the secular head of the Jewish community.

Who were "the Sages"? Here we face a stylistic characteristic of the Mishnah. In recording the diverse views that were expressed on any subject under discussion, the view that was adopted as authoritative was usually ascribed to "the Sages," or the consensus of the scholars, though the original proponent of that opinion might have been only an individual. The usual disputant of Rabbi Eliezer was Rabbi Joshua ben Hananiah, and his opinion was generally preferred over that of Rabbi Eliezer. We may assume that "the Sages" cited here refers to Rabbi Joshua. But his view is given anonymously, in the name of the collective authority of the scholars, to indicate that this is the authoritative view. The rejected view is preserved for posterity and is usually cited first.

What of the view of Rabban Gamaliel? This, too, is a rejected view, preserved for posterity as an illustration of the legal dialectic in action, but not as a source of practice. His view is placed last as a kind of appendix because it is more extended in statement, and it includes an anecdote and some general observations on the rabbinic method in dealing with problems in the law. His eminence as religious and secular leader of Jewry helped to invest his view with interest and with concern to preserve it. But it did not endow his views with priority. The deliberations that led to the determination of the law are omitted in the Mishnah, but the results are documented. The voice of authority is spoken by "the Sages." The other voices are respectfully listened to, but they remain the voices of two individuals who have not been able to convince the court and therefore remain in the role of dissenters who were outvoted by their colleagues.

What was the basis for the disagreement among the three authorities? Not a word is said about this, and we really cannot be certain But it has been suggested that the three scholars each reflected their particular environments. Rabbi Eliezer was a farmer and lived in the countryside where people retired early and rose early. He, accordingly, asked that the *Shema* be completed by the end of the "first watch," which was around ten o'clock (Eliezer divided the night into three "watches"). Rabban Gamaliel was an aristocrat, accustomed to a busy round of social events that often proceeded throughout the night, and for him even until dawn was properly the time of "lying down" or retiring. Rabbi Joshua was of the urban middle class and he fixed the retiring time until midnight, reflecting the general habits of city life.

Here is a *mishnah* taken from the order *Moed*, "Festivals." It is the first *mishnah* in the tractate *Yoma* (literally "the Day"), which deals with the Day of Atonement: "Seven days prior to the Day of Atonement they separated the High Priest from his home and placed him in the Counsellors' chamber. They prepared another priest to officiate in his place lest anything happen to the incumbent High Priest which might render him unfit to officiate. Rabbi Judah says, They also prepared another wife for him lest his wife should die, since it is written [Leviticus 16:6], 'He shall make atonement for himself and his household,' and a household includes a wife. They replied to him, If so, then there would be no end to the matter" (Mishnah Yoma 1:1).

This *mishnah* calls for clarification if we are to see the points at issue. It is clearly an attempt at historical reconstruction, to preserve the proccdure of a time-hallowed institution that had been destroyed by the march of events. The details of the procedure that are described in the rest of the first chapter of this tractate make it clear that the seven-day period spent by the High Priest in the Counsellors' Chamber was a period of consecration. Its purpose was to assure that the High Priest would conduct the service in accordance with Pharisaic principles.

There had been a bitter clash of parties in the Judaism of that epoch, with Sadducees and Pharisees battling for supremacy. In general the Sadducees stood for a literal interpretation of the Bible, challenging the far-reaching developments in law and doctrine which had occurred under the sponsorship of the Pharisees. There were differences between the two sects as to the Temple ritual during the Day of Atonement service. The priestly caste had generally sided with the Sadducees, but during the reign of Salome Alexandra (76–67 B.C.E.), there had been a showdown and the Pharisees won the day. The Temple came under their authority and they expected the priests to conduct the service in accordance with their instructions.

It was during this seven-day vigil that representatives of the Pharisaic authorities met with the High Priest and conducted intensive discussions on the awesome events in which the High Priest was to be the central figure on the Day of Atonement. Thus when the vigil was over they declared to the High Priest: " 'My Lord High Priest, we are representatives of the Court and you are our representative and the representative of the Court. We adjure you by Him who caused His name to dwell in this House that you change nothing from what has been imparted to you.' He turned aside and wept, and they turned aside and wept" (Mishnah Yoma 1:5).

The preparation of another High Priest was precautionary. The theater prepares an understudy for its chief actors. In all vital areas of government and business, provision is made for deputies to replace chief officers in case of emergency. But what was the sense of Rabbi Judah's suggestion concerning the preparation of an understudy for the High Priest's wife?

It is apparent from the context that Rabbi Judah was not describing a fact. The retort of his colleagues, "If so, there would be no end to the matter," makes this clear. We must assume that what Rabbi Judah really meant is that they should have prepared a deputy for the High Priest's wife, not that they really did. What motivated Rabbi Judah's strange opinion? The proof text is a convenient method of bolstering an opinion, but as a rule other motivations create the cogency for the opinion expressed. The proof text is a reinforcement, but it is not always the primary or sufficient consideration to direct a jurist to take the position he does on a question under consideration.

It is difficult to conjecture motives when none are directly indicated. Nevertheless, a consideration of some of the ideological issues under question in Rabbi Judah's time may help us understand his position.

Marriage is a sacred state in Judaism. The duty to marry and procreate is the first commandment in the Torah. The first injunction God imparted to Adam was to "be fruitful and multiply." The life of sex, when lived within the purity of the family, is a basic fulfillment of God's design for man. But the Hellenistic world often saw sex in another light. Gnostic mysticism, which disparaged this world, also disparaged the act by which life was perpetuated. Asceticism was in vogue in many circles where celibacy was preached and practiced as a virtue. The Essenes in Judaism reflected the same outlook on sex; they practiced celibacy. The Christains did not insist on this for their adherents, but they certainly regarded it as a higher, a "holier" state. This may well have contributed to the Christian insistence that Jesus was conceived without the usual sex act. His birth of a virgin, through an immaculate conception, withdrew him from the taint of sex.

These views on sex and marriage were abhorrent to the Rabbis. They challenged them directly by extolling the virtues of the family and the life of sex within the family. Celibates were regarded as incomplete persons. The High Priest officiating in the Holy of Holies on the Day of Atonement was a representative of his entire people. He had to be a "whole" man, a family man. Rabbi Judah's suggestion, whether seriously meant or not, was an attempt to give dramatic emphasis to the need for the state of matrimony. It underscores the view that a wifeless man is not a whole man, and is therefore unfit to serve in the exalted office of High Priest.

The suggestion of Rabbi Judah illustrates an important characteristic of the Oral Torah in dealing with offensive ideologies. The Rabbis avoided direct denunciations. New Testament writers continually upbraided the Jews who remained unwilling to follow the new faith. They used the sharpest invective against the Pharisees who led the Jews in their tenacious refusal to accept Jesus as the messiah. The Rabbis, however, avoided such polemic expressions. Their method was to strengthen their faith from within, and one special device was to lay added stress on institutions and ideas which were under challenge.

We cite a *mishnah* from the third order, *Nashim*, "Women." It is taken from the tractate *Gittin*, "Divorces":

"A person who is half-slave and half-free labors for his master one day and for himself one day. This is the view of the School of Hillel. The School of Shammai said to them, You have provided well for the master, but not for him. He cannot marry a slave because he is half free. He cannot marry a free woman either, because he is half slave. Shall he never marry? But was not the world created for procreation, as it is written [Isaiah 45:18], 'He did not create it to be a waste but that it be inhabited'? Therefore, for the sake of the perfection of the world, we force the master to free him, and he gives him [the master] a note for half his worth. The School of Hillel reversed themselves and concurred in the view of the School of Shammai" (Mishnah Gittin 4:5).

The *mishnah* we have cited discloses many characteristics of this literature. The first impression to be gained is that the tractates lack homogeneity. They are not strictly limited to the subject to which they are dedicated. *Gittin* deals with divorce but here we have a discussion of the status of the slave. What principle governed the inclusion of this discussion concerning slaves in a tractate dealing with divorce? It was the circumstance that the termination of the marriage, like the termination of the state of bondage, was accomplished by means of a *get* (literally, "a legal document"), in the one case issued by the husband, in the other by the master. The verbiage in the document varied, but the substance was the same in both cases, a grant of freedom. The woman gained her freedom from her husband, and the slave gained his freedom from the master.

The mishnaic discussion presupposes, of course, the existence of slavery. A slave, in some respects, was property and could be owned by two partners. It could thus transpire that one owner would emancipate his half-possession of the slave, while the other would not.

Our *mishnah* makes it clear, however, that while the slave is in some respects property, he is in other respects a person who shares the same responsibilities as other men. We have already noted that one of the basic human responsibilities is to marry and raise a family. In the case cited, we have a conflict between the property rights of the master and the human rights of this half slave. The two schools quoted often differed in the rabbinical academies but it is significant that in the end both concurred in giving priority to human rights. The master had to content himself with compensation to be paid by the half slave after regaining his freedom.

It is interesting to note that the School of Shammai, in arguing for the half slave's need to be free to marry, does not invoke the more authoritative injunction issued to Adam: "Be fruitful and multiply, fill the earth and master it." The injunction in Genesis (1:28) was addressed to Adam, who was a free man, and only a free man could be construed as having a mandate to "master the earth." The latter injunction then might be interpreted as applicable only to a free man, not a slave or a half slave. The verse in Isaiah, however, defines the goal of creation, that the world was made to be settled, and life to be perpetuated. If any person were excluded from marriage and procreation he would be in effect a "vain" creature, not sharing in life's purpose. This concept is more inclusive in scope, and a more cogent basis for the position taken by the Shammaites.

The concept of "the perfection of the world" (*tikkun ha-olam*) for the sake of which the master is forced to emancipate the half slave, is introduced into Jewish law as a general juridical principle by the teachers of the Mishnah. The principle does not occur in the Bible, and its formulation illustrates the sophistication and juridical maturity assumed by the law in the intervening period between the close of the Bible and the rise of the Mishnah.

We cite a *mishnah* taken from the tractate *Baba Metzia* (literally, the "Middle Gate") in the order of *Nezikin*, "Damages," which deals with civil law:

"If one found scrolls, he should read in them once in thirty days. If he cannot read, then he should roll them out. However, he must not study from them a subject for the first time, nor may he permit another person to read with him.

"If he found a garment, he should shake it out once in thirty days; he should spread it out for its benefit, but not so as to add to his own prestige.

"Silver and copper vessels he may use if it is for their benefit, but not to the point where they become worn. Golden and glass vessels he is not to touch but leave them until the coming of Elijah.

"If he came upon a sack or a basket or any object which he would not normally carry, he need not take it" (Mishnah Baba Metzia 2:8).

This *mishnah* is an illustration of the far-reaching development of Jewish law under the direction of the Rabbis. The Bible (Deuteronomy 22:1–5) speaks of a person's duty to restore a lost object to its owner. If the owner cannot be readily identified, then the finder is told that he is to bring the found object "to thy house, and it shall be with thee, till thy brother ask for it, and thou shalt restore it to him."

The *mishnah* considers the further obligation which a person has to protect the found object against deterioration or loss during the time of waiting for the owner's identification. The books of antiquity were in the form of scrolls, and the finder is advised that he must air the books periodically against deterioration. Where use will protect the object he is to use it, but he must be careful that the use is for the benefit of the object, not for his own benefit. Studying a subject for the first time requires the intensive use of a book and this may damage it. Two readers using a book together may lead to pulling one side or the other which again may damage the book. Silver or copper vessels will tarnish, but overuse may wear down the metal. Gold and glass vessels do not tarnish and therefore they are to be left unused.

Our text speaks of leaving them until "the coming of Elijah." This alludes to the tradition that Elijah, who will come to announce the advent of the messiah, will resolve all unsettled questions of fact and law. The phrase is an idiom which suggests that these objects are to be left unused indefinitely, until the loser is discovered.

But our *mishnah* qualifies a person's obligation to restore a lost article. If the article were of a nature that it is inconsistent with his dignity to occupy himself with it, then he is relieved of this obligation.

This *mishnah* illustrates a characteristic of rabbinic law to which we have alluded previously. It presupposes a will to be ethical as a motivation in obedience. The provisions of this *mishnah* define the measure of an ethical obligation. In the nature of things it cannot be expected that an external authority will compel performance of this obligation. While rabbinic law has not dispensed with the use of force altogether to secure compliance, it operates on the assumption that there exists a wide margin of voluntary obedience, and that men need only to be told what is right and they will proceed freely to do it.

The entire *mishnah* states its provisions anonymously. This indicates that the jurists who had discussed the subject had reached unanimity. None had challenged those rulings. Whoever had taken the initiative in formulating those rulings cannot be determined from the *mishnah*. The greatest triumph of a jurist was to have the court adopt his views and propound them as its own.

How did the jurists reach their decision in areas where the Bible is silent? An ingenious dialectic sometimes developed inferences from what is given in the biblical text. But beyond this dialectic there was the intrinsic logic of a situation which recommended certain courses of action as reasonable and equitable. The Rabbis of course preferred to cite proof texts, but in some instances the "proof" is only a gesture to reinforce what had previously been established as reasonable.

It is in the nature of the Mishnah to ignore the considerations underlying a decision. Its rulings are presented categorically, as codified formulae of what should or should not be done. As we shall have occasion to discover, the search for the reasons underlying the rulings of the Mishnah was to stimulate the creation of another branch in the literature of the Oral Torah.

We now cite a *mishnah* from the tractate *Hullin* ("Non-Consecrated"), which is part of the order *Kodoshim* or "Holy Things":

"A man may not take a mother bird with her young even for the sake of cleansing the leper. If then because of so light a precept which involves but the worth of an *issar* the Torah has said [Deuteronomy 22:7] 'that it may be well with thee and that thou mayest prolong thy days,' how much greater must be the merit of keeping the weightier precepts of the Torah" (Mishnah Hullin 12:5).

This *mishnah* discloses an additional characteristic of rabbinic law. It embraces in its concern man's obligation to the animal kingdom. The Bible had ordained the protection of the mother bird from the pain of watching a raid on her nest. The *mishnah* fortifies the biblical admonition. A leper, after completing his period of isolation and therapy was readmitted to the community. The readmission was preceded by a rite which involved two birds, one to be slaughtered and the other to be set free in the open field (Leviticus 14:4–7). But even for so meritorious an action the mother bird could not be touched. The concern of Jewish law with protecting the animal kingdom led eventually to a prohibition of the sport of hunting.

On completing a tractate, the Mishnah often expressed some edifying thought, and in this *mishnah*, which completes the tractate Hullin, we have, in this spirit, the observation concerning the merit of keeping the precepts of the Torah. The biblical exhortation to protect the mother bird adds the promise that such compassion would bring a person well-being and length of days, though the mother bird herself involved a value of no more than the small coin of antiquity, the *issar*. Surely, the *mishnah* suggests, even where no reference to merit or reward appears in the Bible, we must assume that great reward will come to those who are zealous in keeping the law.

We must not assume that the Mishnah encourages a pragmatic motivation for keeping the law. The *Ethics of the Fathers* sums up an often repeated rabbinic admonition: "Be not like servants who serve a master for the sake of reward, but rather be like those who serve the master without the expectation of reward." But while the Rabbis cautioned against a service of God based on the expectation of rewards, they certainly believed that obedience and disobedience bring with them positive or negative consequences for a person's life. It is the recognition that such consequences do follow which comes to expression in our *mishnah*.

Our final citation is from the tractate *Kelim* ("Vessels") in the order *Taharot*, "Clean Things":

"If an oven was cut up into rings and sand was inserted between the rings, Rabbi Eliezer rules it unsusceptible to impurity, while the Sages ruled it susceptible. Such was the oven of Akhnai. As for the cauldron of the Arabs—which are hollows dug in the ground and plastered over with clay—if the plastering can stand independently it is susceptible to impurity, otherwise, not. Such was the oven of Ben Dinai" (Mishnah Kelim 5:10).

This *mishnah* deals with a highly specialized phase of Jewish law, the law of ritual purity. The Bible provides (Leviticus 11:32) that a vessel may become impure through contact with the dead body of a person or an insect, requiring that it be withdrawn from use for a specified time and cleansed with water before it may be restored to a state of purity. The basis for all the rules concerning ritual purity of persons and objects is difficult to determine, but these rules certainly served—among other things—a hygienic end, limiting exposure to contact with infectious agents.

The biblical law speaks of a "vessel," and the problem dealt with in the *mishnah* centers on the definition of the term "vessel." The "Akhnai" stove had been cut by the owner into rings which were separated from each other by sand but externally plastered over with cement. Rabbi Eliezer saw this as a broken vessel, and as such, free of contamination by impurity. The Sages, ignoring the objective appearance, considered the fact that the owner continued to use it as a stove, and this fact of continued use made it a vessel and therefore subject to the impurity of a vessel. The same principle is involved in the "Ben Dinai" stove. If the clay form that has hardened to the shape of the hollow dug in the ground is firm enough to stand independently, then it is a vessel. Even Rabbi Eliezer apparently agreed that this stove was subject to the rules bearing on vessels generally.

To the layman this discussion may seem abstruse, but weighty principles of law are often expounded through consideration of seemingly trivial cases. The principle at stake in our *mishnah* is certainly important. Shall the law take into consideration subjective states, or shall it ignore the intention of the exceptional individual and decide solely on the basis of objective facts? If the vessel is broken it is no longer a vessel, argued Rabbi Eliezer, but the Sages saw the owner's action as clearly reflecting his subjective state in which he continued to regard it as a vessel.

It is necessary again to divorce ourselves from the conventional notion that law is concerned with the conflict of persons or with the conflict of the person and society. Rabbinic law, as we have noted, is an attempt to guide man in doing what is right. Any subject in which man may be helped by such guidance is embraced by the law. And the help rendered often takes the form of a definition of what is right. The rest, in many cases, is left to the individual, who, as a law-abiding person, is inwardly directed to heed the law without constraint from outside sources.

Rabbinic literature includes a work that parallels the Mishnah in content and in form; it is known as *Tosefta*, literally, a "supplement."

It is not easy to offer a precise definition of this work in relation to the Mishnah. The editors of the Mishnah had apparently omitted much material in order to make their text as concise and brief as possible. Material excluded from the Mishnah was called *baraita*, Aramaic for "outside." The omitted material was also of interest to scholars, and in time a collection of some of this material was produced to create the Tosefta as a supplement to the mishnaic text. Subsequent editions of the Mishnah re-admitted certain passages from the Tosefta to make for a fuller text. The Tosefta itself is divided, like the Mishnah, into orders and tractates that bear the same names as parallel divisions of the Mishnah.

We cite a passage from the Tosefta to illustrate some of the characteristics of this branch of the Oral Torah and its relation to the Mishnah. The passage is taken from the tractate *Avodah Zarah* ("Idolatrous Worship") and it deals with one of the most grievous predicaments faced by the Jews in the Roman Empire:

"It is forbidden to go to the amphitheatres of the gentiles because of idolatry, so says Rabbi Meir. The Sages say, When they offer sacrifices, it is forbidden because of idolatry, when they do not offer sacrifices it is forbidden as 'a seat of the scornful' [Psalms 1:1].

"One who goes to stadiums or army camps and sees the sorcerers and charmers or the performances of *bukion* and *mukion*, *lulion* and *mullion*, *blurin* and *salgurin* is guilty of sitting in 'the seat of the scornful' denounced in Scripture [Psalms 1:1–2], 'Happy is the man who has not walked in the council of the wicked, nor stood in the way of sinners, nor sat in the seat of the scornful.' From this you may infer that those pursuits undermine one's devotion to the study of the Torah.

"One who goes to the amphitheatres of the gentiles, if he is to participate in public affairs it is permitted. However, if he is a person of prominence in the Jewish community it is forbidden. One who sits in the stadium is guilty of bloodshed. Rabbi Nathan permits it because as a spectator he may shout for mercy and thus save lives and he may be able to testify so as to enable a woman to remarry. One may go to the stadium because he may shout for mercy and save lives, and to an army camp for various business transactions. However, if he is a person of prominence in the Jewish community, it is forbidden" (Tosefta Avodah Zarah 2:5–7).

The passage we have quoted seeks to define the attitude which a Jew may adopt toward the two characteristic institutions of the Roman way of life—the amphitheater and the army camp. The Roman theater centered in the arena where gladiators fought, often to death, against one another, or against wild beasts, while the crowd watched and enjoyed the brutal spectacle. The scope of these games may be gauged by the following figures: at the inauguration of the Colosseum in Rome 5,000 wild beasts and 4,000 tame animals were killed, and to commemorate one of Trajan's victories there was a butchery of 11,000 beasts. How many human victims were involved in these brutal performances? It has been said by one historian that "nothing so clearly brings before us the vein of coarseness and inhumanity running through the character of the Roman as his passion for gladiatorial shows." [1] The theater was also the setting for sacrifices to various Roman gods.

The popularity of the amphitheaters made them into general places of assembly, for socializing, and for the transaction of private and public affairs. Amphitheaters were established in the Roman provinces in imitation of those in Rome.

The Roman army camp was situated anywhere in the Roman Empire where their armies were needed to safeguard the hold of power. Sometimes the camp was established around a city under siege. At the same time civilians had occasion to visit the camp to trade with the soldiers and to render them various other services, and also to deal with the Roman command. The camp was a miniature Rome, and typical Roman sports and entertainment as well

[1] "Games, Classical," *Encyclopaedia Britannica* (14th edn.), X, 10.

as idolatrous exercises were arranged for the pleasure and edification of the soldiers.

The Rabbis forbade a Jew to go to the amphitheater or to the Roman army camp where he would be involved in morally degenerate pastimes. The general prohibition of going to the amphitheater was, however, waived in the case of a person going on a mission to meet with the officials on the public welfare. But this was further limited by excluding a Jew of prominence, who should not be seen at the amphitheater at all. And the Tosefta adds the remark that to be a spectator at the games tainted one with the crime of bloodshed.

But Rabbi Nathan called attention to extenuating circumstances, because of which attendance should be permitted. The rules of the gladiatorial combats left it to the spectators to decide whether a wounded gladiator was to be spared or to be pressed on to the bitter end. By shouting in favor of mercy the gladiator would be saved. There was another service that might be rendered by a spectator. The gladiators were often those the Roman courts had condemned to death or those taken prisoner after skirmishes with the Roman garrisons. There were tens of thousands of Jewish prisoners after the war against Rome who were sentenced to fight and die in the arena. One who witnessed the bloody spectacle might therefore be in a position to certify to the death of the victim, which would render his wife a widow and thus free to remarry. Without such certification she might be left for years, ignorant of her husband's fate, doomed sometimes to a lifetime of fruitless waiting.

Finally our passage offers a concluding statement. Adopting the view of Rabbi Nathan, it permits going to the amphitheater and adds permission to visit the army camp, but limits these to the ordinary person. The prominent individual is asked to live by a standard of greater sensitivity, and he must not be seen in such places under any circumstances.

The entire discussion we have quoted from the Tosefta is absent in the Mishnah. Why did not the editor of the Mishnah include this material in his collection? We cannot really know, though we may conjecture it. The Roman games were a crime against man and beast, but the Mishnah reflects life in Palestine, where Jews lived in concentrated areas, and therefore remote from these centers of Roman pastime. The Roman camps, too, were away from the centers of native population and constituted a kind of Roman reservation with which civilians had little contact.

Other aspects of the subject are, however, touched on in two *mishnayot:* one in the tractate Baba Kamma, and one in the tractate Avodah Zarah. The *mishnah* in Baba Kamma expresses pity for the animals used in the games. Biblical law provided that "when an ox gores a man or a woman to death, the ox shall be stoned and its flesh shall not be eaten; but the owner of the ox shall be clear" (Exodus 21:28). The *mishnah* exempts from this rule an ox used in the games, as the viciousness of such an ox is not innate, but a result of conditioning by the trainer. In the words of the *mishnah:* "An ox from the stadium is not liable to be put to death, for it is written, 'If an ox gore,' and not, 'If it be made to gore' " (Mishnah Baba Kamma 4:4).

The *mishnah* in Avodah Zarah discusses the propriety of doing business with the Romans to help them import their game animals or to help them build the edifices where their violent way of life was centered. This *mishnah* speaks eloquently for the contempt felt by the Rabbis for the Roman way of life and it illustrates the measures taken by them to insulate the Jews against its influence:

"One may not sell them bears and lions or any other item which may result in injury to the public. One may not build with them a basilica, a prison house, a stadium, and a podium. But one may build with them pedestals and bath houses. But one must desist when reaching the vaulted area where the idol is placed" (Mishnah Avodah Zarah 1:7).

The prohibition to sell them "bears and lions" was no doubt due to the use of these animals in the arena. The basilica was the administrative building of the Roman authority and the scene where its courts of law deliberated and meted out their harsh sentences; the prison house was usually near the basilica, and it was notorious for the torture of prisoners; the stadium was the principal feature of the amphitheater, the scene where the spectators viewed the games; the podium was the platform from which the official proceedings of the games or other administrative procedures were directed.

The public bath was another characteristic institution of the Romans. Here the problem was that these baths were dedicated to various deities and adorned with idols. The Mishnah allows helping to construct a bath house. The bath house was, in a sense, similar to our country club. It had all kinds of facilities for the bathers' pleasure and edification, in addition to the areas for bathing. It had a lounge, a dining area, games, and sometimes even lectures and entertainment. Various pedestals were set in the room for the placement of decorative statues or as seats for distinguished guests. But a Jew was directed to show his dissociation from idolatry by refusing to share in the construction of the vaulted area, which was reserved for the location of the idol.

In the illustrations cited the Mishnah and the Tosefta supplement each other, but each may be read independently. In some instances the relationship between the two is much closer. This is well seen by examining Mishnah Shekalim 1:1 and Tosefta Shekalim 1:1. Thus the Mishnah: "On the first day of the month of Adar announcements are made concerning the half-shekel due to the Temple treasury [Exodus 30:13 ff.]. . . . And on the fifteenth day of the month the roads are repaired. . . ." Apparently presupposing this *mishnah* the Tosefta merely adds: "On the fifteenth day of that month emissaries of the court attend to the repair of the roads, which have become damaged in the rainy season." Without the Mishnah we would be in the dark as to what is meant by "on the fifteenth day of that month." It is only by drawing on the Mishnah that we may identify "on the fifteenth day of that month" as referring to the month of Adar.

Sometimes the statement in the Tosefta extends the discussion in the Mishnah by citing additional contingencies. Once we understand the Mishnah it becomes a simple matter to continue the discussion in the Tosefta text.

We cite a passage from the Tosefta which parallels the *mishnah* cited above from Baba Metzia, dealing with found property. It illustrates the closeness of the two texts, as well as their divergence.

"If one found scrolls, he should read them once in thirty days. But he is not to read the weekly portion from Scripture and review it, nor is he to read it and then translate it. Three are not to read from one volume, nor is he to unroll more than three folios at a time. Simkus said, In the case of new books, he is to read them once in thirty days, but in the case of old books, he is to read from them once in twelve months (Tosefta Baba Metzia 2:21).

The other statements of the above *mishnah* are similarly supplemented in the Tosefta, with additional provisions or illustrations, and, in some cases, with additional opinions by teachers whom the Mishnah had ignored.

The Mishnah and Tosefta are the two classic sources for the succinct formulations of rabbinic law. But the Mishnah was by far the more influential work and it has remained a basic landmark in the literary flowering of the Bible. To be sure, the Bible is not generally cited in the text of the Mishnah, but the Bible is the silent, invisible spring from which it flows on the far-reaching course of its development.

Chapter VI
The Gemara

The human spirit is an uncertain master. Now it demands of us one thing, and now another. Sometimes we are impatient with long discussions; we want the brief, the succinct statement. But then when we have succeeded in producing these triumphs of brevity our spirit craves the freer, the more profuse and leisurely exposition. The Mishnah was a triumph in the history of Jewish tradition. In brief and succinct formulations it preserved for posterity the great treasures of rabbinic law. Zealously, students pored over its contents. By studying the Mishnah they were able to master the distillation of tradition which had grown from biblical beginnings. But in due time the literary history of tradition turned in a new direction and yielded us a new harvest, what we call the *Gemara* (from the Aramaic *gamor*, which means "to learn"), or "The Teaching."

How was the Mishnah studied? The first objective was to master its immediate contents, to learn the formula itself, and to know how to associate the names of the scholars represented in the Mishnah with the views expressed by them. But the rabbinic mind was always impatient with the arbitrary, the dogmatic. It sought underlying principles; it sought a logic and rationale in man's life within the beliefs and practices of the Jewish faith. The Rabbis sought a basis for the law in Scripture or in the exigencies of life and they sought a consistency in the various legal opinions of jurists who created the system by which Jewish life was governed. They also allowed themselves to digress, to tell an anecdote, a parable, or a piece of folklore, or to recall some historic event, or invoke some religious or moral observation, at times only remotely bearing on the subject under discussion.

The Mishnah also served as the basis for legal decisions by jurists who held judicial positions within the Jewish community. The Mishnah, as we noted previously, was edited in the third century C.E. Jewry then lived within a larger non-Jewish world, in Palestine as part of the Roman Empire, and in Babylonia as part of the Parthian Empire. But both these empires allowed the Jews a large measure of autonomy, which included the right to maintain their own courts where the Jewish law was administered. The Mishnah was the source book of law, but no legal formula applies itself automatically. There is always the continuing need of discussion and argument in which judges draw on their own discretion, as well as on the knowledge of the law, to assess the precedents of another age and evaluate their relevance for the new facts of life, in which there is always some element of novelty not anticipated by ancient formulations.

The Mishnah became the center of a vast intellectual endeavor spread over the centuries in the leading academies of Palestine and Babylonia, where the major Jewish communities existed. Various unofficial records were kept of these discussions but it was inevitable that these records should receive a more formal recognition, as a supplement commenting on and clarifying the Mishnah. As the Mishnah and Gemara are presently arranged, each individual *mishnah* was followed by its appropriate *gemara*. Not every tractate of the Mishnah was supplemented by the Gemara, only those that were of interest to the teachers who created the Gemara. The Palestinian Gemara, frequently called *Yerushalmi*, or "Jerusalem Gemara," supplements thirty-nine of the sixty-three tractates of the Mishnah; the Babylonian (the *Bavli*), only thirty-seven. In scope, however, the latter is three times as large as the former, the Babylonian Gemara being more elaborate in its discussions. The same teachers are often represented in the two Gemaras, for the academies in both countries maintained contact and sought to bring their labors into mutual harmony. The Palestinian academies enjoyed the prestige of functioning in the Holy Land, while the Babylonian academies enjoyed the advantage of a more flourishing Jewish community. For in post-mishnaic times the Jewish community of Babylonia had overtaken Palestine as a center of Jewish culture and life.

The teachers who are represented in the Mishnah are called *tannaim*, those represented in the Gemara are called *amoraim*. Both terms are Aramaic. *Tanna* means "a teacher," *amora* means "a lecturer."

The Mishnah has often been edited as an independent text, but the Gemara does not appear separately. It is broken down into sections relevant to the individual *mishnayot* to which they are added as a supplement. The Mishnah and Gemara as an integrated text constitute what we call the Talmud. The Palestinian Talmud was edited sometime in the fifth century, while the Babylonian Talmud was given its literary form by teachers who lived toward the end of the same century. In the two versions of the Talmud we have the vast intellectual resources of one of the most brilliant epochs in the history of Judaism.

We shall cite representative selections from the two Gemaras to gain from them a recognition of the major characteristics of this great classic in the history of Jewish tradition.

Here is a *mishnah* taken from the tractate Yevamot, in the order *Nashim*, "Women":

"A man is commanded concerning the duty of procreation, but not a woman. Rabbi Yohanan ben Beroka said, Concerning both of them it is written [Genesis 1:28], 'And the Lord blessed them and said to them, Be fruitful and multiply' " (Yevamot 6:6).

We now quote the discussion in the Gemara which follows upon this *mishnah:*

"Whence do we derive it that only the male is subject to the duty of procreation? Rabbi Ilea said in the name of Rabbi Eleazar the son of Rabbi Simeon, Scripture added [Genesis 1:28], *and fill the earth and subdue it*, it is man's nature to *subdue* but it is not a woman's nature to *subdue*.

"But on the contrary! *And subdue it* is read as a plural form (*vekivshuah*). Rabbi Nahman bar Yizhak replied, As written in the Torah, *and subdue it* may be taken as a masculine singular form (*vekavshah*).

"Rabbi Joseph said, We may infer this from the following verse [Genesis 34:11]: '*I am God Almighty, be thou fruitful and multiply*'; it does not say in the plural form, 'Be you fruitful and multiply.'

"It was stated: Rabbi Johanan and Rabbi Joshua ben Levi disagreed. One held that the law was to follow Rabbi Johanan ben Beroka and the other said that it was not to follow Rabbi Johanan ben Beroka. . . . Now, what is the decision? Come and listen to what Rabbi Aba ben Hanina reported in the name of Rabbi Abbahu, who, in turn, reported in the name of Rabbi Asi: A woman once came before Rabbi Johanan at the synagogue in Caeserea and sued for divorce on the ground that she had borne no issue from her husband. He decided that her husband divorce her and also pay her the amount promised in her *ketubah* as a settlement in the event of divorce. On what ground did he decide this if the woman is not subject to the law of procreation? Perhaps she submitted a special plea, as did a certain woman who once came with a similar suit to Rabbi Ammi? When he replied, I dismiss your suit because the commandment to procreate does not apply to you, she exclaimed, 'What is to become of a woman like myself in my old age?' The master then reversed himself and said, In a case such as this we surely direct the husband . . . to grant a divorce and pay the provision in the *ketubah*.

". . . But does not the commandment apply to women? Did not Rabbi Aha bar Katina report in the name of Rabbi Isaac the case of a woman who had been half slave and half free and her master was forced to liberate her so that she might be enabled to marry a free man? Said Rabbi Nahman bar Yizhak, The problem with this woman was that people were taking liberties with her" (Yevamot 65b–66a).

A number of vital characteristics of the Gemara are illustrated for us by the passage quoted. The Rabbis understood the verse in Genesis 1:28 as prescribing a commandment. Man is obligated to raise a family in order to collaborate with God in the perpetuation of the species. But they disagreed as to whether the commandment applied equally to the female as well as the male. The view given anonymously, which thus bore the consensus of the scholars discussing the question, restricted the commandment to the male only, while Rabbi Johanan ben Beroka extended it to the female as well.

The first preoccupation of the Gemara is to find a scriptural basis for the two interpretations. The discussion in the Gemara presents several possibilities. We have the casuistic approach of analyzing minutely the linguistic forms used in Scripture to prescribe the duty of procreation. We have noted previously that the original biblical text consists of consonants solely. The Hebrew term for "subdue it," without its vowels, is *VKVSHH* which may, therefore, be read *VeKiVSHuaH* or *VeKaVSHaH*, the former being a second person plural and the latter a second person masculine singular form. A later tradition decided on the former reading and the appropriate vowels were then added to the word. The inclusion of both sexes in the duty to procreate followed the traditional reading. But since this reading is, strictly speaking, not in the text, those who restrict the commandment to the male only had the retort that we go only by the original text which permits reading the word as a masculine singular, *VeKaVSHaH*. This means "and thou shalt subdue it." One opinion, that of Rabbi Ilea, goes beyond the casuistry of textual analysis. It considers the facts of human nature as well as the provision of Scripture. Scripture joins in one sentence the call to "be fruitful and multiply" with the call to "fill the earth and *subdue* it." It is a fact of nature that the *subduing* of the earth—the conquest of the wild, untamed earth, and the extension of civilization—is a work which normally rests on the male initiative. We must, accordingly, understand the demand to procreate as part of the same context, thus limiting it to the male.

We have had occasion to note that whenever the Mishnah quoted two opinions, one anonymously and one in the name of a particular jurist, the anonymous view generally was deemed the more authoritative. But here we note that this was not always the case. Rabbi Judah the Prince, who edited the Mishnah, must indeed have viewed the two opinions in these terms. Teachers of a later generation who are quoted in the Gemara did not feel bound by this rule, and they felt free to review the question and to decide between the opinions quoted. A teacher of the time of the Gemara, an Amora, as he was called, felt bound to respect the views of the masters of the Mishnah, the Tannaim. But he was not bound to respect Rabbi Judah's determination between the views of the Tannaim. As long as an Amora found some basis in the views of a Tanna, even if that Tanna had been rejected by his contemporaries, he was within the bounds of propriety in choosing those views and making them the basis of his own position whether as a teacher or as a practicing judge.

The Gemara tells us that two Amoraim, Rabbi Johanan and Rabbi Joshua ben Levi, disagreed whether the law was to follow the views of Rabbi Johanan ben Beroka in the Mishnah or not. We are not told who of the two Amoraim favored Rabbi Johanan ben Beroka and who opposed him. The Gemara attempts to derive this on the basis of circumstantial evidence in a portion of the passage which we deleted from our quotation. But this is a frequent problem we encounter in the Gemara. The traditions transmitted are not altogether precise, and the teachers in the academy seek to authenticate the record. Sometimes they seek to fix the authority behind a given statement, while sometimes the statement itself is uncertain and they seek to establish the more accurate text.

The jurists quoted in the Gemara spoke with a wide sense of authority. In the passage cited we have the hypothesis that several teachers rendered decisions on grounds of compassion, ignoring the strict provisions of the law. It is an interesting indication both of the authority enjoyed by the Rabbis and of the recognition they accorded to human welfare as a factor in the law. The Gemara, incidentally, did not resolve the question. It leaves us with the conflicting opinions of two teachers, one of whom accepted the anonymous provision of the Mishnah, and one of whom rejected it. This is an important aspect of the truth about the Talmud. It is a source book for the study of law, but it is not in itself a legal code setting forth the final decisions. The codification of rabbinic law was to be a labor for a later generation of jurists who created another branch in the literature of Jewish tradition.

The passage in the Gemara we have quoted above is interrupted with the following discussion, which appears to be a sharp digression into an altogether unrelated theme. For the sake of simplification we have withdrawn it from its original setting to cite it here:

"Rabbi Ilea further stated in the name of Rabbi Eleazar, the son of Rabbi Simeon, As it is meritorious for a person to speak words of rebuke when he will be heeded, so is it meritorious for him not to speak knowing that he will not be heeded. Rabbi Abba said, It is a duty to heed this, as it is written [Proverbs 9:8], 'Reprove not a cynic lest he hate you, reprove a wise man and he will love you.'

"Rabbi Ilea further stated in the name of Rabbi Eleazar the son of Simeon, It is permissible for a person to misquote for the sake of peace, for it is written [Genesis 50:16, 17], 'Thy father did command . . . so shall you say to Joseph, Forgive I pray thee now.' Rabbi Nathan said, It is a duty, for it is written [I Samuel 16:2], 'And Samuel said, How can I go, if Saul hear of it, he will kill me.' And the Lord said, 'Take a heifer with thee, and say: I am to sacrifice to the Lord.'

"At the school of Rabbi Ishmael it was taught, Great is the cause of peace, for God Himself misquoted for its sake: the original report read, 'My lord being old,' while afterward it is quoted as, 'And I am old'" (Genesis 18:12, 13).

This passage is a good illustration of the element of digression which often appears in the discussions of the Gemara. The statements by Rabbi Ilea limiting the duty to rebuke a neighbor and granting permission to misquote have no direct connection with the preceding theme under discussion. These statements are introduced because they too were expounded by Rabbi Ilea in the name of Rabbi Eleazar the son of Rabbi Simeon. It was he, speaking in the name of Rabbi Eleazar the son of Simeon, who had shared in the exposition of the main theme of the Gemara, and when the main theme was concluded two other statements dealing with aspects of the ethical life that he transmitted in the name of Rabbi Eleazar the son of Rabbi Simeon were likewise introduced. The element these statements have in common with the preceding is the same authorship, and this creates a continuity for the Gemara, though the subject itself is, in fact, a digression from the main theme. The Gemara was long preserved orally, and the practice of keeping together statements by the same master was an important aid to memory.

The two ethical statements cited by Rabbi Ilea illustrate the creative initiative exercised by the Rabbis in dealing with the ethical life. The Bible bids us chastise a person for his faults (Leviticus 19:7), but there are instances when we know that our chastisement will be of no avail, and the advice given under such circumstances is to forbear.

The more daring statement suspends the usual admonition to tell the truth. The Rabbis certainly prized the truth, but under conditions when telling the truth will create rancor between people it is better to preserve peace by compromising on the truth. This position is supported by scriptural passages. In one, Joseph's brothers told him that their father, Jacob, prior to his death, had spoken against any resumption of the ancient feud, that he hoped Joseph would continue his forgiving attitude toward his brothers. Their father had not spoken of this at all, but they took the liberty to ascribe these words to him for the sake of peace. In the second instance, when Samuel hesitated to crown David king lest Saul learn of his mission and put him to death, God allowed Samuel to pretend that he was going on another mission, to offer sacrifices to the Lord. The most dramatic instance involved Abraham and Sarah. When the "stranger" promised that she would yet be the mother of a child, she was incredulous and added in her retort "and my lord [husband] being old." When God quoted her to Abraham, He changed it to "and I am old." As interpreted here the misquotation was deliberate. God was sensitive to the possibility that Abraham might be angry with his wife for thinking him too old to be a father. It was to avoid a disturbance of the domestic harmony in Abraham's household that God Himself misquoted, placing the alleged disability of old age on Sarah herself rather than on Abraham, and thus setting an example of the primacy which the pursuit of peace must have in the scale of our values.

Sometimes the language of a *mishnah* was not precise and it needed clarification. Sometimes a particular *mishnah* appeared inconsistent with another *mishnah* or a teacher quoted in a given *mishnah* seemed to contradict his own views quoted elsewhere in the Tannaitic tradition. The Gemara deals with these questions, seeking in every instance clarity and consistency. This phase of the Gemara will be made clear for us through an examination of several passages.

The *mishnah* in Makkot 1:10 quotes a discussion on capital punishment. The Rabbis did not formally abolish it but they circumscribed it to a point where it had in effect become inoperative. The anonymous view of the *mishnah* is given thus: "A sanhedrin which sentences a person to death once in seven years is branded destructive." To this statement we have the following addendum: "Rabbi Elazar ben Azariah says, Once in seventy years."

The following is now given in the Gemara: "The question was raised whether the comment of Rabbi Elazar was to enlarge on the position stated anonymously, that an execution once in seventy years would also mark the court as 'destructive,' or to define the normal, that an execution once in seventy years would be deemed acceptable. The question was left undecided."

The Mishnah Berakot 4:4 quotes Rabbi Eliezer as saying: "Whoever treats his prayer as a perfunctory obligation—his prayer is not genuine prayer." The Mishnah does not define what is meant by "perfunctory obligation." The teachers of the Gemara found it necessary, if not to give a formal definition, to illustrate the term so that the concept might be more readily understood.

Here is the discussion of the Gemara: "What is meant by a perfunctory obligation? Rabbi Jacob the son of Idi said in the name of Rabbi Oshayah, Anyone who treats his prayer as a heavy burden. The Sages say, Anyone who does not recite it in a supplicating spirit. Rabbah and Rabbi Joseph both say, Whoever is unable to include something original in it. Rab Zera said, I can insert something original in the set prayers, but I am afraid to do so lest I become diverted. Abaye the son of Abin and Rabbi Hanina the son of Abin said, Whoever does not pray at dawn or sunset. For Rabbi Hiya the son of Abba said in the name of Rabbi Johanan, It is meritorious to pray at dawn and sunset. Rabbi Zera further said, What text confirms this? 'They shall fear Thee with the rising of the sun, and before the noon throughout the generations' [Psalms 72:5]. In the West [Palestine] they berated anyone who delayed the Minhah [afternoon] prayer to the time of sunset. For what reason? Because of the apprehension that he may miss the time altogether" (Berakot 29b).

The Mishnah's discussion of prayer referred, of course, not to the free, improvised prayer which the individual could offer any time, or the occasional prayer for special events in personal life, but to the formalized prayers in the morning and at the declining of the day, the *Shaharit* and *Minhah* services, recited publicly in the synagogue and privately by the individual. There was a third service, the *Ma'ariv,* in the evening, but the Mishnah was still to decide whether this service, too, was obligatory. The *Shaharit* and *Minhah* services had long been established as obligatory, but the Mishnah did not want these services to be recited in a perfunctory spirit, and the Gemara offers various illustrations as to what might be deemed perfunctory. The various suggestions illustrate the freedom of the scholars to give diverse answers to a question. This freedom contributes to the intellectual stimulation one finds in the Talmud, but it also has an element of frustration. For whoever wants clear-cut answers will be disappointed. The truth, of course, is that there are endless ways in which prayer may become perfunctory. The scholars offer us illustrations, which, in turn, may serve as analogies in the light of which other ways of distorting prayer into perfunctory exercise may be identified.

Our passage also illustrates the variation in practice between the Babylonian and Palestinian communities. The freedom of a community to express itself by developing its own customs was a characteristic of Jewish life in talmudic times. They exercised this freedom within the general bounds of a common tradition and a common method in developing the Oral Torah. This helped to maintain a general unity among Jews, despite some variation in practice among local communities.

It is also appropriate to note that the scholars often reflected their own world. Prayer at sunrise has an exhilarating quality but in an urban society where people rise at a later hour, this would be clearly impossible and it could not have been held up as the norm. The urging of prayer at that hour presupposes a rural setting or perhaps working habits of people in the cities where it is customary to awake at early hours.

A frequent preoccupation of the Gemara is to resolve apparent contradictions between several *mishnayot* or between a *mishnah* and a tannaitic statement (a baraita) in another stratum of this literature, or between a *mishnah* and the views of an Amora for whom the consensus reached in the *mishnah* should have been authoritative law. We cite an illustration of the Gemara's attempt to resolve a conflict between a *mishnah* and the views of an Amora. A *mishnah* cited earlier from the tractate Baba Metzia prescribes that whoever finds books must read in them once in thirty days, or, if he cannot read, unroll them (because ancient books came in the form of scrolls), as a precaution against their becoming moldy or moth-eaten.

The Gemara, commenting on this, cites a seemingly similar case where an Amora ruled otherwise: "Samuel said, If one find phylacteries [a receptacle with parchment inserted on which is inscribed the paragraph of the Shema, and still worn by Jewish men on arm and forehead during weekday morning prayer] in the market place, he appraises their values, sells them, and puts the money aside until a claimant should announce himself. Ravina raised an objection: According to the Mishnah [2:8], If one finds books he reads from them once in thirty days; if he cannot read, he must unroll them. Thus we see that he may only unroll them, but he may not sell them and put aside the money. Abaye replied, Phylacteries are easily obtainable at Bar Hahu, while books are rare" (Baba Metzia 29b).

The phase of law discussed here presupposes a person's zeal in doing what is right, provided the right is clarified to him. The problem is to define a person's duty in safeguarding a found object so as to be able to return it intact to the loser. A ruling of the Amora Samuel seemed to be contradicted by the Mishnah. Samuel allowed a finder to sell phylacteries found in the market place and to keep the money, while the Mishnah imposes on the finder of books the duty to keep them and watch against their deterioration, not allowing him to sell them and keep the money for the claimant. The reply is based not on any scriptural provision but on prevalent conditions. Phylacteries are easily obtainable and the finder would have no difficulty getting another pair, while books were rare and not easily restored. This is the reason imputed to the Amora Samuel who allowed the sale of phylacteries, but insisted that the books be held intact.

Some of the most precious information we have concerning the lives and times of the talmudic epoch have come down to us in historical notes scattered in the pages of the Gemara, as *obiter dicta*, incidental observations or digressions from the main theme. The decadence of the priesthood in the days of the Second Temple is documented for us in a number of occasional notes in the Gemara, which were introduced incidentally and not for the primary purpose of recording history.

Here, for example, is the *mishnah* in Yoma (1:3) telling us that the Sages instructed the High Priest in the Yom Kippur ritual: "They said to him, My lord High Priest, read by yourself, with your own mouth, perhaps you have forgotten or perhaps you never learnt. . . ."

This statement drew the following comment from the Gemara: "It is understandable that they might assume that he had forgotten, but would a High Priest be appointed if he had never learnt? Has it not been taught, The Torah describes the High Priest as 'the priest who is the highest among his brethren' [Leviticus 21:10, 14], which means that he must excel his colleagues in vigor, in appearance, in wisdom and in wealth. Others say: How do we know that if he does not have possessions his brother priests endow him? From the verse, 'the priest that is highest among his brethren,' which may be interpreted, 'make him the highest *through* his brethren.' Rabbi Joseph explained: This is no difficulty. The one characterization refers to the High Priests who served in the First Temple, the other to the High Priests who served in the Second Temple. For Rabbi Asi reported that Martha, the daughter of Boethus gave a *tarkubful* of dinars [coins] as a bribe to King Jannai to appoint Joshua ben Gamala as one of the High Priests" (Yoma 18a).

We have here a rabbinic conception of the ideal High Priest. To meet the rigors of his office, he had to be of strong constitution, of an attractive personality, wise and financially independent. The opinion that his fellow priests endow him with the means of financial independence is an interesting proposal as to how to deal with a suitable candidate for the office who was without means, but there is no reference anywhere to indicate that this was ever put into practice.

The incident reported by Rabbi Asi is confirmed from other sources. Martha was the wife of Joshua ben Gamala (Yevamot 61a), and the king she bribed was Agrippa II rather than Jannai. The Gemara sometimes used the name Jannai as a general family name for the Hasmonean or Herodian rulers. The parallel account in Josephus, who was a more careful historian [*Antiquities* XX 9:4], helps us to authenticate some of the details, but it is invaluable to have the same incident alluded to in the pages of the Gemara.[1]

The corruption of the High Priests in the days of the Second Temple is discussed in another passage in the Gemara (Pesahim 57a), again in a digression from the main theme. The Mishnah tells us of certain practices in connection with Passover which were followed by the people of the city of Jericho against the wishes of the Sages. Presumably as another illustration of practices pursued against the wishes of the Sages, the Gemara refers to the shocking behavior of the priests.

There are two reports cited in the same passage of the Gemara. One teacher, Abba Jose the son of Hanin, is quoted as having lamented thus about the various high priestly families of his day: "Woe is me for the House of Boethus, woe is me because of their clubs, woe is me for the House of Hanin, woe is me because of their whisperings. Woe is me for the House of Kathros, woe is me because of their pens. Woe is me for the House of Ishmael the son of Phabi, woe is me because of their fists. For they are High Priests, and their sons are Temple treasurers, and their sons-in-law are Temple trustees, and their servants beat the people with clubs."

The other report quoted anonymously speaks in highly hyperbolic language: "Four cries did the Temple courtyard cry out. The first, 'Depart hence, children of Eli, for they defiled the sanc-

[1] Cf. Derenbourg: *Essai sur l'histoire et la géographie de la Palestine* (Paris; 1867), pp. 2, 4, 8.

tuary of the Lord.' Another cry, 'Depart hence, Issachar the son of Barkai, who glorifies himself while desecrating the sacred rites of the divine sacrifices,' for he used to wrap his hands with silks and thus perform the sacrificial service. . . . The Temple courtyard also cried out, 'Lift up your heads, O gates, and let Johanan the son of Narbai, the disciple of Pinkai, enter and fill his stomach with the divine sacrifices.' It was said of Johanan the son of Narbai that he ate three hundred calves and drank three hundred barrels of wine and ate forty *seah* of young birds as a dessert for his meal. It was said of Johanan the son of Narbai that as long as he lived there were no left-overs from the priestly portions of the sacrificial foods in the Temple."

These reports, too, while important sources for our knowledge of the state of the priesthood during the Second Temple, are highly inexact. We have here satire and exaggeration. No one could really perform the feats ascribed to Johanan the son of Narbai. But the exaggerations are based on a core of genuine truth. The gentleman was surely rapacious and self-indulgent, to have occasioned the legends about his sumptuous table. The offenses of the other High Priests are not spelled out, but we may surmise them. Wielding political power under the Roman procurators, they impressed their contemporaries as cruel, self-seeking men, who abused the people with their clubs, their whispered machinations, their penning of evil decrees, and their fists. Their nepotism expressed itself in the appointment of members of their families to various Temple offices, which became a source of self-enrichment to them.

During this period High Priests were made and unmade by the Roman authorities who ruled in Palestine. But having once served as High Priest a person kept the title and some of the power that went with it. This would explain the reference to a number of High Priests within the same historic period.

The teachers of the Gemara, in some cases, invented parables to speak for them. When reflecting on Roman power they felt especially inhibited against speaking directly. Shifting their observations to another epoch, reading the incident into the behavior of other historic personalities, they achieved an apparent dissociation from the world around them, though the knowledgeable person could have had little difficulty in recognizing their meaning. We have such a passage in the Palestinian Talmud (Yerushalmi Baba Metzia 2:5). It satirizes the rapaciousness of Alexander the Great, but the reflection is probably pointed to the Roman power, whose rapaciousness was notorious. Against the rapaciousness of the reigning power, the Rabbis pictured the utopian justice of an ideal king.

The Mishnah's discussion of found property (Baba Metzia 2:5) evoked the following story from the teachers of the Gemara (Yerushalmi Baba Metzia 2:5): "Alexander of Macedon visited King Katzya, who displayed to him an abundance of gold and silver. Alexander said to him, 'I have no need of your gold and silver. My only purpose is to see your customs, how you act and administer justice.' While they were engaged in conversation, a man came before the king with a case against his fellow from whom he had bought a field with its scrap-heap and in it discovered a bundle of coins. The purchaser contended, 'I bought the heap but not the treasure hidden in it' and the vendor asserted, 'I sold the heap and all it contained.' While they were arguing thus, the king turned to one of them and asked, 'Have you a son?' 'Yes,' he replied. He asked the other, 'Have you a daughter?' and he answered, 'Yes.' 'Let them marry and give them the treasure,' was the king's decision. Alexander began to laugh, and Katzya inquired, 'Why do you laugh? Did I not judge well? Suppose such a case came before you, how would you have dealt with it?' He replied 'I would have put them both to death and confiscated the treasure.' 'Do you, then, love gold so much?' said Katzya. Katzya made a feast for Alexander at which he was served with golden cutlets and golden poultry. 'I do not eat gold,' Alexander exclaimed; and the king retorted, 'A curse on you! If you do not eat gold, why do you love it so intensely?' He continued to ask, 'Does the sun shine in your country?' 'Certainly,' was the reply. 'Does rain descend in your country?' 'Of course,' Alexander replied. 'Are there small animals in your country?' 'Of course,' Alexander again replied. 'A curse on you! You only live, then, by the merit of those animals!' Katzya finally retorted.

The Gemara is the fascinating labyrinth in which the details of a legal system are spun out for all to see. But sometimes the masters of the Gemara are reminded of the peril posed by an overconcentration on details, which obscures the larger goals served by the law. They therefore seek to relate those details to the general value concepts expressed by them. The particularities of practice demanded by the detailed provision of the law are thus shown to be a means to a larger end. This end is the larger goal of justice, or mercy, or love—the love of God and the love of man.

We have such a discussion in the Gemara, in the tractate Makkot which is part of the order *Nezikin* ("Damages"), dealing with civil and criminal law.

The Mishnah (3:16, as explained in the commentary of Maimonides) made the point that while the Torah includes many commandments, a person's standing in the eyes of God is not determined by tabulating statistics as to how many commandments he has fulfilled or violated. Every commandment is its own pathway that enables a person to enter into divine grace. The numerous commandments therefore represent so many opportunities open to a person by which to gain the rewards of fulfillment.

This *mishnah* evoked extended discussion in the Gemara (Makkot 23b–24a). We quote part of this discussion, which attempts to restate all the commandments of the Torah in more general categories: "Six hundred and thirteen commandments were given to Moses—three hundred and sixty-five prohibitions corresponding to the days of the solar year, and two hundred and forty-eight positive commandments corresponding to the number of limbs in the human body. David came and reduced them to eleven principles [which are enumerated in Psalm 15]. Isaiah came and reduced them to six, as is said, 'He that walketh righteously and speaketh uprightly, he that despiseth the gain of oppression, that shaketh his hands from holding bribes, that stoppeth his ears from hearing of blood, and shutteth his eyes from looking upon evil' [Isaiah 33:15]. Micah came and reduced them to three, as it is written, 'It hath been told thee, O man, what is good and what the Lord doth require of thee: Only do justly, and to love mercy and to walk humbly with thy God' [Micah 6:8]. Isaiah subsequently reduced them to two, as it is said, 'Thus saith the

Lord, "Keep ye justice and do righteousness" ' [Isaiah 56:1]. Lastly came Habakkuk and reduced them to one, as it is said, 'The righteous shall live by his faith' " (Habakkuk 2:4).

The Gemara is the richest treasury we have of classic Jewish thought. It embraces everything—law, theology, ethics, ritual, history, folklore. The Gemara became, in turn, a new subject for commentaries and supercommentaries, which have continued to be written by zealous students of this mighty branch of Jewish literature. But with the completion of the Gemara we have reached the most important landmark. Together with the Mishnah, around which it is embroidered as a clarifying supplement, it makes up the Talmud, into which all previous literary creations of Judaism flowed and from which all subsequent creations derived their major direction and scope.

Chapter VII

The Talmud and Sectarian Polemics

The earliest record which reflects the Jewish-Christian polemic is the Talmud in the case of Judaism, and the New Testament in the case of Christianity. We have noted a number of instances, recorded in the New Testament, in which Jesus is pictured as clashing with the rabbinic figures of his time. The Talmud is not mentioned by name. As a literature the Talmud took shape long after the time when those clashes occurred. But the earliest layer of the Talmud was forged in the oral discussions of the Palestinian academies, which began prior to the time of Jesus. The leading figures in those discussions were the Pharisaic teachers, who debated among themselves and with the sectarian adversaries, especially the Sadducees. The arguments between Jesus and the scribes and Pharisees constitute one of the main themes in the writings of the New Testament.

The terms "scribes" and "Pharisees" have been invested with

negative connotations in Christian writings. They imply pedantry and formalism, a narrow concentration on the trivial rather than the major aspects of the spiritual life. It would be well, therefore, to see these terms in their original meaning. The term "scribe" is a literal translation of the Hebrew word *sopher*. The sopher was primarily a narrator or teacher, an expounder of tradition, and his work was essentially oral. Thus the word *sofer*, which describes the sopher's work, designates in modern as in biblical Hebrew the oral activity of narration and instruction. The art of writing was rare in antiquity and the sopher, as a leader of culture, usually possessed this rare art. But the sopher's role as a "scribe" was a derivative and secondary role. His primary role was that of a teacher, and this is really what the term designates. The sopheric movement flourished during the years that Persia was the imperialist master of Palestine, from 563 to 332 B.C.E.

The successors of the sopherim who carried on the interpretation and development of the Torah during the Maccabean times were called *Perushim*, or Pharisees. The primary meaning of the root *parosh*—from which "Pharisees" derives—is "separate," and some historians have rendered Pharisees as "separatists," men who because of their excessive piety tended to separate themselves from the common people. But historically the Pharisees were the popular spokesmen of the people, and therefore could not have kept themselves aloof from them. *Perushim* may also be related to a secondary meaning of *parosh*, "interpret," as it is used in Leviticus 24:12. (*Perushim* is a passive construction of the verb *parosh*, but Talmudic Hebrew frequently uses the passive form with an active meaning as in Mishnah Berakot 4:5, Tosefta Berakot 2:6, 3:18, Ketubot 26a, 66b). *Perushim* may thus be rendered as "expounders" or "interpreters." Like the sopherim, they derived their name from their function, the interpretation of the written Torah.

The Pharisees supplemented the written Torah with new clarifications, with new religious and ethical concepts, and new legal formulations. They taught the beliefs in retribution in a life hereafter, the immortality of the soul, the resurrection of the dead, and an extensive angelology. They elaborated the Temple ritual with new ceremonials, like the impressive water libation before the altar on the Sukkot festival. They ordained that the daily *Tamid* sacrifice in the Temple be purchased not from the funds donated by the wealthy few, but from the shekel collections which were contributed by all Jews. To counteract a popular superstition that God's physical presence resided in the inner shrine of the Temple, they insisted that the High Priest, in his annual entrance to enact the solemn Day of Atonement ritual, omit the incense whose smoke was to screen him from gazing upon God; he was to prepare that incense after his entry into the shrine. Their conception of God was so exalted that they proscribed the pronunciation of His proper name, *YHWH*. They moderated the code of Jewish criminal law. All these and various other measures adopted by them were grounded in the recognition that the written Torah must be supplemented by a continuing new tradition, which can apply the written Torah's ultimate purposes to the changing facts of life.

The Pharisaic period in the development of the Torah came to an end with the rebellion against Rome in 66 C.E. Then there began the epoch of the Rabbis. The term *rabbi* means "master," and it refers of course to mastery in the knowledge of the Torah. The Talmud preserves some references to the work of the sopherim and the Pharisees, but it is primarily a record of the work of the Rabbis, who became the architects of normative Judaism.

In the New Testament, Jesus and his apostles, especially Paul, are repeatedly described as engaged in discussions with Jewish leaders concerning the new teachings. They invoke the aid of scriptural texts and of rational considerations to maintain the soundness of their cause. The words that Jesus spoke we really do not know with any certainty, as many scholars have reminded us. The record in the Gospels was written more than a generation after the events, and often reflects the editorial hand of the Gospel writers. But as far as the record goes, these "dialogues" are really not dialogues at all. They are more in the nature of outright denunciations. The pattern is invariably the same. The Jewish spokesmen refuse to be persuaded, and the other participants in the discussion become indignant and abusive, invoking curses and invectives against them.

The invectives imputed to Jesus against the Pharisees are well known, and they make melancholy reading. We cite one illustration—it is mild and restrained in comparison with others: "While he was speaking, a Pharisee asked him to dine with him; so he went in, and sat at the table. The Pharisee was astonished to see that he did not first wash before dinner. And the Lord said to him, 'Now you Pharisees cleanse the outside of the cup and of the dish, but inside you are full of extortion and wickedness. You fools! Did not he who made the outside make the inside also? But give for alms those things which are within; and behold, everything is clean for you'" (Luke 11:37–41). Once, after a disagreement on the interpretation of a biblical verse, Jesus is quoted as having denounced the Pharisees as "hypocrites," "serpents," "brood of vipers," who are sure to be "sentenced to hell." This denunciation fills all of chapter 23 in the Gospel According to Matthew.

It was long assumed by Christian commentators that Jesus was only calling a spade a spade. There were all kinds of Pharisees, as there have been all kinds of Christians. Some Pharisees undoubtedly failed to fulfill the highest ideals of their party. The Talmud itself speaks out against Pharisees who are insincere and ostentatious, whose piety is motivated by ulterior considerations, such as fear of divine judgment, rather than the pure and disinterested love of God. But Christian scholars such as R. Travers Herford, Herbert Danby, and George Foot Moore, who have studied the rabbinic sources where Pharisaism is exemplified, have acknowledged that the sweeping denunciation of Pharisaism as such represents a historic injustice.

A movement embracing large numbers of people will include individuals of varying qualities. If the movement attains public recognition it is always in danger of drawing to itself opportunists who will want to put on themselves an honorable label. But Pharisaism as such was a noble ideal, and the few opportunists who dishonored it must not blind us to the dedicated and selfless numbers who sought to live up to the pharisaic ideal to the best of their ability. In the words of George Foot Moore: "Men who make a show of more piety or virtue than they possess are not peculiar to any creed or age, and the higher the value set on religiousness, the more they have flourished. The Pharisees had endeavored by teaching and example to establish a higher standard of religion in Judaism, and had gained the reputation of being more religious than their Sadducean opponents or the ignorant and negligent mass of the people. That many men cared more for the reputation than for the reality, is only what human nature would lead us to expect. . . . But that the Pharisees, as a whole, were conscious or calculating hypocrites whose ostentatious piety was a cloak for deliberate secret villainy is unimaginable in view of the subsequent history of Judaism. . . . Judaism is the monument of the Pharisees." [1]

Students of the New Testament have questioned whether the sharp words against the Pharisees could really have been spoken by Jesus himself. The suggestion has been made that the invective, certainly in its extreme expressions, represents the addition of the Gospel writers, who wrote long after the events, when the hostility of Christians toward Jews had hardened. But whether uttered by Jesus or by the Gospel writers, what can account for this intemperate language? It becomes understandable if seen against the setting of the passions aroused by polemics. In religion as in politics, polemics breed overstatement and exaggeration. The controversies aroused by Marxism, the debates aroused by an American Presidential campaign afford us a good illustration of how far facts will be exceeded in order to score a point. But the function of dialogue is not to score points; it is rather to seek truth.

The failure of dialogue is well illustrated throughout the New Testament, but it is especially pronounced in the writings of Paul. He was an energetic and resourceful missionary who traveled extensively to propagate his new faith. He mingled with Jews, attending their synagogues, and used every opportunity to engage them in conversation. But he himself admits that his statements were not forthright, that he often dissembled so as to gain the confidence of his listeners. He was an early practitioner of an art popularized in modern revolutionary movements of boring from within. In the words of Paul (I Corinthians 9:19–24): "For though I am free from all men, I have made myself a slave to all,

[1] George F. Moore: *Judaism* (Cambridge, Mass.: Harvard University Press; 1927), pp. 11, 193.

that I might win the more. To the Jews I became as a Jew, in order to win Jews; to those under the law I became as one under the law—though not being myself under the law—that I might win those under the law. To those outside the law I became as one outside the law . . . that I might win those outside the law. To the weak I became weak, that I might win the weak. I have become all things to all men. . . . Do you not know that in a race all the runners compete, but only one receives the prize? So run that you may obtain it."

Paul certainly tried hard but his successes were with the non-Jews; his prize was won as apostle to the gentiles. The Jews resisted his efforts, and in frustration he developed the thesis that God had somehow blinded the Jewish people, that a veil rests on their eyes so that they cannot see the truth (II Corinthians 3:12–15). This notion is turned into a more sinister direction by the author of the Gospel According to John. The Jews refuse to listen because they are the children of the devil who cast a spell on them. John attributes these words to Jesus: "You are of your father the devil, and your will is to do your father's desires. . . . If I tell the truth, why do you not believe me? He who is of God hears the words of God; the reason why you do not hear them is that you are not of God" (John 8:39–47).

The New Testament is a Christian record, and its accounts are written from the point of view of the missionary goals of the young Church. It does not enable us to reconstruct the reactions which this propaganda aroused in the Jewish community. The contemporary Jewish sources are the writings of the Talmud, and here we find what developed into the normative Jewish attitude to the interreligious polemics as conceived by its Christian proponents. The Talmud is singularly free of polemics. There are occasional discussions of points of law or doctrine that were at issue between the two communities. There are a few dubious references to Jesus. But there is no Jewish polemic which is to serve as a counterpart to the Christian polemic. The Rabbis believed in expounding their own faith, in strengthening its institutions, in deepening its doctrines and translating them into a law cogent enough to guide life. They apparently shunned the negative approach of exposing and denouncing a competing faith.

In the early centuries C.E., the Christian community was but one sect among other Jewish sects. Its adherents regarded themselves as Jews who added to their normal Jewish piety a belief in the messiahship of Jesus, which they deemed indispensable for salvation and which they read into various verses in Scripture, through ingenious interpretations of the text. With Paul especially there was also added the abrogation of the traditional Jewish law and its replacement by faith in Jesus as messiah and as son of God, and by two new rites, the Eucharist and baptism, which were said to have charismatic effect on the faithful, to guarantee them sinlessness and life eternal.

These claims created confusion in the Jewish community. In the rabbinic tradition a man could not be "saved" by faith alone. Nor could the performance of rites—any rites, including those prescribed in Judaism—assure a person of meeting God's claim on his life. Faith and rites have their place in the economy of the religious life, but moral and spiritual values are not automatically reached because a person has been won emotionally to a certain faith and has expressed this faith by the performance of certain rites. While the Rabbis prized highly the life of faith and the commandments prescribed in the Torah to express this faith, they acknowledged that life is above doctrine and rite and that we must never lose sight of what is primary—the quality of life itself. As one rabbinic dictum expressed it (Yalkut on Judges 4:1): "Heaven and earth I call to witness that whether it be gentile or Jew, man or woman, slave or handmaid, according to the deeds one does, will the holy spirit rest on him."

The Rabbis were accustomed to free discussion in matters of religion; they did not prescribe any dogmas to be adhered to on faith; they demanded that their people study the Torah and practice its commandments; the unity of the people, deemed especially urgent after the destruction of the Temple, was to be maintained through a common law. The splintering of the people through the rise of sects which rigidly proclaimed a particular doctrine and developed their own rites was deemed a menace. It is in this context that the Rabbis looked upon the Christians—they were a sect, contributing to the splintering of their people and their faith through sectarian beliefs and practices.

The Rabbis spoke out against *minut*, which means sectarianism, and *minim*, which means sectarians. They added a prayer to the Amidah, the central portion of the Jewish liturgy recited at each weekday morning and evening service, invoking God's aid against sectarianism. The prayer reads thus: "Frustrate the hope of slanderers; and may all sectarians [*minim*] come to an end, speedily; let all the enemies of Thy people soon be cut off; and mayest Thou uproot, crush, and subdue the arrogant government, speedily, in our time. Praised be Thou, O Lord, who dost break the adversaries and humble the arrogant." Sectarianism, the fragmentation of a people into ideologically differentiated communities that live in mutual hostility to one another, has often proven a vexing problem in secular as well as religious history. The prayer against *minut* reflects the deep concern that sectarianism had created in the Jewish world of the first century. It was the hope of those who originally framed this prayer that its recitation would discourage the further proliferation of sectarianism.

The prayer against *minim* proved troublesome to many Jewish authorities. It appears, in its familiar phraseology, as an imprecation against erring men rather than at the state of error. Because *minim* was sometimes identified with a particular sectarianism, that of Christianity, there were those who saw in this prayer an imprecation against Christians. Rabbi Judah Loew of Prague dealt with this subject at some length. He recalled the lesson taught by Beruriah, the wife of Rabbi Meir, that one must not pray for the death of wicked men, but rather for their conversion to righteousness, since wickedness is only a temporary state from which men may be reclaimed (Berakot 6a). It is in the same spirit, he maintained, that we must interpret the prayer against *minim*. " 'And may all sectarians *come to an end speedily*,' is to be understood in the sense that there be no more sectarianism in the world, and thus will sectarians come to an end. If the prayer read 'and may all sectarians die (*yamutu*) speedily,' it would mean that we prayed for the downfall of the sectarians. But it does not read thus. It reads 'and may all sectarians come to an end (*yovedu*, literally, "be lost") speedily,' which suggests its intent is that there be no more sectarianism" (*Beer ha-Golah*, ch. 7).

In most modern editions of the Jewish Prayerbook the text of this prayer has been changed, replacing the term *minim*, "sectarians," with the term *rishah*, "wickedness." This prayer is thus modified to read: "Frustrate the hope of slanderers, and may all wickedness come to an end, speedily. . . ." In this formulation the prayer has been detached from its historical context, but it has been given a more universal significance.

The Rabbis did not, of course, leave the issue of sectarianism to God alone. What strategy did they develop to help their people against this disrupting force? They counseled their people to avoid discussions with sectarians, not to engage in conversations with them. They quoted Proverbs 5:8: "Remove thy way far from her [an alien woman] and come not nigh near her house." "Remove thy way far from her" the Rabbis applied to *minut*, sectarianism; "come not nigh near her house" they applied to the occupation government which ruled the country by force (Avodah Zarah 17a).

There are altogether two references to Christianity as such in the Babylonian Talmud and none in the Palestinian Talmud. The text in both instances has been tampered with by the Christian censor, but it is possible to recover the substance of the original discussion. In one case an Amora suggests that the principle enunciated by Rabbi Ishmael, which calls for withdrawal of contact with pagans on the days of their festivals, should by right be extended to the Christian Sunday—a view which was never adopted in rabbinic law. In the other case a rule was cited which precludes intercessionary fasting by certain Temple functionaries on Fridays, Saturdays, and Sundays. Various explanations are suggested for the inclusion of Sunday among the non-fasting days. Among them is that of Rabbi Johanan who suggests that it is "because of the Nazarenes." Presumably he means that for Jewish representatives to turn the Christian Sunday into a fast day would have aroused resentment in the Christian community (Avodah Zarah 6b, 7b, and Taanit, ed. Henry Malter, 27b).

Some Rabbis expounded certain doctrinal positions which have been interpreted as reactions to Christian beliefs. Thus we shall note[2] that the rabbinic emphasis on the rite of circumcision has been explained by some scholars as a reaction to the abroga-

[2] See below, p. 170.

tion of this rite by the Judeo-Christians. But there is no direct confrontation of Christianity as such anywhere in talmudic literature.

Why does the Talmud say so little about Jesus himself, and about Christianity? A number of considerations will account for it. The primary interest of the Talmud is law and doctrine, and not history as such. The Talmud does not mention Judah the Maccabee, though he is the hero of the Hanukkah festival, which the Talmud discusses by prescribing the rites for commemorating it. Here and there the Talmud inadvertently alludes to a historical event, and such allusions are often invaluable to us. But the Talmudists were not concerned with the preservation of historical records.

As a chapter of history—Jewish as well as world history—Christianity was destined to become of paramount importance in later centuries. But in the early period of the Talmud it was a sect among numerous other Jewish sects, like the Essenes or the Qumran community, and the Rabbis dealt with them as part of the general problem of sectarianism. When Christianity became a world movement, it was no longer a sect within Judaism. It had become a part of the religious ferment of the larger non-Jewish world.

Jesus himself made a deep impression on his disciples, but there were other prophets and messiahs who agitated the Jewish scene, especially in Galilee, as anyone who reads the contemporary historian Josephus will readily note. Even his death by crucifixion did not constitute anything unique in the history of the period. This was the common method by which the Roman authorities dealt with those who seemed a danger to the public order. Thousands of Jews were crucified by them during that period as part of their reign of terror in Judea. In one instance the procurator Florus (64–66) crucified some 3,600 Jews, including women and children, in order to terrorize the Jewish population into a more ready acceptance of the Roman occupation. As Josephus, who was a contemporary of those events, described it, Florus, who had been mocked by the populace for his greed and rapaciousness, let his soldiers loose on the people to plunder at will. In addition "they also caught many of the quiet people and brought them before Florus, whom he first chastised with stripes and then crucified. Accordingly the whole number of those that were destroyed that day, with their wives and children (for they did not spare the infants themselves), was about three thousand six hundred. . . ." (*Wars* II 19).

The failure on the part of the Rabbis to transmit authentic information about Jesus has robbed us of what would undoubtedly have been an important source of information on a critically important chapter in Jewish—and world—history. It has, moreover, left a vacuum which invited legendary substitutes to take the place of historical information. Various legendary accounts were indeed created, offering an answer to the Jewish popular mind on this subject, and some of these legends found their way into the pages of the Talmud.

In the absence of authentic information from Jewish sources, and in the absence of a body of scholarly research to reconstruct the historical elements from the legendary accounts in the Gospels, there were only the Gospels in their further Christian embroidery. The Jewish legends therefore accepted the substance of the Christian legends—but they changed their idealizing perspective. Some of these legends accepted the traditions of the Gospels that Jesus performed miracles—but they attribute his power to witchcraft. In some of these legends it is assumed that the Gospel account of a Jewish trial and sentence must have occurred as pictured in conventional Christian teaching, but they try to find a justification for the sentence imposed. A Christian censorship on Jewish books was introduced in the sixteenth century, and all these legends were deleted from the Talmud. This censorship has, of course, been discontinued in modern times, but the legends concerning Jesus were not reintroduced into the Talmud, since they were only peripheral to the talmudic teachings. Much of this material is explored by R. Travers Herford.[3] It is important to note however that this legendary material does not generally mention Jesus by name and it is by no means certain that he is really its subject. There were various claimants to prophecy and

[3] *Christianity in Talmud and Midrash* (London: William and Norgate; 1903).

messiahship during the centuries reflected in talmudic writings, and it would be rash to assume that every discussion of a would-be messiah is necessarily directed at Jesus.

The Talmud as a body of literature became a target for Christian attacks in the Middle Ages. After Christianity had consolidated its power, the Jews were the only dissident element who insisted on retaining their distinctiveness, thereby challenging the claim of Christianity to total religious sway over European civilization. Considering the basic logic by which the Church was guided, the opposition to the Talmud becomes understandable.

The Talmud is the basic source in which the Oral Torah is preserved, and the Oral Torah is the dividing line between Judaism and Christianity. The original text of Scripture was to be interpreted by Christianity in one way, and by Judaism in another way. Faithful to the Oral Torah, the Jews dismissed the Christian interpretations as untenable. The resistance of the Jews to Christianity thus centered in the literature of the Talmud, which defined the distinctiveness of the Jewish faith and the criteria by which an authentic interpretation of Scripture might be differentiated from a false one. It became the bulwark of Judaism and the basis of its rejection of the competing claims of Christianity. It therefore seemed to Christians that if they could overcome the hold of the Talmud on the Jews they would automatically break the resistance to the missionary efforts of the Church.

The following characterization of the Talmud addressed by Pope Innocent in 1244 to the king of France illustrates the real objection of the Church to this important literature of Judaism: "Ungrateful to the Lord Jesus Christ who, His forebearance overflowing, patiently awaits their conversion; they manifest no shame for their guilt, nor do they reverence the dignity of the Christian faith. Omitting or contemning the Mosaic Law and the prophets, they follow certain traditions of their elders, the very ones for which the Lord took them to task in the Gospel, saying: 'Why is it that you yourselves violate the commandment of God with your traditions?' [Matthew 15:3]. It is traditions of this stripe-in Hebrew they call them 'Thalamuth,' and an immense book it is, exceeding the text of the Bible in size, and in it are blasphemies against God and His Christ, and against the blessed

Virgin, fables that are manifestly beyond all explanation, erroneous abuses, and unheard-of stupidities—yet this is what they teach and feed their children . . . and render them totally alien to the teaching of the Law and the prophets, fearing lest the Truth, which is understood in the same Law and Prophets, bearing patent testimony to the only-begotten Son of God, who was to come in flesh, they be converted to the faith, and return humbly to their Redeemer." [4]

Rev. E. H. Flannery, a modern Catholic writer on anti-Semitism, quotes with approval the following statement by A. Lovsky to explain Christian objections to the Talmud: "On the whole, the Talmud sins much more by an evidently well guarded silence with respect to Christianity than by tendencious insults or accusations." To which the Reverend Flannery adds this observation: "The Talmud served the cause of anti-Semitism indirectly insofar as it reinforced Israel's traditional separation." [5] The offense of the Talmud to Christianity stems, in other words, from its refusal to acknowledge the claims of Christianity and from its positive contributions to the strengthening of Judaism as a distinctive faith.

In the Middle Ages, when religious disputations were popular, the Talmud became a frequent subject of controversy. Jews were forced to select their champions to public disputations on the merits of the two faiths. The most important of these disputations were those held between Rabbi Yehiel of Paris against Nicholas Donin in 1239; between Rabbi Moses Nahmonides and Fra Pablo Christiani at Barcelona in 1263; and the Tartosa disputation between a group of Spanish rabbis and Antipope Benedict XIII and Gerónimo de Santa Fe during 1413–14. The Talmud was a frequent subject for argumentation. Some Christian spokesmen tried to prove the messiahship and divine sonship of Jesus from the Talmud itself. Usually the Talmud was subjected to abuse and denunciation.

It may seem paradoxical that the Christians should have as-

[4] Cited by Edward A. Synan: *The Popes and the Jews in the Middle Ages*, p. 112.

[5] H. Flannery: *The Anguish of the Jews* (New York: The Macmillan Company; 1964), p. 105.

sumed that the Talmud contained references to the messiahship and divine sonship of Jesus. But this fitted in with the conception of the Jew as a perverse creature. For if the Talmudists knew that Jesus was the messiah and God's son, and yet refused to give him due reverence, then this could only mean that the Jew was diabolical and satanic, knowing the truth yet spurning it out of his hate for all that Jesus represented.[6]

Perhaps the most serious charge against the Talmud was that it is irreverent toward the beliefs and practices of the Church. The Talmud arose during the epoch when Christianity began its secession from Judaism, and when the Christians were looked upon as dissident Jews. Against that background there must have been extensive controversy between the adherents of traditional Judaism and the advocates of the new doctrine. The Talmud, as we noted, generally avoids polemics; but some echoes of that controversy survived in the Talmud, principally in the denunciation of sectarianism, such as the prayer against *minim*, which was added to the Jewish liturgy. This now became a cause of serious charges against Judaism, above all against its revered classic, the Talmud.

The animosity toward the Talmud was often instigated by renegades from Judaism who exhibited the converts' customary zeal by a villification of the faith they had deserted. The apostate Nicholas Donin laid before Pope Gregory IX the charge that the Talmud was a pernicious and blasphemous work. The Pope responded with an order to seize all copies of the Talmud for an inquiry into their content. In consequence of this agitation twenty-four cartloads of Hebrew books and manuscripts were publicly burned in Paris on June 17, 1242. In the sixteenth century there were six burnings of talmudic books, in 1553, 1555, 1559, 1566, 1592, and 1599. A Christian censorship of Hebrew books was instituted in 1562. Most editions of the Talmud now extant still carry the censor's assurance that these volumes are free of "offensive" material.

There were voices in the Jewish community that spoke out in

[6] Cf. Cecil Roth: "The Medieval Conception of the Jew," in *Essays and Studies in Memory of Linda R. Miller* (New York: Jewish Theological Seminary; 1938), pp. 171–90.

defense of the Talmud. Some defended the particular passages of the Talmud that had been attacked. Others addressed themselves to the larger issue involved—they spoke out boldly for religious freedom. One of the most courageous pleas for freedom came from Rabbi Judah Loew of Prague (1512–1609). After analyzing the usual charges against the Talmud in detail and refuting them, he adds: "One ought not reject the words of an opponent. It is preferable to seek them out and study them. Thus shall a person arrive at the . . . full truth. Such words should not be suppressed. For every man of valor who wants to wrestle with another and to show his strength is eager that his opponent shall have every opportunity to demonstrate his real powers. But what strength does he show when he forbids his opponent to defend himself and to fight against him? Therefore it is wrong to suppress anyone who wants to speak against religion and say to him: 'Do not speak thus.' The very converse is true. This itself weakens religion. Suppose the Talmudists did speak against Christian doctrine, expressing publicly what was in their hearts. Is this an evil thing? Not at all. It is possible to reply to them. . . . The conclusion of the matter is that it would be most unworthy to suppress books in order to silence teachers. . . ." (*Beer ha-Golah*, ch. 7).

The Talmud also found a champion in the Christian community itself in the person of the humanist Johann von Reuchlin (1455–1542). Reuchlin had studied the Bible in the original Hebrew and this led him also to study the Talmud and the Cabbalah. In 1509 the emperor Maximilian of Germany issued an order for the destruction of all Hebrew books found among the Jews of Cologne and Frankfurt. He had been instigated by a baptized Jew of Cologne, Pfefferkorn, who had behind him the support of the Dominican friars. Pfefferkorn posed as an expert in Jewish literature and he maintained that the Talmud, especially, teaches Jews to be hostile to Christianity and at the same time serves as a force to keep them faithful to their own religion and inhibits them from entering the Church. The Jews appealed the edict, and Reuchlin was asked by the emperor to submit an opinion in the case. Reuchlin's report was that the Talmud and the other great classics of

Judaism deserved to be spared because they were useful for theological studies and they were free of heresy. The edict was rescinded in 1510.

Reuchlin then became embroiled in controversy with the Dominicans, and pamphlets for and against him kept the issue alive before the Christian community. The matter was brought before the Lateran Council at its session in 1516 which ruled in favor of Reuchlin. But this decision was reversed in 1520 by Pope Leo X who condemned Reuchlin's writings as heretical. Pope Leo X himself was a humanist and had pursued Hebrew studies under the Jewish scholar Elijah Levita. His decision against Reuchlin was largely a concession won by the king of France and Emperor Charles IV of Germany who sided with the Dominicans against the spread of the Reformation in Germany.

It is indicative of the episodic nature of the persecutions against the Talmud that during the very time when the Pfefferkorn-Reuchlin controversy raged, a Christian humanist Daniel Bomberg founded in Venice a great printing house for the publication of Hebrew books, beginning with the great rabbinic Bible which appeared in 1517–18. Pope Leo X was asked to intervene on the ground that the works being produced were heretical and blasphemous. The Pope ordered an inquiry, with instructions to punish those responsible if the accusations were proven true. But nothing came of this. Moreover, Bomberg even obtained from the Pope a formal authorization to publish the Talmud, which began to appear from the Bomberg press in 1519. The decline of Christian humanism in the wake of the Counter Reformation brought fresh attacks against the Talmud, and as we noted earlier there were six burnings of the Talmud in the latter part of the sixteenth century.

The rise of modern anti-Semitism gave fresh impetus to the attacks against the Talmud. The father of the modern calumnies upon the Talmud was the German polemicist John Andreas Eisenmenger (1654–1704). Eisenmenger offered to suppress his work, *Entdecktes Judentum* (*Jewry Unmasked*), for a consideration of 30,000 florins, but the Jews refused to be blackmailed into paying this sum. The book has been described as "a collection of scandals" by the *Allgemeine Deutsche Bibliographie*, an official encyclopedia of German bibliography published by the German Imperial Academy of Science in 1876. "Some passages," the appraisal continues, "are misinterpreted; some distorted; others are insinuations based on one-sided inferences."

The most spectacular campaign against the Talmud was led by August Rohling (1839–1931), a professor of Hebrew Antiquities at the University of Prague. His *Der Talmudjude* (*The Talmud Jew*) went through seventeen editions, reaching a circulation of 200,000 copies in Austria alone. Rohling repeatedly prefaced his slanderous material with the offer of 1,000 taler "if Judah managed to get a verdict from the German Association of Orientalists that the quotations were fictitious and untrue." The challenge was taken up by Joseph S. Bloch, Rabbi at Florisdorf and later a member of the Austrian Parliament, who offered 3,000 taler if Rohling could prove that he was able to read a single page of the Talmud chosen at random by Rohling himself. Accusing Rohling of ignorance and perjury, Bloch dared him to bring a libel suit. Because of his professional standing, Rohling could not evade the issue and finally charged Bloch with libel before a Vienna magistrate.

The court was anxious to make a thorough study of the subject and requested the rector of the University of Vienna, Hofrat Zscholk, and the German Association of Orientalists to appoint two experts. It conceded to Rohling's request that both these experts be "full-blooded" Christians. Professor Theodor Noeldeke of the University of Strassburg and Professor August Wünsche of Dresden were selected. From time to time additional experts were called in. After two and a half years the report was ready. The trial was to start November 18, 1885, but before the hearings began, Rohling, afraid of an open exposure, withdrew all his charges. The court sentenced him to pay the cost of the trial and, disgraced, he was retired from his university post. The entire story of this dramatic encounter is told by Rabbi Bloch in his *Israel and the Nations*.[7]

Another such Talmud "authority" was Aaron Briman, alias Dr. Justus. He was born a Jew and had aspirations for a career as a Jewish scholar. But when he lost face with the Jewish community

[7] (Berlin and Vienna: Benjamin Harz Verlag; 1927).

for deserting his wife and children, he became a Protestant. Subsequently he became a Catholic and then a Protestant again, and finally tried to return to Judaism. Toward the end of his career he once again joined the Catholic Church. His principal work, published anonymously, was *Der Judenspiegel* (*The Mirror of the Jew*), a compilation of a hundred laws taken from the *Shulhan Aruk*, to show the animosity of this Jewish law code toward Christians. In a book about the Cabbalah, which Briman subsequently wrote under his true name, he said that the whole anti-Semitic literature, including the *Judenspiegel* (his own work!) had been written by stupid and ignorant men. In 1885 he was sentenced by a Vienna court to a long term in prison and expulsion from Austria for forgery of documents. Professor Franz Delitzsch, the famous Protestant theologian, pronounced the *Judenspiegel* "a concoction of damnable lies." Following his expulsion Briman took up medical studies in Paris. These same forgeries of Justus-Briman were later published by another adventurer, Jacob Ecker, who offered them as his own work under the title *The Hundred Laws of the Jewish Catechism.*

Czarist Russia made its contribution to this gallery of literary swindlers in the person of the notorious Justin Pranaitis, a Catholic clergyman. His monograph, *The Christian in the Jewish Talmud*, was based on the works of Eisenmenger and Rohling. To create the impression of authenticity he cites many passages in the original Hebrew and Aramaic, but they are all lifted from Eisenmenger, errors and misprints included. By identifying as references to Christians and Christianity such epithets in the Talmud as *am ha-aretz* (literally, a peasant, but more generally, an illiterate person), *akum* (pagan or idol worshipper), *apikoros* (epicurean, but applied to heretics generally), and *kuthim* (the Samaritans), he "proves" widespread prejudice on the part of the Talmud toward Christianity.

In spite of his office as a Catholic clergyman, Pranaitis became involved in a series of financial scandals. A picture in a frame he wanted gilded at the workshop of a certain Avanzo in Petersburg was accidentally damaged, whereupon he tried to extort 3,000 rubles from the owner of the shop on the alleged ground that the picture had been painted by the seventeenth-century artist Murillo and that it was part of the collection of Cardinal Gintovt. Both allegations proved false. On another occasion he was charged by the board of a local Catholic welfare society in his home parish at Tashkent with misappropriating the sum of 1,500 rubles.

It was in 1912 during the trial of Mendel Beiliss on the ritual-murder libel that Pranaitis drew world notoriety upon himself by offering his services as an expert for the prosecution. When confronted by the bulls of Popes Innocent IV and Clement XIV, which denounced ritual-murder charges against Jews as libels and slander and which called upon Christians to desist from the staging of ritual-murder trials, Pranaitis denied the authenticity of the documents. Cardinal Merry del Val, the Papal Secretary of State, examined the originals at the Vatican and certified that they were genuine. Pranaitis was unable to answer the simplest questions about Judaism. Beiliss was of course acquitted, but the prosecution remunerated the star "expert" with five hundred rubles.

Pranaitis died on January 29, 1917. It took more than a month for the Czarist government to issue the permit for the removal of his body from Petersburg to Tashkent. Objections had to be overcome of local officials in Tashkent who were anxious to avoid a public demonstration at his funeral and urged an inconspicuous burial in Petersburg.[8]

The inability to sustain any serious charges against the Talmud led to the accusation that the Talmud was really a secret literature to which Christians had no access. This accusation, too, found its proponents, mostly in Germany. Hermann L. Strack, the Protestant scholar who wrote the most celebrated introductory study of the Talmud, took note of this in the preface to the fourth edition of his work (1908): "Even at the present time, certain ignorant agitators (most of them are at the same time malevolent) seek to make the Christian-German people believe that the Jews 'are solicitous, with every possible means at their hands, to keep the Talmud a secret book,' for fear lest its contents should become known, in-

[8] See Maurice Samuel: *Blood Accusation: The Strange History of the Beiliss Case* (New York: Alfred A. Knopf; 1966), a recent study of the Beiliss case, which includes all the data concerning the role of Pranaitis.

deed, that they consider it a crime worthy of death for any Jew to make its contents known. . . . *The Talmud* (I repeat a statement which I have been solemnly making for many years) *contains no report or utterance which . . . any Christian scholar, who is at home in the language and subject matter, is not able to find.* . . . Among the entire body of Jews there is not a single piece of literature or an oral tradition which is inaccessible to learned Christians. The Jews make no effort whatever to conceal anything from Christians, nor could they if they would." [9]

These diatribes against talmudic literature produced a reaction, and some of the noblest works in appreciation of the Talmud were written by non-Jews. We recall that Reuchlin and his circle of Christian Hebraists carried on a campaign in the sixteenth century in defense of Hebrew books. The libels of August Rohling were answered by the famous Protestant theologian, Franz Delitzsch, in his work *Was D. Aug. Rohling beschwören hat und beschwören will* (*What August Rohling Has Sworn to And Is Prepared to Swear to*).[1]

The hostility toward the Talmud which had long been fostered in Western culture made it a convenient target of Nazi propaganda. The old accusations against the Talmud were reinforced, however, by extensive falsifications of the original text, which were cited to "prove" the perversity of this literature. Some of this material appeared in crude leaflets, full of abusive and scurrilous references, whose character could be readily identified. An anonymous pamphlet, *Thus Speaks the Talmud*, with evidence from "Jewish Rabbi Scriptures" was distributed in large quantities in the United States. It openly acknowledged as its authorities the "experts" Eisenmenger, Rohling, and Ecker! *Why Are the Jews Persecuted for Their Religion?*, another anonymous leaflet following the same pattern, was also used extensively in Nazi anti-Semitic propaganda in this country. The quality of the "scholarship" which went into producing it may be judged from the fact that it identified *Yom Kippur* (Day of Atonement) as "the Jewish New Year" and fixed its date on the seventeenth of

[9] Hermann Strack: *Introduction to the Talmud and Midrash* (Philadelphia: Jewish Publication Society; 1931), p. vii.

[1] (Leipzig; 1883).

September! In spite of their repudiation by many competent scholars, including noted Catholic theologians, these slanders against the Talmud were repeated almost verbatim in an article published in the issue of December 12, 1938, of Father Coughlin's publication, *Social Justice*.

Some Nazi works on the Talmud, on the other hand, gave the impression of being serious works of scholarship; they were written in academic language, documenting their assertion with learned references and footnotes. But a closer examination revealed the same hand of the unscrupulous propagandist. One such "scholarly" work on the Talmud was Walter Fasolt's *Die Grundlagen des Talmud*.[2] Fasolt admitted unblushingly in the introduction to his work: "In issuing this work our purpose is purely political. . . . As a political tract it is necessarily one-sided. It, therefore, deals with talmudic law only at the point where it may prove helpful in illuminating the attitude of Germany to Jewry."

It is interesting to note that most of these Talmud baiters are also the violent enemies of Christianity. Rohling, one of the pillars of the "science" of Talmud falsification, was a fanatical anti-Protestant. In his *Der Antichrist und das Ende der Welt* (*The Anti-Christ and the End of the World*),[3] he bluntly declared: "Wherever Protestantism gains a foothold it causes a spiritual vacuity, a decline in . . . morality. A Protestant . . . is a monstrosity. . . . Vandalism and Protestantism are identical concepts."

The Nazi Talmud baiters showed a particular bitterness toward the Catholic Church. Thus an article by Dr. Johannes Pohl, "Der Talmud," in the *Nationalsozialistische Monathefte*, after repeating the usual performance against the Talmud, continued with a violent attack against the Catholic Church: "One can only compare all this," he writes, "to the system of the Roman Catholic Church which, in true Talmudic spirit, seeks to regulate the lives of its adherents through an external counting, calculating and balancing. . . . Exactly like the Talmud so does the Catholic Church reduce the principles of the ethical life to an endless series of questions which the average Catholic cannot decide himself but must seek the guidance of the priest, as the Jew must seek the

[2] (Breslau; 1935).
[3] (St. Louis; 1874), pp. 58, 59, 61.

guidance of one of the 2,500 Talmud rabbis or some contemporary rabbi. . . . The Jesuits also concentrate their speculations on the intimacies of sex life. . . ." [4] The editor of this periodical, and one of the prime movers in the campaign against Judaism, was Alfred Rosenberg, the arch-enemy of Christianity, and one of the prophets of the neopaganism of Nazi Germany. His *Myth of the Twentieth Century* and other neopagan works were placed on the Catholic Index.

The utilization of the attack on the Talmud by Nazi propaganda evoked a defense from those sensitive to the peril of Nazism. Protestant as well as Catholic voices were raised in defense of talmudic literature. The noted Protestant scholar Herbert Danby, writing in the introduction to Publication 54 of the series "Friends of Europe," pointed out that all quotations cited in the anti-talmudic propaganda are "chosen in a spirit of malice and malignity. We pass over the type of mentality which finds it proper to approach an ancient document solely with the object of ferreting out absurdities and fatuities or details which offend against present-day fashions of reticence. The same process can be applied with equal effect to any other ancient literatures, oriental or classical; but it is a process which is not admirable and is more characteristic of prurient and misguided adolescence than of objective scholarship. What may not, however, be passed over is the contented ignorance or irresponsible malice which—as happens in many of these extracts—presents passages in such a manner that their intended damaging effect depends on (a) being misunderstood in themselves, (b) being given a false sense owing to separation from their context, or, (c) being wrongly quoted."

The Nazi attacks against the Talmud also evoked a number of replies from Catholic sources. Among these was the very lucid study by Rev. A. H. Dirksen, "The Talmud and Anti-Semitism," in the January 1939 issue of *The Ecclesiastical Review*, a publication of the Catholic University of America, and the pamphlet *A Fact About the Jews*, written by the famous Catholic scholar Joseph N. Moody and distributed by the Paulist Fathers. A more elaborate study of the Talmud was written by the Polish Catholic scholar Thadeus Zaderecki. He began his researches in

[4] *Nationalsozialistische Monathefte* (March 1939), pp. 226–37.

the Talmud under the inspiration of anti-Semitic libels, but what he learned made him into an admirer of this great literature. His work, *The Talmud in the Crucible of the Centuries*,[5] is a brilliant appreciation of the moral values of talmudic literature and a refutation of the libels against it, especially those of Rohling and Pranaitis.

There is a splendid English translation of the Mishnah, published in 1933, by Rev. Herbert Danby, Canon of Christ Church and Regius Professor of Hebrew at the University of Oxford, England. There is a German translation of the Babylonian Talmud by Lazarus Goldschmidt. The Palestinian Talmud is available in a French translation by M. Schwab. The Soncino Press in London has recently published a new translation of the Babylonian Talmud in English under the very competent editorship of Dr. I. Epstein.

The El Am edition of the Talmud presently being produced in Israel under the editorship of Dr. Arnost Ehrmann offers a vocalized and punctuated original text with a fine English translation and commentary. Portions of the tractate Berakot were published in 1965–6, but the entire work as projected will include both the Babylonian and the Palestinian Talmud.

Among the well-known studies of talmudic literature in English is the *Introduction to the Talmud and Midrash* by Hermann L. Strack, prominent Protestant theologian and professor at the University of Berlin, and *Talmud and Apocrypha* by the well-known British scholar R. Travers Herford, and also the short but popularly written essay by Arsene Darmesteter, *The Talmud*. An accurate and exhaustive survey of the world outlook of talmudic Judaism is available in the monumental work *Judaism in the First Centuries of the Christian Era* by the eminent Protestant scholar and professor of religion at Harvard University, the late George Foot Moore. A brief digest of the contents of the Talmud, with copious quotations, is available in Abraham Cohen's *Everyman's Talmud*. A short history of talmudic times is available in Judah Goldin's essay "The Period of the Talmud" in volume I of *The Jews: Their History, Culture, and Religion*, edited by Dr. Louis

[5] It is available in the original Polish and in a German translation by Mina Safier, published in Vienna in 1937.

Finkelstein. *The Wisdom of the Talmud* by the present author is a popular presentation of the literary and historical aspects of talmudic literature, and a brief characterization of its teachings.

A splendid study of the Palestinian Talmud is offered us in Dr. Louis Ginzberg's recent work, *Pirushim ve-Hidushim b'Yirushalmi* (*A Commentary on the Palestinian Talmud*). Its three volumes cover the first four chapters of the tractate Berakot, but its extended notes and an introductory essay in Hebrew and English offer invaluable insight into the general nature of the Palestinian Talmud and its relationship to the parallel literature which emanated from the Babylonian academies. A fourth volume extending the commentary to the fifth chapter of the tractate Berakot was published posthumously under the editorship of David Halivni.

Rev. A. H. Dirksen wrote as follows concerning the Talmud: "The rising tide of anti-Semitism which is sweeping some portions of the modern world has again focused attention on that mysterious body of literature known as the Talmud. . . . By falsifying and misinterpreting texts, by tearing others from their context or removing them from their historical setting, the Talmud has been made to yield a rich mine of material for the rabid anti-Semite in his campaign by villifying the Jew. . . . It [the Talmud] contains much religious teaching, and a wide range of religious ideas, but also much of a purely secular quality. It contains much historical and cultural material, but it also abounds in legal decisions and opinions. It is in greater part valuable, but there is also much idle speculation and fantastic legend in it. . . . Its unlimited scope takes in human living in all its complexity and bewildering detail. . . . Without some knowledge of it we shall never sympathetically approach Judaism and never fully understand the New Testament. . . ."[6]

The hysterical hostility to the Talmud reached its zenith with Nazism and it has abated with the decline of Nazism. But Christian writers continue to show an antipathy to the Talmud, and their characterizations of talmudic teachings reveal various distortions and falsifications. The Jesuit scholar Joseph Bonsirven has charged that "the most annoying consequence of the system of

[6] "The Talmud and Anti-Semitism," *The Ecclesiastical Review* (January 1939), pp 3–13.

the Torah [he means the Oral Torah] was that genuinely moral obligations were put on the same level as ritual and external observances. . . . Pharisaism, the most accurate expression of Palestinian Judaism of this period, did not escape the conviction that one can satisfy one's duties to God by fulfilling external rituals, which may easily be emptied of all love. Such formalism and hypocrisy—which inevitably derive from it—were called in ancient times 'the plague of the Pharisees.'" [7]

The Reverend Bonsirven's characterization is of course a total distortion of the truth. It is part of his general endeavor to exalt Christianity through the degradation of Judaism. The Oral Torah as exemplified in the writings of the Talmud made it very clear that the apex in the value system which constituted rabbinic Judaism was the sanctity of human life, that the ethical ideal enjoys a higher priority than any ritual obligation. The derisive term, "the plague of the Pharisees" was coined by the teachers of the Talmud, and it was their denunciation of a piety that was devoid of moral and spiritual depth. While Jesus summed up the law in two commandments, the duty to love God and to love one's fellow man, Rabbi Akiba was content to embrace all of Judaism in the commandment (Leviticus 19:18) to love one's neighbor as oneself. Hillel simplified this commandment when he summed up all of Judaism to a pagan: "That which is hateful to you, don't do unto others, the rest is commentary." Hillel advised the pagan to study the commentary, but he made it clear that the highest ideal of his faith was the ethical imperative. This emphasis on the primacy of the ethical ideal is characteristic of the value system taught in all branches of talmudic literature.

The malignity against the Talmud owes its inception to the Christian polemics against Judaism. But the prejudice it has engendered has left its mark even on those who have repudiated their Christian heritage. Thus the Communist campaign against Judaism did not fail to produce an anti-Talmudic tract, as part of its effort to degrade the Jewish religion. Trophim K. Kichko's *Judaism Without Embellishment*, published in the Soviet Union in 1963, presented a series of Talmudic forgeries purporting to

[7] Joseph Bonsirven: *Palestinian Judaism in the Time of Jesus Christ* (New York: Holt, Rinehart and Winston; 1964), p. 96.

show that Judaism teaches a tribal morality, sanctioning theft, deception, and exploitation if practiced against non-Jews. An outcry from the non-Communist world, and more feeble protests from timid critics in the Soviet Union itself, led to the suppression of this work.

Ghosts die hard. Early Christianity turned the image of the Jew into a ghostlike being. As often as this ghost has been dispelled by causing the light of truth to shine on the dark areas it inhabits, it has returned to haunt the credulous. And this ghost still hovers over the dark areas where prejudice and ill-will hold sway over the minds of men.

Chapter VIII
The Bible in Judaism

Judaism is *not* the religion of the Bible. It is *founded* on the Bible but is not identical with it. Biblical religion differs from classic Judaism as the seed differs from the flower that finally has blossomed from it. Judaism has been a living faith that never became static and unchanging. Each generation has deposited something of its own experience to enrich the total treasury of Jewish wisdom that comprises the Jewish tradition. The classic character of Judaism was given form by the Sages who created the Midrash and the Talmud. A more generic name for the Sages is "Rabbis," and we call the Judaism as formulated by them, "rabbinic Judaism."

It will be helpful to review the transformation that biblical religion underwent in the process of becoming classic, or rabbinic, Judaism.

The Hebrew Bible seeks to teach man how to live in the existential world, the world of nature, the world of history, the world of social relations. The different books of the Bible reflect diverse interests and tastes; they reveal both the divergent minds of the men who gave them literary form and the particular setting of locale and of historical circumstances in which they arose. But those who determined the selection of the books to be included in the biblical canon sought unity amidst diversity. And there is indeed such a unity that underlies the varied experiences recorded in biblical literature. This unity consists in the conviction that the existential world is man's home, that finite existence fulfills a divine vocation, and that man, by ordering his life within a certain discipline, vindicates his own life as well as that of the world which God saw fit to bring into being.

The Bible begins with the story of Creation (Genesis 1, 2:1–3). It is not a detailed report of the incidents of the creative process. It is rather a general statement whose primary objective is clear. It is to declare the world of material being, the world of man and nature, as a divine creation, as an embodiment of "good." It is to declare the dignity of man, his primacy in the order of existence. It is to declare that his life is subject to divine imperatives, that he is under obligation "to be fruitful and multiply, to fill the earth and subdue it." It is to place the institution of the Sabbath at the center of man's response to his place in a divinely created and ordered universe.

Other biblical stories help round out the vision of man, of his place in the world, of the eminence to which he is called as well as of the depths to which he may fall, of his need to struggle in order to meet the claim of his Creator which continues to press on him. There are the stories (Genesis 3, 4) of man's disobedience of God and of his subsequent banishment, of the frightful consequence of a brotherly rift, of the terrifying fact of murder committed by brother against brother, and of its tragic consequences. We are given (Genesis 6:5–7, 8, 9; 11:1–9) a portrayal of man's continued straying from the course marked out for him, and of God's continued efforts to frustrate his false designs by various acts of retributive judgment. God is described as destroying His world in a final step to undo the evil wrought by man. But always God persists in His dream for a good man in a good world. The world is destroyed, but one good man is left to be the nucleus for a new race of men to develop, men who will fulfill the ideal set for them. Finally God is pictured (Genesis 12:1–9) as charging one man and his family, in whom He sees an embodiment of His dream, to go forth to the world as His emissary, to lead the families of the earth to the knowledge of God and His law of righteousness. The one man and his family become the founder of the Jewish people, who are given the mandate to continue the work till it shall finally be accomplished.

The Jewish people are described as going through all kinds of experiences in order to be fitted for its task. They are given a law, enter a convenant at Mount Sinai to be faithful to the charge laid on it, and then move on to the two directions of their destiny—to find a secure basis of their own historical existence as a people and to serve the larger goal of witnessing to the truths taught by their founder.

This, in a sense, is the prologue of the Bible. Its major theme is the promulgation of the law by which the Jewish people are to live. The law is the primary medium chosen for directing man toward his responsibilities, charting the way he must go amidst the pressures and conflicts in the existential world. The rest of the Bible is a record of the experiences of the Jewish people in its endeavor to move in the two directions set for it: to find itself as a people and to be faithful to the law and the visions to which it is dedicated.

The historical books and the prophetic books are all inspired by this goal. They recall the past, but it is a past one sees from the perspective of a destiny. They tell of the successes and failures in Israel's stuggles to settle on the land and to build a viable society, and of its successes and failures in keeping the covenant formed at Sinai. The so-called "wisdom" books of the Bible add the testimony of common human experience to reinforce the visions and precepts which make up the view of the world and man's place in it as defined in the earlier scriptural works.

The Bible affirms the hope that the travail of the centuries will finally bear fruit, that the world will respond to the leadership of God's chosen witness and emissary, the people of Israel. The world will finally learn to acknowledge God as King over all the earth, and build a world community faithful to the demands of His sovereignty. Sometimes the Bible links this hope with the mediating work of the *messiah*, a term which means literally an "anointed one," an allusion to the ancient practice of investing a leader in his office by a ceremony of anointment. Kings Saul, David, and Zedekiah, and even a pagan king, Cyrus the Persian, are called in the Bible *meshiah*, from which derives the term *messiah* (I Samuel 24:7, II Samuel 22:51, Lamentations 4:20, Isaiah 45:1). In other instances the Bible does not refer to a mediating leader, but speaks directly of a golden age of the future which would climax historic development by inaugurating a world order of universal enlightenment and peace (Isaiah 2 and Micah 4). It is the messianic hope that inspires the all-pervading optimism of the Hebrew Bible. The present was often bitter and disillusioning, but the biblical writers were always animated by the faith that history was moving, by slow and sometimes faltering steps, away from idolatry and falsehood and unrighteousness, toward the ascendant triumph of enlightenment, justice, mercy, and peace.

The Oral Torah, as it developed in Judaism, remained within the basic conceptions of the Bible. It only sought to clarify and to implement these conceptions. The goal that underlies the Oral Torah is the same goal that pervades the written Bible. It is to define man's way as a child of God and as a citizen of the world. It is to define more clearly his responsibilities to God and to the rest of creation, and to chart his duties toward the emergent goals of history, the establishment of the messianic age of justice, freedom, and peace, of the universal knowledge of God and the universal obedience to His will. "There is a living bond between rabbinic thought and the Bible. This can only mean that the character of rabbinic thought and the character of Biblical thought are not essentially different," [1] Dr. Max Kadushin recently declared.

The Oral Torah, as we noted previously, arose as a natural evocation of the written biblical text. A word, a thought is forever fluid and incomplete and it interacts with the mind of one who is exposed to it, and out of this interaction there occurs the phenomenon of intellectual germination. The Bible, for instance, reports to us that Noah was saved from the fate of his generations, who perished in the flood, introducing the account with these terse words (Genesis 6:9): "These are the generations [descendants] of Noah. Noah was a righteous and wholehearted man in his

[1] Max Kadushin: *The Rabbinic Mind* (New York: Jewish Theological Seminary of America; 1952), p. 300.

generation; Noah walked with God." The Rabbis saw in this introduction a characterization of Noah which presumably accounts for his deliverance. But how vague the scriptural text is! The Rabbis were stimulated to speculate, suggesting one thing or another, on the basis of clues or hints in the text, that might explain Noah's merit. One Rabbi finds the secret of his merit in the fact that he raised a family, as is alluded in the text's opening reference to his "generations," or descendants, in contrast to his contemporaries to whom sex was a thing of play and dissipation. Others find the clue in the compassionate disposition he revealed when he attended to the needs of the animal world, which he saved with him in the ark. The biblical story is allowed to stand in its basic function of helping to set the value structure of the biblical view of life. The Rabbis add, they elaborate, they clarify, they make explicit what the text sometimes only assumes or states in the most fragmentary fashion.

The Rabbis concern themselves with law, because the law plays so important a role in the Bible. The biblical assumption concerning the nature of man and his need of law to serve his spiritual goals remains unquestioned. The Rabbis again amplify, elaborate, clarify. The Bible states its legal enactments without always providing a rationale. Sometimes it states a general imperative without providing procedural details crucial for the fulfillment of the law in practice. Sometimes the Bible, reflecting its own world, fails to make provision for altered circumstances. Occasionally, the Bible appears to reflect a survival of the primitive, which the Rabbis found offensive and in need of correction. In dealing with these problems the Rabbis did not supersede the Bible; they enabled the Bible to function in its basic role as man's guide for living in the world of concrete existence.

The Bible prescribes laws without stating the larger goals they were to serve; the Rabbis point to these goals. "The commandments," the Rabbis say, "were given only for the purpose of refining human nature" (Genesis Rabbah 44:1). The commandments are seen as a means of sanctifying life (Sifra on Leviticus 20:7). Though imposing rigorous demands on human behavior, the commandments are a means to freedom, for they liberate a person from servitude to lower preoccupations (Avot 6:2). The law serves life, but it must not stifle it, and in the face of hazards to life all laws were to be superseded, except the prohibition of idolatry, incest, and murder, which were to be defended with life itself. One Rabbi limits the exception to the case of murder, but includes the others with those which in a time of persecution one may temporarily violate in order to save his life (Sanhedrin 74a).

The Rabbis grouped the law into comprehensive categories. The two major categories that they recognized in the law were *ben adam lamakom* and *ben adam lahavero*, precepts that deal with man's obligation to God and his obligation to his fellow man (Yoma 85b). The Bible often promulgates laws that interfere with the rights of property. The Rabbis derived a general principle from these precedents, *hefker bet din hefker*, that the court has the authority to displace the property rights of the individual in order to serve the common good (Gittin 36b). The Bible assumes that a marriage may terminate in divorce. The Rabbis attempt to define the grounds for divorce and they specify the measures that must be taken to protect the woman and her children (Gittin 90a, Ketubot 52b, 82b). The Bible forbids work on the Sabbath. The Rabbis try to define what is meant by work, and they speculate on the circumstances which would justify ignoring the prohibition, because in some cases life's work must go on and cannot be subject to a day's interruption each week (Shabbat 89b, 150a). Biblical law, as it emerges from the rabbinic discussions, is more sophisticated, more complex, but more viable for dealing with life.

The Rabbis reckoned with new conditions and when they deemed it vital, modified the procedures of biblical law. They circumvented the cancelation of debts on the sabbatical year, as ordained in the Bible, because the law proved unduly burdensome. They allowed the creditor to assign his debts to the court which was technically free to exact payment since the biblical law is directed only at the creditor himself (Mishnah Sheviit 10:3, 4). They disregarded the biblical requirement of two witnesses to establish a legal fact and admitted indirect evidence, the testimony of one witness, even that of a woman, of a slave or a maidservant, to the death of a husband, in order to permit his wife to remarry.

In the unsettled conditions of the first century, as a result of continued fighting against Rome, it was common for men to disappear without leaving a trace. There was a good presumption that they were dead, though it was not always possible to produce two witnesses who could prove it. The biblical law was modified to ameliorate the condition of the woman (Mishnah Yevamot 16:7).

The Rabbis were aware that the Bible could not have forseen all the vicissitudes of circumstance that faced the Jewish people in subsequent generations. Without recourse to biblical precedent, they felt free to enact various measures to deal with emergency situations that they faced in their day.

The Rabbis, in some cases, sought to mitigate the severity in the primitive provisions of biblical law. The Bible (Deuteronomy 21:18–21) decrees the death penalty for a "rebellious son," without defining the nature of his rebellion. The Rabbis define the nature of his rebelliousness, but finding the law itself excessively harsh, declare that this law "was never carried out in practice, and never would be" (Sanhedrin 71a). The Bible decrees the death penalty for numerous categories of crime. The Rabbis hedged the application of this rule with so many restrictions that they in effect, nullified the death penalty altogether (Mishnah Makkot 1:10).

The most dramatic modification of biblical law under rabbinic sponsorship was the development of the synagogue and the democratization of Jewish piety. The rabbinic period began with the Temple in Jerusalem still in existence and the sacrificial system still operative. Retaining the sacrificial system, the Rabbis, however, bent their efforts to democratize its character. They demanded that the layman, contributing the sacrificial offering, perform a personal act of placing his hands on it prior to its offering by the priest. They divided the country into zones and arranged that a representative of each zone in rotation be present at the Temple services, so that the general populace could achieve a measure of representation and participation at those services. It was also arranged that, simultaneously with the sacrificial offerings, prayers be recited in local communities by the zonal representatives who were not on duty at the Temple. At the same time, under rabbinic sponsorship, the synagogue came into its own, and a liturgy of prayer developed for weekdays, the Sabbath, and the festivals, creating a viable religious life outside the Jerusalem Temple and its sacrificial system. When the Temple was destroyed, the new piety replaced it, and the Rabbis voiced the assurance that this new piety was fully efficacious, that the Temple and the sacrifices were not indispensable. Indeed the Rabbis declared prayer, the study of Torah, and the performance of good deeds as far more efficacious than sacrifices (Berakot 32b, Menahot 110a). Rabban Johanan ben Zaccai, arguing for the dispensability of the sacrificial system, quoted Hosea 6:6: "For I desire loving kindness rather than sacrifice, and the knowledge of God rather than burnt-offerings" (Yalkut Shimeoni, *ad locum*).

The Rabbis broadened the biblical recognition of the universal worth of all men, regardless of religious affiliation. The Bible recognizes the spiritual significance of the Jewish people itself which is the historic bearer of the covenant at Sinai. The preoccupation with its own life as a historical community sometimes obscures the transcendent end toward which the Jewish community is committed. But the dimension of universality is always present in the Bible, whether expressed or not. Abraham's call has as its motivation that "all the families of the earth shall be blessed" through him (Genesis 12:3). The prophetic writings, especially the Book of Jonah, are emphatic in their inclusion of the non-Jewish world in God's concern and in the recognition that all men have the capacity to respond to God's word in deeds of penitence and in growth toward moral and spiritual perfection.

The Rabbis placed the dimension of Jewish universalism into doctrinal terms. Probing into all the implications of the verse "Ye shall therefore keep My statutes and Mine ordinances, which if a man do he shall live by them" (Leviticus 18:5), one teacher asked "Whence may it be demonstrated that a pagan, when he conforms to the moral law of the Torah, becomes the equal of a High Priest in Israel? From the words, 'which if a man do he shall live by them' [the term man being universal and referring equally to Jew and pagan]. Similarly it is said 'This is the law of mankind, Lord God' [II Samuel 7:19, a possible rendition of the original

Hebrew]—it is not stated, 'This is the law of Priests, Levites and Israelites, but [the more inclusive term] the law of mankind.' In similar manner, too, Scripture does not say, 'Open the gates, that Priests, Levites and Israelites may enter,' but, 'Open the gates that a righteous *goy*, keeping faithfulness, may enter' [Isaiah 26:2 *goy* means a people or nation generally, Jewish or pagan]. And again, it does not say, 'This is the gate of the Lord, Priests, Levites and Israelites shall enter into it,' but, 'the righteous shall enter it,' [Psalms 118:20, which is more universal]. Likewise, it does not say, 'Rejoice in the Lord, O ye Priests, Levites and Israelites,' but, 'Rejoice in the Lord, O ye righteous' [Psalms 33:1]. And finally it does not say, 'Do good, O Lord, to the Priests, Levites and Israelites,' but, 'unto the good' [Psalms 125:4, which clearly refers to good men among all nations]. It is thus abundantly demonstrated that even a pagan, provided he adheres to the moral discipline of the Torah, is the equal of the highest ranking priest in Israel" (Yalkut Shimeoni on Leviticus 18:5).

The Rabbis found biblical support for their conviction that men outside the Jewish faith might rise to high spiritual and moral attainments, to win divine approval. In what sense, then, were we to understand the conception that the entire Torah which describes specific forms of the Jewish religion was divinely commanded? If the entire complex of beliefs and disciplines that constitute Judaism are commanded us, are they not all necessary, and how could one who does not abide by them be deemed as having satisfied God's will for man?

The Rabbis resolved this apparent paradox by differentiating between a universal and a particular dimension in the Jewish religious system. The universal dimension was summed up by the so-called seven Noahide commandments (Sanhedrin 56a). These include the practices of equity in human relations and the prohibition of blasphemy, idolatry, unchastity, bloodshed, robbery, and cruelty to animals. These universal principles of religion could be followed by people of other faiths or by those with no formal religious faith at all. The particular dimension of religion was the differentiating expression of these principles through the unique forms of rite and law that each people develops through its own historic experience. Judaism represents the universal religion expressed through the unique system of rite and law that are native to the historic experiences of the Jewish people.

There were Jewish missionaries in the ancient world who sought to make converts for their faith among the pagans. But their efforts were not always bent on making formal converts, on calling people to detach themselves from their particular customs to enter the Jewish faith. Those willing to enter the Jewish faith were received after due preparation and initiation. But we have, for instance, the case of the Jewish missionary Ananias, who actually dissuaded the prince of Adiabene from taking this step when the latter was anxious to become a convert to Judaism. Ananias urged him to follow the universal principles of Judaism without formal conversion, telling him "that he might worship God without being circumcised even though he did resolve to follow the Jewish law entirely; which worship of God was of a superior value to circumcision" (Josephus, *Antiquities* XX 2:4). Within their own native religions it was possible for people to achieve spiritual and moral progress, shed superstition and falsehood, and acknowledge God's universal sovereignty and the primacy of the moral order, becoming in spirit at one with the Jewish people though technically not a part of it.

A modern teacher of Judaism expressed this doctrine succinctly when he said: "As to the other religions . . . neither their absorption nor their destruction is the aim and hope of Israel, just as it is not our aim to do away with the world's national entities. Our aim is to aid them toward higher development and the removal of their baser elements. Thus they will be joined to the source from which Israel is nourished and come under the influence of its fructifying truths. . . . This applies even to pagan cults and certainly so to those religions which are founded, in part, on the teachings of Israel's Torah. And the brotherly love between Esau and Jacob [Christianity and Judaism] and between Isaac and Ishmael [Judaism and Islam] will rise above all the confusions engendered by the evil of their present temporal strivings. It will triumph over them and turn them to truth and eternal love. This broad view, which reflects the sweetness of the truth at the heart of the Torah, must accompany us in all our efforts in the end of days, to seal our faith with the demands of the messianic kingdom, thereby turning bitterness to pleasantness and darkness to light." [2]

This vision of the universal worth of man before God flourished side by side with the conviction that the Jewish people was the vital ground where God performed His wonders of redemption and revelation, and on which men were to build a historical community that would realize the goals of justice and mercy, the love of God and the love of man. The experiences of the Jewish people, the incidents in its life, which illustrated the divine involvement, furnished the occasion where men could express their devotion to God, their quest for nearness to Him, and their yearning for a deepened awareness of His will.

The festivals of Judaism which were given their fullest form under rabbinic sponsorship were the historical festivals, whose roots were to be found in the Bible. They commemorated historical events in the life of the Jewish people, but the meanings they expressed transcended the boundary of the group; they were the universal values of Judaism which summoned men to larger human loyalties. Those loyalties included loyalty to the Jewish people, but they directed men to rise beyond it, to the universal love of God and the universal love of all His creation, at the apex of which was man. Indeed these loyalties were not separate elements, but each was suffused with the other. For the Jewish people was seen as a holy community through which God worked His purpose in history, and through which men could meet the divine imperative pressing on their life.

These two dimensions of Judaism remained a permanent characteristic of its essence. It is universal in its value system, and in its form it remains rooted in the existential particularities of a historical community, the Jewish people.

The Rabbis elaborated on the biblical hope for the ultimate triumph of God's plan for human life. These elaborations flow in diverse directions, sometimes not charted by the Bible. The biblical formulation of this hope often occurred at a time when the Jewish people was set on its own soil, living as a nation among nations. This hope therefore accented the universal note, the

[2] Abraham Isaac Kook: *Igrot Harayah* (Jerusalem; 1823), p. 18.

larger liberation of all mankind. In the rabbinic period the Jews were dispersed among the nations, often persecuted by alien empires. The hope therefore stressed ultimate Jewish restoration in the Holy Land. Through all its proliferations, however, the Jewish hope, as expressed by the Rabbis, remained faithful to the biblical ideal. It was a hope for a change in the historical order, for a change in the lives of men and nations. "The messianic age will differ from the present order only in the absence of oppressive empires," one Sage declared (Berakot 34b). The messianic age will be characterized, in other words, by a prevalence of freedom, and the absence of oppressive violence.

There were instances in which the biblical value system came under challenge in the contemporary world, and the Rabbis reacted with words of defense. Christians had developed the theory that God had rejected the Jewish people because they did not follow the new faith, and they cited the lowly conditions of Jews in exile as "proof" of this rejection. The Rabbis reacted by quoting God's self-designation, so often expressed in the Bible, as a Father to the children of Israel; and a father, if he attain the full ideal of fatherhood, never rejects his children. The conditions of persecution and exile endured by the Jewish people proved that the world was in an unregenerate state and they reaffirmed the faith in eventual restoration. They called on their people to strive for a higher moral and spiritual state so as to contribute by their merit toward hastening the day of the restoration.

Some Jewish rites came under sharp attack from pagans and Christians. This was especially true of the rite of circumcision over which there had been much controversy in the early Church. In its inception as a sect within Judaism, Christianity demanded that its adherents follow prescribed Jewish practice and submit to circumcision. But as it moved away from its Jewish base, it gradually relaxed this requirement. And the defense of this relaxation took the form of an attack against the rite as unnecessary and "unspiritual," since what was done to the flesh could not affect the condition of the soul. In the polemics which ensued it was argued that if God really wanted man to be circumcised, He would not have created him uncircumcised. The rabbinic retort (Genesis Rabbah 11:7) was that all God's work comes to us in a state of incompletion, waiting for man to complete and perfect it. Even the grain we harvest needs to be ground before it can be baked into bread. rabbinic literature (Mishnah Nedarim 3:11, Nedarim 31b, 32a) continually reiterates the importance of the rite of circumcision, and it has been maintained that this stress was, in part, defensive, to counteract the disparagement to which this rite was subject in the polemics of the period.

The Rabbis dealt with the problem of mysticism, which was widespread in the Hellenistic world and which had also gained a following in Jewish circles. The core of this mysticism was the belief that certain representations of divine elements were scattered in the mundane world, whose mastery would give a man a link to the divine and a command of vast resources of theurgic power. There were various subjects on which the mystics centered their interest. One theme in these mystical preoccupations was the pronunciation of God's proper name. For Jewish mystics this meant the pronunciation of the Tetragrammaton, *YHWH*. The Rabbis, to discourage this, forbade the pronunciation of the divine name, and whenever *YHWH* occurred in Scripture, they asked that it be read as though written *Adonai*, "Lord" (Mishnah Sanhedrin 10:1, Avodah Zarah 18a).

Another theme in contemporary mysticism was the idealization of the color blue. Its resemblance to the sky, which in all ancient cultures was deemed the abode of the deity, invested it with divine associations. Jewish mystics saw a confirmation of this in the biblical commandment that a thread of blue be added to the fringe in each corner of a garment (Numbers 15:37–41). Mystics saw the efficacy of the fringe solely in the thread of blue, which they invested with all kinds of sacred associations. The Rabbis appear to have been troubled by this development and they took measures to discourage it. The Mishnah (Mishnah Menahot 4:1, Menahot 38a, 40a) ruled that the blue and the white of the fringe were not both indispensable, that a fringe consisting of either color entirely is satisfactory. The blue dye, which was especially prized in antiquity, was made from the anal glands of a mollusk found in the Mediterranean, the murex, called by the Rabbis *halozon*. When the murex became rare, instead of substituting a vegetable-based dye, the so-called *kela ilan,* which was also current, the

Rabbis discouraged the use of the blue thread altogether (Midrash Tanhuma and Numbers Rabbah on Numbers 15:37–41).[3]

Some Rabbis were drawn toward mysticism, and their views are reflected in the Talmud. But the consensus of rabbinic thought defended a more rational faith, and sought to discourage the flight to mysticism, which opened the door to magic and superstition. Mysticism finally came into its own in the Cabbalah, which developed its own literature, whose best known work was the Zohar. The Cabbalah remained a minor episode in Judaism, thanks to the force of the rabbinic tradition, with its emphasis on *conduct* as the way to meet God's claim on man rather than through secret formulae of esoteric wisdom laden with theurgic potentialities.

The comment which the study of the Bible evoked from the Rabbis is vast in scope and diverse in content. But its over-all contribution is to make the Bible more relevant and more viable as man's guide to the problems facing him in the world of concrete existence.

The Rabbis regarded the Bible as the revealed word of God, but this did not inhibit them from examining the purely literary aspects of the books included in the Bible. They sought to fix the identity of the biblical writers who were the mediators of the divine revelation by giving it a disciplined literary form (Baba Batra 15a). They accounted for the variation of style in the prophetic writings by the varying cultural backgrounds of the prophetic writers (Hagigah 13b). They noted that biblical language is adapted to the necessities of human comprehension, permitting itself, for instance, to characterize God in human attributes, by various metaphors and analogies which seek to interpret the Creator by reference to experiences drawn from His creation (Genesis Rabbah 27:1, Midrash Tehillim on Psalms 1:1). The Bible becomes a much more readable and comprehensible work as a result of these clarifying comments of the Rabbis.

The Rabbis reminded us that biblical statements give us occasionally but a fractional truth, that they depend on the balancing

[3] For a fuller treatment of this subject, see the author's "The Thread of Blue," *Proceedings*, American Academy for Jewish Research, XXXI (1963), 1–32.

lessons from other parts of Scripture. Thus the Rabbis were troubled by the psalmist's comparing of God to a shepherd (Psalms 23:1). The analogy might be taken literally, that man need not exert himself, that he can depend on God to sustain him. The Rabbis denied this by quoting Deuteronomy 2:7, to shed light on the verse in Psalms. The verse in Deuteronomy declares: "For the Lord thy God hath blessed thee in all the work of thy hand." One of the Rabbis inferred from this that "if man worked he would be blessed but he would not be blessed if he did not work" (Midrash Tehillim on Psalms 23:1).

The Bible was greatly enriched by the embroidery of comment that makes up the substance of the Oral Torah, but not always without a price, for the comment was sometimes farfetched, and the inference drawn of dubious cogency. The concern to give added weight to a proposition by relating it to a hallowed text sometimes led an author to press his point by forcing his interpretation into the text, in clear violation of its obvious meaning. The text itself, unencumbered by commentary, was frequently obscured, losing its authentic, original sense, and it came to be understood in the light of the meaning later commentators assigned to it.

In Genesis 32:5 Jacob is quoted as instucting his messengers to tell Esau: "Thus saith thy servant Jacob, I have sojourned with Laban and stayed until now." The numerical equivalent of the word "sojourned" (*garti*) is 613, corresponding to the rabbinic calculation of the number of the commandments in the Pentateuch. This led the Rabbis to suggest that Jacob really told Esau that though he had spent many years with Laban, he had nevertheless kept all the precepts of the Torah (Midrash Lekah Tov, *ad lucum*)! But the Pentateuch and its laws were not promulgated until a later epoch, and how could the coincidental equivalence of the numerical value of a word justify such an interpretation? The Rabbis wove their embroidery of legendary embellishment around their heroes, and they gave the imagination free reign, undaunted by the facts. They may have been inspired, too, by the desire to point a lesson to their own contemporaries who were often forced to live in alien lands under pressures to abandon their faith. Jacob's faithfulness could then serve as an example to emulate. We treat such comments as imaginative exuberance, but we cannot take them as authentic versions of what the text has to say.

We have quoted previously the interpretation of the Midrash on Deuteronomy 16:18–22: "Judges and officers shalt thou make thee in all thy gates . . . and they shall judge the people with righteous judgment." The Midrash quotes several interpretations, one of which turns this verse into a definition of the criteria for the selection of judges. One Rabbi sees this verse as declaring that a judge must possess good moral character so that his influence will be a force for obedience to the law. Such a judge is at the same time an "officer," an agent of enforcement, one who by the sway of his influence and example guarantees the execution of the law. Another interpretation suggests that this verse asked that judges be selected who are sympathetic in judgment, who can render on their people a judgment that finds them righteous. These ideas are interesting in themselves, and we may wish to accept them as valid. But do they not depart from the obvious meaning of a text?

These excursions from text to commentary were in some instances challenged by Rabbis when they saw in the interpretation a dangerous distortion of the text. We have an instance of this in a discussion evoked by Zechariah 9:1: "The burden of the word of the Lord. In the land of *Hadrach*, and in Damascus, shall be His resting place. For the eye of man will belong to the Lord, and all the tribes of Israel."

The meaning of this verse is not entirely clear. The prophet here seems to envision a time when all men will turn to the Lord, together with the tribes of Israel, when God's presence will be acknowledged beyond the frontiers of the land of Israel, reaching to Hadrach and Damascus, which were located in the north. It is typical of the messianic hope that is often expressed by this prophet. The term *Hadrach*, however, may be taken as a compound of *had* and *rach*, the former meaning "harsh" and the latter, "soft." One Rabbi seizing upon this coincidence interpreted *Hadrach* as referring to the messiah who will be *harsh* with the pagan nations and *soft* with the Israelites. Rabbi Judah ben Durmascis protested to the author of this interpretation with the retort, "Why do you distort the text! I declare by heaven and earth that I am from Damascus and there is a place in that region called Hadrach" (Sifre, Devarim 1).

The Rabbis were aware that the elaborations proposed sometimes exceeded the bounds of authenticity, that the meanings expounded from texts occasionally departed from the text's genuine sense, and they asked that a line of demarcation be drawn. Let the *derash*, or the elaboration, proceed as it may, but the authentic interpretation must not be subverted, they declared (Shabbat 63a). In such a case the elaboration was to be treated largely for its own merits, but it was not to be mistaken for the genuine meaning, which is to remain intact. The text was thus to be studied in a two-dimensional sense, for its simple meaning as well as for its evocations in the secondary literature of rabbinic commentary.

The superstructure of interpretations which was raised on the original text of the Bible embraced the most significant contributions in Jewish thought, in ethics, theology, and law. A tendency developed in medieval Judaism to center the chief concern of students on this superstructure, on the vast body of talmudic and midrashic writings, sometimes to the neglect of the Bible itself. The very elaborateness of these interpretations made them intellectually challenging and all the more attractive to those inclined toward the intellectual life. The Pentateuch was read in the synagogue as part of the religious service, and so were selected passages from other parts of the Bible. These were studied diligently, usually with the commentary of Rashi (eleventh century, France), which made extensive allusions to the interpretations of the Rabbis, and they were studied in an order corresponding to the cycle of readings in the synagogue. But the whole Bible, as a continuous work with its own level of meaning, was often lost to sight.

There were reactions in Judaism against the overemphasis on the Talmud and its related literature, to the neglect of the Bible. In the latter half of the eighth century there arose a revolt against the Talmud, led by Anan ben David, of a notable Babylonian Jewish family. He demanded a return to the Bible. The movement he led developed into a sect which broke with official Judaism. Followers of this sect were called *Karaim* or *Bene Mikra*, or *Baale*

Mikra, which means "scripturalists," the term *Mikra* being a designation for Scripture, and *Kara,* for the study of Scripture. We generally refer to them, in short, as Karaites. They repudiated the authority of the Oral Torah, and sought to base their version of Judaism on the Bible alone.

It proved impossible to remain within the rigid confines of the Bible, and the Karaites were soon forced to create an interpretive tradition of their own. Their method remained simpler, however, than the one developed by the Rabbis. They followed three principles of interpretation: the literal meaning of the biblical text, inference derived from analogy to provisions in the biblical text, and the consensus of opinion in the Karaite community, where neither the explicit statement of the text nor its extension through logical analogy proved adequate.

The surrender of the adaptation to life that had been achieved by rabbinic law made Karaism in many cases unduly harsh and burdensome. Thus Anan prohibited medical treatment of the sick, as incompatible with the implicit faith in the healing power of God (Exodus 15:26). One of the major contributions of Karaism was the stimulus it offered rabbinic Judaism to restate its case in the face of challenge.

The excess of attention to the dialectics of rabbinic law was countered by Saadia Gaon (882–942), whose labors were in part stimulated by the Karaite revolt. He wrote on the Bible, both commentaries and translations into the vernacular, and he inaugurated the philosophic exposition of Judaism in his *Emunot ve-Deot*, "Beliefs and Opinions."

The excesses of legalism were also countered by a school of moralists whose writings stress the elements of belief, devotion, and moral concern. The best known among these writers was Bahya ben Joseph ibn Pakuda, who lived in Saragossa, Spain, probably toward the end of the eleventh century. His *Hovot ha-Levavot,* "Duties of the Heart," has remained a classic of Jewish piety. It accepts the totality of the Oral tradition, but centers its attention on the realm of faith, on the interior life, on the hidden meanings of the commandments. It is replete with quotations from the Bible, especially those of the prophets.

One of the great voices calling for a balanced view of Jewish tradition was Rabbi Judah Loew of Prague, who protested against this trend as a narrowing of Jewish tradition. He was one of the great educational reformers in the history of Judaism. He advocated a graded education, beginning with the mastery of the Hebrew language, then the Bible, which was to be studied as a continuous text, regardless of the cycle of weekly scriptural readings in the synagogue, and without the customary addition of the Rashi commentary, which obscured the simple meaning of the text with elaborations and digressions. Then was to follow the study of the Mishnah, and then the Gemara. But Rabbi Judah's counsel went unheeded and the study of the Oral Torah continued to displace the written Torah from a place of primacy in Jewish life and thought.

Rabbi Judah Loew of Prague was a formative influence on the rise of *Hasidism*, a folk movement of Jewish mysticism which arose in the first half of the eighteenth century in the southwestern region of Eastern Europe. The term *hasid* (plural *hasidim*) means "zealous" or "devout," and it is so used frequently in the Bible. Hasidism was in part a reaction against the overintellectualization of Judaism through concentration on the study of the Talmud. Hasidism taught God's accessibility through every deed, every experience, in all walks of life. Hasidim believed that every event of nature seen in depth reveals an inner essence, a divine dimension, and they believed similarly concerning every precept, every utterance of Scripture. The sense of God's nearness suffused the piety of the Hasidim with joy, and this was enhanced by emotion stirring elements which Hasidism introduced into Jewish ritual, such as singing, dancing, and the fellowship meal. The head of a Hasidic circle was a *tzadik*, "a righteous man," from whom his followers derived inspiration and practical direction for problems of piety as well as practical affairs. The quest for hidden meanings in Scripture led the Hasidim to develop a figurative and sometimes allegorical interpretation of Scripture, but the Hasidim respected the traditional precepts which they observed faithfully, indeed, often with greater devotion than non-Hasidic Jews. Hasidism stressed the study of the Pentateuch and especially the study and devotional recitation of the psalms.

The founder of Hasidism was Israel ben Eliezer, known as the

Baal Shem-Tov (*c.* 1700–60), and he was followed by other leaders who developed his doctrines and enriched the movement with many of their own original insights. Hasidism, especially its parables, and its teaching of God's accessibility through all of life's experiences, and its stress on joy as a service to God, found an eloquent expounder in Martin Buber (1878–1965), who introduced its basic concepts and ideas into the mainstream of modern thought.

The rise of various modernist movements in Judaism have invariably affirmed the need of a return to the plain text of the Bible, which was to be liberated from the superstructure of commentary represented by the Oral Torah. This was one of the goals of the movement for cultural modernization known as *Haskalah*, as well as of the movements for religious modernization represented by Reform and Conservative Judaism. The greatest impetus to the recovery of the original Bible came from the new state of Israel. Israeli Jewry has revived the Hebrew language, which has become the spoken idiom of the new state, and the Hebrew Bible —without midrashic elaboration—is studied in all the schools and in various projects of adult education that are pursued throughout the country.

The movement for the return to the biblical text itself has sometimes included critical judgments against the Oral Torah as a distortion of the original Bible. Most critics, however, have taken a broader view, conceding the legitimacy of the literary proliferation which created the Oral Torah, but at the same time insisting on the necessity of studying the original biblical text for its authentic meaning, without embroidery or elaboration. Many have recognized too that the rabbinic *midrash* often sheds valuable light on the *peshat*, the literal meaning of the biblical text.

The recognition of distinctive levels in Jewish tradition, the separation of the biblical world from the rabbinic, is a phase of the historical approach to the study of culture. The historical sense inhibits the random reading of the present into the past. It insists that a text has a certain legitimate meaning that cannot be subverted by subtleties of interpretation. The historical sense, at the same time, in looking at every literary creation by the light of the particular world in which it arose, has gained for us a new appreciation of both the biblical, as well as the rabbinic writings. For it has given to each a particular context, a dimension of the reality against which those who wrote them struggled to shape their world to ideal ends.

The discovery that the biblical (as well as the rabbinic) writers were real people struggling with the problems of the real world has authenticated the biblical and the rabbinic works as historic documents. It has disclosed for us with great cogency the sublimity of thought, the depths of feeling and imagination, the zealous commitment to moral and spiritual values that inspired those writers. Even one who reads these works as literature rather than as testaments of religious faith will cherish them for their unique qualities as literary masterpieces. The modernist movements in Judaism have sometimes been critical of the Jewish religious tradition, but the interest in the Bible has survived this criticism. The book on which the Jewish tradition was founded remains central to every concept of modern Judaism as it was to the Judaism of all the ages preceding us.

Two new translations of the Hebrew Bible into English have appeared recently, which illustrate the two attitudes toward the Hebrew Bible. The new translation of the Pentateuch called *The Torah*, published by the Jewish Publication Society of America, seeks to define the meaning of the original text, the *peshat* as it has been called. Another translation of the Pentateuch, called *Torah Yesharah*, the work of Rabbi Charles Kahane, attempts to read the Midrash into the language of the original text, with the result that the simple meaning is sometimes lost in far-reaching digressions and occasional distortions. Here are the opening two verses in Genesis, as rendered in the translation by Rabbi Kahane: "In the beginning the Almighty, in His wisdom, created out of nothingness the heaven and the earth together with their inherent potentials. But the earth was still formless and without system, and the darkness of the various gases which the Almighty created were on the face of the abyss; and mighty winds blew over the face of the water but were controlled by the merciful spirit of the Almighty." The new Jewish Publication Society version reads thus: "When God began to create the heaven and the earth—the earth being unformed and void, with darkness over the face of the deep and a wind from God sweeping over the water. . . ." The corresponding translation in the Jewish Publication Society (old) version is: "In the beginning God created the heaven and the earth. Now the earth was unformed and void, and darkness was on the face of the deep; and the spirit of God hovered over the face of the waters."

The Bible remains the foundation of Judaism, but it is not in itself a complete statement of it. The Bible was regarded as unfinished, in the sense in which every work that bears the stamp of a finite dimension in its creation must be unfinished. It is unfinished because life, out of which it arose and to which it addresses itself, is unfinished. Witnessing to the fecundity of the Bible is a secondary literature whose creation it stimulated. The problem confronting students of Judaism is to disentangle these processes so that each element be given its legitimate scope. It is to keep the Bible for what it is in itself, and at the same time to permit it to enter as a factor in the fermentation of thought. It is to permit the Oral Torah and the written Torah to flow together in a higher unity in which the seed lives on in its fruit, and at the same time to keep the two apart so as to see them in their distinctiveness for the unique historic phenomenon each represents and for the unique word which each has spoken to man.

Chapter IX

Jesus: Jew or Christian?

The Hebrew Bible was the source that fed the living tradition of Judaism. But there were two tributaries that also flowed from the same source, Christianity and Islam. There were influences other than the Bible that helped shape the Christian and Islamic traditions, but the Hebrew Bible was the cornerstone on which they were reared. And the process by which these traditions transformed the biblical element into their own image was also a process of interpretation analagous to the *midrash* by which the Rabbis created the Oral Torah. The Islamic tradition falls outside our present inquiry, but we shall study the Hebrew Bible as the formative elment in the rise of Christianity. The directing force behind the origin of Christianity was of course the ministry of Jesus.

A mist of legend hovers over the historical personality of Jesus and the teachings he imparted to his disciples and left as his legacy to posterity. There are no reports written from a detached and objective viewpoint on the basis of which to reconstruct those events in which he was the central figure. Our knowledge must be drawn from the New Testament writings, principally the synoptic Gospels—Mark, Matthew, and Luke. But none of the Gospels were written by an immediate disciple of Jesus, nor did they originate in the primitive Christian community where firsthand reports might have been preserved as oral tradition. They originated in the Greek Christian community and were composed by people who were more than one generation removed from the events chronicled.

The Gospel writers sought to defend the dogmas which the Church had woven about the role of Jesus in the scheme of salvation. The Gospels are both polemical and defensive. They are not directed at an objective portrayal of the master's life and of his work. In the words of the noted contemporary New Testament scholar Rudolf Bultmann: "We conclude that the whole framework of the history of Jesus must be viewed as an editorial construction, and that therewith a whole series of typical scenes which, because of their ecclesiastical use and their poetic and artistic associations, we had looked upon as scenes in the life of Jesus, must be viewed as creations of the evangelists." [1]

The commingling of a kernel of historical fact with homiletical embroidery in the Gospel narrative was recently touched on by Msg. Myles M. Bourke of St. Joseph's Seminary in an article in the *Catholic Biblical Quarterly*. Writing on "The Literary Genus of Matthew 1–2," he declared: "Admittedly, the gospel presents Jesus' ministry, death and resurrection as events which really happened. But that the author of such a work might have introduced it by a midrash of deep theological insight, in which Jesus appears as the new Israel and the new Moses (thus containing the theme of the entire gospel), and in which the historical element is very slight seems to be a thoroughly probable hypothesis." [2]

The Gospel portrayal of Jews is generally hostile, as many Christians as well as Jewish scholars have observed. The Gospels were written after the Christian community had broken with Judaism, after Jewish practices had been repudiated as ineffectual

[1] Rudolf Bultmann and Karl Kundsin: *Form Criticism,* Frederick C. Grant (trans.) (New York: Harper & Row; 1962), p. 28.

[2] Quoted by James M. Robinson in *Ecumenical Dialogue at Harvard,* Samuel H. Miller and G. Ernest Wright (ed.), (Cambridge, Mass.: The Belknap Press of Harvard University Press; 1964), p. 102.

at best, and new formulae for man's salvation, faith in Jesus, the rites of the Eucharist meal and baptism had been developed by Church authorities. They were written, too, after Christian leaders had resigned themselves to the realization that the Jewish community by and large would remain adamant in rejecting the claims of Christianity, and that the future of the Christian movement was therefore to be sought among the pagans of the Roman Empire. It therefore suited the purpose of the Gospel writers to present Jesus as a noble figure who struck out against the spiritual decadence of the Jewish faith, and who was consistently at war with the Jews and with their leaders. The events were so shaped as to suggest that the Jews were the prime movers in the tragedy of the crucifixion, while the involvement of the Romans was played down.

It is significant therefore that when subjected to searching inquiry, the Gospel accounts themselves disclose to us that Jesus lived and died as a Jew, within the framework of Jewish belief and Jewish practice. "The schematic representation according to which the Pharisees and scribes are from the outset the sworn enemies of Jesus is certainly unhistorical," declared Bultmann. He even doubts that Jesus himself thought of himself as the messiah: "Indeed, it must remain questionable whether Jesus regarded himself as the messiah, and did not rather first become messiah in the faith of the community." [3]

A detailed examination of the teachings of Jesus disclosed him to have been within the mainstream of the living tradition of Judaism. The pioneer of critical studies in the Old and New Testaments, Julius Wellhausen, declared categorically: "Jesus was not a Christian; he was a Jew. He did not preach a new faith, but taught men to do the will of God; and in his opinion, as also in that of the Jews, the will of God was to be found in the Law of Moses and in the other books of Scripture." [4] Some of the findings of Wellhausen, especially in his Old Testament studies, have been questioned by contemporary historians, but his judgment on the Jewishness of Jesus is fully supported by modern scholarship.

[3] Bultmann and Kundsin: *Form Criticism*, pp. 35, 71.

[4] Julius Wellhausen: *Einleitung in die drei ersten Evangelien* (n.p.: Berlin; 1905), p. 113.

The New Testament portrayal of Jesus, Joseph Klausner has noted, shows him to have been obedient to the traditional practices of Judaism.[5] He attended the Temple and respected the institution of sacrifices. He was a regular worshipper in the synagogue. He wore fringes on the corners of his garment, as prescribd by Jewish tradition. He celebrated the religious festivals and recited the prayers customary at such occasions.

When asked to define the way one might earn eternal life he replied (Mark 10:17–19): "You know the commandments: 'Do not kill, Do not commit adultery, Do not steal, Do not bear false witness, Do not defraud, Honor your father and mother' " (Exodus 20:12–16, Deuteronomy 5:16–20). When asked to single out the primary commandments he replied (Mark 12:29–31): "The first is [Deuteronomy 6:4–5] 'Hear, O Israel: The Lord our God, the Lord is one; and you shall love the Lord your God with all your heart, and with all your soul, and with all your mind, and with all your strength.' The second is this [Leviticus 19:18], 'You shall love your neighbor as yourself.' There is no other commandment greater than these." The commandments quoted by Jesus as the way to gain eternal life are selected from the Ten Commandments. But "Do not defraud," included in the Gospel of Mark, does not appear in either version of the Decalogue. The parallel discussion in Matthew 19:17–19 omits "Do not defraud" and substitutes for it "You shall love your neighbor as yourself" (Leviticus 19:18). This discussion is also paralleled in Luke 18:18–23, and here, too, "Do not defraud" is omitted, but Luke did not substitute any other commandment for it.

We also face difficulty in the formulation of the two primary commandments (the love of God and the love of neighbor). In the original Hebrew the verse commanding the love of God does not have "with all your mind." The parallel passage in Matthew 22:37 has "with all your mind," but it omits "with all your strength." In Luke 10:37 the passage reads: "With all your heart, and with all your soul, and with all your strength, and with all your mind."

[5] Joseph Klausner: *Jesus of Nazareth*, Herbert Danby (trans.) (New York: The Macmillan Company; 1953), pp. 363–8.

The disagreement of the Gospels in quoting the words of Jesus and the slight deviation of each version from the original Hebrew is readily understood when we recall that one of the Gospel writers personally witnessed the events they describe. Dependence on an oral tradition going back to events more than a generation earlier leads to inaccuracy—in which the Gospel abounds. While it is thus impossible to fix the precise words of Jesus, it remains clear that he walked firmly on the ground of Jewish piety and the authority that he invoked as a guide to life was the authority of Scripture, which was embodied for him in the Hebrew Bible.

The distinction that Jesus made in the relative importance of the commandments was also in the spirit of Judaism. The Rabbis discussed this subject often. Rabbi Akiba, for example, dealt with the same question, but his answer was more radical than that of Jesus. He was content with singling out one commandment—the one which Jesus quoted from Leviticus (19:18)—as the summation of the whole Torah: "You shall love your neighbor as yourself."

Some have seen a cleavage between Jesus and his Jewish heritage in the sharp invective that he is quoted as having spoken against the Pharisees, who were presumably the official representatives of Jewish piety in his time. We have already noted that historians tend to doubt whether the denunciations of the Pharisees that the Gospels put into Jesus' mouth are really genuine. They are rather inclined to think that these denunciations reflect the later hostility between the early Church and the Jews, after the Jews had confounded the hopes of Christian leaders by refusing to acknowledge the messiahship of Jesus. Indeed, Jesus appears to have lived his life in conformity to Pharisaic teachings. But apart from this, a critical attitude toward the Pharisees was not inconsistent with loyalty to Judaism. The name Pharisee was, indeed, an honorable name in Judaism, but there were instances when the name became a mask and a pretense, a byword for shallow and insincere faith, for a rigorous attention to the externals of religion and an unconcern for its inner essence.

The Talmud, too, was impatient with such Pharisees and

spoke out sharply against them. The Talmud (Yerushalmi Berakot 9:7 and Sotah 5:7) speaks derisively of the "shoulder Pharisee," who exhibits his good works on his shoulder for public view; the "wait-a-bit Pharisee," who announces to people with whom he is engaged in business that he must interrupt himself to do a good work; the "calculating Pharisee," who seeks to keep statistics on his transgressions and his good works; the "economizing Pharisee," who asks, What economy can I practice to save a little for the purpose of doing a good deed; the "show-me-my-fault Pharisee," who says, Show me my fault and I will correct it by a balancing good deed; the Pharisee who serves out of fear, like Job. Only one kind of Pharisee is dear to God, the Talmud adds, one who serves out of love, like father Abraham.

The Pharisees were the architects of popular Jewish piety. In the ideological battle they had once waged with the Sadducees, they won the people to their side. But the Pharisees remained a distinct party, with customs and disciplines of their own which set them apart from the rest of the people. While the people recognized them as the custodians of the tradition, this did not prevent the people, in some instances, from resenting the Pharisees as a group apart in the community. Jesus, as Yehezkel Kaufmann suggested, followed the Pharisaic tradition without formally being a member of the group.[6] This would explain his general adherence to Pharisaic principles, as well as the freedom of criticism which he voiced against them.

The Gospels, W. D. Davies reminds us, preserve "only the whisper of the voice of Jesus." [7] It is difficult to believe that Jesus could really have employed against the Pharisees the abusive language imputed to him in the Gospels. Did he not denounce anger as a vile emotion? Did he not advocate returning good for evil and turning "the other cheek"? But wide is the margin between what good men preach and what they are able to practice in their own life. The most dedicated and selfless idealists in religious and ethical pursuits have often made fierce adversaries of those with

[6] Yehezkel Kaufmann: *Goleh ve-Nekar* (Tel-Aviv; 1929), I, 353.

[7] W. D. Davies: *The Setting of the Sermon on the Mount* (New York: Cambridge University Press; 1964), p. 436.

whom they disagreed. A contemporary of Jesus, Rabbi Eliezer the son of Hyrcanus, had a favorite maxim: "Let your friend's honor be as precious to you as your own, and be not easily provoked to anger" (Avot 2:15). But when he became engaged in debate over some principle he proved a most recalcitrant opponent. In one instance he defied the consensus of his colleagues and sabotaged the proceedings of the academy with bitter and unyielding words. In the end he was voted in contempt of the academy and excommunicated from its deliberations.

Some have grounded the Jewish opposition to Jesus in his claims to being the messiah. The sources in the New Testament are by no means clear that Jesus himself laid claim to messianic status. Julius Wellhausen, Rudolf Bultmann, and Charles Guignebert, among others, tend to doubt this, attributing this claim to the Christian community after his death. Adolf Harnack and others believe that he did make such a claim.[8] Assuming that Jesus himself laid claim to being the messiah, this would not automatically have made him a heretic to bring the wrath of the Jewish authorities against him. Preceding Jesus and following him, there were various figures in Jewish history who were imbued with the redeemer's zeal and thought of themselves as messiahs. The best known of these was Bar Kokba, whose cause won a following among the highest circles of religious leadership in Judaism, including Rabbi Akiba, one of the most renowned teachers in the rabbinic academies of his time. Bar Kokba became the central figure in a movement for the liberation of Jewish Palestine from the Roman yoke which had its heyday in 135 C.E. Jesus conceived of messiahship in other terms than did Bar Kokba; his was otherwordly in emphasis and was less concerned with the injustices of Roman imperialism. But however he conceived his messiahship, this could not have created an impassable barrier between him and the Jewish authorities of his day.

Jesus has on occasions been presented as a universal spirit who was impatient with the introverted, narrow Jewish piety of his

[8] Adolf Harnack: *What Is Christianity?* (New York: G. P. Putnam's Sons; 1904), p. 133. (Now available in a Harper Torchbook soft-cover edition.)

time. The record, however, points clearly in the opposite direction. The Pharisees were concerned with bringing the message of their faith to the outside non-Jewish world. The New Testament itself states that the Pharisees would travel over land and sea to make a single convert for their faith (Matthew 23:15).

The Jewish missionary effort as guided by Pharisaic principles, we have noted earlier, did not concentrate primarily on seeking formal conversions to Judaism. It was content to make "God fearers," men who acknowledged the existence of a universal God and the claims of the moral law, even though they remained technically within their ancestral faith. Jesus, on the other hand, did not concern himself with the non-Jewish world. He centered his interests on his own people. He was reluctant to help a Canaanite woman because, as he explained to his disciples, he was sent "only to the lost sheep of the house of Israel" and that "it was not meet to take the children's bread and cast it to the dogs" (Matthew 15:21–27). He instructed his disciples when charging them to continue his ministry (Matthew 10:5–6): "Go nowhere among the Gentiles, and enter no town of the Samaritans, but go rather to the lost sheep of the house of Israel."

A contrary position is expressed in Jesus' parting message to his disciples, where he is quoted as charging them: "Go therefore and make disciples of all nations, baptizing them in the name of the Father and of the Son and of the Holy Spirit" (Matthew 28:19). But Jesus is here quoted as speaking after his resurrection, as an apparition seen by his disciples. It cannot therefore have the authenticity of the earlier encounters reported in his lifetime. The reference to the three persons of the trinity also stamps the final scene as a later formulation, after the trinitarian doctrine had been established. John C. Fenton, in his commentary on Matthew, cites the actual hesitation of the first disciples of Jesus to preach to gentiles, as reported in Acts 11:1–2, 19, and concludes that "it is improbable that Jesus said this." [9] He notes also that the first disciples of Jesus baptized in the name of Jesus, and not in the name of the trinity (Acts 2:38). D. E. Nineham, in his commentary on

[9] J. C. Fenton: *The Gospel of St. Matthew* (Baltimore: Penguin Books; 1963), p. 453.

Mark, regards the call to preach to all the nations "a saying current in a Gentile Church but not an actual saying of Jesus" [1] Indeed, the verses in Mark charging the disciples to preach to all the nations (16:14–16) are regarded by most scholars, Protestant as well as Catholic, as spurious. They relegate them as part of an appendix to the Gospel of Mark, written sometime in the second century.

Some have maintained that the God of Judaism is remote and austere, and that Jesus broke new ground in religion by proclaiming the nearness of God, and His accessibility to man, no matter what his condition. Thus it has been pointed out that Jesus called God *abba*, "father," a term of nearness and endearment. Joachim Jeremias, a prominent German Lutheran scholar of both Testaments, put it thus: "As a form of address to God the word abba is without parallel in the whole of late Jewish devotional literature. . . . There is no parallel to the authority with which he dares to address God as *abba*. . . ." [2] It is difficult to know where Professor Jeremias received his information, but he is of course very much mistaken. He is a noted authority on the history of Christianity, but his knowledge of post-biblical Judaism is limited. Jewish devotional literature abounds in the use of "father," as a term of address to God. It generally uses the Hebrew terms *avinu* or *av*, rather than the Aramaic *abba*. One prayer, recited on fast days and the Day of Atonement, consists of some forty verses, each of which begins with *avinu*. Sometimes the term appears in combinations as *av harahamim*, "Merciful Father"; *av shebashamayim*, "Heavenly Father"; *av lekol ha-olam*, "Father to the Whole World"; *avinu av harahamim* "Father, Merciful Father." In the words of Martin Buber: "The pious Jews of pre-Christian times called their God 'Father'. . . . It is not as though these men did not know that God is also utterly distant; it is rather that they know at the same time that however far away God is, he is never unrelated to them, and that even the man who is farthest away

[1] D. E. Nineham: *The Gospel of St. Mark* (Baltimore: Penguin Books; 1963), p. 449.

[2] Joachim Jeremias: *The Problem of Historical Jesus*, Norman Perrin (trans.) (Philadelphia: Fortress Press; 1964), pp. 18–21.

from God cannot cut himself off from the mutual relationship." [3] The Rabbis' use of the term "Father" in various combinations, when addressing God, is well documented by A. Marmorstein in his *The Old Rabbinic Doctrine of God*.[4] Jesus was no innovator when he used this term; he merely drew on one of the basic concepts of Jewish piety.

The Sermon on the Mount has sometimes been cited as a pronouncement by Jesus which appears to abrogate the old law in favor of a new law propounded by him. Our principal source for this body of teachings is Matthew 5–7. Commentators on the Gospels tend to believe however that, as formulated, these teachings express the editorial hand of the evangelist himself and are not to be seen as a direct utterance of Jesus. John C. Fenton, principal of Lichfield Theological College in England, and editor of the Gospel of Matthew, put it thus: "Whatever the pattern of this block of teachings is, it has almost certainly been contrived by the Evangelist himself, because it is almost certain that Matthew has collected together here sayings of Jesus which were not all spoken on the same occasion. The words and deeds of Jesus seem to have been remembered and preserved in the period before they were written down as isolated small units of not more than a paragraph each; and the arrangement of these paragraphs and sayings was the work of the Evangelists." [5]

The Sermon on the Mount proceeds in the form of antithesis: "You have heard. . . . But I say unto you." We cite a passage from this sermon to illustrate its method as well as its substantive direction: "You have heard that it was said to the men of old, 'You shall not kill [Exodus 20:13, Deuteronomy 5:17]; and whoever kills shall be liable to judgment.' But I say to you that everyone who is angry with his brother shall be liable to judgment; whoever insults his brother shall be liable to the council, and whoever says, 'You fool!' shall be liable to the hell of fire. . . . You have heard that it was said [Exodus 21:21, Leviticus 24:20, Deuteronomy 19:21], 'An eye for an eye and a tooth for a tooth.'

[3] *The Writings of Martin Buber*, Will Herberg (ed.) (New York: Meridian Books; 1956), p. 268.

[4] (London: Oxford University Press; 1927), pp. 56–62.

[5] Fenton. *The Gospel of St. Matthew*, p. 78.

But I say to you, Do not resist one who is evil. But if anyone strike you on the right cheek, turn to him the other also; and if anyone would sue you and take your coat, let him have your cloak as well; and if anyone forces you to go one mile, go with him two miles. Give to him who begs from you, and do not refuse him who would borrow from you" (Matthew 5:21–22, 38–42).

An analysis of this passage and of the Sermon as a whole does not support the impression that we have here an abrogation of the old law taught by Judaism in favor of a new law propounded by Jesus. The Sermon on the Mount does not abrogate the original commandments of Judaism but seeks to remind us that law in itself does not fulfill the full demand of our moral responsibilities, that there is a zone of moral concern beyond the law which a good man must attend to.

Moshe Greenberg, Ellis Professor of Biblical Studies at the University of Pennsylvania, expressed it thus "The New Testament does not contain a corpus of criminal laws. While several sayings of Jesus touch upon points of biblical law, they do not themselves take the form of law, but of exhortation to saintly behavior (e.g., Matthew 5:21–32, note vs. 20). Jesus' pronouncement on talion is a case in point: what is rejected is far more than the literal application of 'an eye for an eye and a tooth for a tooth,' which, as suggested above, can hardly have been a juridical penalty even in ancient Israel. The Tannaitic understanding that monetary compensation alone is implied (Mekilta at Exodus 21:23; Misnah Baba Kamma 8:1) would be no less repugnant to Matthew 5:38–41. For the demand here is that the injured waive his rights to sue for reparations of any sort whatever. This saintly teaching is, of course, the very antithesis of a legal prescription." [6]

In protesting the moral insufficiency of law as such, Jesus expressed a familiar doctrine in rabbinic Judaism. The Rabbis often emphasized the importance of the law, but they were well aware that a morally sensitive person cannot content himself with merely conforming to the law, but must often go beyond it. In

[6] Moshe Greenberg [erroneously cited as J. Greenberg]: "Crimes and Punishments," *The Interpreter's Dictionary of the Bible* (Nashville, Tenn.: Abingdon Press; 1962), I, 742 ff.

one instance the Rabbis declared that Jerusalem was destroyed because the people therein were content to act in accordance with the strict demands of the law (Baba Metzia 88a). Good people must act *lifnim mishurat ha-din*, "beyond the letter of the law" (Mekilta on Exodus 18:20).

In the Sermon on the Mount Jesus expressed what the Rabbis called *midat hasidut*, "a standard of saintliness," by which rare spirits live. The Rabbis idealized the person who accepts offense without retaliation and submits to suffering cheerfully (Yoma 23a). Does not the Amidah include in the final liturgical meditation these words: *venafshi keafar lakol tihyeh*, "and may I be like dust to all." It is a strange idiom but it is obviously a prayer for a state of self-effacement that would make a person wholly non-responsive to injury. In the *Ethics of the Fathers* we have the following evaluation of human character (5:13): "He who says, What is mine is mine, and what is yours is yours, is a medium type, and some say that his type is like that of the wicked city of Sodom. . . . He who says, What is mine is yours and what is yours is yours, is a saintly man." The Mishnah (Sotah 3:4), in one instance, cautioned against excessive "saintliness" because it may prove quite unrealitic, but there have always been "unrealistic saints" in the history of Judaism.

The exhortation to the "standard of saintliness" presupposes an existing social order with a system of justice to protect the innocent and judge the guilty. But good men render a precious service to the world by reminding us of a higher standard where men are protected by a more potent safeguard, a mutuality of love, a degree of self-effacement and non-retaliation to hurt which establishes peace through love rather than the fear of force. In projecting such a standard Jesus did not necessarily negate the right of men—even their duty, in some circumstances—to resist aggression. He was within the tradition of his people in projecting another order of life in which saintliness would render the dependence on force a moral anachronism.

This interpretation of the two major elements by which the structure of this sermon is developed will account for an otherwise insoluble problem in its text. As David Daube noted: "Twice in the sermon on the mount, 'Ye have heard' leads up to a quotation not really found in the Old Testament: 'Ye have heard, Thou shalt not kill, and [only] he who kills shall be in danger of the judgment,' and 'Ye have heard, Thou shalt love thy neighbor and hate thine enemy' [Matthew 5:21]. The clauses, 'and only he who kills shall be in danger of the judgment' and 'thou shalt hate thine enemy,' do not occur in the Pentateuch at all. However, as soon as we proceed from the translation 'You have literally understood,' the additions cease to be troublesome."[7] It was not the Pentateuchal law as such which Jesus castigated, but its vulgarization by an interpretation of strict literalism. The clauses missing in the Pentateuchal text are simply an interpretation of that text which Jesus found offensive.

Those who have studied the Sermon on the Mount critically tend to see it not as a call to abrogate the law of Judaism but as an effort to redefine that law in terms of the higher demands of its inner spirit. "You have heard. . . . But I say unto you," according to Professor Daube, is not meant to oppose the old law with a new law, but rather to contrast two interpretations of the old law; the conventional interpretation, which is literal and narrow, and the interpretation advocated by Jesus, which seeks to fulfill not only the letter but also the spirit and the underlying ideal of that law. In the words of Professor Daube: "In Matthew, in the sermon on the mount, we find a series of injunctions intended to illustrate Jesus as upholder, not destroyer of the Law. They all, more or less, follow this pattern: 'Ye have heard what was said by them of old time, Thou shalt not kill. But I say unto you, That whosoever is angry with his brother shall be in danger of the judgment.' This form falls into two parts. The first gives a Scriptural rule narrowly interpreted, the second a wider demand made by Jesus. . . . The relationship between the two members of the form is not one of pure contrast; the demand that you must not be angry with your brother is not thought of as utterly irreconcilable with the prohibition of killing. On the contrary, wider and deeper though it may be, it is thought of as, in a sense, resulting from, and certainly including, the old rule."[8] W. D. Davies,

[7] David Daube: *The New Testament and Rabbinic Judaism* (London: University of London; 1956), p. 56.

[8] Ibid., p. 60.

after quoting the statement of Daube, adds the following: "To interpret on the side of stringency is not to annul the Law, but to change it in accordance with its own intention. From this point of view . . . we cannot speak of the Law being annulled in the antithesis, but only of its being intensified in its demand, or reinterpreted in a higher key." [9]

Elwyn E. Tilden, Jr., of Lafayette College, Easton, Pennsylvania, in his brief commentary on Matthew (5:21–48) in the *Oxford Annotated Bible*, regards the Sermon on the Mount similarly as an exposition of what the old law really demands and as a protest against its narrowing by conventional interpretations. He describes the provisions of this Sermon as "illustrations of the true understanding of the Law." The theme was a common one among the Rabbis as well, who were ever seeking to lift the spiritual vistas of their people by showing them the wider implications of the law, and the broader principles which lie beyond the zone of law. Principles or laws once adopted shrink or broaden in scope depending on the people who live by them.

The ground of authority on which Jesus took his stand was the Hebrew Bible, but for him too, just as for the Rabbis, the Bible was not a rigid document. Jesus supplemented the biblical word with a kind of *midrash*, an interpretive elaboration, which made the Bible an efficacious instrument for dealing with life as he understood it. The Oral Torah is of wide latitude and it permitted diverse interpretations. This diversity was balanced by the unity of a common adherence to the authority of the scriptural word itself and to the principles of hermeneutics by which the text was expounded to yield new inferences. The interpretations quoted in the name of Jesus are not incompatible with the structure of the Oral Torah or with the method by which its provisions were drawn from the written text.

Jesus is quoted in the Gospels as expounding the biblical text on a number of subjects. We quote his exposition concerning the Sabbath. The report in Mark 2:23–28 is as follows: "One sabbath he was going through the grain fields; and as they made their way his disciples began to pluck ears of grain. And the Pharisees said to him, 'Look, why are they doing what is not lawful on the Sab-

[9] Davies: *Setting of the Sermon on the Mount*, p. 102.

bath?' And he said to them, 'Have you not read what David did [I Samuel 21:1–6, II Samuel 8:17], when he was in need and hungry, he and those who were with him: how he entered the house of God, when Abiathar was high priest, and ate the bread of the Presence, which it is not lawful for any but the priests to eat, and also gave it to those who were with him?' And he said to them, 'The sabbath is made for man, not man for the sabbath; so the Son of man is, also lord even of the sabbath.' "

The same report is quoted in Luke 6:1–5. This report is also cited in Matthew 12:1–8, but with a slight change. After quoting the precedent of David, who ate the "bread of the Presence," he cites an additional consideration: "Or have you not read in the law [Numbers 28:9–10] how on the sabbath the priests profane the sabbath, and are guiltless? I tell you, something greater than the temple is here. And if you had known what this means [Hosea 6:6], 'I desire mercy and not sacrifice,' you would not have condemned the guiltless. For the Son of man is lord of the sabbath."

Another case involving the Sabbath law is reported in Mark 3:1–6, and it is also reported in substantially the same form in Luke 6:6–11. As reported in Mark the case was as follows: "Again he entered the synagogue, and a man was there who had a withered hand. And they watched him to see whether he would heal on the sabbath, so that they might accuse him. And he said to the man who had the withered hand, 'Come here.' And he said to them, 'Is it lawful on the sabbath to do good or to do harm, to save life or to kill?' But they were silent. And he looked around at them with anger, grieved at their hardness of heart, and said to the man, 'Stretch out your hand.' He stretched it out, and his hand was restored."

The issue under discussion is the application of the scriptural law which forbids work on the Sabbath. Jesus is quoted as propounding the view that the prohibition was not meant in an absolute sense, that it was not to be applicable where the work contemplated was to assuage hunger, to heal the sick, to save life. In the case of the disciples who plucked grain on the Sabbath, Jesus is quoted as citing scriptural support for condoning it. Had not David and his associates violated a law to assuage their hunger?

The priests in the Temple regularly ignored the Sabbath to perform the sacrificial rites. Since Scripture itself testifies that an act of mercy is preferable in the eyes of God to the rites of sacrifices, it should certainly be proper to set aside the usual Sabbath restrictions to meet human needs, such as assuaging hunger. In the second case cited, no specific scriptural text is quoted, but it is implied. Since there is nothing higher than saving life, healing cannot be forbidden on the Sabbath.

The principle propounded by Jesus acknowledges the authority of the biblical prohibition to labor on the Sabbath, but it surrounds it with qualifications. This is precisely how the Sabbath law is treated by the Rabbis. The rabbinic principle is *pikuah nefesh dohe shabbat*, "the saving of life supersedes the Sabbath." And this principle is given even broader scope in several well-known maxims: "The Sabbath has been given for you, you were not given for the Sabbath" (Mekilta on Exodus 31:13) and "the Sabbath has been placed under your authority, you have not been placed under its authority" (Yoma 85b).

The Rabbis specifically permitted various categories of communal business on the Sabbath, such as meeting for the purpose of making grants to charity, and when necessary, they allowed attending meetings with Roman officials on the Sabbath, even if this meant going to see them at "theaters, circuses, and basilicas." They likewise allowed making arrangements on the Sabbath for the betrothal of a young girl, or for a child's education, including training for a trade.

The Rabbis quoted Isaiah 58:13 as a source for their views: "If you honor it [the Sabbath], not going your own ways, or pursuing your own business. . . ." One's own "business" must not be attended to on the Sabbath, but acts of service to others—good deeds—are the Lord's "business" and are therefore permitted (Shabbat 150a).

The additional statement attributed to Jesus, "The Son of man is lord of the sabbath," is of uncertain meaning. Some have taken it as directed at Jesus himself, that he, in his role as "Son of man," is Lord of the Sabbath. This would imply that the authority to break the Sabbath derives from the special status of Jesus, but is not the point of the homily that it is the fact of human *need* which sanctions labor on the Sabbath, and if so, is not *any* man in such instance justified in ignoring the restriction against work on the Sabbath? The Rabbis made it a point to emphasize that the suspension of Sabbath restrictions in order to save life does not require specific sanction from religious authorities, but that each individual must act on his own and "the quicker one does so, the more praiseworthy he is" (Yoma 84b). Professor Morton Scott Enslin and others have suggested that "Son of man" in the present passage is to be understood simply as *man*, any man, in other words, and it does not refer to Jesus at all.[1] If *any man* be acknowledged as lord over the Sabbath, then the statement attributed to Jesus would be an exact parallel to the maxim of the Rabbis. The discourse of Jesus on the Sabbath law, as quoted in the Gospels, is thus within the general pattern of thought developed by the Rabbis in the Oral Torah.

The principle attributed to Jesus in qualifying the law of the Sabbath is clearly the principle well recognized in rabbinic Judaism, but the application given it in the Gospels is less certain. If the disciples were in a state of starvation to the point where their health was really imperiled, or if the man with the withered hand faced some special jeopardy through the persistence of his condition, then the principle enunciated would be clearly applicable. On the other hand, if this were not the case, then there was no real cogency for the action *on the Sabbath*. There would have been no serious loss in delay. D. E. Nineham has noted this point when he declared: "The difficulty with this is that the man with the withered hand was in no danger of death; there was no question of saving or destroying life; if there had been, the rabbis themselves would have been completely at one with Jesus, for they were quite clear that the sabbath law might and must be broken in cases of danger to life. But Jesus seems to extend this principle so as to make it justify healing work of all kinds—and, indeed, all other kinds of benevolent work—on the sabbath. If that was his meaning the effect would have been to supersede the sabbath law entirely, for the prohibition on sabbath work would

[1] Morton S. Enslin: "Son of Man," *An Encyclopedia of Religion* (New York: Philosophical Library; 1945), p. 726; cf. Nineham: *The Gospel of St. Mark*, p. 108.

become simply a prohibition of evil and life-destroying activity on the sabbath, and that is forbidden on any day." [2]

Students of the Gospel texts have indeed questioned whether these reports may be considered historical. One may, for example, question the rather strange coincidence that the Pharisees were present as Jesus and his disciples passed the cornfield. The coincidence suggests rather a deliberate stage setting, in other words, the work of the evangelist who wrote the Gospel.

Rudolf Bultmann is of the opinion that these reports reflect not the practice of Jesus himself but that of the later Christian community, which had broken with the practices of Judaism. To justify their action, they told stories to show that their master had sanctioned their conduct. As Bultmann puts it: "The 'disciples,' i.e. the primitive Christian church, have broken with the old customs in this matter, and they are defending themselves against criticism by means of the stories, through which they make their appeal to a saying of Jesus." [3]

Another incident in which Jesus is involved in what appears to be an attack on Jewish practice deals with the question of divorce. The report is quoted in Mark 10:2–12: "And Pharisees came up and in order to test him asked, 'Is it lawful for a man to divorce his wife?' He answered them, 'What did Moses command you?' They said, 'Moses allowed a man to write a certificate of divorce, and to put her away' [Deuteronomy 24:1–4]. But Jesus said to them, 'For your hardness of heart he wrote you this commandment. But from the beginning of creation, "God made them male and female." "For this reason a man shall leave his father and mother and be joined to his wife, and the two shall become one" [Genesis 1:27, 5:2, 2:24]. So they are no longer two but one. What, therefore, God has joined together let no man put asunder.' And in the house the disciples asked him again about this matter. And he said to them, 'Whoever divorces his wife and marries another, commits adultery against her; and if she divorces her husband and marries another, she commits adultery.' "

The same case is reported in Matthew 19:1–9, with the usual variation in details. But here a radical difference appears in the

[2] Nineham: *St. Mark*, p. 109.

[3] Bultmann and Kundsin: *Form Criticism*, p. 44.

concluding statement of Jesus. In the Matthew version, Jesus is quoted thus: "And I say to you: whoever divorces his wife, except for unchastity, and marries another, commits adultery." According to Matthew, the rejection of divorce is not absolute. Divorce is sanctioned on grounds of unchastity.

The differences between Matthew and Mark on so crucial an aspect of the views of Jesus are a dramatic reminder of the uncertainty we face in defining what is authentic in the views of Jesus. But both reports proceed clearly on the common ground of scriptural authority. The moral element in the position of Jesus derives from the biblical conception of marriage as founded in the design of creation, which intended male and female to separate themselves from their respective fathers and mothers and to join themselves to one another, as one flesh (Genesis 1:27, 2:24).

The apparent sanction of divorce which reflected current Jewish practice and which was rooted in Deuteronomy 24:1–4, where it is taken for granted that a man may give his wife a bill of divorcement and send her away and she may then marry another, is cited as a challenge to Jesus. He replies by redefining the provision in Deuteronomy in a manner typical of the Midrash, by an interpretive supplement. The sanction of divorce in Deuteronomy, he expounds, does not represent the true scriptural ideal. It is a concession granted to men, because of their weakness. Jesus, however, asks his followers to rise above the compromise and reach out for the scriptural ideal, which is less permissive. The entire exposition proceeds with all the presuppositions of the Oral Torah and with its basic methodology of defining a scriptural text in the light of other texts, and in the light of our general understanding of what the Torah really wants for human life.

Not only in method but in the substance of his thought, the position of Jesus remains in consonance with general rabbinic thinking on the subject. Even more explicit than the verses from Genesis quoted by Jesus is the declaration of the prophet Malachi (2:13–16): "And this again you do. You cover the Lord's altar with tears, with weeping and groaning because he no longer regards the offering or accepts it with favor at your hand. You ask, 'Why does he not?' Because the Lord was witness to the covenant between you and the wife of your youth, to whom you have been faithless, though she is your companion and your wife by covenant. . . . So take heed to yourselves, let none be faithless to the wife of his youth. For hateful is [literally, he hates] divorce says the Lord, the God of Israel, and covering one's garment with violence, says the Lord of hosts. So take heed to yourselves and do not be faithless." The Rabbis took the verse from Malachi as the occasion for many touching statements in abhorrence of divorce. Said Rabbi Elazar: "Whoever divorces the wife of his youth, causes even the altar to shed tears for his treachery, as it is written, 'And this again you do. You cover the Lord's altar with tears . . . because the Lord was witness to the covenant between you and the wife of your youth, to whom you have been faithless.' " Rabbi Johanan read his exhortation into the very words of the prophet: "Hateful is divorce" (quoted in Yalkut Shimeoni *ad locum*).

There was no division of opinion among the Rabbis on the moral issues involved in divorce. The severance of the marriage bond is a tragic event, which desecrates a covenant meant to be holy and binding for all time. But the facts of life sometimes confront us with grievous situations, in which the ideal is defeated or compromised. The unity of marriage is founded ultimately on the love that should relate husband and wife to each other. Sometimes, however, one partner may be unfaithful to the other. Sometimes even without formal grounds, husband and wife prove unsuited for each other, and love turns to hate. In the face of certain tragic circumstances, is not the dissolution of a marriage a preferable alternative? Shall the law shut its eyes to these realities and insist that husband and wife must continue to live with each other in a marriage which has in truth ceased to exist?

Rabbinic jurists were realistic and under certain circumstances sanctioned divorce. The School of Hillel, which was also joined by Rabbi Akiba, was not concerned with objective considerations. Given the subjective fact of incompatibility, the law must acknowledge what life has wrought, and must permit the dissolution of the marriage. The School of Shammai, on the other hand, insisted on objective grounds, and it sanctioned divorce only for reasons of unchastity. The formal basis of these divergent opinions was centered in the interpretation of Deuteronomy 24:1:

"When a man takes a wife and marries her, if then she finds no favor in his eyes because he has found some indecency in her, and he writes her a bill of divorce. . . ." The School of Shammai saw the term "indecency" as implying a case of unchastity; Rabbi Akiba quoted, "if then she finds no favor in his eyes" as the significant consideration, which is all subjective; the School of Hillel cited "some indecency," the qualification *some* implying to them *any* fault which the husband deems an indecency (Mishnah Gittin 9:10).

If Matthew's version be correct and Jesus allowed divorce on grounds of unchastity, then he would be in agreement with the views of the School of Shammai. If so, it may appear strange that Jesus did not follow the scriptural interpretation of the Shammaites, and base his view on the word "indecency." Jesus may well have agreed that the verse in Deuteronomy has the more permissive meaning, especially since the general practice followed the School of Hillel. Jesus found firmer ground for his views, whether as reported in Matthew or in Mark, by calling for the higher ideal which Scripture clearly affirmed, rather than the compromise sanctioned by the law. The theory that biblical law sometimes accommodates itself to human weakness and demands of man less than the highest was a familiar view in rabbinic circles. It was invoked, for example, to account for the permission granted by the Bible (Deuteronomy 21:10–14) to Israelite warriors to marry women taken captive in war (Kiddushin 21b).

Another exemplification of the method of the Oral Torah, precisely as taught by the Rabbis, is afforded us in Matthew 22:23–23, with a close parallel in Mark 12:18–27: "The same day Sadducees came to him, who say there is no resurrection; and they asked him a question, saying, 'Teacher, Moses said [Deuteronomy 25:5], If a man dies, having no children, his brother must marry the widow, and raise up children for his brother. Now there were seven brothers among us; the first married, and died, and having no children left his wife to his brother. So, too, the second and third, down to the seventh. After them all, the woman died. In the resurrection, therefore, to which of the seven will she be wife? For they all had her.' But Jesus answered them, 'You are wrong, because you know neither Scriptures nor the power of God. For in the resurrection they neither marry nor are given in marriage, but are like angels in heaven. And as for the resurrection of the dead, have you not read what was told to you by God [Exodus 3:6], I am the Lord God of Abraham, and the God of Isaac, and the God of Jacob. He is not God of the dead, but of the living.' And when the crowd heard it, they were astonished at his teaching."

The Sadducees as we know from Josephus and from rabbinic sources did not believe in the resurrection as the crowning event of "the end of days." They did not believe in the general extension of the teachings of the Torah through the method of *midrash*, which had been developed by the Pharisees. They were strict constructionists of the biblical text, and they accepted only what was explicitly in the text. In the passage quoted, Jesus stands as the champion of Pharisaic teachings, which in his time had become normative in general Jewish doctrine. He affirms the resurrection, and he affirms the method of *midrash* by which the doctrine of the resurrection found support in the biblical text.

The statement of Jesus is paralleled substantively in the teachings of the Rabbis. One teacher put it thus (Berakot 17a): "In the world to come there is no eating or drinking, no begetting of children, no commerce, no envy, no jealousy no hatred and no competition—there is only this, that the righteous sit with crowns on their heads and take delight in the splendor of God's presence."

The proofs cited by the Rabbis for the resurrection do not differ in substance from the proof given by Jesus. Here is one such proof quoted in the Talmud (Sanhedrin 90b) in the name of Rabbi Simlai: "Whence do we infer the belief in the resurrection from the Torah? From the verse [Exodus 6:4], 'And I also have established My covenant with them [the Patriarchs] to give them the land of Canaan.' It does not say 'to give you,' but 'to give them,' implying that they would be restored so that the land might really be given to them." These "proofs" are all of one character—they are attempts to find some scriptural allusion, to confirm a doctrine deemed vital, but which some circles continued to challenge.

The exponents of the Oral Torah did not confine themselves

to scriptural interpretations. They often expressed views directly, without reference to proof texts. The Torah was conceived in broad terms allowing for new insights which were in harmony with its basic teachings, though they might not flow directly from a text. Jesus, too, expounded many ideas directly, not relating them to Scripture, though they were always within the spirit of the Bible and the rabbinic tradition which had grown out of it. Jesus extolled poverty, he spoke for the simple life, he attacked involvement in mundane concerns and asked for a concentration on the life of the spirit, on faith in God, and the pursuits of mercy and love. The most important of his teachings was the messianic doctrine. Whether he himself believed that he was the promised messiah is still a subject of speculation among scholars. But he believed and taught as a basic article of his faith that the messianic promise, long spoken of by the prophets, was reaching fulfillment, that the present world was about to end, and the eschatological visions of a divine kingdom to supersede the present order, were about to become a reality. The change, he taught, was to be effected through God's intervention, and then would follow the Last Judgment, and the promised bliss for the righteous and retribution for the wicked. Jesus called on his adherents to prepare for the end by penitence (cf. Matthew 25:31–46). The ascetic trend in his teachings, and the apparent disdain for the world and its problems, stemmed in great part from this belief in the imminent destruction of the present order and the inauguration of the new order, the Kingdom of God.[4]

Jesus is quoted as having said that the Kingdom would be established in his own generation (Mark 13:30, Matthew 10:23), and to have assured his listeners that some among them would "not taste death before they see the Kingdom of God come with power" (Mark 9:1). Those who took his prophecy of the imminent end seriously could not but respond with a radical shift in their center of interest; the world paled in its appeal for them. The Thessalonian Christians concluded from this belief that it was foolish to work. This faith fostered an uprootedness from the existential world, its claims and its responsibilities.

[4] Nineham: *St. Mark*, p. 48; Fenton: *St. Matthew*, p. 21; Bultmann and Kundsin: *Form Criticism*, p. 101.

The sources from which the belief in imminent world destruction was drawn were varied. In part it represented the action of an innate mystical tendency that is especially pronounced in certain natures. In part it was an influence of apocalyptic visionaries who were then active in the Jewish world and who were preoccupied with pointing to the impending end of the present epoch and its replacement by a new heavenly order which would cancel all mundane existence with its effrontery to the life of the spirit. The call of Jesus for recognition of his own role as mediator of divine power in healing, in forgiveness of sin, and in the qualification of those who are to be admitted to God's kingdom, if historical, is a parallel to the conceptions found in apocalyptic writings.

This belief was also fed, no doubt, by the evils of the Roman occupation and the yoke which bore heavily on the land, which set Jews to dream of redemption and deliverance. There were some who were aware that the work of redemption depended at least in part on human initiative. But Jesus belonged to those who waited for a miraculous deliverance through an intervention by God and His angelic hosts. For Jesus, as Maurice Goguel put it, "the entry into the Messianic Kingdom depends on divine and not on human initiative." [5]

According to some scholars, the journey of Jesus and his followers to Jerusalem was to witness and share in the epochal event which was to inaugurate the new order, the Kingdom of God. According to Paul Winter, the entry to Jerusalem "has the appearance of an unmistakable messianic demonstration. As such it would have been an open defiance of imperial authority—a proclamation of the will to national independence from Roman rule." [6] The kingdom which Jesus proclaimed was not of this world, but spirit does not exist in total detachment from substance. Certainly for his followers, this "kingdom" could not but appear as the antithesis of the existing power structure, and a reinauguration of the ideal kingdom of ancient days, the kingdom of

[5] Maurice Goguel: *The Life of Jesus,* Olive Wyon (trans.) (New York: Barnes & Noble; 1958), p. 314.

[6] Paul Winter: *On the Trial of Jesus* (Berlin: Walter de Gruyter & Co.; 1961), p. 141.

David. No wonder his followers greeted Jesus with royal acclaim, shouting among other things (Mark 11:10): "Blessed be the name of the kingdom of our father David, that cometh in the name of the Lord; Hosanna in the highest."

It was his messianic proclamation which brought on the tragedy of Calvary. As Professor Solomon Zeitlin reminds us: "On the cross was inscribed in Hebrew, Greek and Latin: *Jesus Nazarenus, Rex Judaeorum,* 'Jesus of Nazareth, the King of the Jews.' It was the Roman custom to write the reason for the execution on a placard and attach it to the body of the victim. Pilate followed the established method. Jesus was crucified for claiming to be the king of the Judeans." [7]

As we shall have occasion to note later on, the offense of Jesus was clearly an offense against the existing order. Jewish officials no doubt played a part in the proceedings, but they were Roman appointees and served as collaborators of the Roman authorities. Charles Guignebert, professor of the History of Christianity at the University of Paris, tends to doubt that Jesus regarded himself as a messiah. But it was the messianic movement, the call to expect an immediate end to the existing order and the dawn of the heavenly kingdom, which made Jesus a menace to the Roman authorities. The account in the Gospels that places the blame for the crucifixion on the Jews, Professor Guignebert further maintains, is clearly inaccurate and represents an anti-Jewish bias, as well as a desire to curry favor at the hands of the Roman authorities: "According to all appearances, the efforts of our Evangelists to absolve the Roman of guilt, and lay upon the Jews the entire responsibility for the crime, are not inspired by a desire to be true to the facts, but by a desire to humor the Roman authorities, for they were writing at a time when these authorities were the sole support of the Christians against the animosity displayed toward them by the synagogues." [8]

Paul Winter, in his more recent study of the trial of Jesus, offers us the same conclusion: "The Gospel records, when criti-

[7] Solomon Zeitlin: "The Dates of the Birth and the Crucifixion of Jesus," *Jewish Quarterly Review,* LV:1 (July 1964), 56 ff.

[8] Charles Guignebert: *Christianity, Past and Present* (New York: The Macmillan Company; 1927), pp. 37, 38, 43.

cally examined, furnish clear evidence of the fact that Jesus was executed on a charge of sedition at the order of the Emperor's representative. . . . That he was executed as a rebel, together with others who were executed on the same charge, by no means proves that he did work for the overthrow of the existing political system. So far as the procurator [Pontius Pilate] was concerned, it would have been sufficient reason for ordering the crucifixion if he had come to the conclusion that Jesus' itinerant preaching tended to excite the masses to expect the end of the existing order." [9]

Our primary concern, however, is not the personal destiny of Jesus, but his exemplification of the Jewish interpretive tradition in the study of Scripture. We have noted that the teachings of Jesus, insofar as it is possible to reconstruct them from layers of later New Testament reinterpretations, are expressive of the method and the substance of the Oral Torah as developed by the great masters of rabbinic Judaism. If, in some details Jesus hewed an independent line, this was normal in rabbinic Judaism, which allowed a wide latitude for individual teachers to think independently. If, in some instances, his views might have aroused opposition from contemporary teachers, this, too, was a normal phenomenon in Judaism. The debates between the School of Shammai and the School of Hillel on the interpretation of tradition and its application to contemporary life were sometimes fiercely acrimonious, but there was never any doubt that both were legitimate lines for the exposition of Judaism. Jesus, declared Professor Guignebert, "did not come bearing a new religion, nor even a new rite, but only a conception personal rather than original of the piety embedded in the Jewish religion. Nor did he aim at changing either its creed or its Law or its worship. The central point of his teaching was the Messianic idea, which was common property of all his compatriots as much as to him, and only his conception of it was his own. . . . To attribute to him the desire to found a Church, his Church, to provide it with rites and sacraments, visible signs of his grace, and to prepare it for the conquest of the whole world—these are just anachronisms. I prefer to say

[9] Winter: *On the Trial of Jesus*, p. 148.

that they are distortions of his ideas which would have shocked him, had he known them." [1]

Jesus himself declared his loyalty to the institutions of Judaism when he said (Matthew 5:17–18): "Think not that I have come to abolish the law and the prophets; I have come not to abolish them but to fulfill them. For truly, I say to you, till heaven and earth pass, not an iota, not a dot shall pass from the law until all is accomplished." But the process of seeking to fulfill the law often involved going beyond it, to supplement the written word with new elaborations. This process of supplementation and elaboration was achieved primarily through an interpretive technique represented by the Midrash, and exemplified in the Oral Torah.

The Jesus of history was a son of his people, who shared their dreams, who was loyal to their way of life, who died a martyr's death because of a commitment to his vision of their highest destiny. The image of Jesus as depicted in Christian writings was not founded on historical reality. It is rather a work of idealization and myth-building, reflecting the faith, primarily, of those who were under the influence of the non-Jewish, Hellenistic world, and who conceived Jesus in accordance with their own understanding of the hero in the drama of salvation. Professor Frederick C. Grant, writing in the language of Christian piety, but also as a historian, puts it thus: "In a profoundly true sense it is not—and never has been—the Jesus of history who is the redeemer of men and the hope of the world, but the spiritual Christ, the risen and exalted Lord of the church's faith." [2] Rudolf Bultmann reached the same conclusion. Summarizing Bultmann's views, Joachim Jeremias put it bluntly: "For Bultmann, the history of Jesus is part of Judaism, not of Christianity. . . . The study of Jesus and his message may be very interesting and instructive for the historical understanding of the rise of Christianity, but it has no significance for faith." [3] Bultmann himself expressed it thus: "The message of Jesus belongs to the presuppositions of the the-

[1] Guignebert: *Christianity, Past and Present,* p. 44.

[2] *The Gospels: Their Origin and Their Growth* (New York: Harper & Brothers; 1957), p. 9.

[3] Jeremias: *Historical Jesus,* pp. 9–10.

ology of the New Testament and is not a part of that theology itself." [4] In other words, the teaching of Jesus is only a preface to Christianity, which does not really begin until after the death of Jesus.

Indeed, many Christian scholars have abandoned the quest for the historical Jesus because this leads to Judaism and not to Christianity. Christianity was a work of construction by Jesus' disciples, who made him the center of an original conceptual system, which included among its formative elements "the Easter experiences of the disciples, the Messianic expectations of Judaism and the mythology of the pagan world with which Jesus of Nazareth was to be clothed." [5]

The question may well be raised as to why the teachings of Jesus did not enter the classic literature of Torah supplementation. In the time of Jesus, as Professor Harry A. Wolfson has pointed out,[6] Jewish teachers were officially affiliated with schools, the School of Shammai or the School of Hillel. Those schools preserved the teachings of affiliated masters. In the official literature preserved from this period, the heads of the schools are quoted by name, while the individual masters are quoted collectively, in the consensus which eventually summed up their views. Independent teachers, like Jesus, were free to teach, but their words were often lost to posterity. The recent discovery of the Dead Sea Scrolls is a reminder that a literature of vast scope flourished in Judea, which was lost until our own day.

The teachings of Jesus were preserved by his followers—but in a context that obscured their original character. They were reinterpreted to conform to the new role that Jesus assumed after his death, as the central figure in a new religion that was essentially hostile to Judaism. But the historical Jesus, to the extent that we can envision him from the reinterpreted versions left by his followers, represents a point of development running unbroken from the Hebrew Bible and linked to it through an interpretive supplement that is characteristic of the great literary creation of the Rabbis, the Oral Torah. As Yehezkel Kaufmann put it: "The

[4] Cited by Jeremias: ibid., p. 9.
[5] Ibid., pp. 9 ff.
[6] *Menorah Journal*, XLIX (1962), 25–31.

attitude of Jesus to the Torah is the very same attitude one finds among the masters of *halakah* and *haggadah* who followed in the Pharisaic tradition. The Torah is the everlasting foundation on which they base their own views and doctrines, even when they appear to digress sharply from its literal meaning. . . . Jesus believed that his teachings were only a completion or a clarification of the teachings of the Torah, guideposts inviting man how to live and conduct himself in its spirit." [7]

[7] Kaufmann: *Goleh ve-Nekar*, p. 342.

Chapter X

The Perversion of History

The trial of Jesus and his subsequent crucifixion has become a primary issue in the Jewish-Christian dialogue. For Christianity these events are fraught with grave doctrinal significance. For Jews these events are of deep concern because they constitute a chief amalgam in the religious and cultural influences that have conditioned the world to hatred for the Jews. Is it possible to disentangle those events from the web of later embellishment and theological refinement, to see them as they were, in the context of history?

The basic sources for the events of the crucifixion are the four Gospels of Matthew, Mark, Luke, and John. These records parallel each other, but they diverge and sometimes contradict each other in critical details. The Gospels were not written by eyewitnesses to the events they describe, nor were they written by historians who were anxious to authenticate the facts. They were written by missionaries who felt free to edit the record for the sake of religious exhortation. A layer of tradition in which there resides some kernel of fact underlies each of the Gospel accounts, but great care must be taken to reach for this kernel of fact out of the elaborations and alterations to which the older traditions were subjected by the editorial hand of the writers. This is at best a hazardous task and we cannot ever be sure that what we establish as fact is indeed so.

Our quest is aided by a knowledge of the general historical context in which the crucifixion is set. Here we are on surer ground. We know from contemporary sources the general complexion of life under the Roman occupation of Palestine. We know of the seething unrest in Judea, of the frustrations felt by the Jews under Roman domination, of the dreams of freedom which inspired some to eschatological visions, to a divine annuling of the predatory empire and its replacement by God's own kingdom of righteousness, and which inspired others to resist the predatory empire, and with their own hands to put an end to its ungodly rule. We know of the Roman administration in the country, of the procurators and their Jewish collaborators. Above all we know a great deal about Pontius Pilate, who was to play the central role in the tragedy of the crucifixion.

The Romans respected Jewish autonomy in all cultural and religious affairs. The heavy hand of their oppression was economic and political. There was the enormously heavy taxation, particularly upon the people least able to pay it. Specifically the levies included the *annona*, a tax on crops and other farm produce, delivered in kind; a poll tax on males from fourteen years and females from twelve years to sixty-five years; a market tax on necessities of life like meat and salt; various tolls, such as those exacted for crossing a bridge or entering a city; forced labor and compulsory requisitions of farmers' animals. The greatest burden of this taxation clearly fell upon lower classes, particularly the rural population. Indeed, beginning with Caesar, the Roman tax was as high as 25 per cent of the total crops in the country. Some of these taxes were collected directly, under the general supervision of native officials from nearby cities. Other levies were farmed out to the *publican*, whose rapaciousness made him a byword for sin in Jewish society.

The Pharisees called upon their people to keep aloof from their imperialist masters and to spurn their offers of collaboration. Shemaya, who lived shortly after the Romans became masters of

Palestine, counseled his people: "Love work; hate mastery over others; and avoid intimacy with the government." The exponents of Torah during this period denounced the Jewish tax farmer as a reprobate and a robber because he collaborated with the Roman system of extortion and oppression. Deceiving the Roman tax collector they put on a par with deceiving a pirate, for Rome had no moral right to the country which she had occupied by force. As the Mishnah put it: "Men may vow to murderers, robbers, or tax gatherers that what they have is Heave-offering even though it is not Heave-offering; or that they belong to the king's household even though they do not belong to the king's household . . ." (Avot 1:10; Mishnah Nedarim 3:4).

Rome opened vast markets for enterprising merchants and her fiscal policies encouraged shipping and industry with the result that individual families amassed great wealth—but the masses suffered. Discriminatory taxation forced many farmers to abandon the land. Some became laborers on the big estates or moved to the cities where they joined the urban proletariat.

The fate of the urban working people was equally tragic. Slave labor never flourished in Palestine as it did in other parts of the empire; and the humanitarian legislation of the Bible tended to raise the living standard of the slave and the laborer alike. But the absence of a united labor front made for extremely low wages throughout the ancient world, and Palestine was no exception. The skilled worker was not entirely helpless. Thus the Garmu and Abtimas families, Temple bakers and chemists respectively, were able to win substantial wage increases by striking. Their highly specialized work could not be duplicated by strikebreakers who had been imported from Alexandria; and the Temple authorities were forced to accede to their demands (Yoma 39a). The laborer who did not command such specialized skills was entirely at the mercy of his employer, and his earnings could not have been much above the level of mere subsistence.

The laborer in addition suffered from the constant threat of unemployment. Josephus records a pathetic attempt to check unemployment through a public works project. To quote Josephus: ". . . So when the people saw that the workmen were unemployed, who were above eighteen thousand and that they, receiving no wages, were in want . . . and while they were unwilling to keep them by their treasuries that were there [in the Temple] deposited, out of fear of their being carried away by the Romans . . . so they persuaded him [King Agrippa] to rebuild the eastern cloisters . . . [Agrippa] denied the petitioners their request in the matter; but he did not obstruct them when they desired the city might be paved with white stone . . ." (*Antiquities* XX 9:7).

The Romans concealed their imperialist rule behind a façade of local autonomy, which was administered by native collaborators. Heading these collaborators in Jewish Palestine was the High Priest. For a time, the administration of Palestine was entrusted to native vassal kings, the most important of whom was Herod the Great, who reigned from 37 to 4 B.C.E. In 6 C.E. the country was placed under the direct administration of Roman governors or procurators. But both the Jewish puppet kings as well as the Roman procurators manipulated the selection of the High Priest so as to have in that influential position a friend and willing collaborator of government policy. Herod made and unmade seven High Priests in the course of his reign. Valerius Gratus, who served as procurator from 15–26 C.E., made and deposed five High Priests in succession.

The kind of men who would serve in such capacity were politicians of low moral character to whom the rewards of power took precedence over their duties to their people and their faith. Many of them did not even know how to perform the Temple ritual, and it became customary for a committee of Pharisaic teachers to coach the High Priest in the performance of the Day of Atonement service for a full week before each holiday. The Mishnah records that this committee would always depart from its mission in tears (Mishnah Yoma 1:1).

The worldliness of these High Priests is well described in a number of talmudic satires. One teacher lamented sadly that the various high priestly families of his day were a source of woe to their people: "For they are the High Priests, their sons the tax collectors, their sons-in-law the Temple officers, and their servants beat the people with their staves" (Pesahim 57a, Yoma 35b).

The High Priests oppressed not only the people at large but also the humbler members of their own caste, robbing them often of their due share in the priestly perquisites. As Josephus describes the High Priests of his time: "They had the hardness to send their servants into the threshing floors to take away these *tithes* that were due to the priests, with the result that the poorer sort of priests died for want" (*Antiquities* XX 8:8, 9:2).

Stirred by a host of unbearable evils, a revolutionary sentiment was developing in the country and reached its apex in 66 C.E. The pioneer of the revolutionary movement was the Galilean peasant leader Judas, who "prevailed with his countrymen to revolt and said they were cowards if they would endure to pay taxes to Rome and after God submit to mortal men as their lords" (Josephus: *Wars* II 8:1, and *Antiquities* XVIII 1:6). The spearhead of the rebellion was the hard-pressed peasantry, but they were aided by the masses of the people generally, who suffered with them degradation and exploitation. The actual precipitation of the struggle was the work of the lower order of priests. They deposed the reigning High Priest and by lots designated his successor, the rural priest Phanias ben Samuel of the village Aphta. With the Temple in their control, the insurgent priests proclaimed the defiance of Rome by rejecting the special Temple sacrifice which had always been offered in the name of the emperor.

The issues ran deeper than the acceptance or rejection of a Temple sacrifice. This may be seen by the fact that one of the first acts of the rebels, according to Josephus (*Wars* II 17:6), was to set fire "to the place where the archives were deposited, and made haste to burn the contracts belonging to their creditors, and thereby to dissolve their obligations for paying their debts." As to the role of the High Priest, it suffices to note that even before burning the archives the rebels "set fire to the house of Ananias, the High Priest," states the same report of Josephus. The High Priest was a primary target of the people's hatred because he was the most direct and visible instrument of Roman oppression.

The Gospels, read carefully, offer many indications that the drama surrounding the execution and arrest of Jesus was part of the larger drama of the Roman endeavor to crush Jewish resistance to Roman rule.

We quote from the Gospel of Mark, the oldest of the Gospels

(14:43–72, 15:1–15): "And immediately, while he was still speaking, Judas came, one of the twelve, and with him a crowd with swords and clubs, from the chief priests and the scribes and the elders. Now the betrayer had given them a sign, saying, 'The one I shall kiss is the man; seize him and lead him away safely.' And when he came, he went up to him at once, and said, 'Master!' And he kissed him. And they laid hands on him and seized him. . . . And they led Jesus to the high priest; and all the chief priests and the elders were assembled. . . . Now, the chief priest, and the whole council sought testimony against Jesus to put him to death; but they found none. . . . And some stood up and bore false witness against him, saying, 'We heard him say, I will destroy this Temple that is made with hands, and in three days I will build another, not made with hands.' Yet not even so did their testimony agree. And the high priest stood up in the midst, and asked Jesus, 'Have you no answer to make? What is it that these men testify against you?' But he was silent and made no answer. Again the high priest asked him, 'Are you the Christ, the son of the Blessed?' And Jesus said, 'I am; and you will see the son of man sitting at the right hand of Power, and coming with the clouds of heaven.' And the high priest tore his mantle, and said, 'Why do we still need witnesses? You have heard his blasphemy. What is your decision?' And they all condemned him as deserving death. . . . And as soon as it was morning the chief priests, with the elders and scribes and the whole council held a consultation; and they bound Jesus and led him away and delivered him to Pilate. And Pilate asked him, 'Are you the King of the Jews?' And he answered him, 'You have said so.' And the chief priests accused him of many things. And Pilate again asked him, 'Have you no answer to make? See how many charges they bring against you.' But Jesus made no further answer, so that Pilate wondered. Now at the feast he used to release for them any one prisoner whom they asked. And among the rebels in prison, who had committed murder in the insurrection, there was a man called Barabbas. And the crowd came up and began to ask Pilate to do as he was wont to do for them. And he answered them, 'Do you want me to release for you the King of the Jews?' For he perceived that it was out of envy that the chief priests had delivered him up. But the chief priests stirred up the crowd to have him release for them Barabbas instead. And Pilate again said to them, 'Then what shall I do with the man whom you call King of the Jews?' And they cried out again, 'Crucify him.' And Pilate said to them, 'Why, what evil has he done?' But they shouted all the more, 'Crucify him.' So Pilate, wishing to satisfy the crowd, released for them Barabbas; and having scourged Jesus, he delivered him to be crucified."

The account as reported in Mark—and it is likewise true about the accounts given in the other Gospels—presents various problems that have baffled historians. There is the difficulty concerning the episode with Judas. In Mark he identifies Jesus by actually kissing him; in Luke he only "drew near to Jesus to kiss him," and Jesus at once rebuffed him (Luke 22:47–48); in Mark "they promised to give him money for betraying his master" (14:11); in Matthew he was actually given "thirty pieces of silver" (26:16). The episode is, however, baffling for other reasons. Was not Jesus a known figure among the people, who taught openly in Temple and synagogue? What need was there for a special device to betray his identity? B. W. Bacon, the noted historian of the Gospels, was led by these considerations to deny the historicity of the Judas episode as reported in the Gospels.[1] Instead he relates the betrayal of Judas to the incident reported earlier, in Mark 14:3–10, which forms an introduction to the passion narrative. Here we are told of an unnamed woman who poured a jar of ointment on the head of Jesus, in an act of anointment; and Jesus is quoted as approving her deed. To the woman this must have been a token of coronation as king, as messiah, and Bacon suggests that it must have been this which Judas betrayed—that Jesus had been invested with the title of king, that he was now a claimant to messianic prerogative. This event made Jesus a dangerous figure in the eyes of the authorities, a threat to the existing order, and it precipitated the action against him.[2] Alfred Loisy calls attention to the connotation of the name Judas which may readily be equated with the Jewish people, and he raises the question

[1] B. W. Bacon: "What Did Judas Betray?" *Hibbert Journal*, XIX (1920–1), 486.

[2] Ibid., pp. 486–93.

"whether the role assigned to Judas is not fictitious from beginning to end, a symbol of Judaism as the villain of the piece." [3]

Following his arrest, Jesus is alleged to have been taken to the residence of the High Priest, where he was tried that very night by the council—the *synedrion,* as it is called in the Greek original—with the High Priest acting in the role of presiding officer. But the details of this trial present many irregularities. If the proceedings had been concluded during the night session, why did the council deliberate again "as soon as it was morning"? More baffling is the divergence of this account from the record describing the procedure by which the Sanhedrin conducted its sessions, which has been preserved in the Mishnah (Sanhedrin 4:1). Here the court is described as sitting only in the daytime, and never on a day of a festival or a day preceding a festival. It is unthinkable that the Sanhedrin would have met on the night of Passover. The Roman authorities themselves exempted Jews from appearing before Roman courts on Sabbaths and festivals and on days preceding them. An edict by Augustus Caesar exempting Jews from appearing before any judge "on the Sabbath day" or "on the day of preparation to it after the ninth hour" has been preserved in the memoirs of Josephus (*Antiquities* XVI 6:2). The Mishnah rules, too, that a verdict of guilty in a capital case could not be promulgated the same day. It was to be deferred for the day following. The procedure also required that the trial begin with a consideration of circumstances favorable to the defendant, and only subsequently was the prosecution to be presented. As Hugo Mantel has recently shown,[4] all the evidence in rabbinic sources, moreover, indicates that the presiding officer of the Sanhedrin was a Pharisaic scholar, not the High Priest, and that this Sanhedrin never met in the residence of the High Priest. Its regular meeting place was in the "Gazit" chamber in the Temple precincts.

The Sanhedrin is alleged to have found Jesus guilty of "blasphemy." This is a grave offense in biblical and rabbinic law, punishable by death. But blasphemy is defined as a deliberate vilifica-

[3] Alfred Loisy: *The Origins of the New Testament* (London: George Allen and Unwin; 1950), p. 100.

[4] Hugo Mantel: *Studies in the History of the Sanhedrin* (Cambridge, Mass.: Harvard Theological Press; 1965), pp. 176 ff., 254.

tion of God's ineffable name, *YHWH* (Mishnah Sanhedrin 7:5). Jesus never vilified God's name. On the contrary, his conduct, while critical of some current practices in Judaism, showed the utmost reverence for God. The accusations with which Jesus was charged, the prediction of the Temple's destruction and the claim to being the messiah, even if completely substantiated, did not constitute blasphemy and involved no culpability in Jewish law. Jeremiah and Ezekiel had predicted the destruction of the first Temple (Jeremiah 7:14, Ezekiel 24:21) and Rabban Johanan ben Zaccai (Yoma 39b), among others, predicted the fall of the second Temple. Similarly there were claimants to messiahship before Jesus and after him, and there is no record of any sanctions taken against them by Jewish authorities. Bar Kokba, who led the Jewish revolt against Rome in 132–135 C.E., claimed to be the messiah, and Rabbi Akiba apparently endorsed the claim.[5]

If Jesus had really been charged and found guilty of blasphemy, it is also puzzling why the Jewish court itself did not impose the death penalty. Most scholars are in agreement that the Jewish courts of that time were competent to impose the death penalty for capital offenses, if of a religious nature. Indeed, according to the Gospel of John, Pilate suggested to the deputation of the High Priest that Jesus be dealt with by the Jews themselves. They replied that it was not within their authority to execute anyone (18:31). But how could Pilate have suggested that they perform an act which Roman law itself had forbidden? Pilate's statement becomes intelligible if we assume that he originally judged the complaint against Jesus as religious in nature and therefore asked that the Jewish authorities assume jurisdiction. Some commentators have also found it strange that here (18:62) Jesus is quoted as making a public acknowledgment of his messiahship. This runs counter to the general plan of the Gospel of Mark, according to which the messiahship of Jesus was a secret known only to the chosen few, which was to become common knowledge only after the crucifixion.

We face a more serious difficulty in comprehending the behavior of Pilate, the Jewish leaders, and the Jerusalem crowd. Pilate is here portrayed as a weak but kindly man, one who has a strong

[5] Ibid., pp. 273, 275.

sense of equity but who allows outside pressures to deflect him from doing what is right. He is described as convinced that Jesus is innocent and as anxious to release him, but the crowd, instigated by the Jewish authorities, presses him to execute Jesus, and he yields to them.

All this runs counter to the facts as we know them concerning Jewish Palestine under the Roman occupation, especially under the stern procuratorship of Pilate. As Dominic M. Crossan of Loyola University noted in his lead article in the Jesuit scholarly magazine *Theological Studies* entitled "Anti-Semitism and the Gospel": "Jerusalem was the occupied capital of an occupied country. At the time of any great feast it was a tinder-box needing only a spark to start the flames; just how swiftly the Roman garrison was poised to descend on any mob may be deduced from Acts 21:31–39. It is then a priori not too likely that the Roman *praefectus* would allow a mob to gather, let alone work itself into a fury at such a time. And if any other Roman might have tolerated this, Pontius Pilate would hardly have done so. The three main incidents which Flavius Josephus chooses to narrate about this man all concern one topic: his somewhat gleeful and certainly vicious dispersal of the crowds. The multitude importuned him at Caeserea to remove the standards from the Holy City. He had them secretly surrounded, and only their open willingness for unresisting martyrdom deflected his purpose (*Antiquities* XVIII 3:1). The people gathered to protest the use of Temple funds for the construction of an aqueduct; they are secretly surrounded and slaughtered (*Antiquities* XVIII 3:2). Finally he is sent back to Rome to answer charges made against him after he has killed a group of Samaritans gathered to find the sacred vessels hidden by Moses on Mt. Gerizim (*Antiquities* XVIII 4:2). So we should not too readily accept the idea of a mob shouting at Pilate during the Passion." [6]

The behavior of the Jewish authorities is likewise inexplicable. What was their motivation in opposing Jesus and turning him over to Pilate? One can of course see their conduct as simply satanic, as an unreasoned hate of Jesus precisely because he represented the great spiritual figure against whom their carnal natures

[6] *Theological Studies* XXVI:2 (June 1965), 200.

were in rebellion. But the sources speak not of one man, but of a number of men.

Would they all have been motivated by this unreasoned hate? Their action against Jesus was not without its hazards. There were the people who were sensitive to arrests, and often rioted when popular leaders came afoul of the law. Indeed we have the revealing note in Mark 14:2 that the arrest was planned so as to evade the peoples' notice lest it arouse their anger and provoke a riot. The action had to be justified before Pilate, too, and it is not likely that they would have courted his displeasure by venting unreasoned hate against an innocent man. It is significant, too, that in the early polemics with Jewish leaders when the issue was a disagreement over the interpretation of Judaism, Jesus is pictured as contending with religious leaders, principally with the Pharisees. In the encounter that led to his arrest, he faces another group of adversaries—the High Priests and their associates. The synoptic Gospels speak of the chief priests and their associates solely. The Gospel of John (11:47–49) includes the Pharisees in the group that acts against Jesus but he, too, places "the chief priests" in the major role. Is this shift only coincidental or does it betoken something special about the identity of the Jewish authorities and the considerations which sent them to make the arrest and initiate the steps that eventually led to the crucifixion?

Mark imputes to Pilate the perception that it was "out of envy that the chief priests had delivered him up." But Jesus was a teacher, a preacher, a visionary. His career did not run parallel to that of "the chief priests," who, during this period, were generally Roman appointees and collaborators in ruling the country. Men who exercise power generally envy those who exercise more power than they; they do not as a rule envy those who have chosen to live by the spirit.

Two passages in the Gospel of John place another complexion on the behavior of the Jewish authorities. In John 11:47–49 we are told: "The chief priests, therefore, and the Pharisees gathered a council, and said, What do we? For this man doeth many signs. If we let him thus alone, all men will believe on him: and the Romans will come and take away both our place and our nation. But a certain one of them Caiphas, being high priest that year, said unto them, Ye know nothing at all, nor do ye take account that it is expedient for you that one man should die for the people, and that the whole nation perish not." In 18:14 John repeats the tradition that Caiphas had advised that it was expedient to permit one man to die in order to save the nation.

The Gospel of John is alone in associating the Pharisees with "the chief priests" in considering some action to deal with the threat posed by Jesus. The Gospels of Matthew, Mark, and Luke, as we noted earlier, exclude the Pharisees from the deliberation. On the face of it one is inclined to discount John's report, in favor of the report as given in the synoptic Gospels. The chief concern of the Pharisees was spiritual and academic. They generally stayed aloof from the problems of state, which was the chief concern of the priestly clan and their associates.

Raymond E. Brown, professor of New Testament at St. Mary's Seminary, in his commentary on John, which he published with a new translation from the Greek for the Anchor Bible series, notes the implausibility of Pharisaic involvement in the proceedings against Jesus. His explanation is that John drew on a name which had long been identified with the hostility to Jesus: "John would have been more exact in speaking of priests and *Scribes* (Mark XIV 43, 53); but, as we have stressed, John does not attempt to be precise about the Jewish groups that existed before the destruction of the Temple. The Judaism of the Pharisees survived, and it was this Judaism that presented the challenge to Christianity when the Fourth Gospel was being written. The reference to the Pharisees is more a question of simplification than of error." [7]

But John's report may nevertheless rest on fact. The Pharisees were aloof from the power struggle as such; they were scandalized by the High Priests and the oligarchy over which he presided for making common cause with Rome. But the Pharisees were opposed to the armed uprising against Rome. They knew that its outcome was likely to be total disaster for the nation. The Talmud has preserved the account of Rabban Johanan ben Zaccai's efforts to persuade the people against rebellion, but his counsel

[7] *The Gospel According to John*, Raymond E. Brown (ed. and trans.) (New York: Doubleday and Company; 1966), IXXX, 439.

was unheeded. Josephus also speaks of "the principal of the Pharisees" (*Wars* II 17:3) as joining in the attempt to ward off the final conflict. The crisis may well have brought Pharisaic leaders and members of the ruling oligarchy in a common concern to act against the unrest in the country, but for different reasons. The Pharisees were against the rebellion because they feared its consequences, while the High Priests and their associates opposed it because they had become part of the status quo. The primary role in the effort to discourage the unrest in the country—and the movement inspired by Jesus contributed to that unrest—must be judged, however, as having been the work of the priestly aristocracy and those who shared in the administration of the country under Rome.

R. H. Lightfoot's commentary on the Gospel of John, which is singularly indifferent to the social and political realities that underlie the Gospels, nevertheless takes note of the allusion to the fear of Roman reprisals in this passage we have cited from John. He interprets it to mean that the Jewish leaders were afraid that if Jesus remained unhindered in his activity the result would have been that the occupying power would have deprived the Jews of "both their temple worship and their national existence." [8]

The fear that the Romans would be moved by the activity of Jesus to deprive the Jews of "both their temple worship and their national existence" is based on John 11:48. Literally John's words are: "If we let him thus . . . alone the Romans will . . . take away both *our place* and *our nation*." *Our place* has generally been taken as a reference to the Temple, and some translations interpolate the word "holy" before place, to remove the ambiguity of the original text. The translators of *The New English Bible* allowed themselves even greater liberty with the text, rendering the phrase as *our temple*, instead of *our place*. Paul Winter, however, interprets *our place* as referring to the positions held by the members of the council who served as auxiliary officials with the High Priest, and who held office at the pleasure of the Romans. The term *our nation* he understands in the sense of "national status."

We quote Paul Winter's interpretation of the same passage:

[8] R. H. Lightfoot: *St. John's Gospel* (London: Oxford University Press, 1963), p. 227

"The high priest shows himself apprehensive for the rights and status he and his colleagues enjoyed as members of an autonomous organ of the Jewish community in Judea. He betrays fears lest the Romans, perturbed by commotions occasioned by Jesus' activities, should deprive the holders of senatorial office of their positions, and perhaps even abolish Jewish autonomy. As a precaution against this eventuality, the high priest recommends that Jesus be arrested. . . . The political situation in Judea under procuratorial rule was tense. Jewish factions of all sorts were stirring the people to defy foreign domination. The more widespread outbreaks of disorder became, the more frequent discontent was voiced, the greater would become the probability that the procurator would take countermeasures, and in so doing encroach upon the authority that had remained in the hands of the Sanhedrin." [9]

The behavior of the Jewish authorities becomes intelligible when it is recalled that they exercised their authority by the grace of the Romans. At the apex of this group was the High Priest. He presided over the Temple rites, but his ecclesiastical duties were in fact subordinate to his civil and political responsibilities. He was appointed by the Romans who looked to him to help maintain tranquillity in the country. He was charged with ferreting out subversion either directly or by bringing it to the attention of the Romans. Sometimes he convened a council of elders and fellow priests with whom he took counsel on various matters before him. The vestments of the High Priest were kept in the custody of the Roman procurator; they were given to the High Priest for use on official occasions, and after each such use they had to be returned to the Romans—a clear reminder that the Romans were the true masters in the country (Josephus, *Antiquities* XX 1:1).

The people continued to respect the Temple as an ancient institution in Judaism, but they often showed their disdain for the High Priest whom they regarded as a collaborator of Rome. We have noted the sharp words used by the Rabbis of the Talmud against the High Priests of this period. When the rebellion finally broke out against Rome, the High Priest and his associates did their best to thwart its course. He subsequently went into hiding

[9] Paul Winter: *On the Trial of Jesus* (Berlin: Walter De Gruyter & Co.; 1961), p. 40.

to escape the wrath of the revolution. In the end he and his brother were caught by the rebels and executed as traitors to the Jewish cause (Josephus, *Wars* II 17:9).

But it is significant for the deep feelings which prevailed in the country over the issue of resistance to Rome that Eleazar, the son of the slain High Priest whom Josephus described as "a very bold youth" (*Wars* II 17:2) turned against the collaborators and served as a leader of the rebellion. It is not an uncommon phenomenon in times of revolutionary upheaval for men to turn against their own households in order to pursue the patriotic cause.

The revolutionary fever which was to erupt in 66 C.E. was not yet at the breaking point during the procuratorship of Pontius Pilate, which lasted from 26 to 36 C.E. But the ferment of disaffection and unrest was at work throughout the land. There were various expressions for this unrest, and the movement inspired by Jesus was one of them. It is only natural that "the Jewish authorities," sensitive to the explosive possibilities latent in this unrest and anxious to spare their people a final confrontation with Roman power, would take precautionary measures. The arrest of Jesus, one focal point of this unrest, was such a precautionary measure. But if the action of the Jewish authorities against Jesus was inspired by the fear that this action would provoke Roman reprisals against the country as a whole, then their responsibility was only secondary and derivative. The primary responsibility was clearly with the Roman authorities who were the true masters of the situation.

There are two additional statements in John that support the motivation suggested for the behavior of the Jewish authorities. The force which brings Jesus under arrest is said to consist of "the band and the chief captain, and the officers of the Jews" (John 18:12). *The New English Bible* translation renders this verse: "The troops with their commander, and the Jewish police now arrested Jesus." Roman troops, under a Roman commander, shared this operation with Jewish officers, a clear intimation that we are dealing here with a political rather than a religious offense. Romans would not have involved themselves in ferreting out a purely religious offender. The second statement of John describes the High Priest's protest to Pilate's characterization of Jesus as "King of the Jews": "We have no king but Caesar" (19:15). This sounds like a reaffirmation of loyalty to Rome, a disclaimer of sympathy for the movement represented by Jesus which was apparently considered politically subversive.

These references in John have led S. G. F. Brandon to conclude "that part of the sub-Apostolic Church, of which the Johannine writings are representative, had inherited a tradition which shows remarkable agreement with the evidence we have deduced from the relevant New Testament documents and other sources to the effect that in its origins the movement which was initiated by Jesus of Nazareth was invested with an essentially political aspect expressive of Jewish nationalistic aspirations to be rid of the yoke of heathen Rome." [1]

Why did John, who is the most anti-Jewish of the Gospel writers, preserve this tradition which implicates the Romans in the action against Jews? It is difficult to say. It is well to bear in mind that John turned the warning of Caiphas into a prophecy, that Jesus would indeed die for his whole nation, indeed for all men. He took his words as an intimation of the later doctrine that the death of Jesus was a divinely willed sacrifice by which all men would attain vicarious atonement for their sinful natures. John, who was primarily a theologian, may have preferred to fortify a dogma even though he thereby softened the guilt of the Jews. But the report itself must be judged as resting on ancient tradition, and cannot be regarded as an invention of John. Maurice Goguel has reasoned thus: "The philo-Roman tendency being still stronger in the Fourth Gospel than in the Synoptic Gospels, it is impossible to suppose that the cohort and the centurion have been introduced into the narrative by John. Thus we must admit that he is here following a source which mentioned a collaboration between the Jews and the Romans, or which may have mentioned the Romans only. The Jews will have been added by the evangelist under the influence of the Synoptic Narratives." [2]

[1] S. G. F. Brandon: *The Fall of Jerusalem and the Christian Church*, p. 125.

[2] Maurice Goguel: *The Life of Jesus* (New York: Barnes & Noble, 1958), pp. 468 ff.

Some scholars have questioned the historicity of *any* trial before the Sanhedrin. Thus Nineham has argued that Mark's account was a later development, an attempt by the early Church to answer why Jesus was rejected by his own people. And he sees in this report a reflection of the Church's subtle effort to shift the blame for the crucifixion on the Jews. In the words of Nineham: "The indisputable fact that he died by crucifixion shows that his formal trial and sentence were the work of a Roman court, for crucifixion was essentially a *Roman* penalty. What then was the point of the proceedings before the Sanhedrin? . . . The early church, as we have seen, exhibited a steadily growing tendency to transfer the responsibility for Jesus' death from the Romans to the Jews, and so it is natural that they should have come to posit a Jewish trial, at least as formal and decisive as that before Pilate, in which the Jewish authorities incurred the responsibility for Jesus' death . . . Increasingly (and supremely in the fourth Gospel) the Jews were seen by Christians as having deliberately rejected Christ in full knowledge of his claims and evidence in their support (cf. e.g. John 15:24 and 12:37). This is probably the point being made here; what the Sanhedrin did, it did in full awareness of the facts. In view of Jesus' solemn declarations, the scene depicts the Jews, as represented by their duly constituted leaders, deliberately and with full knowledge casting out the 'name' of Jesus and rejecting their Messiah."

It is difficult to dismiss the entire account of an action by the Sanhedrin against Jesus as unhistorical, as some scholars have done, especially since this account is repeated in each of the Gospels, with varying details. A simpler solution is available, but it will involve us in a re-examination of the nature of the Sanhedrin which acted against Jesus. The term *sanhedrin*, the Greek *synedrion*, is a common rather than a proper noun; it means "council" or "assembly." In our rabbinic sources the term is also used to designate a court of law. There were many such Sanhedrins (the Greek plural, *synedria*) in Palestine. According to Josephus, Gabinius divided Judea into five provinces, each to be administered by a Sanhedrin (*Antiquities* XIV 5:4). The Mishnah (Sanhedrin 1:6) specifies that in addition to the seventy-one-member Sanhedrin there was to be one of twenty-three. It moreover provides that a Sanhedrin was to be appointed for every town and village, even it it had a population of no more than one hundred and twenty. Another view requires a population of two hundred and thirty. As Harry A. Wolfson expressed it: "During the Roman period all such governing bodies among the Jews in Palestine came to be known, even among Jews who did not speak Greek, by the Greek name *synedrion* or in its Hebraized form, Sanhedrin." [3]

The two principal Sanhedrins that concern us here and that have become confused in the usual interpretation of the Gospels is the Great Sanhedrin, which rested on the authority of Jewish law, and a Sanhedrin that served as an auxiliary body to the High Priest in administering the country.[4] The Sanhedrin that rested on Jewish law was governed by procedures that are discussed in the Mishnah. Shorn of much of its power by the Romans, this Sanhedrin nevertheless remained competent to administer the death penalty for certain limited offenses of a religious nature.

The Sanhedrin alluded to by Josephus and in the New Testament, as the noted Hellenistic scholar E. J. Bickerman has observed, "always refers to a council associated with the head of state, summoned and constituted by him." This will explain the close identification of the High Priest with the affairs of this body, for this council or Sanhedrin shared his governmental responsibilities. But its decisions were not final since it was not a court of law but a political body and supreme political power was in the hands of the Romans.

Professor Bickerman has offered us a plausible reconstruction of the events that followed the arrest of Jesus, on the basis of a fresh interpretation of the Greek text in Gospel narrative. The proceedings before the Sanhedrin were not a formal trial; they were a hearing to determine whether there were grounds for a trial. The consensus of the council condemning him "as deserving of death" is not to be seen as an actual sentence of death, but as a

[3] Harry A. Wolfson: Philo: *Foundations of Religious Philosophy in Judaism, Christianity, and Islam*, 2 vols. (Cambridge, Mass.: Harvard University Press; 1947), II, 349.

[4] Mantel: *Studies in the History of the Sanhedrin*, pp. 54–101, 254.

conclusion that a capital offense was to be charged to him, that the facts warranted a formal trial, the trial, of course, to be conducted by the Roman authorities. And Bickerman suggests that blasphemy as used in the charge against Jesus be understood not in a technical sense, but as meaning "an enormity," "an outrage," "a gross impropriety." In the words of Bickerman: "In truth, the sentence was rendered solely by the procurator. For the Sanhedrin had not pronounced a verdict, but having established a case involving the death penalty, it withdrew from the case by transferring the accused before the Roman tribunal, as was customary in provincial jurisdiction." [5] It is difficult to decide whether the events followed precisely the reconstruction suggested by one scholar or another. It is clear however that the trial itself in which Jesus was condemned to die on the cross was not a trial before a Jewish court but before a Roman one, that the sentence was carried out under Roman jurisdiction and by Roman officials. It is clear, too, that the offense for which Jesus died was not religious. The death of Jesus was actually a miscarriage of justice when judged by the standards of Jewish law. Something other than religious considerations must have inspired the action taken against him. The method of execution by which Jesus died itself proclaims Roman responsibility. Crucifixion was the typical method used by the Romans to do away with those who threatened the existing political order. It was inadmissible in Jewish penal jurisprudence.

It is noteworthy that in Luke's account the charges made by the Jewish authorities are political rather than religious. Jesus is accused of "perverting our nation and forbidding us to give tribute to Caesar, and saying that he himself is Christ the King" (23:2). After some give and take before Pilate they reiterate the charge that "he stirs up people teaching throughout all Judea, from Galilee even to this place" (23:5). The charge that Jesus kept the people from paying tribute recalls the passage in Mark 12:13–17: "And they sent to him some of the Pharisees and some of the Herodians to entrap him in his talk. And they came and

[5] Elias J. Bickerman: "Al ha-Sanhedrin," *Zion*, III:4 (1934), 359 and "Utilitas Crucis," *Revue de l'histoire des religions*, CXII (1935), 180, 182, 199.

said to him . . . Is it lawful to pay taxes to Caesar, or not? Should we pay them, or should we not? . . . Jesus said to them, Render to Caesar the things that are Caesar's and to God the things that are God's." The answer given by Jesus placed him in opposition to a program of immediate defiance of Roman authority. But that the question arose at all suggests that the position of Jesus could have been interpreted as favoring defiance.

Does our inquiry suggest that Jesus was a political messiah whose ministry was directed toward the overthrow of Roman rule? Theories to this effect have indeed been proposed, the earliest by Hermann Samuel Reimarus (1694–1768). Barrows Dunham in his *The Heretics* is the latest to adopt this hypothesis. To substantiate his views Dunham cites, among other considerations, Luke 22:35–38 where Jesus instructs his followers to sell their belongings and buy a sword, and Mark 10:29–31 where Jesus promises his followers a recompense *in this* world (as well as in the next) for their faith in him, and for the sacrifices with which they sustained that faith: "I tell you this: there is no one who has given up home, brothers or sisters, mother, father, or children, or land, for my sake and for the Gospel, who will not receive *in this age* a hundred times as much—houses, brothers and sisters, mothers and children, and land. . . . and in the age to come eternal life. But many who are first will be last and the last first." [6]

It would be rash to press the teachings of Jesus into the sole mold of a political category. Much of what he had to say—at least as reported in the Gospels—is clearly pietistic and eschatological or otherworldly in character. But his vision of the kingdom of God undoubtedly had its political implications as well. As S. G. F. Brandon noted: "Although it is generally impossible to distinguish what Jesus actually taught from the earliest interpretations of his teachings recorded in the Gospels, it is evident that the original disciples expected that the order of things in Palestine, as they knew it, would soon be brought to an end by some signal intervention of God. . . . As the political fortunes of Israel had

[6] Barrows Dunham, *The Heretics* (London: Eyre & Spottiswoode; 1963), pp. 45, 47. Dunham's quotations are from the *New English Bible* version.

worsened, the belief strengthened that Yahweh would vindicate his honor by a marvellous restoration of his chosen people. . . . The form it might take ranged from the restoration of Israel's national independence to the replacement of the present cosmic order by a new world, created by God, with a heavenly Jerusalem as its centre. . . . The original Jewish Christians evidently shared in both these conceptions of the achievement of the divine purpose. According to the record of Acts, the disciples asked the Risen Jesus: 'Lord, wilt thou at this time restore the kingdom unto Israel?' (1:6), thereby implying a political fulfillment of the Messianic hope." [7]

What further differentiated Jesus from the usual political or social revolutionary was the method envisioned for effecting the inauguration of the new order. The evidence does not indicate that Jesus favored an insurrection. It appears rather that he expected the transformation to occur through the miracle of divine intervention. Alfred Loisy has characterized the hope of Jesus thus: "The ideal of Jesus was national in its setting, religious and moral in its spirit, the mystical programme of a universal revolution of which the execution was left to the omnipotence of the Eternal." [8]

The truth, of course, is that freedom dreamers were just as abhorrent to Rome as freedom fighters. Every messianic vision, even if expressed in eschatological terms, becomes a *judgment against* the status quo; every vision of the kingdom of God when presented as due for imminent realization constituted a threat against the kingdom of Caesar. Rome was secure in a quiescent people, and the dream of freedom, no matter how conceived and no matter how its fulfillment was envisioned, fed unrest and engendered a feeling of insecurity. Rome knew only one way to deal with freedom dreamers and freedom fighters—to nail them on the cross.

It is therefore readily understandable that those charged with maintaining peace in a turbulent province like Judea would look

[7] S. G. F. Brandon: *History, Time and Deity* (New York: Barnes & Noble; 1965), p. 152 ff.

[8] Alfred Loisy: "The Christian Mystery," *Hibbert Journal*, X (1911–12), 46.

upon Jesus and the intense unrest he inspired as a threat to the state. In the words of Maurice Goguel: "From the very outset the proceedings against Jesus were not purely Jewish in character, since the Roman cohort was present when Jesus was arrested. Thus Jesus was not arrested for blasphemy but as an agitator, or as a person who might furnish a pretext for, or become the occasion of, a political agitation." [9]

Our final consideration is the behavior of the "crowd." The conventional story of the crucifixion assigns to the crowd a crucial role. The crowd is deemed to represent the people of Jerusalem, if not the Jewish people generally. They are supposedly introduced by the Jewish authorities as part of the plot against Jesus. And since it is their screamed demands which lead Pilate to doom Jesus, the Jewish people as a whole are thereby linked in the culpability for the crucifixion.

A careful reading of the Gospels discloses, however, that the people of Jerusalem were generally sympathetic to the teachings of Jesus. His parables and his moralizing homilies were close to their spirit. His vision of a new world order partook of the apocalyptic tradition, which was one expression of their frustration at the hands of Roman power. The most telling reference is Mark 14:2. Here the authorities are pictured as plotting the arrest of Jesus and they agree that this must be done "not during the festival, or a riot may break out among the people." This was only two days before Passover, two days, as it turned out, before his actual arrest! As Dominic M. Crossan sums it up: "Their considered opinion is that it is impossible to take Him 'secretly' during the festival, and the obvious reason is that the people are on His side and a riot could easily start at such a time. This appears in Mark 14:1–2, Matthew 26:3–5, Luke 22:2. . . . In the light of these explicit statements, the burden of proof must rest with him who would have the authorities introduce the Jerusalem crowd into the proceedings against Jesus. It is precisely this they cannot risk." [1]

The Marcan account of the crowd's role before Pilate and

[9] Goguel: *The Life of Jesus*, p. 481.

[1] Dominic M. Crossan: "Anti-Semitism and the Gospel," *Theological Studies*, XXVI:2 (June 1965), 201 f.

their shouting for the release of Barabbas poses serious difficulties. Scholars can find no substantiation of a custom among the Romans to release a prisoner during a feast. D. E. Nineham in his commentary on Mark concludes that the Marcan assertion of a regular custom to release a prisoner must be judged erroneous. The procurator was, of course, free to grant an amnesty in a *particular case*, "and several partial parallels are known, one of them providing a fairly close analogy to our own." [2]

Nineham notes other difficulties: "Not only is it unlikely . . . that a man of Pilate's position and character would be found bandying words with a mob of subject people in the way pictured in 9 ff., but the content and dialogue presents problems; it seems to presuppose that Pilate is faced with a choice between two condemned prisoners, so that if one is released, the other must be executed; but at the end of vv. 2–5 Jesus has not been condemned, and, as the story stands, there is nothing to prevent Pilate, if he believed in Jesus' innocence, from acquitting him and granting an amnesty to Barabbas as well."

Mark tells us that "the chief priests stirred up the crowd to have him [Pilate] release for them Barabbas instead" of Jesus. But, as Nineham notes, "it is not clear how the priests could have had time to influence the crowd's attitude to Jesus between the suggestion of Pilate (v. 9) and the people's reply." [3] The entire scene was enacted in Pilate's presence. Would the priests have dared to incite the crowd, in Pilate's very presence, to thwart the procurator's clear intentions?

The Reverend Crossan puts a totally different complexion on this passage. A careful reading of the text in Mark has convinced him that the crowd came primarily to seek amnesty for Barabbas, who was apparently a leader in some anti-Roman action. The text speaks of him as being "among the rebels in prison, who had committed murder in the insurrection." In the words of Crossan: "This text is quite clear—against the background of an occupied city. Barabbas and his companions had risen against the Roman

[2] D. E. Nineham: *The Gospel of St. Mark* (Baltimore: Penguin Books; 1963), p. 414.

[3] Ibid., pp. 416 ff.

domination and killed some Roman soldiers or Jewish quislings during their revolt. Thus John 18:40b describes Barabbas as a *lestes;* and Jesus is crucified along with two *lestai* (Mark 51:27, 32; Matthew 27:38, 44; Luke 23:32–33, 39–43). This term does not mean a robber in our sense of the term, but rather an insurgent, a rebel, a guerrilla fighter against the occupation authorities. Barabbas and two followers were, then, to be crucified that day; 'the crowd' came up to ask for the rebel's release according to the customary amnesty. There is no indication from Mark that they came up as a mob or that they came up against Jesus or that they were gathered by the authorities from the populace. . . . One can reasonably presume that they are friends or followers of the rebel leader and that they are a small band; neither the character of Pilate nor the use of 'the crowd' in Mark 15:18 warrants the idea of a very large group. They find themselves faced with a possible disappointment; there is now somebody else in prison and we cannot even be certain that adherents of Barabbas would necessarily know who Jesus is. Pilate knows that Barabbas is more dangerous than Jesus and tries to release the latter to them. . . . This would seem to be the picture which emerges with relative clarity from Mark; later the tradition (e.g., Luke) seems to have taken the crowd as being a mob from the populace, but this cannot be substantiated from Matthew or John." [4]

The Reverend Crossan shows the subtle changes that occur in later New Testament writings to enlarge the scope of Jewish involvement and Jewish guilt. Luke uses the term "the crowds" as a substitute for the specified Jewish authorities, be they Pharisees or Sadducees who are the early opponents of Jesus. John is more sweeping: he employs the term "the Jews," as he often uses the term "the world," synonymously with those in authority who opposed Jesus. Indeed in John the term "the Jews" has become a symbol "for those who rejected Jesus in the earthly ministry and engineered his death." The Reverend Crossan notes the danger in the conversion of the term "the Jews" into a symbol of all forces

[4] Crossan: "Anti-Semitism and the Gospel," *Theological Studies*, XXVI:2 (June 1965), 203 ff.

that were hostile to Jesus: "But it is also a very dangerous symbolic term, and one cannot but wonder if it might be a root of anti-Semitism in the Christian subconscious." [5]

Once the evil seed had been planted, it continued to yield its ignoble harvest. The myth of Jewish guilt in the crucifixion continued to proliferate in the later Gospels and subsequent Christian writings, while the primary responsibility of the Romans was all but forgotten. There is a continued reduction of Pilate's involvement. Indeed Christian legend has sometimes even glorified him. Every year on June 25, the Ethiopian Christian Church commemorates the sainthood of Pilate and his wife.

In the scene before Pilate, as we move from Gospel to Gospel, this trend is vividly clear: the later Gospels continue to play down the Roman involvement and to magnify that of the Jews. Matthew speaks of Barabbas simply as a "notorious prisoner" (27:16), omitting his connection with the revolutionary movement against Rome. This makes the preference of the crowd for him over Jesus all the more heinous. Matthew, moreover, elaborates on Pilate's anxiety to free Jesus. He introduces Pilate's wife who sent word to him while he was sitting on the judgment seat that she had "suffered much over him [Jesus] today in a dream" and that he is therefore to "have nothing to do with that righteous man." It is Matthew who has Pilate wash his hands before the crowd to proclaim that he was "innocent of this man's blood." Following this act he has the gruesome footnote: "And all the people answered, 'His blood be on us and on our children.'" By "all the people" Matthew presumably meant all the people present before Pilate, the "crowd," as described by Mark, but he uses a term that carries allusions to the entire Jewish people. Pilate finally yields Jesus to his soldiers to be crucified, because he was afraid of a riot by the people! (27:24–26). A. J. Grieve has noted the anti-Semitic overtones in the Matthew narrative: "The whole narrative intensifies the guilt of the Jews; there is little doubt that [verse] 25 has been largely responsible for the malignity with which 'Christian' communities and individuals long pursued

[5] Ibid., pp. 190–9.

Jews."[6] According to the Jesuit scholar Gerald G. O'Collins of Cambridge University, Matthew 27:25 "has done more than any other sentence in the New Testament to feed the fires of anti-Semitism."[7]

Luke's account enlarges the Barabbas group to a representative segment of people of Jerusalem and their primary concern is not the release of Barabbas but the death of Jesus.

The Reverend Crossan is disinclined to charge Luke with deliberate anti-Semitism. His verbiage was simply more suited to the Roman audience for whom he wrote. But he acknowledges that the objective effect of Luke's terminology is to give ground for anti-Semitic bias. In the words of Crossan: "As the tradition went out from a Palestinian milieu, where words like 'Scribes, Pharisees, Sadducees' meant something to the audience, it moved into a Gentile world, where these terms had little relevance. So, gradually these specific expressions were erased from the tradition and more general terms such as 'the crowds' took their place. This had the advantage of warnings to a new audience, new 'crowds,' that they faced a like challenge as had the 'crowds' in Palestine. But the obvious fact is that where anti-Semitism was not inserted by design, some can easily be extracted by mistake."[8]

The Gospel of John carries this process to its final logic. Here Pilate refuses to order the crucifixion, but allows "the Jews" to do so; and it is they, "the Jews," who take Jesus and lead him to be crucified (19:13–17). But even John does not altogether succeed in effacing Roman responsibility from the record. For John retains the petition by Joseph (19:38) that had to be addressed to Pilate to permit removing the body of Jesus from the cross, to give it honorable burial, in accordance with Jewish rites. The jurisdiction of the Roman authorities over the body of an executed prisoner was only an extension of their jurisdiction over the exe-

[6] A. J. Grieve: Commentary on Matthew 27:11–16, in A. S. Peake (ed.): *A Commentary on the Bible* (London: Thomas Nelson & Sons; 1919).

[7] Gerald G. O'Collins: "Anti-Semitism in the Gospels," *Theological Studies*, XXVI:4 (December 1965), 663.

[8] Crossan: "Anti-Semitism and the Gospel," *Theological Studies*, XXVI:2 (June 1965), 192.

cution itself. And John follows the other Gospels in having the soldiers—obviously Roman soldiers—effect the deed itself.

It is saddening to see how far John's mythical interpretation of the Jews has insinuated itself into Christian thinking. Even a humanist like Jacques Maritain, in a book written to combat anti-Semitism, reveals that he has not freed himself of it. Speaking of the "vocation of Israel," he has this to say: "And we must say that, if St. Paul be right, what is called the *Jewish problem* is an *insoluble* problem, that is, one without definitive solution until the great reconciliation foretold by the apostle. . . . Israel . . . is in the world but not of the world. But since the day when, because its leaders chose the world, it stumbled, it is bound to the world, prisoner and victim of that world which it *loves*, but of *which* it is not, shall not be and never can be. Thus is the mystery of Israel understood from a Christian viewpoint." [9]

Maritain's meaning is always cast in a gracious and eloquent prose, but it is not difficult to discern it. The Jewish leaders *chose the world*, the Jewish people *love* the world—here is an echo of John's identification of "the Jews" and "the world" as the forces of evil which are antithetical to Jesus; because the Jewish leaders chose the world, a euphemism for rejecting Jesus, the Jewish people *stumbled*—here is a reaffirmation of corporate guilt which rests on the Jewish people for all time; the Jews, because they *stumbled*, are fated to be *prisoner and victim* of the world—here is the notion that Jewish suffering is an expiation of their guilt for having rejected Jesus; and Professor Maritain is resigned to the thought that the problem will remain insoluble until *the great reconciliation* foretold by Paul—which means the conversion of the Jews to Christianity. As a talmudic aphorism puts it: "If the flame bring down a mighty cedar tree, how can the frail grass stand up?" Maritain is a foremost exponent of neoscholasticism, a renowned Catholic humanist. If the mythical conception of Jewish destiny maintains its hold on him, how can we be shocked at its persistence among the less educated multitude?

Why did the evangelists pervert the facts, thereby misleading generations of Christians into an unreasoned hostility toward

[9] Jacques Maritain: *A Christian Looks at the Jewish Question* (New York: Longmans, Green and Co.; 1939), pp. 25, 27.

Jews? They were not historians of course and their works were not chronicles of history. They were meant to be aids to their missionary labors. Emotions color one's perspective. They cherished hostile feelings toward Jews for their resistance to the claims of the Church, and they could not be unduly perturbed if their "enemies" were being presented in a lurid light. On the contrary, the more evil the image of the Jew, the more understandable became his refusal to embrace the "true" faith. But the evangelists had another motive—"to represent the Roman authorities as having no essential quarrel with Jesus and no fault to find with him or his movement. This point was of overwhelming importance to Christians living and evangelizing in a Roman environment, for if the imperial authorities had discovered no harm in the founder of the religion it might be assumed that his followers were harmless too." [1]

The conception of the Jew as a sinister figure actuated by hate to seek the death of Jesus invited the belief that these characteristics were a permanent trait of the Jew, and that he is continually engaged in secret plots against Christendom. The Jews then became a frequent target of charges of all sorts of nefarious activities against their Christian neighbors. Throughout the Middle Ages one continues to encounter various libels against the Jews, that they poisoned the wells, that they desecrated the wafer used as the Host in the Christian mass, that they slew Christians, especially Christian children, to use their blood for ritual purposes. Torture produced confessions from those accused, and one such libel became evidence for the perpetration of another libel.

The Vatican acted recently to withdraw one such libel which was perpetrated against Jews in Trent, Italy, in 1475. The case was typical and bears recounting in detail. The report, written by Robert C. Doty, and carried on page 1 of *The New York Times* on November 1, 1965, speaks for itself:

> ROME, OCT. 31—A group of Jews executed nearly five centuries ago for the supposed "ritual murder" of a 2-year-old child has been declared innocent by the Roman Catholic Church.

[1] Nineham: *St. Mark*, p. 412.

The Most Rev. Alessandro Gottardi, Archbishop of Trent, where the incident took place in 1475, acknowledged in a pastoral letter the Jews' innocence in the death of the Blessed Little Simon of Trent. At least 12 Jews were executed.

The letter was dated Oct. 28 to coincide with the promulgation by Pope Paul VI of the Ecumenical Council declaration in which the Jewish people are absolved of any collective guilt for the Crucifixion of Jesus.

Archbishop Gottardi noted the "happy coincidence" of the Council declaration and the withdrawal of the status of martyr from Simon by the Vatican Sacred Congregation of Rites.

The Congregation of Rites, which has jurisdiction over the ceremonies of the church and the process of beatification and canonization, forbade any further veneration of relics or saying of masses in Simon's name.

Simon, 2 years 4 months old when he was found dead, has been recognized for centuries as a Blessed [eligible for local veneration] without ever having been formally beatified by the Congregation of Rites.

Detective work on the 490-year-old case was conducted by the Rev. P. Eckert, a Dominican, and published in Trentine Studies of Historical Science earlier this year.

The child, son of a tanner, vanished on March 24, 1475. His body was found two days later by one of the 25 Jews of the city.

A "trial" of virtually all of the Jews was carried out under the authority of the Prince-Bishop of Trent. Most of the accused were tortured to death.

Christian superstition of the time held that the Jews carried out "ritual murder" of Christian children as part of their worship.

For the record, and despite the obvious implausibility of the charge in 20th-century eyes, Father Eckert made a careful examination of the "evidence" in archives in Trent, Rome and Vienna and concluded that "the trial of Trent had led to a judicial assassination." [2]

[2] *The New York Times*, November 1, 1965, p. 1.

The allegation of Jewish guilt in the crucifixion was eventually formalized into the charge of "deicide." The Jews were branded as "murderers" of God, since Christians identified Jesus with God. This guilt was said to rest on the entire Jewish people collectively and for all time. And the persecution of Jews often perpetrated by Christians—was taught to be a divine retribution visited on them as a consequence of this guilt.

There are theological difficulties in this charge of "deicide" against the Jews. It implies a primitive conception of God, that the Deity can be "slain" by mortal hands; it implies the primitive notion of corporate guilt, that the actions of some can involve guilt on an entire people; it implies the primitive notion that guilt is transmitted by heredity to generations still unborn; it implies that a human agent who performs God's purpose can then be deemed guilty for having performed this purpose, since Jesus, according to Christian theology, died to fulfill God's purpose, as a sacrifice of atonement for the sins of all men.

Most contemporary Christian efforts to remove the allegation of Jewish guilt in the crucifixion base themselves on one or another of the theological inconsistencies in the allegation. But they leave the historical distortion untouched. Christian theologians and ecclesiastical leaders owe it to the truth to correct the perversion of history. The Christian public continues to entertain a version of the crucifixion in which Jews bear the primary responsibility in the making of that tragedy. A five-year study of anti-Semitism in the United States conducted by Dr. Charles Y. Glock of the Survey Research Center of the University of California with the aid of a grant from the Anti-Defamation League of B'nai B'rith has disclosed that 60 per cent of those tested in the Protestant community and 61 per cent in the Catholic community regarded the Jews as bearing the greatest responsibility for the crucifixion of Jesus.[3] A study of textbooks used in Catholic and Protestant schools conducted by St. Louis University (a Jesuit institution) and Yale University in cooperation with the American Jewish Committee showed one of the primary sources from which the

[3] The first volume of this study, *Christian Beliefs and Anti-Semitism*, written by Charles Glock and Rodney Stark, was published in May 1966 by Harper & Row.

Christian public derived its misinformation. The Jews are often presented in these texts as the major culprit in the events of the crucifixion.[4]

The theological considerations against the allegation of Jewish guilt in the crucifixion of Jesus have a certain cogency in themselves, and the fact that they are being brought forth is significant as an indication of theological development in Christianity, away from the primitivism of its conventional doctrine. But the application of these considerations to Jewish "guilt" is largely irrelevant, for the allegation of this guilt is simply a case of false testimony against the Jewish people. As Dominic M. Crossan, the Jesuit scholar we have quoted earlier, summed it up: "The often repeated statement that the Jews rejected Jesus and had Him crucified is *historically* untenable and must, therefore, be removed from our thinking, and our writing, our teaching, preaching, and liturgy." [5]

The re-examination of the events leading up to the crucifixion is not really germane to the issue of anti-Semitism. Even if the conventional version of the crucifixion were correct, this would not justify the imputation of guilt to the Jewish people. Religious as well as secular societies have often dealt harshly with rebels and heretics. Shall we impute guilt to all Christendom because the medieval Church did in fact condemn thousands as heretics, torture them to obtain confessions, and then send them to die a miserable death at the stake? To his countrymen Jesus was a man like other men, subject to the laws, whether benign or harsh, by which the existing order was safeguarded. But the conventional version of the crucifixion is false and represents one of the most grievous distortions of history.

It is pertinent to note that the conflict between Jesus and the Roman power structure persisted after the crucifixion of Jesus. The persecutions of Paul and other followers of Jesus have some-

[4] The Yale study is summed up in Dr. Bernhard E. Olson's *Faith and Prejudice* (New Haven: Yale University Press; 1963). The St. Louis study is discussed by James W. Arnold in "Religious Text Books . . . Primers in Bigotry," *Ave Maria* (October 10 and 17, 1964).

[5] Crossan: "Anti-Semitism and the Gospel," *Theological Studies*, XXVI:2 (June 1965), 189.

times been blamed on the Jews, but as in the case of Jesus himself the source of conflict was no doubt the sensitivity of the Roman authorities (and their Jewish collaborators headed by the High Priest) to any phenomenon which fostered unrest within the social order. And the Christians with their dreams of another kingdom to supersede the kingdom of Caesar were such a phenomenon. The arrests of Paul in Jerusalem, of Peter and John, and of Stephen and James (who were executed), were all instigated by the High Priest and his associates—the very men who were part of the power structure of the Roman administration. In every instance the Pharisees are either not mentioned at all or are cited as opposing the persecution (Acts 6:34, 23:9, and Josephus, *Antiquities* XX 9:1).

Stephen and James died as Christian martyrs and the report left to us does not indicate any Roman involvement in the proceedings against them. The omission of Roman action in the case of Stephen has been explained by the fact that his execution occurred at the end of 35 or the beginning of 36 C.E., when there was no Roman procurator in the country. Pilate had been recalled to Rome and his successor had not yet arrived to replace him. Law and order had to be maintained, and the High Priest may have decided to act on his own authority.[6]

What is significant, however, in the trial of Stephen is the fact that it is the High Priest who presides and conducts the interrogation. The Sanhedrin is mentioned as sitting with him. Here, too, the term does not refer to the august tribunal which functioned as the supreme religious tribunal of Judaism. As F. J. Foakes Jackson in his commentary on Acts cautions us: "It may not be superfluous to remind the reader that the word Sanhedrin is Greek transliterated into Hebrew characters, and may signify no more than an assembly.

"The author of Acts consistently represents the Pharisees as upon the whole well-disposed to the believers. . . . We must always remember that, according to Acts, the followers of Jesus were, at first, decidedly popular in Jerusalem; and that the priests

[6] Wilfred L. Knox: *St. Paul and the Church of Jerusalem* (Cambridge: Cambridge University Press; 1925), pp. 42, 160 *n.*

who controlled the Temple were greatly disliked." [7]

The execution of James (a brother of Jesus) also occurred without the authority of the procurator's office, but here Josephus tells us explicitly that the High Priest acted alone because the Roman procurator was out of the country. The procurator Festus had died and Albinus who was to succeed him had not yet arrived in Jerusalem to take office. Following the execution there was a storm of indignation from "those who seemed most equitable of the citizens and such as were most uneasy at the breach of the laws." This description suggests that Josephus was referring to the Pharisees; the High Priest who instigated the action against James is described by Josephus as a Sadducee. As a result the High Priest Ananus was deposed from his office. He had become too unpopular with the Jewish public to continue serving as a facade of Roman power. He was replaced by another puppet High Priest, Jesus the Son of Demneus.

Christianity was looked on as a subversive movement by the Romans, and whoever came under suspicion of adhering to it was often persecuted by the authorities. One of the most renowned sages of Israel, Rabbi Eliezer ben Hyrcanus, who had helped in the founding of the rabbinical academy in Jabneh after 70 C.E., was once suspected of Christian sympathies and he had to stand trial before a Roman magistrate (Avodah Zarah 16b, Tosefta Hullin 2:24).

A careful examination of the primary Christian records bearing on the fate of Jesus as well as of his disciples has led S. G. F. Brandon to conclude: "Jesus of Nazareth was executed by the Roman governmental authorities as a rebel against the Roman suzerainty in Palestine. In the Gospel narratives there is clear evidence of a tendency to shift the responsibility from the Romans to the Jews by representing the destruction of Jesus as initially the work of the Jewish leaders and its ultimate accomplishment as only achieved by their criminal overbearing of the resistance of Pilate to what he knew would be an outrage upon justice. However, despite this tendency, and indeed the more significant because of it, the crucial fact remains uncontested that the fatal

[7] F. J. Foakes Jackson: *The Acts of the Apostles* (New York: Harper & Bros., 1931), pp. 45 ff.

sentence was pronounced by the Roman governor and its execution carried out by Roman officials.

"The Christian tradition is strong that Jesus carefully eschewed any involvement with the political issues then at stake in Palestine, and the significance of that tradition must be respected, although its origins need to be closely investigated. Nevertheless, whatever may have been the degree to which Jesus had become involved in the cause of Jewish freedom, it is certain that the movement connected with him had at least sufficient semblance of sedition to cause the Roman authorities both to regard him as a possible revolutionary and, after trial, to execute him as guilty on such a charge." [8]

The crucifixion of Jesus was an incident in the Roman oppression of the Jewish people. Some Jewish leaders were involved in the events, but they were colonial administrators serving under an occupation government; they were an auxiliary element in the Roman administration. They did not represent their own people; they were, in fact, part of the apparatus by which the Roman administration operated. Jesus was crucified because his movement threatened the stability of the existing order, and the existing order in this context was the political order over which presided the Roman procurator. The initiative for the action against Jesus in an ultimate sense, however the sequence of events really occurred, was with the Romans whose order was threatened, and not with the Jews who, as a people, were themselves the victims of that order.

[8] *The Fall of Jerusalem and the Christian Church* (London: Society for Propagation of Christian Knowledge; 1957), pp. 101 ff.

Chapter XI The Old Testament and the New Testament

Christianity began after the death of Jesus. The turning point in the new development was the refusal by his disciples to acknowledge the finality of his death. It was not long before they announced to the world that their master had indeed died on the cross, but that after three days he was resurrected, that he now sat in glory in the heavenly realm, beside God, and he would soon return to bring to completion his redemptive ministry, to establish the messianic kingdom.

Scholars who are inclined to rationalism see in the account of the resurrection a triumph of faith over reality. Hermann Samuel Reimarus, David Friedrich Strauss, Ernest Renan, Theodor Keim, among others, regard the belief in the resurrection as based on a subjective experience, which occurred in the mental processes of the disciples and was not associated with objective fact. But is it possible to envision the steps by which this faith arose and spread its way among the faithful, to become a cardinal doctrine of Christendom?

Charles Guignebert, the noted historian of early Christianity, has stressed at least two factors which helped shape this faith. In part it was the afterglow of the original faith which had sustained the disciples of Jesus while their master was alive. Their belief in his mission was so deep that it was difficult for them to accept his death, for on the face of it, his death belied all his claims and his promises on which they had staked their own lives. In the words of Professor Guignebert: "Their faith fixed itself upon, and one might say, was hypnotized by this one idea: 'it is simply impossible that he should have abandoned us, that he should be actually dead.' The inevitable culmination of concentration on the same constant or fixed idea in the brains of men both uncultered and mystical, is a vision. That is why Peter *sees* Jesus, and the others afterward see him as Peter has seen him. Whether it is an open case of visual hallucination or of visual appearances interpreted as hallucinations, matters little; fishermen from the Sea of Galilee would be equally foiled by both these phenomena. . . . Assuming that the apostles thought at first the apparitions which they had seen were of his *spirit* only, they could not, we may be sure, retain this opinion long, since popular belief construed resurrection to mean complete resumption of the life on earth." [1]

It is well to remember that there was some support in Judaism for those who refused to believe in the finality of the death of Jesus. The prophet Elijah, according to II Kings 2:11, was taken up to heaven without suffering death. There was a tradition too among the mystics that Enoch, the seventh of the ten antediluvian patriarchs, likewise was spared the fate of a mortal and was taken in a living state to heaven. This was inferred from the indirect way in which Scripture describes his end (Genesis 5:24): "Enoch walked with God; then he was no more, for God took him." [2] Enoch was said to have become a kind of vice regent under God, the angel *metatron*, who rules the sublunar world.

[1] Charles Guignebert: *Christianity, Past and Present* (New York: The Macmillan Company; 1927), pp. 45–60.

[2] New Jewish Publication Society translation.

The ascension of Enoch to heaven is the theme of two apocalyptic works, I Enoch and II Enoch. Both books recount the journeyings of Enoch through all the earth and through the seven heavens, where all the mysteries of heaven and earth are revealed to him, so that he in turn might teach them to the rest of mankind. I Enoch was written in Palestine, in all likelihood in Aramaic, between the third and first centuries B.C.E.

It is of interest to note that the Midrash quotes a discussion between *minim*, members of a "sect," in other words, which sometimes refers to Christians, and Rabbi Abbahu, a third-generation Amora, on the very subject of Enoch's ascension to heaven: "The *minim* asked Rabbi Abbahu, But there is no mention of death in the case of Enoch! He said to them, How so? They replied, Of Enoch it is written that the Lord 'took' him, and of Elijah [who ascended to heaven while alive] it is also written [II Kings 2:3]: 'And the sons of the prophets who were in Bethel came out to Elisha, and said to him, Do you know that the Lord will *take* away your master [Elijah] from over you?' He replied to them, If your inference is from the term *take*, this term is also used to mean death, as in Ezekiel 24:16: 'Son of man, behold, I am about to *take* the delight of your eyes [his wife] away from you at a stroke . . .'" (Genesis Rabbah 25:1).

The voices that spoke for a more rational faith gained ascendancy in Judaism, but all kinds of mystical speculations were assiduously pursued in other circles, and some of the beliefs about Jesus that seem so strange when viewed from the perspective of classic Judaism may well have found some antecedence in the mythical motifs that were being spun by Jewish mystics.

There was a second factor that helped shape the belief in the resurrection. It was the influence of the mystery religions, which were prevalent in the Hellenistic world. There were a number of deities revered in these religions: Attis in Phrygia, Adonis in Syria, Melkart in Phoenicia, Tammuz and Marduk in Mesopotamia, Osiris in Egypt, Dionysus in Greece, and Mithra in Persia. Mithraism also had a wide following in Rome. A common characteristic of all these divinities was their alleged death at a certain time of the year, followed soon by a rebirth. It was apparently the experience of the seasons—the waning of summer and the death of vegetation in winter—which inspired the myth of the death of the god associated with that particular phase of nature. And it was the renewal of spring with the promise of renewed vegetation which, in turn, inspired the belief in the god's rebirth. The various rites associated with these deities were vicarious reenactments of the myth, and their effect was to flood the faithful alternately with intense grief and intense joy. They felt themselves dying with the god and reborn in his rebirth. The god's death, moreover, was seen as a willing self-sacrifice for the sake of his faithful to whom he offered the promise of his own rebirth, and of the renewal of nature on which they depended. Death is of course the common lot of mortals, but the experience of rebirth through identification with a deity seemed to save mortals from their mortal destiny; it seemed to offer them eternal life.

The belief in the resurrection of Jesus rounded out his entire career with the elements of miracle and mystery. We quote again from Professor Guignebert: "It is through it [the belief in the resurrection of Jesus] that faith in the Lord Jesus became the foundation of a new religion which shortly after separated from Judaism and was offered to all men as the Divine Way of Salvation. Through it again, the influence of the old Oriental myth of the god dying and rising again to lead his followers to life immortal will penetrate the consciousness of Christian communities, at any rate, the Hellenizing ones and promptly take the Jewish Messiah, a national hero, unintelligible and a matter of indifference to the Greeks, and transform him into Jesus Christ, the Lord and Savior, the Son of God and his ambassador in the world, upon whose name, as St. Peter says again, all believers call, and before whom the entire creation ought to bow to kneel." [3]

An illustration of the influence of the mystery religions on Christianity is offered us in the celebration of Christmas, according to Joseph Blau, professor of religion at Columbia University. It was some time in the fourth century that the Church selected December 25 to recite the mass celebrating the birth of Jesus, but there is no Christian tradition which claims that Jesus was actually born on that date. The decisive factor for the selection of this date was apparently "to distract the attention of Christians from

[3] Guignebert: *Christianity, Past and Present*, pp. 47–8.

the old pagan feast days." December 24 was the last of the ten days of the Saturnalia, a festival abounding in licentiousness, associated with the cult of Saturn, while December 25 was celebrated in Mithraism as the *dies natalis solis*, the Birthday of the Vanquished Sun. In the words of Dr. Blau: "Undoubtedly the Saturnalia, as well as the *dies natalis solis invicti*, enters into the background of the selection of December 25 as the date on which to celebrate the Feast of the Nativity. The Mithraic observance was probably the most important element, for in the Clementine Homilies an equation was made between Christ and the sun, an equation that may itself reveal the syncretistic spirit at work trying to incorporate Mithraic ideas into the young Christian faith." Professor Blau notes the struggle of the Puritans against Christmas. In the Puritan Massachusetts Bay Colony it was a crime, punishable by the stocks, to observe Christmas. He quotes from the English writer William Prynne, who in his *Histriomastix* (1633) expressed the Puritan view of the Christmas celebration: "The affinity between Christmas revels and Saturnalia is so close both in time of celebration and in the manner of observance, that all pious Christians should eternally abominate them." [4]

Acknowledging that the belief in the miraculous elements in the career of Jesus are mythical, Arnold J. Toynbee cautions us not to dismiss them as naïve; they are to be seen as symbolic statements of deep spiritual significance. But we must beware against taking them as literal descriptions of reality: "Though shrines, rituals, tokens and social conventions are highly charged with feeling, they do not come so close to the heart of a religion as its myths: the portrayal of death as the seed of life in the figure of Tammuz—Adonis—Osiris—Attis, embodying the fruitfulness of the year that dies to be born again; the portrayal of self-sacrifice for the salvation of fellow-sufferers in the figure of Christ . . . the portrayal of super-human spiritual nature in the figure of a hero whose mother is human but whose father is divine (the birth story that is told of Jesus, Augustus, Alexander, Plato, and every Pharaoh of Egypt since, at least, the beginning of the Fifth Dynasty). Can these myths be discarded without taking the heart out

[4] Joseph Blau: "On the Celebration of Christmas," *Columbia University Rapport* (1964–5), pp. 3 ff.

of the faiths whose essence the myths convey? If the universe is a mystery, and if the key to this mystery is hidden, are not myths an indispensable means for expressing as much as we can express of the Ineffable? . . . This is true, and it does mean that myths are indispensable to man for probing a mystery that is beyond his intellectual horizon. Yet no particular myth can be sacrosanct; for myths are woven out of poetic images borrowed from this world's passing scene. . . ." [5]

This new conception of Jesus is the motif that guided the evangelists who wrote the Gospels. They were not creating faithful reconstructions of the master's life and teaching. They were rather reconstructing the past in the light of the new doctrine. His life was portrayed in terms that accentuated its divine character. He was said to have been born of a virgin, in immaculate conception; his early years were spent under providential protection; he taught with a rare authority and he was able to perform miracles, to heal the sick, to drive out demons, to make the lame walk and the blind see. On the third day after his crucifixion he was said to have risen from the dead and to be sitting in divine splendor at the right hand of God. The Christians waited for his return to usher in the divine kingdom over which he would reign as King Messiah, but the faithful experienced the efficacy of his life and death and rebirth immediately. They were reborn, vicariously, with him, reborn from sin and mortality. Their old selves died with his death, and in his resurrection they, too, were resurrected and endowed with eternal life.

This new belief represented a break with Judaism. At the center of Judaism is a law, a way of life. For Christianity Jesus himself is the way of life. At the center is faith in Jesus, and certain rites through which the faithful re-enact his passion and his resurrection. Jews sensed the break, but Christians refused to acknowledge it, insisting that their new doctrine was consistent with the Jewish Scriptures, even maintaining that it was mandated by those Scriptures. Jesus himself had recognized the authority of the Hebrew Bible. His apostles were Jews and they directed their propaganda initially to Jews for whom the Bible was the word of

[5] Arnold J. Toynbee: *A Historian's Approach to Religion* (New York, Toronto, and London: Oxford University Press; 1956), p. 282.

God. Even the Hellenistic communities to whom they eventually carried their propaganda regarded the Hebrew Bible with great veneration. Christian spokesmen therefore presented their new doctrine as a continuation of Judaism, as its logical development and completion. But this was a claim that needed substantiation, and the ultimate authority through which this substantiation could be effected was the Hebrew Bible.

The Christian apostles sought to accomplish this through a Christian version of the Midrash, similar to the Midrash by which the Rabbis effected a link between their interpretations and the scriptural text. The rabbinic Midrash is richer in scope, because the Rabbis shared the richly diverse interests reflected in the Hebrew Bible, the world of nature, the world of human history, the problems and conflicts of men acting in society and exposed to the dilemmas of the existential world. The Christian "Midrash" is by comparison narrower in scope. The problems of creation, of the natural order, of the historical order, did not primarily concern its creators. Their interests center on effecting a bridge between Judaism and the cult which was centered in Jesus. Their "Midrash" concerns itself with finding prophecies for the messiahship of Jesus, with supporting the claim that Judaism in its older form lacked sufficiency and completeness, and presupposed a subsequent fruition, and with the finding of polemic invective against the Jews who insisted on clinging to the old way and refused to embrace the new and fuller truth ushered in by Jesus.

This Christian "Midrash" served a crucial role in the Christian rationalization of its place in the scheme of salvation. It enabled Christianity to "legitimitize" its secession from Judaism. It enabled Christians to claim that they were the true heirs of the patriarchs and prophets of ancient Israel. It enabled Christianity to "obliterate" Judaism in a theological sense. Judaism had made a deep impression on the world with its teaching of a pure monotheism, and an exalted standard of ethics. Now Christianity was able to concede the efficacy of Judaism, indeed to claim it for itself. The efficacy of Judaism, it was maintained, came to an end when the Jews rejected the gospel of Jesus, and all that it had ever meant to the world, in a refined and perfected form, was to be found in the Church.

The Judaism which continued to maintain a vibrant life after the secession of Christianity was simply ignored. This bias has lived to this day, and it may be discerned readily in the tendency of Christian historians and educators to terminate their considerations of Judaism after the first century. The story of the Jewish people in the intervening two thousand years between the birth of Christianity and the present is told but sparsely in theological seminaries, colleges, and universities, not to speak of high schools and church schools. Christianity was able to achieve all this by the dialectical resourcefulness of its "Midrash" on the Hebrew Bible.

The basic source where this Christian "Midrash" may be found are the Scriptures which comprise the New Testament. There are twenty-seven works in the New Testament, all originally written in Greek, most of them in the sixty years between 50 and 110 C.E. They are all related to the practical needs of the early Church: to give authoritative information about Jesus, to define its doctrine, to answer the views of its opponents, or to encourage the faithful who often faced persecution because of their Christian affiliation.

The order of books in the New Testament begins with the three synoptic Gospels—Matthew, Mark, and Luke. They are called synoptic because they cover the same material, often using the same words. It is possible to arrange the three Gospels in parallel columns to get at once a synopsis of their contents. Matthew and Luke drew on Mark as one of their primary sources. There is a fourth Gospel, John, but this differs radically from the other three in presentation as well as in conception. The fourth Gospel presents Jesus as a divine figure, and sets him in a doctrinal context that reflects another stage of Christian teaching. The authors of the Gospels were evangelists or missionaries and their writings were intended to help in the instruction of new converts. The Book of Acts tells of the work of the apostles of Jesus, principally that of Paul and Peter, and is presumed to have been composed by the same hand that wrote the Gospel According to Luke.

The Epistles of Paul follow. Fourteen Epistles have been ascribed to Paul, but New Testament scholars credit him only with ten, in the following order: Romans, I and II Corinthians,

Galatians, Ephesians, Philipians, Colossians, I and II Thessalonians, I and II Timothy, Titus, Philomen, and Hebrews. Modern New Testament scholarship has rejected the tradition that links Paul with the authorship of Hebrews. The identity of its author remains uncertain. There is doubt among scholars whether Paul wrote I and II Timothy and Titus (the so-called "pastoral Epistles"). But the latter three Epistles embody notes left by Paul and reflect his views. The Epistles of Paul attempt to guide various Christian communities in doctrinal, as well as practical, problems faced by the early churches. His views proved a decisive influence in molding the theology which became dominant in classical Christianity.

Five works included in the New Testament are usually grouped together under the designation of Catholic, or general, Epistles: James, Jude, I and II Peter, and I John. The last work is the Book of Revelation, whose author was John, though it is difficult to identify which John. Its purpose is to encourage the Christians to fortitude in resisting the cult of Caesar-worship which was being enforced in the reign of the Emperor Domitian, about the year 95 C.E.

These writings of varying lengths that make up the New Testament give us a composite of history and doctrine on which Christianity based its appeal to the world.

We shall cite a number of passages from the New Testament illustrating the use of the Hebrew Bible as a source of support for Christianity, and for the derogation of Judaism.

The most celebrated proof text for the truth of Christianity concerns the virgin birth of Jesus. The Gospel According to Matthew recounts how an angel announced to Joseph that his wife, Mary, still a virgin, was conceived "of the Holy Spirit" and he was to name the child she bore Jesus, "for he will save his people from their sins" (the Hebrew for "Jesus," *Yehoshua*, means "he will save"). All this took place to fulfill what the Lord had spoken by the prophet, "Behold, a virgin shall conceive and bear a son and his name shall be called Emmanuel," which means "God with us" (Matthew 1:18–23).

The prophet alluded to by Matthew is Isaiah, and the passage allegedly predictive of the virgin birth is Isaiah 7:14. As rendered in the King James and the Douay Versions of the Bible, both based on the translation of the Septuagint Greek, this verse reads: "Therefore the Lord Himself shall give you a sign; Behold, a virgin shall conceive, and bear a son, and shall call his name Immanuel."

This version of Isaiah's prophecy appears to be impressively confirmed by the circumstances of the birth of Jesus as described in Christian tradition. But the passage in the original Hebrew of Isaiah is quite different from what is presupposed in the King James (or Douay) Version. The Hebrew text does not have the word *betulah*, which means a "virgin." It has instead *ha-almah* which means "young woman," with no reference at all to her state of virginity. The Hebrew word moreover has the definite article prefixed to it, thus meaning "*the* young woman," a particular young woman, in other words, one presumably known to the prophet and his contemporaries.

The context makes it clear that Isaiah, who lived in the eighth century B.C.E. was addressing himself to his own time, and was not projecting a prophecy for over seven hundred years beyond it. The city of Jerusalem had been besieged by the armies of Syria and Ephraim, and Ahaz, king of Judah, feared that his capital would fall to the besiegers. The prophet Isaiah urged him to trust in God's deliverance, and he invited the king to ask a "sign" that might bolster his faith, but the king refused to ask. The prophet then offered an unasked sign. The text does not identify the young woman to whom the prophet referred, and we cannot be altogether sure how we are to interpret this sign. Commentators have suggested that she was either the wife of the prophet or of the king, or possibly some other young woman not related to the two. The sign consisted in the assurance that within a brief period the siege would be lifted and the child soon to be born would accordingly be given a name to celebrate God's deliverance of Jerusalem. It was common in that period to give children symbolic and didactic names. Here the term *Immanuel*, "God is with us," was to denote a triumphant vindication of God's presence as protector and savior. Another interpretation of that sign is that the woman, in giving her child a name proclaiming her faith in God's protection, was to serve as a token of faith for the king, that he might do likewise.

Modern Christian scholarship has admitted the difficulty of taking the passage in Isaiah as proof text for the belief in the virgin birth. In the words of H. H. Rowley: "The first Gospel says that the birth of Jesus was a fulfillment of the prophecy of Isaiah. Attention is commonly centered on the word 'virgin' in the verse quoted in the New Testament, and modern writers point out that Isaiah did not prophesy a Virgin Birth at all. The Hebrew word which he used simply means a mature young woman, whether she be a virgin or married. But more important than any philological study is the whole impact of Isaiah's prophecy. When King Ahaz was filled with terror through the attack of Ephraim and Syria, he assured him that they were not to be feared, and then gave him a sign from God, whereby he might know that his word was to be believed. If that sign was something which could only be tested in something over seven hundred years, it would have been quite futile for its purpose." [6]

The belief in virgin birth poses another difficulty for Christians. The New Testament (Matthew 1:2-16), as part of its confirmation of the messiahship of Jesus, claims his descent from King David. But the line of descent is traced through his father, Joseph. If Mary conceived Jesus "by the Holy Spirit" and while still a virgin, then Joseph was not really his father.

The belief that Jesus was conceived by impregnation from the deity is paralleled by similar claims in other religious mythologies. In ancient Egypt the priests proclaimed that Queen Hatshepset was the offspring of the god Amon and a mortal mother. One of the founders of Rome, Romulus, was also said to have been virgin born, being the child of a vestal priestess and the god Mars. Cyrus, Julius Caesar, Pythagoras, Plato, Zoroaster, as well as many others, were alleged to have had a similarly semi-divine birth. There is no precedent for such a claim in Judaism, but the pagan conception of the hero was widespread in Hellenistic culture, which was a decisive force in the development of Christian doctrine.

The Revised Standard Version of the Old Testament ignores the proof texts cited by Matthew and renders the passage in Isaiah more accurately: "Behold, a *young woman* shall conceive and

[6] Harold H. Rowley: *Rediscovery of the Old Testament* (Philadelphia: Westminister Press; 1945), p. 293.

bear a son. . . ." The Confraternity Version renders the word *ha-almah* as "the virgin," but the commentary questions it and notes that *almah* means "a young maiden" or "a young woman."

The homily of Matthew on the verification of the virgin birth through a text in the Hebrew Bible is characteristic of much of this type of Christian exposition. It proceeds by lifting Old Testament verses out of their original context, frequently ignoring the rules of philology and Hebrew syntax. But it gave to its listeners who were often raised on the Jewish Scriptures, a feeling of continuity with Judaism, and of a higher faithfulness to its precepts.

In another instance, Matthew relates a prophecy in Jeremiah to the tragedy of Herod's slaying the children in Bethlehem. According to the Gospel account, Herod had expected the wise men from the East who had come to worship the new-born babe Jesus to inform him precisely where the babe was to be found, so that he might slay him. But the wise men eluded Herod and in anger the king slew "all the male children in Bethlehem and in all that region who were two years old or under." The Gospel then adds: "Then was fulfilled what was spoken by the prophet Jeremiah, 'A voice was heard in Ramah, wailing and loud lamentation, Rachel weeping for her children; she refused to be consoled because they were no more' " (Matthew 2:16–18).

The passage in Jeremiah alluded to by Matthew is 31:14. The New Testament use of this prophecy, too, represents a radical distortion of a text in order to bolster the beliefs of the Christian faithful. The prophet Jeremiah (who lived some six hundred years before the birth of Jesus) dealt in the section of the chapter from which this verse is quoted with the fate of the kingdom of Israel, which had been destroyed by the Assyrians in 722 B.C.E. and her people banished into exile. The road of the exiles, according to tradition, passed near the grave of Mother Rachel. In the verse under discussion the prophet envisions Rachel—who had given birth to Joseph and Benjamin, the tribes which had formed the nucleus of the kingdom of Israel—as watching her children cruelly marched to exile and degradation, weeping and interceding for them. The prophet in the continuation of his vision sees Rachel's intercession as efficacious and he projects a promise of their return. The second part of the vision given in verses sixteen and seventeen is as follows: "Thus says the Lord: 'Keep your voice from weeping and your eyes from tears; for your work shall be rewarded, says the Lord, and they shall come back from the land of the enemy. There is hope for your future, says the Lord, and your children shall come back to their own country.' "

A case of outright misquotation is offered us in the homily (which is repeated in each of the Gospels) concerning the ministry of John the Baptist, whom Christians regarded as the forerunner of Jesus. Jewish tradition had pictured the messiah as preceded by a prophet, usually identified as Elijah. It was important for Christians, in establishing the messiahship of Jesus, to point to a prophetic forerunner, and they found him in John.

We quote the opening lines of the Gospel According to Mark: "The beginning of the Gospel of Jesus Christ, the Son of God. As it is written in Isaiah the prophet, 'Behold, I send my messenger before thy face, which shall prepare thy way; the voice of one crying in the wilderness: Prepare ye the way of the Lord, make his paths straight.' John the baptizer appeared in the wilderness, preaching a baptism of repentance for the forgiveness of sins. . . . Now John was clothed with camel's hair, and had a leather girdle around his waist; and he ate locusts and wild honey. And he preached, saying, 'After me comes one who is mightier than I . . . I have baptized you with water; but he will baptize you with the Holy Spirit' " (Mark 1:1–8). In this opening passage, Mark was obviously concerned with confirming the credentials of Jesus as the messiah. He sought to accomplish this by showing that Jesus was preceded by a forerunner who made his appearance in the wilderness, exactly as had been foretold by the prophets. The description of the clothing worn by the forerunner corresponds to the clothing worn by the prophet Elijah as described in II Kings 1:8, thus suggesting that this forerunner was truly Elijah returned to earth, a further fulfillment of ancient prophecy.

The first and second passages, as quoted by Mark, diverge from the original Hebrew. The first part is based on Malachi 3:1, rather than Isaiah, but the original reads thus: "Behold I will send my messenger and he shall prepare the way before me. . . ." In

Malachi the messenger was to prepare the way for God and not for the messiah.

The second part is based on Isaiah 40:3. It appears in the original Hebrew as: "A voice cries, 'In the wilderness prepare the way of the Lord, make straight in the desert a path for our God.' " The correspondence between John's ministry "in the wilderness," and the voice calling "in the wilderness" is therefore absent in the original text. Mark probably quoted from the Septuagint translation, which deviates from the punctuation of the original and has the wilderness as the setting for the voice that cries. But the critical issue is the meaning of the term "Lord" in the opening half of the verse, for whom "the way" is to be prepared. The original Hebrew, as well as the Septuagint translation, make it clear that "Lord" is here used as a synonym for God, since the second half of the verse calls specifically to make straight "the paths of God." Mark changed the Isaiah passage in the second half of the verse to read "his paths" rather than "paths of God." This subtle change enabled him to apply the term "Lord" to Jesus. In the Isaiah passage, the original as well as the Septuagint translation, exactly as in the Malachi passage, the forerunner was to prepare the way *for God*, not the *messiah*. In the words of D. E. Nineham: "In the Old Testament it was God himself for whom the forerunner was to prepare, and certain small changes have been introduced into the texts to make the quotations refer to Christ" [7] (Mark 1:2–3). Even small changes in a text are inadmissible when it is through these changes that the text is given a meaning which diverges from the original. Mark's quotation from Isaiah is repeated by Matthew 3:1–4, Luke 3:4, and John 1:23, but they omitted the verse from the prophet Malachi.

The critical passage cited by Mark are the verses from Isaiah. The context makes it clear that Isaiah addressed his remarks to the exiled Judeans who languished in Babylonia as exiles, following the destruction of Judah in 586 B.C.E. In this chapter he prophesies a forthcoming return, and poetically asks that the wilderness turn into a highway on which the redeemed Judeans would march on

[7] D. E. Nineham: *The Gospel of St. Mark* (Baltimore: Penguin Books; 1963), p. 60.

the way to their renewal and restoration. The passage quoted in the Gospels is preceded in the original with the following: "Comfort, comfort my people, says your God, speak tenderly to Jerusalem and cry to her that her warfare is ended, that her iniquity is pardoned, that she has received from the Lord's hand double for all her sins."

The verses from Malachi carry a similar message of reassurance to the people of his time, that God would soon intervene to execute justice upon His world.

Christian documents were not immune to textual tampering in the interests of doctrinal confirmation. Matthew tampered with his New Testament sources in order to effect a clearer correspondence between "Old Testament prophecies" and incidents in the life of Jesus. Thus, in the description of the events preceding the crucifixion, the Gospel of Mark, which served as one of the sources for Matthew's own work, reads "they offered him wine mingled with *myrrh*" (Mark 15:23). Matthew changed "myrrh" to "gall" (27:34). According to J. C. Fenton, in his commentary on Matthew, this is clearly an allusion to Psalms 69:22 (in the Septuagint version), where a pious man cries out against his persecutors saying, "They put gall into my food; and in my thirst they gave me vinegar to drink." Matthew took this psalm as referring to Jesus, and he modified the account he found in Mark to correspond more fully to the description in the psalm.

Professor Nineham has suggested that many stories about Jesus may indeed have been contrived as inferences from Old Testament prophecies: "Since the Old Testament was regarded as completely accurate down to the last detail, it followed that everything it predicted concerning this final event must have found fulfillment at some point in Christ's ministry. . . . There are passages in Mark where it is impossible to be certain whether a particular story rests on a tradition derived from witnesses or whether it represents a deduction from Old Testament prophecy about what must have happened when the messiah came." [8]

The Book of Psalms was another source from which Christian teachers often drew texts prophesying the appearance of Jesus. The psalmist writes in varying moods. Sometimes he strikes

[8] Ibid., p. 21.

a triumphant note, writing of his favorite hero, the king who reigns under God's special providence, whose victories are divinely ordained, and whose enemies are sure to fail as their schemes run counter to the divine order. Such psalms lend themselves readily for appropriation into Christian prophecies. The one telling objection to such appropriations is of course the divergence in time, that the psalmist lived many centuries before the Christian epoch, but Christian commentators had allowed themselves to ignore the boundary of the centuries, and they had no hesitation in putting references to later events on the lips of earlier historical figures.

Psalm 2 is a good illustration of this process. We cite the full text of this psalm (Revised Standard Version): "Why do the nations conspire, and the peoples plot in vain? The kings of the earth set themselves, and the rulers take counsel together, against the Lord and his anointed, saying, 'Let us burst their bands asunder, and cast their cords from us.' He who sits in the heavens laughs; the Lord has them in derision. Then he will speak to them in his wrath, and terrify them in his fury, saying, 'I have set my king on Zion, my holy hill.' I will tell of the decree of the Lord: He said to me, 'You are my *son*, today I have begotten you. Ask of me, and I will make the nations your heritage; and the ends of the earth your possession. You will break them with a rod of iron, and dash them in pieces like a potter's vessel.' Now, therefore, O kings, be wise; be warned, O rulers of the earth. Serve the Lord with fear, with trembling *kiss his feet* [italics mine], lest he be angry and you perish in the way; for his wrath is quickly kindled. Blessed are all who take refuge in him."

The Book of Acts (4:25–29, 13:33) sees in this psalm a prophecy of Jesus. He is "the anointed one" against whom the nations rage in vain; he is God's begotten son, destined to rule the world. Guided by this interpretation, translations of the Psalms under Christian auspices read the identification with Jesus into the text of the psalm. We have italicized the critical words which are tendentiously translated to strengthen the claimed allusion to Jesus. The King James Version of Psalms (American Bible Society edition) introduces this psalm with the following superscription: "The kingdom of Christ; kings exhorted to accept it." It capitalizes the words "anointed" and "son" clearly to suggest that these allude to a divine being—Jesus, in other words. The phrase "kiss his feet" is a rendition of the Hebrew *nashku var*, which is uncertain in meaning, but the term *var* appears in Aramaic where it means "son." Ignoring the fact that the psalm is written in Hebrew, the King James translators seized on the Aramaic meaning of *var* and translated this phrase as "kiss the Son," again an allusion to Jesus.

The Douay translation of the Bible is even more pointed in identifying this psalm as a prophecy of Jesus. The superscription to this psalm reads: "The vain efforts of persecutors against Christ and his church." The opening two sentences of the psalm in this translation read thus: "Why have the Gentiles raged, and the people devised vain things? The kings of the earth stood up, and the princes met together, against the Lord, and against his Christ." The term "Gentiles" suggests a religious category, reinforced by the use of the term "his Christ." The original Hebrew has the term *meshiho*, literally "his anointed," which may refer to any leader whose installation in office was marked by a ceremony of anointment. A secular ruler was elevated to the throne by such a ceremony and the term is often used in the Hebrew Bible to refer to a king. *Christ* is of course the Greek term for "anointed" but its usage has been given a more specialized meaning, limiting it to Jesus.

The identification of the hero of this psalm with Jesus naturally invited the identification of his enemies with the Jews (Acts 2:28), and threats proclaimed against his enemies suggested themselves as a prophecy of the retribution which was to be visited on the Jews for having resisted Jesus. After the destruction of Jewish autonomy and the dispersion of the Jews by the Roman conquerors, this psalm was cited as a prophecy that had actually been fulfilled in history and thus a "proof" of Christianity. Christian commentators often elaborated on this. Thomas Scott, whose commentary was popular in the last century, wrote in part as follows: "After a time, the Roman legions, the executioners of divine vengeance, surrounded Jerusalem, and at length destroyed the city and temple, and subverted both their civil and ecclesiastical state, with the most dreadful miseries and destruction of the devoted Jews; the wretched remains of whom to this day, scattered throughout the nations, unwittingly attest the fulfillment of this ancient prophecy."[9]

William R Taylor, principal and professor of Semitics, University College, University of Toronto, in his commentary on Psalms in *The Interpreter's Bible*, notes the interpretation of this psalm as a prophecy of Jesus, but dismisses it as untenable: "The fact is that the messianic interpretation cannot be sustained. The New Testament quotations are in this respect not decisive, since the Old Testament passages used by New Testament writers with a messianic connotation are frequently selected without regard to the original context (cf. Mark 1:2–3). The character of the rule to be initiated by the king (vss. 9–11) scarcely comports with the messianic ideal. In the psalm the king is confronted with a disaffection of states that have already been subjected to him. That the messiah's rule, once established, should be threatened by revolt is a situation outside messianic thought (cf. Rev. 11:15)." Professor Taylor takes this psalm as "an oracle or a poem written to express confidence of, or to give confidence to, one of the royal line at the time of his accession or on an anniversary of his enthronement (vss. 6–7)."[1]

The more recent commentary in the *Oxford Annotated Bible* by Robert C. Dentan of the General Theological Seminary (Episcopal) interprets this psalm similarly. He gives the following as a general characterization of the psalm: "The Lord gives universal dominion to his king (a royal psalm, composed for a coronation)."[2] The issue to which the psalm addresses itself is a rebellion: "Israel's subject peoples plot against the new king." He takes the term *anointed* as "one of the titles of an Israelite king."

The Confraternity Version, of this psalm has also ignored the Christological interpretation, but the editor's superscription nevertheless characterizes it as messianic: "The universal reign of the Messiah." Rev. Joseph Grispino's commentary notes the repu-

[9] *Scott's Bible* (Boston: Samuel T. Armstrong; 1830), III, 119.

[1] William R. Taylor: Commentary on Psalms in *The Interpreter's Bible*, 12 vols. (Nashville, Tenn.: Abingdon Press; 1956), IV, 23.

[2] *Oxford Annotated Bible* (New York: Oxford University Press; 1962), p. 657.

diation of the Christological interpretation by modern biblical scholarship: "Many moderns hold that this psalm does not predict that a divine Messia called Christ will come hundreds of years later and rule over a spiritual kingdom forever, but that the psalm speaks of a historical king, a successor of David, before the sixth century exile. In this modern view the psalm was most likely written to celebrate his accession to the throne of David." The commentary follows this interpretation of modern scholarship.

Robert C. Dentan's commentary on Psalms in the *Oxford Annotated Bible* interprets *you are my son* in Psalm 2 as "a formula of adoption whereby the king became God's son." There is no need, however, to invoke the formality of an adoption rite to account for the phrase *you are my son*. This is not an uncommon epithet in the Bible to characterize its heroes. Thus we have in Exodus 4:22: "Thus saith the Lord: Israel is My son, My first born." In II Samuel 7:14 David is assured that his son Solomon who would succeed him as king would be looked upon as God's son: "I will be to him a Father, and he shall be to Me for a son." The Rabbis discussed the sense in which a mortal may be called God's son. They held the phrase to be purely metaphoric and intended to convey a sense of endearment. The assertion of God's fatherhood, which is a metaphor for His creatorship, carries with it as a correlative metaphor the characterization of His creatures as His children (Midrash Tehillim, ed. Buber, Abraham ibn Ezra and Rashi on Psalms 2:7). The Targum reads this interpretation into the Aramaic translation of this verse: "You are as dear to me as a son to his father." The concept became a problem for Christian theology because it was applied to Jesus in a literal rather than a metaphoric sense.

On the Hebrew phrase *nashku var* translated in the Confraternity Version as "pay homage," the Reverend Grispino notes: "The poet urges his people to pay 'homage' (v. 12), which literally means in Hebrew 'kiss his feet.' In the Orient this is the highest mark of respect from subjects to their kings, for it is a sign of subjection." It was the translation of this phrase as "kiss the Son," which was to give this psalm its most cogent allusion to Jesus.

Sometimes the psalmist is inspired by a different mood. He writes as a humble man, unswervingly loyal to his God, but beset by the hostility of the wicked who conspire to destroy him, and he sings of his faith in God's deliverance. This mood of the psalmist is often paralled in the experiences of other men. It is this parallelism which has made the Psalms the great treasury of faith for all mankind. They express the universal pathos of life, its struggles, its trials and frustrations, and the miracle of renewal after defeat and failure. All men can identify with the mood of the psalmist and voice their feelings through his words. This parallelism is also often reflected in the career of Jesus as well. New Testament writers, seizing on these parallels, insisted that the original was in truth a "prophecy," that it referred not to the historical person who is clearly the subject of the text, but to Jesus and Jesus alone.

The Christological interpretation of Psalm 16:8–10 is a good illustration of numerous biblical texts which were emptied of their original sense and turned into prophecies concerning Jesus.

As quoted in Acts 2:25–28 these verses read: "I saw the Lord always before me, for he is at my right hand that I may not be shaken; therefore, my heart was glad, and my tongue rejoiced; moreover, my flesh will dwell in hope. For thou wilt not abandon my soul to Hades, nor let thy Holy One see corruption."

The author of Acts interpreted these verses as a prophecy of the resurrection of Jesus. In support of this interpretation we are given the following argumentation: "Brethren, I may say to you confidently of the patriarch David that he hath died and was buried, and his tomb is with us to this day. Being, therefore, a prophet, and knowing that God had sworn with an oath to him that he would set one of his descendants upon his throne, he foresaw and spoke of the resurrection of the Christ, that he was not abandoned to Hades, nor did his flesh see corruption" (Acts 2:29–31).

The author of Acts argues that David could not have written this psalm about himself, because he was mortal, and he died and was buried. This psalm, which speaks of escape from "Hades" and "corruption" and which affirms seeing "the Lord always before me," must, the author continues to argue, therefore have another as its subject, and he finds its characterization satisfied in Jesus, who was resurrected after his death on the cross. Supporting this interpretation is the phrase "thy Holy One" in the last line. The Hebrew original of this phrase is *hasidka,* which means "one who is faithful," or "one who is zealous." The Revised Standard Version of the Book of Psalms (and similarly the Jewish Publication Society version) translates this phrase as *thy godly one*. The Confraternity edition renders it "your faithful one."

A careful study of this psalm makes it clear that its theme is not immortality or resurrection after death. It is rather the deliverance from premature death, due to perils which the author knows might otherwise have destroyed him. And he sings in gratitude to God whom he credits with his deliverance.

This meaning emerges more clearly when we read the same lines in their original source, in the Book of Psalms, in the same Revised Standard Version of the Bible: "I keep the Lord always before me; because he is at my right hand, I shall not be moved. Therefore, my heart is glad, and my soul rejoices; my body also dwells secure. For thou dost not give me up to Sheol, or let thy godly one see the Pit."

This meaning is even more explicit in the Confraternity Version: "I set the Lord ever before me; with Him at my right hand I shall not be disturbed. Therefore, my heart is glad and my soul rejoices, my body, too, abides in confidence; because you will not abandon my soul to the nether world, nor will you suffer your faithful one to undergo corruption."

William R. Taylor, commenting on this psalm in *The Interpreter's Bible*, makes it very clear that the New Testament interpretation misreads the clear intention of the psalmist. As Professor Taylor succinctly puts it: "The Psalmist fills out the alloted span of years, shielded from wasting sickness and sudden death. . . . There is no reference to a resurrection after death. . . . *Thy Godly One* is the Psalmist himself." Robert C. Dentan, in his commentary in the *Oxford Annotated Bible*, offers us a similar interpretation: "*Godly one* means devout adherent." The theme of the psalm is not the hope for resurrection; it is rather the psalmist's confidence "that God will not permit him to perish," that "he will survive his ordeal and through God's help enjoy life's pleasures again."

Once again we find modern Christian Bible scholarship, in

translation as well as commentary, repudiating the reading of a psalm as a prophecy of Jesus. The interpretation adopted reaches out for authenticity, for faithfulness to the original text, and eliminates sectarian considerations from the study of Scripture.

We quote another passage from Acts (3:19–24): "Repent, therefore, and turn again, that your sins may be blotted out, that times of refreshing may come from the presence of the Lord, and that he may send the Christ appointed for you, Jesus, whom heaven must receive until the time for establishing all that God spoke by the mouth of his holy prophets from of old. Moses said, 'The Lord God will raise up for you a prophet from your brethren as he raised me up. You shall listen to him in whatever he tells you. And it shall be that every soul that does not listen to that prophet shall be destroyed from the people.' And all the prophets who have spoken, from Samuel and those who came afterward, also proclaimed these days." In this passage Moses is made to prophecy the coming of Jesus!

The verses quoted in the name of Moses appear in Deuteronomy 18:9–10, 15–16. A simple examination of the context indicates clearly that the application of this prophecy to Jesus represents a gross misinterpretation. The passage deals with the problems which were due to face the Israelites after entering Canaan.

When God attempted to communicate His will to them directly, as He did at Mount Sinai, the Israelites found the experience awesome. After the divine voice had completed the Ten Commandments, they asked that it cease, and that Moses speak to them instead (Exodus 20:15–16). But with Moses gone, who would speak to them? There was the danger that they might follow the ancient pagan practice of resorting to divination and magic. Moses therefore assured them that God would provide for them other prophets to continue his unfinished ministry.

All this is made abundantly clear by reading the original passage: "When you come into the land which the Lord your God gives you, you shall not learn to follow the abominable practices of the nations. There shall not be found among you anyone who burns his son or his daughter as an offering, anyone who practices divination, a soothsayer, or an augur, or a sorcerer, or a charmer, or a medium, or a wizard or a necromancer. The Lord your God will raise up for you a prophet like me from among you, from your brethren—him shall you heed—just as you desired of the Lord your God at Horeb, on the day of the assembly, when you said, 'Let me not hear again the voice of the Lord my God, or see this great fire any more, lest I die.' And the Lord said to me, 'They have rightly said all that they have spoken. I will raise up for them a prophet like you from among their brethren; and I will put my words in his mouth, and he shall speak to them all that I command him.' "

The inadmissibility of the interpretation in the Book of Acts is acknowledged by Rev. Samuel R. Driver, Regius Professor of Hebrew and Canon of Christ Church, Oxford, in his commentary on the Book of Deuteronomy: "The exclusively Messianic reference of v. 15–18, adopted by many of the older commentators (cf. Acts 3:22 f, 7:37) is inconsistent with the context; and has been deservedly abandoned by the great majority of modern commentators and theologians. . . . The promised prophet is to meet a *continuous* and *permanent* need of the people after they are settled in Canaan (v. 9): he is to supersede the necessity either of God's addressing Israel directly Himself (v. 16–18), or of Israel having recourse, like their neighbours, to the acts of divination (v. 14 f). The argument of the passage shows that the 'prophet' contemplated is not a single individual, belonging to a distant future, but *Moses' representative for the time being*, whose office it would be to supply Israel, whenever in its history occasion should arise, with needful guidance and advice; in other words, that the reference is not to an individual prophet but to a prophetical *order*. . . ." [3]

The refusal of the Jews to accept the Christian Gospel was a source of embarrassment to Christian apologists, who made use of the type of scriptural interpretation which had long been familiar in Judaism to bolster their adherence to the new faith. Paul, especially, was a master of this type of scriptural dialectics, and his writings abound in proof texts of Christian doctrine, most of them farfetched when examined in the light of the Hebrew original.

[3] Samuel R. Driver: *A Critical and Exegetical Commentary on Deuteronomy* (Edinburgh: T. & T. Clark; 1902), pp. 228 ff.

In one instance Paul contrasted the Christian use of "great plainness of speech" with the method of Moses, "which put a veil over his face, that the children of Israel could not steadfastly look to the end of that which is abolished. But their minds were blinded; for until this day remaineth the same veil untaken away in the reading of the Old Testament, which veil is done away in Christ. But even unto this day, when Moses is read, the veil is upon their heart" (II Corinthians 3:12–15, King James Version).

Paul does not quote the full passage from the Hebrew Bible which recounts how Moses put a veil on his face. The passage appears in Exodus 34:29–35. It tells of a divine effulgence which became visible on the skin of Moses. After coming down from Mount Sinai his face became radiant, and the people were awe-struck and feared to come near him. When Moses discovered this, he put a veil on his face to blunt the light. The King James Version of the Bible translates these crucial verses in Exodus (34:33–34) to conform to Paul's homily in II Corinthians: "And till Moses had done speaking with them, he put a vail on his face. But when Moses went in before the Lord to speak with him, he took the vail off, until he came out."

Paul's homily turned the action of Moses into a metaphor. The veil Moses put on his face is turned by Paul into a metaphoric statement that Moses had concealed his teachings from the people. The Jewish people were incapable of apprehending the full truth of the teachings conveyed to them. The full truth taught in the Old Testament consisted for Paul in the Christian allusions, in the prophecies centering in the birth, the ministry, and the passion of Jesus. The veil obscuring these truths is removed only for one who has embraced the Christian dispensation.

It is in the nature of language to permit the conversion of a literal fact into a metaphor conveying a more general but analogous truth, but the use of a literal fact in metaphoric terms conveys no cogency. The cogency must rest on the intrinsic elements in the new situation itself. Thus the fact that Moses put a veil on his face to hide his radiance does not really establish that he deliberately concealed an aspect of the truth from his teachings, and that the truths so concealed involved Jesus who was to be born over a thousand years later!

The homily of Paul is, however, implausible for another and more basic reason. *The Hebrew text does not say that Moses veiled his face while speaking to the people. It says, on the contrary, that whenever he addressed the people, whenever he performed the act of teaching them or admonishing them, he removed the veil!* The veil was on only when he was not engaged in official acts. Once again we find the Revised Standard Version (and similarly the Confraternity Version) ignoring the claims of Christian apologetics. Here is the rendition of the same verse in the Revised Standard Version (Exodus 34:33): "And when Moses had finished speaking with them, he put a veil on his face." The Confraternity Version reads: "When he finished speaking with them, he put a veil over his face."

It is noteworthy that this farfetched interpretation of Paul was used in later centuries as evidence of the depraved nature of the Jewish people, an assertion that entered the mainstream of anti-Semitic disparagements of Jews and Judaism. Here is a comment by one Christian commentator on the passage in Paul, and it indicates the stimulus given to anti-Jewish pronouncements: "The glory of Moses' face is anti-typically Christ's glory shining behind the veil of legal ordinances. The veil which has been taken off to the believer is left on to the unbelieving Jew. . . . He stops short at the letter of the law, not seeing the end of it. The evangelical glory of the law, like the shining of Moses' face, cannot be borne by a carnal people. . . ."[4] A dubious interpretation of a passage in the Hebrew Bible, sustained only by the necessities of sectarian apologetics, has here been turned into evidence that the Jews are a carnal people!

Paul's notion that the Jews refused to follow Jesus because a veil is on their hearts which blinded them to the truth became part of the Christian stereotype of the Jew. In the Middle Ages when the Pope was also the secular ruler of Rome, it was customary for the Jewish community of Rome to participate in his coronation ceremonies. Their delegation, headed by the Chief Rabbi, bearing a Torah scroll, extended greetings to him and offered him acclaim as their sovereign, while asking that he confirm them in

[4] A. R. Fausset: *A Commentary on the Old and New Testament* (New York: S. S. Scranton and Company; 1874), II, 305.

their right to worship in accordance with their own faith. The Pope's response was part of the ritual of the occasion. We have a record of the coronation ceremonies of Pope Innocent II, which took place in 1130. The Pope made a gesture of respect for the Torah and he offered a prayer: "May Almighty God remove the veil from your hearts." Msgr. Franz Wasner, who describes the incident in the Catholic missionary volume *The Bridge*, calls this prayer "tender and merciful." [5] A similar ceremony is reported on the coronation of Pope Boniface VIII in 1295. Cardinal Gaetano Stefanescki described the incident in verse:

> See the Pope, mounted on a horse
> Crossing the Tiber on the Marble Bridge!
> Leaving behind the Tower of the Field,
> He is met by the Jews, singing, but blind of heart,
> To him, the Prince, right here in Parione,
> Moses' Law is shown, pregnant with Christ.
> Him he adored, in this Law prefigured; over
> the shoulder
> He then returned the scroll with measured words.[6]

Monsignor Wasner interprets the ceremony is his own words: "To the pope as to the Church, the Torah is a woman with child, and that child is the Christ. He is hidden in it, enveloped in its words and deeds. It is this center the Church venerates, worships and adores. Without it, the Torah would be like a frame that holds no canvas. The painting is there, but Israel, blinded by the beauty of the frame, does not see the greater beauty that it serves." [7]

This homily of Paul inspired the Roman Catholic prayer for the conversion of Jews, recited on Good Friday, as may be noted from its opening lines: "Let us also pray for the Jews: that our God and Lord would withdraw the veil from their hearts: that they also may acknowledge our Lord Jesus Christ. . . ." Paul's offending verbiage has been deleted from a new version of this

[5] Franz Wasner: *The Bridge*, John M. Oesterreicher (ed.) (New York: Pantheon Books; 1961), IV, 278.

[6] Ibid., p. 281.

[7] Ibid., pp. 281–2.

prayer recently announced by Pope Paul VI, as we have noted earlier.

The characterization of the Jews as "blind" because they insisted that the Hebrew Bible did *not* teach Christian truths is often invoked by Christian writers. It became a popular theme in medieval art. The Synagogue was depicted as a woman with her eyes veiled, her scepter broken, her crown removed, confronting the Church represented as a clear-eyed maiden, zestful and triumphant, with the crown of victory on her head. One can still see this contrasting symbolism on doors and stained-glass windows of Europe's great cathedrals.

A mural by the painter Sargent in the Boston Public Library embodies in two of its panels the same conception of Judaism and Christianity. One panel depicts the Synagogue as "a gray-haired woman of massive frame, seated in the attitude of despair upon the worn and broken step of a temple, above a mosaic pavement; her eyes are blindfolded, the crown is falling from her head, her powerful arms clutch to her breast a broken sceptre and the Tables of the Law . . . The picture presents the loss of vision, which was the medieval view of the fate of the Jewish religion." The other panel, representing the Church, shows sitting on a great throne "a powerful female figure, stiff, solid, statuesque, with mystic gaze fixed on space. . . ." Various Christian symbols are depicted in association with this figure. This panel also expresses the claim that the foundations of Christianity are in Judaism: "On the side of the throne, typifying the foundation of the Christian faith upon Hebrew prophecy, are inscribed the names of Isaiah, Jeremiah, David, and Ezekiel. . . ." [8] Sargent's interpretation is medieval only in its artistic conception. Its ideological motif goes back to the teaching of Paul in the New Testament.

The method of allegory was particularly suitable to the freedom of interpretation necessitated by the conversion of the Old Testament into a handbook of Christian allusions. Paul was a master in this art, and his writings include many allegorical interpre-

[8] *The Boston Public Library; A Handbook of the Library Building, Its Mural Decorations and Collections*, 6th edn., Frank H. Chase (rev.) (Boston: Boston Organization Publications; 1927), pp. 55–8.

tations of the Old Testament, turning the Hebrew Bible into a weapon against the Jews and Judaism.

In his Epistle to the Galatians (21–31, King James Version) Paul has the following homily: "Tell me, ye who desire to be under the law, do ye not hear the law? For it is written that Abraham had two sons, the one by a bondmaid, the other by a free woman. But he who was of the bondmaid was born after the flesh; but he of the free woman was by promise. Which things are an allegory: for these are two covenants; the one from Mount Sinai, which gendereth to bondage, which is Agar. . . . Now we brethren, as Isaac was, are the children of promise. . . . Nevertheless, what saith the Scripture? 'Cast out the bondwoman and her son' [Genesis 29:10]. . . . So then, brethren, we are not children of the bondwoman, but of the free."

Biblical history, as read in the pages of Genesis, traces the Jewish people from Abraham to Isaac and then to Jacob. A process of selection is alleged in the Bible to have occurred at every step. Abraham had a brother, Nahor, but only Abraham was chosen; Isaac had a half brother, Ishmael, but only Isaac was chosen; Jacob had a twin brother, Esau, but Jacob became the father of the Jewish people. Paul ignores the context, defeating the very point of the biblical portrayal. It was Paul's pet dogma that the law was an enslavement, and he called on Christians to shed the law, and find salvation by faith in the messiahship and divinity of Jesus. By a process of verbal equation, the law of Sinai is therefore associated with Ishmael, who was the son of a bondwoman, while Christians are now declared to be the truly chosen, the followers of the son of freedom, Isaac.

Allegories always pose problems if taken seriously. They permit the "establishment" of equivalents where there is no equivalence except for extraneous factors. Philo resorted to allegory in order to read Greek philosophical doctrines into texts from the Hebrew Bible, but he did not sacrifice the *peshat*, the literal meaning, altogether, and he remained faithful to the religious practices of Judaism. The Rabbis, too, sometimes allowed themselves to play with figurative and allegorical interpretations, but they made sure that the original meaning of a verse was respected. The extravagant use of allegory by Christian interpreters defeated the *peshat*, the original meaning altogether, and the text was transvaluated to teach Christianity and to defame Judaism.

The Philonic and rabbinic allegories were never invested with doctrinal importance. They belonged to the realm of the *haggadah*, which carried no binding authority for the conscience of the Jew. They expressed a personal predilection. They reflected the individual imagination and literary taste of the author whose views entered the tradition as literature, but not as authoritative doctrine. Those views were often quoted by contemporaries or later authorities on the basis of their intrinsic appeal, but they remained the respected views of individuals, which were entitled to enter the free market of ideas, to compete with other ideas that circulated in their midst.

Paul's allegories were invested with doctrinal importance, and were made the basis by which Christians assessed themselves and their relationship to their ideological adversaries. The allegory we have quoted fostered the Christian self-assurance that they were truly God's chosen, while the Jewish people and their faith represented an inferior community clinging to an unspiritual and obsolete faith.

Paul did not shrink from carrying his allegory to its fateful climax. "What saith the Scripture? 'Cast out the bondwoman and her son,' " implying that the fate of the Jewish people was to be rejection and banishment. These allegories were futher elaborated on in the Christian commentaries and in Christian preachments, and they helped create an image of the Jew as a sinister figure, subhuman, unspiritual, rejected by God and therefore unworthy of tolerance by men. The Reverend Fausset, whose commentary on the New Testament we have quoted previously, explains the contrast between Isaac as the Christian and Ishmael as the Jew thus: "The language [of Genesis] though referring primarily to Isaac, born in a spiritual way . . . is so framed as especially to refer to believers justified by Gospel grace through faith, as opposed to carnal men, Judaizers, and legalists." [9] In defining the reference to "cast out," the same commentator explains that it is

[9] Fausset: *A Commentary on the Old and New Testament*, II, 305.

directed literally to Ishmael but "spiritually" to the "carnal and legalists."

The dangers inherent in the allegorizing of Scripture was well stated by Professor J. Philip Hyatt: "In skillful and careful hands allegorical interpretation may have some validity, but it should generally be avoided. Its great danger is that it usually has no objective controls, and becomes completely subjective. Once you start with the assumption that a given passage does not mean what it says, but rather 'something else,' you open the cover on a Pandora's box of wild imaginings and bizarre interpretations." [1]

The dialectic by which Christian exegetes interpreted the Hebrew Bible in order to harmonize its teachings with Christian dogma included another method, that of "typology." Events in the two "convenants" were arranged in an order, with those in the Hebrew Bible assumed to be lower and those in the corresponding Christian experience assumed to be higher. The lower was then alleged to be a "type" of the higher, its foreshadowing and its anticipation. Both were thus included in the one design of God, with the Jewish covenant as a stage, a preparation that is finally culminated in the Christian. Thus Paul declares Adam as "a type of the one who was to come" (Romans 5:14). In the words of one Catholic writer: "In its biblical sense a type is a person, thing, action, or event in the Old Testament which the Holy Ghost presents as a foreshadowing of the future. Thus Adam (Romans V, 14), Malchisidek (as priest) [Melchizedek, King of Salem and priest of 'God the Most High,' mentioned in Genesis 14:18 and Psalms 110:4], Jonas (resurrected from the monster) are types of Jesus Christ, the antitype; Jerusalem or Zion is a type of the Heavenly City; the flood of Baptism; the paschal lamb, of the sacrifice of Calvary. There are many other spiritual types, the lower being the figure of the higher, e.g., human marriage is a type of union of Christ with his Church or with the individual soul." [2]

The typological interpretation of the Old Testament was re-

[1] J. Philip Hyatt: *The Heritage of Biblical Faith* (St. Louis: Bethany Press; 1964), pp. 32 ff.

[2] Donald Attwater (ed.): entry on "Type," *A Catholic Dictionary* (New York: The Macmillan Company; 1957).

affirmed by Vatican II. Its statement on the Old Testament expressed it thus: "The principal purpose to which the plan of the Old Covenant was directed was to prepare for the coming both of Christ, the universal Redeemer, and of the messianic kingdom, to announce the coming by prophecy (cf. Lk. 24:44, Jn. 5:39, 1 Peter 1:10), and to indicate its meaning through various types (cf. I Cor. 10:11). . . . God, the inspirer and author of both testaments, wisely arranged that the New Testament be hidden in the Old and the Old be made manifest in the New. . . . The books of the Old Testament with all their parts, caught up into the proclamation of the gospel, acquire and show forth their full meaning in the New Testament and in turn shed light on it and explain it."[3]

The alleged relationship between the two Testaments is of course an assumption. It rests on an act of faith, that act of faith which has led Christianity to seek its legitimacy in Judaism. The typological interpretation yields certain homiletical benefits. It is edifying for the faithful to see an article of their belief reach back into antiquity, to find its place in the design of God Himself. The Rabbis occasionally used this method, as when they saw in the exodus from Egypt a prelude to the final liberation which will witness the end of every oppression of man by man and nation by nation. Such interpretations for the Rabbis carried no doctrinal authority. They were offered for purposes of inspiration and edification. Because Christians assumed that Jesus marked the dawn of the messianic age, ignoring the persistence of the tyranny and violence that have continued to make our world into a vale of tears, they felt constrained to claim that it was precisely the appearance of Jesus which was foreshadowed by the Egyptian exodus. Such claims helped to reconcile the dogmas of the Church with the plan of human destiny as portrayed in the Hebrew Bible.

The linking of two events as types by virtue of some elements they appear to have in common remains, however, a piece of homiletics. It can establish nothing that is not contained in the act of faith which is antecedent to it. A Muslim could, for exam-

[3] Walter M. Abbott (ed.): *The Documents of Vatican II* (New York: Guild Press; 1966), p. 122.

ple, structure the ancient Temple in Jerusalem, the synagogue of later Judaism, and the Church of Christianity, as foreshadowings and anticipations of the ultimate, the mosque. He could place Moses, Jesus, and Muhammad in the same justaposition, claiming finality for the founder of Islam. Christian exegetes drew on the typological interpretation to claim that Judaism had been superseded by Christianity. This is the underlying basis of the claim reiterated so often by Paul, that Judaism, having performed its preparatory role, was now dead, and that Christianity had inherited it. As one Christian teacher put it: "The Synagogue was only a sign (figure) of the Church, and the latter is now the one true chosen people of God. The Church, which was founded by Jesus Christ, has become the successor of the Synagogue." [4]

We have cited illustrative passages from the New Testament. They are typical of an approach to the Hebrew Bible that figures prominently in other Christian writings. The liberties taken with the Hebrew text are indeed even greater in some instances. Some of the Church fathers quote spurious passages from the Hebrew Bible which are not there, and to account for the discrepancy Jews were on occasions accused of having deliberately altered their biblical text. Here, for example, is a passage from Chapter 73 of Justin Martyr's *Dialogue with Trypho:* "Again from the ninety-sixth Psalm of the words spoken by David they have removed this short saying: *from the tree*. For although the word was: Tell it among the Gentiles: the Lord reigned from a tree, they left only: Tell it among the Gentiles the Lord reigned." No edition of the Bible used by any Christian denomination includes the words "from a tree." A. Lukyn Williams, who edited Justin's *Dialogue*, after surveying the evidence, declares: "The phrase ['from a tree'] is doubtless a Christian interpolation." [5] "From a tree" was of course a reference to the figure of Jesus on the cross, and it was inserted into the psalm by some Christian polemicist. A

[4] Gerhard Bellinger: "The Jews in the Roman Catechism," Theodore Filthaut (ed.): *Israel in Christian Religious Education* (Notre Dame: University of Notre Dame Press; 1965), p. 105.

[5] Justin Martyr: *Dialogue*, A. Lukyn Williams (ed.) (London; 1930), p. 154.

psalm—written hundreds of years before the Christian era—was thus made to prophesy that Jesus was triumphant though crucified.

The original verse, as rendered in the Revised Standard Version of the Bible, reads thus: "Say among the nations, 'The Lord reigns! Yea, the world is established, it shall never be moved; he will judge the peoples with equity' " (96:10). The Confraternity Version is: "Say among the nations: The Lord is king. He has made the world firm, not to be moved; he governs the peoples with equity."

In the ancient world Christianity appeared as a Jewish heresy, rather than as an independent religion, and this has truly been its nature. Christians were spiritual Semites who remolded Judaism into a new form and promulgated it as their new faith. Indeed they claimed to be the heirs of the Jewish people, and their successors as the bearers of the Sinaitic revelation in improved and perfected format. The problem that confronted Christian dogmatists was the obvious conflict between the Hebrew Bible, to which they professed their loyalty, and the claims of their new faith. They coped with this problem by a work of reconciliation that was achieved by subjecting the Hebrew Bible to far-reaching "interpretation." Often straining the original text, the Christian interpretation of the Hebrew Bible turned it into a document that proclaimed the obsolescence of the Jewish religion and its replacement by Christianity. The Reverend Fenton, in his commentary on the Gospel of Matthew, has well described the predicament posed by the Christological approach to the Hebrew Bible. He writes of Matthew, but his characterization fits all the writers of the New Testament: "Matthew believed that the events which he was describing had been foretold by God, many years before they happened, in the Old Testament. There, through the prophets (and by 'the prophets' Matthew would understand not only the authors of the books which we call prophetic, but all the Old Testament writers), God had announced beforehand what he would do in the last days; now, with the coming of Jesus, these last days had come, and the events of his life were the events about which the Old Testament writers had been speaking. . . .

"Moreover, so sure was Matthew of the truth of this relationship between the Old Testament and the life of Jesus that he would sometimes change the details of an event as they were recorded in his source, in order to bring out more clearly the correspondence to a prophecy; as in the example given above, where he changed Mark's *myrrh* to *gall*, to make clear the fulfillment of the Greek version Ps. 69:21.

"Modern study of the Old Testament does not support Matthew's understanding of it, nor the use he made of it when he was writing his Gospel. It is now seen that the Old Testament was not a collection of detailed foretellings of future events, which could only be understood centuries later: the Old Testament writers were in fact writing for their contemporaries in a way which could be understood by them, and describing things that would happen more or less in their own lifetime. Thus Matthew's use of the Old Testament, though it was no doubt of first-rate importance to Matthew's original readers, and continued to be helpful until modern historical study enabled us to see the Old Testament in a new way, is now a stumbling-block to the twentieth-century reader of his Gospel." [6]

[6] J. C. Fenton: *The Gospel of St. Matthew* (Baltimore: Penguin Books; 1963), pp. 17–18.

Chapter XII
The Crucifixion

The Christian message to the world was designated by the term "gospel" from the Old English *godspell* ("good spell") or "good news." The equivalent Greek term is *euangelion* and the Latin term is *evangelium,* from which are derived words like "evangelize," "evangelical," and "evangelist." An evangelist was one who wrote or preached concerning the "good news" which Christianity proclaimed about human salvation. The term gospel, originally designating the Christian message, was in time applied especially to the first four books in the New Testament, where the basic elements of the Christian message are set forth and expounded.

The "good news" of Christianity was originally proclaimed to Jews because Christianity began as a movement within Judaism. This "good news" consisted of the announcement that Jesus had come to fulfill the ancient Jewish hope for a deliverer, in conformity with the prophecies of the Hebrew Bible. There were Jews who embraced this announcement, believing that Jesus did indeed represent the long-awaited deliverer of their people. It was among the Jews that Jesus had performed the work of his ministry, and they furnished his first disciples and adherents.

However, the greater number of Jews remained aloof from the Christian movement. To them the claim that Jesus was a fulfillment of ancient prophecies could not but ring hollow. The decisive characteristic of the prophetic hope was a transformation in the existing order, the end of oppression and violence, the dawn of freedom, justice, and peace. Isaiah's graphic description of this hope was before them. It was the vision of a time when men would "beat their swords into plowshares and their spears into pruning hooks," when nation would "not lift up sword against nation," neither "learn war any more" (Isaiah 2:4).

The contemporary world, however, was in startling contradiction to this vision. It was dominated by Roman power, which rested on the sword. At the slightest stirring of opposition to the Roman occupation of the country, there came swift and bloody reprisals. Thousands died on crosses dotting the countryside, which were erected by the Romans to intimidate the people against the dream of freedom. The destruction of the Second Temple in 70 C.E. was followed by a reign of terror against the Jews. Jerusalem was turned into an armed camp, where Jews were forbidden to make their homes. A special tax was levied on the Jews (both in Palestine and in the Diaspora), the *Fiscus Judaicus*, which was used for the maintenance of pagan shrines. Rome added humiliation to injury by erecting an arch of triumph to the conqueror of Jerusalem, Titus, and by issuing a special coin to mark the Jewish disaster. *Judaea Capta, Judaea Devicta,* "Captured Judea," "Vanquished Judea," these coins proclaimed, and they carried as an illustration of the slogan, the image of a decrepit, broken woman, bowing before her proud conqueror. The freedom fighters of the Jewish people renewed their rebellion against Rome in 115 and in 132. There followed more devastation, and more bloody reprisals. The victims, those slain and those deported and sold into slavery, ran into the hundreds of thousands. According to Josephus, Titus killed or captured 1,197,000 in the campaign of 66–70. The Roman historian Tacitus places the fatalities at 600,000.[1] The catastrophe was a glaring reminder that the world was still very much dominated by brute power. The hope foretold by the prophets, if it had any meaning at all, pointed to another time, beyond the present, for its realization.

[1] Cf. Salo W. Baron: *A Social and Religious History of the Jews* (New York: Columbia University Press; 1937), I, 184.

The Christian community felt the challenge in these facts. Indeed the fate of Jesus himself posed a problem to his followers. For how could he be the promised deliverer, if he could not save himself from the Romans and their Jewish puppets who did their masters' will by ferreting out every source of disturbance in the country as posing a threat to the existing order? As conceived in Jewish tradition, the messiah was a heroic, victorious figure. How could the messiahship of Jesus be reconciled with his ignominious death on a cross? The authors of the Gospels and of much of the New Testament generally took this as their burden. They coped with it by showing that the career of Jesus did in fact conform to the messianic expectations of the Hebrew Bible. This conformity could be discerned, they maintained, provided one understood the Hebrew Bible properly and provided one comprehended the true significance of the great events that marked the birth, the ministry and the passion of Jesus. Their writings were an effort to convey this understanding.

Ten times in his Gospel, Matthew employs a formula to relate a statement in the Old Testament to an incident in the career of Jesus; the formula is: "this took place to fulfill what the Lord had spoken by the prophets" (1:22, 2:15, 17, 23, 4:14, 8:17, 12:17, 13:35, 21:4, 27:9). In addition there are numerous other instances where this formula is not used but where the author clearly shapes his narration with a view of establishing conformity to Old Testament prophecies. This is well illustrated by the very opening of his Gospel: "The book of the genealogy of Jesus Christ, the son of David, the son of Abraham." The association of Jesus with David and Abraham, out of the long line of generations from which his origins were traced, was clearly motivated by the effort to relate Jesus to the "promises" which, according to Jewish tradition, had been bestowed on these two, Abraham and David. Abraham had been promised that his offspring would be given the land of Canaan and that he and his offspring would become a source of blessing to all the families of the earth (Genesis 12:7, 22:17–18). The House of David represented for Jews the ideal in royalty and the prophets sometimes envisioned the ideal leader of the future as a descendant of the Davidic line. Paul (Galatians 3:16) found "proof" that Abraham's offspring, upon whom God's promise had been conferred, necessarily pointed to Jesus, rather than the Jewish people as conventionally understood: "Now the promises were made to Abraham and to his offspring. It does not say, 'And to offsprings,' referring to many; but referring to one, 'And to your offspring,' which is Christ." Paul conveniently ignored the philological fact that the Hebrew *zera*, like its English equivalent, "offspring," is a collective noun, and it needs no plural form to have a plural meaning. The genealogy linking Jesus with Abraham and David is in any case of dubious significance because the line of ascent is traced from Joseph, the father of Jesus, and according to Christian tradition, Jesus was virgin-born, so that Joseph was therefore not really his father.

This is the motif of all the Gospel stories about Jesus. They are not historical accounts in the ordinary sense in which we usually view history; they are rather religious tracts in which incidents are recorded and arguments presented so as to aid the claim to the messiahship of Jesus. And each author of the Gospels—as for that matter, all New Testament writers—shape their material with a view to meeting the needs of the particular community for whom they write. Dominant in their endeavor is the quest for parallels between Old Testament prophecies and corresponding incidents in the life of Jesus.

The most telling of the Hebrew prophecies on which New Testament writers drew were those of the prophet Isaiah, recorded in chapters 40–66. Here we have the concept of the suffering servant of the Lord as the hero, who seeks to bring light and salvation to the world and who is requited with abuse and persecution. Christian commentators applied this to Jesus, whose sufferings were thus seen as conforming to ancient prophecy and therefore no longer a challenge to the belief in his messianic status. It will be helpful to see the context in which this prophet developed the concept of the suffering servant in order to judge the propriety of applying it to Jesus. The author of these prophecies (sometimes referred to by Bible scholars as Deutro-Isaiah) lived with the Jewish colony of exiles in Babylonia in the sixth century B.C.E. He had long pondered the fate of his people. They were the custodians of the Torah, the depository of divine truth on which the whole world depended for its salvation. But how lowly was their actual condition. They lived as exiles in Babylonia, banished from their own land. Their Temple was in ruins, having been destroyed by the Babylonians in 586 B.C.E.

The prophet saw them as the servants of the Lord, the bearers of the divine light that the world needed to save itself. But the world failed to realize this. Indeed, the world assumed that their suffering was a mark of divine disfavor and a token of their rejection. The prophet dismissed scornfully these disparagements of the Jewish people. He saw their sufferings as incidental to their service. They suffered because the world was not ready for their ministry and therefore resisted them, as a means of resisting the truths of which they were witnesses and protagonists. But the world will finally respond to the saving truth, and then it will become apparent that the Jewish people did not suffer in vain; through their hurt the world was to find its healing.

The prophet interspersed his characterizations of Israel as the suffering servant with a glowing vision of ultimate vindication, of Israel's restoration as a free people and the response of the world to its ministry, leading to the golden age, when God's truth will ultimately win the hearts of all mankind.

This is how the prophet conceived Israel's vocation as laid upon it by God's choice (Isaiah 42:1–6): "Behold my servant, whom I uphold, my chosen in whom my soul delights; I have put my spirit upon him, he will bring forth justice to the nations. . . . He will not fail nor be discouraged till he has established justice in the earth; and the coastlands wait for his law. . . . I am the Lord, I have called you in righteousness, I have taken you by the hand and kept you; I have given you as a covenant to the people, a light to the nations."

The nations will acknowledge that in Israel they had found the source of their peace, but in looking back they will recall wistfully how in their earlier state they had not realized this and had subjected God's servant Israel to persecution and humiliation. This theme recurs often. The following lines are a good statement of it (Isaiah 53:3–5): "He was despised and rejected by men, a man of sorrows and acquainted with grief; and as one from whom men hide their faces, he was despised and we esteemed him not. Surely he has borne our griefs and carried our sorrows; yet we esteemed him stricken, smitten by God, and afflicted. But he was wounded for our transgressions, he was bruised for our iniquities; upon him was the chastisement that made us whole, and with his strife we were healed."

Christian teachers appropriated these and similar prophecies and turned them into predictions of the fate which befell Jesus. As we noted earlier, the portrayal of Jesus in the Gospels reflects much embellishment by the evangelists, who shaped their portrayals so as to make the correspondence to Old Testament prophecies more striking. But even in its broad outlines the career of Jesus who came to benefit his world and suffered a martyr's fate does indeed bear a resemblance to the Lord's suffering servant described by Isaiah. However, the discovery of parallel elements in two phenomena does not automatically establish a causal relationship between them. A similar parallel may be drawn with the fate that befell Socrates and Mahatma Gandhi, and countless others who came to serve the world and were resisted by those whom they sought to benefit. One may draw a parallel between Isaiah's vision of the Lord's servant and the martyred Jews who died in the holocaust as victims of the Nazis. The Rabbis (Midrash Tanhuma, Vayera 20) noted a general principle often exemplified in all such cases, that those who commit their lives to a righteous cause often suffer great personal grief as an incident in meeting the claims of their mission. But Christian apologists took Isaiah's prophecies as *predictions* of the coming of Jesus and thus a *proof* of his messiahship.

We cite two passages from the New Testament that illustrate the identification of Jesus with the suffering servant in Isaiah. In Luke 22:37 Jesus is quoted as saying: "For I tell you this scripture must be fulfilled in me, 'And he was reckoned with transgressors'; for what is written about me has its fulfillment." Mark's allusion is clearly to Isaiah 53:12: "Therefore, I will divide him a portion with the great, and he shall divide the spoil with the strong; because he poured out his soul to death, and was numbered with the transgressors; yet he bore the sins of many, and made intercession for the transgressors." In Acts 8:26–39, the deacon Philip is described as meeting a worshipper on his way back from Jerusalem who was reading from the prophet Isaiah

(53:7–8): "As a lamb led to the slaughter, or a lamb before its shearer is dumb, so he opens not his mouth. In his humiliation justice was denied him. Who can describe his generation? For his life is taken up from the earth." (The text follows the Greek Septuagint version.) The account in Acts continues to tell us that this worshipper said to Philip, "'About whom, pray, does the prophet say this, about himself or about someone else?' Then Philip opened his mouth, and beginning with this scripture he told him the good news of Jesus." The identification of Jesus with the suffering servant of the Lord is encountered throughout the New Testament. The crucifixion scenes especially are shaped to conform to the characterizations in Isaiah.

As noted previously, the prophet Isaiah, who developed the concept of the servant of the Lord, lived some five hundred years before the birth of Jesus. The prophets sometimes project general visions that bear on the distant future, but they are not prognosticators of detailed incidents in the events after their time. Their primary address is to the people of their own day, of their own world. In Isaiah 41:8–10 the prophet identifies clearly whom he has in mind by "the servant of the Lord": "But you Israel, my servant, Jacob whom I have chosen, the offspring of Abraham my friend, you whom I took from the ends of the earth, and called from its farthest corners, saying to you, 'You are my servant, I have chosen you and not cast you off; fear not, for I am with you, be not dismayed, for I am your God; I will strengthen you, I will help you, I will uphold you with my victorious right hand.'"

It is clear from a careful reading of these prophecies that they are concerned with the fate of the Jewish people, and that they cannot be turned into predictions about Jesus. In the words of the noted Protestant scholar Rev. James Muilenberg, professor of Hebrew and Cognate Languages at the Union Theological Seminary in New York: "Israel, and Israel alone, is able to bear all that is said about the servant of the Lord. For the fundamental fact outweighing all others is the repeated equation of the two in the poems."[2] Professor Julius A. Bewer, also of Union Theological Seminary, contends that Jesus exemplified the characteristics in

[2] Commentary on Isaiah 40–66, in *The Interpreter's Bible* (Nashville, Tenn.. Abingdon Press; 1956), V, 411.

terms of which Deutro-Isaiah described the suffering servant, but he comes to the same conclusion, dismissing any notion that Isaiah "prophesied" or predicted the coming of Jesus: "The interpretation which sees in the Servant of Yahweh the messiah is untenable. Deutro-Isaiah himself called Israel the servant of Yahweh. Compare, *e.g.*, 41:8, 'but thou Israel, My servant, Jacob whom I have chosen,' and 49:3, 'Thou art My servant, Israel, in whom I will be glorified.' Deutro-Isaiah did not prophesy of Jesus Christ. . . ."[3]

Christian teachers drew on another source in the Hebrew Bible to rationalize the death of Jesus. It was the institution of sacrifices. The Hebrew Bible, in the Pentateuchal law, ordains a variety of animal sacrifices which man was to offer God as a means of worship. The patriarchs offered sacrifices; a covenant was usually sealed by slaying an animal which was placed on the altar as an offering to God; the Exodus from Egypt was celebrated by the offering of a paschal lamb; there were a variety of offerings prescribed for the individual and the community to express gratitude for God's blessings or remorse for wrongdoing.

The institution of sacrifice represented a primitive element in religion. It preceded the biblical law. In antiquity it had even more extensive scope than was given it in the Bible, and even included human sacrifices. The Bible forbade human sacrifice as an abomination. The rejection of human sacrifice is the primary theme in the story of the binding of Isaac. Animal sacrifices, and sacrifices of birds and cereals were prescribed, but the law made it clear that the sacrifice was not an end in itself. The law demanded proper motivation indicating that the sacrifice was only a token of surrender to God.

Post-Pentateuchal writings, especially the prophets, and the authors of the Book of Psalms, continually deemphasized sacrifice, placing the order of primacy on the inner feelings of love for God and the love of man as expressed in deeds of mercy and justice.

Some of the noblest expressions in the Hebrew Bible deal with this theme. Here are the well known lines of the prophet Micah

[3] Julius A. Bewer: *The Literature of the Old Testament* (New York: Columbia University Press; 1933), p. 213.

(Micah 6:6–8), which are characteristic of prophetic thinking on this subject: "With what shall I come before the Lord and bow myself before God on high? Shall I come before Him with burnt offerings, with calves a year old? Will the Lord be pleased with thousands of rams, with ten thousands of rivers of oil? Shall I give my first-born for my transgression, the fruit of my body for the sin of my soul? He has shown you, O man, what is good, and what the Lord does require of you, but to do justice and to love kindness, and to walk humbly with your God."

In the rabbinic period, even while the Temple with its cult of sacrifice was still in existence, Jewish piety flowed increasingly in an alternative direction, through the synagogue, the prayer service, the study of the Torah, and the more elaborate rites for observing the Sabbath and the festivals. The Rabbis taught openly that prayer is superior to sacrifices, that the study of the Torah is superior to sacrifices, that deeds of loving kindness are better than sacrifices. As a result of these developments, there was no insurmountable crisis for Jewish piety in the destruction of the Temple in Jerusalem and the cessation of sacrifices. The ground had been prepared for the replacement of sacrifices with other rites which had long been deemed efficacious in serving man's need for a way to commune with his God.

Christian teachers reversed this process by declaring that sacrifices were indispensable, that if animal sacrifices were deemed insufficient to win God's favor, it was not because the blood of the sacrifice was a nonessential, but that something more vital was needed to qualify the sacrifice or perhaps even to replace it. As Christian interpreters viewed it (Hebrews 10:1–10), animal sacrifices were deemed insufficient because God was not satisfied with the blood of an animal. He wanted a more precious blood, the blood of the messiah, who was in truth a divine being robed in the form of humanity; He wanted the blood of Jesus. And the sacrifice, as seen in Christian sources, was not merely a token of reverence for God, as the writers of the Hebrew Bible envisioned it. It was an end in itself, something indispensable to man's salvation.

The Gospels refer to the sacrifice of Jesus as a "ransom." Thus in Mark 10:45 (and similarly in Matthew 20:27) we have the following: "For the son of man came also not to be served but to serve, and to give his life as a ransom for many." The concept of the sacrifice as a ransom harks back to a primitive conception of sacrifices, one that had been superseded by the Hebrew Bible. The re-emphasis of sacrifices in Christian doctrine, in reversal of the trend in the Hebrew Bible (and in the rabbinic teachings as well) was clearly noted by the well-known Orientalist William Robertson Smith: "Christian theologians, looking on the sacrifices of the Old Testament as a type of the sacrifice on the cross, and interpreting the latter as a satisfaction to divine justice, have undoubtedly over-estimated the ethical lessons embodied in the Jewish sacrificial system; as may be inferred even from the fact that, for many centuries, the official theology of the Church was content to interpret the death of Christ as a ransom for mankind paid to the devil, or as a satisfaction to the divine honour (Anselm) rather than as a recognition of the sovereignty of the moral law of justice." In contrast to this Smith notes that "Jewish theology has . . . very little to say about atonement through sacrifice." [4]

The death of Jesus on the cross, as finally interpreted in Christian doctrine, was thus no defeat for his messiahship, but a supreme expression of it. It was an offering freely given, to atone for man's sinful nature, and to win for him divine grace, forgiveness from sin, and freedom from sin's consequences, the terrors of hell which were otherwise waiting to devour him. Those who believed in Jesus were the beneficiaries of the blood of his sacrifice, which carried the old institution to its completion and perfection, rendering obsolete the offering of rams and goats and lambs that could not truly please God.

Sometimes the New Testament presents Jesus as a "paschal lamb." The life lived under the old Jewish law is compared to the age of slavery in Egypt, while the new age inaugurated by Jesus with its liberation from the demands of the law is the time of the Exodus, the new age of freedom. A lamb was sacrificed on the occasion of the exodus from Egypt (Exodus 12:21–28), and Jesus is alleged to have been the offering associated with the new Passover of the Christian dispensation. More generally Jesus is presented as an offering of atonement to expiate man's sinful nature.

[4] W. R. Smith: *Lectures on the Religion of the Semites* (New York and London: The Macmillan Company; 1927), p. 424.

This concept of the death of Jesus pervades all New Testament writings. It is presented in each of the Gospels, especially in the descriptions of the Last Supper. In these accounts Jesus himself is quoted as imparting to his disciples the secret of his impending death (Mark 14:17–25, Matthew 26:26–29, Luke 22:14–23). Here is the statement in Matthew with the accompanying comment by the Reverend Fenton: "Now as they were eating, Jesus took bread, and blessed it, and broke it, and gave it to the disciples and said, 'Take, eat, this is my body.' And he took a cup, and when he had given thanks he gave it to them, saying, 'Drink of it, all of you, for this is my blood of the covenant, which is poured out for many for the forgiveness of sins. I tell you I shall not drink again of the fruit of the vine until the day when I drink it with you in my Father's Kingdom.' "

The Reverend Fenton, in his commentary, puts it thus: "Jesus had said, that he is going to his death in fulfillment of the scriptures; he now explains to his disciples how his death can be within the purpose of God, and what it will effect. He does this by means of a two-fold prophetic action: he compares the bread to his *body*, and the cup of wine to his *blood*. The separation between body and blood suggests sacrifice, because in the Old Testament sacrifices, the blood was separated from the body; and here also Jesus says that his blood is *blood of the covenant, which is poured out for many for the forgiveness of sins*. Therefore, by these words concerning the bread and the wine, Jesus is saying that his coming death will be a sacrifice offered to God, by which a new covenant between God and man will be established; and in telling the disciples to *eat* the bread and to *drink* the cup, he is saying that they will be the beneficiaries of his sacrifice—not only they, but the many, that is the whole world. Moreover, he looks forward to what he will inaugurate by his death—namely his Father's kingdom, the messianic banquet, when he and they will again feast together." [5]

Paul speaks repeatedly of the atoning efficacy of the blood of Jesus, which becomes available to those who believe in him and in his sacrifice. We cite the following passages:

[5] J. C. Fenton: *The Gospel of St. Matthew* (Baltimore: Penguin Books; 1963), p. 417.

Whom God hath set forth to be a propitiation through faith in his blood, to declare his righteousness for the remission of sins that are past, through the forbearance of God (Romans 3:25).

But God commendeth his love towards us, in that, while we were yet sinners, Christ died for us. Much more then, being now justified by his blood, we shall be saved from wrath through him (Romans 5:8–9).

Purge out therefore the old leaven, that ye may be a new lump, as ye are unleavened. For even Christ our Passover is sacrificed for us (I Corinthians 5:7).

In whom we have redemption through his blood, the forgiveness of sins, according to the riches of his grace (Ephesians 1:7).

But now in Christ Jesus ye who sometimes were far off are made nigh by the blood of Christ (Ephesians 2:13).

In whom we have redemption through his blood, even the forgiveness of sins (Colossians 1:14).

And having made peace through the blood of his Cross, by him to reconcile all things unto himself (Colossians 1:20).

The author of the Epistle to the Hebrews states categorically (Hebrews 9:22) that "without shedding of blood is no remission" of sin, and he imputes this view to the Old Testament (Exodus 24:8). And he draws a dramatic contrast between the old order of sacrifices and the new order, inaugurated by the sacrifice of Jesus (Hebrews 9:6–12): "Now when these things [the rites of sacrifice, as described in the Hebrew Bible] were thus ordained the priests went always into the first tabernacle [the anterior chamber], accomplishing the service of God. But into the second [the interior chamber, called the Holy of Holies] went the high priest alone once every year, not without blood, which he offered for himself and for the errors of the people . . . which was a figure for the time then present, in which were offered both gifts and sacrifices, that could not make him that did the service perfect.

. . . But Christ being come an high priest of good things to come, by a greater and more perfect tabernacle, not made with hands. . . . Neither by the blood of goats and calves, but by his own blood he entered in once into the holy place, having obtained eternal redemption for us."

In John's Gospel, Jesus is described as preaching at a synagogue in Capernaum on this theme of his sacrifice, and on the necessity of benefiting by it through partaking of his flesh and his blood. Jesus is quoted as saying (John 6:53–45): "Truly, truly, I say to you, unless you eat the flesh of the Son of man and drink his blood, you have no life in you; he who eats my flesh and drinks my blood abides in me, and I in him."

A modern interpreter of the Catholic Mass has restated the basic conception of the death of Jesus for modern Christians. In the words of Bishop Fulton J. Sheen: "All the sacrifices of bullocks, and goats, and sheep, and particularly the sacrifice of the paschal lamb, found their completion in the cross. . . . Up until the coming of the Son of God, there were many sacrifices offered for sins. . . . Among all peoples, in addition to the Jews who had the greatest advantage of Divine revelation, there were, therefore, priests who offered victims of sacrifice. . . . But when our Lord came He became at one and the same time *Priest* and *Victim*, He became both the Offerer and the One Who was offered. . . . It is to be noted that there is no such thing as Communion without a sacrifice. . . . That is why the Mass is not just a Communion service; it is a sacrifice which ends in Communion. Communion is the consequence of Calvary, we live by what we slay." [6]

The action ascribed by the New Testament to Jesus at the Last Supper in giving his disciples bread and wine, which they were to eat and drink, with the accompanying interpretation that these were truly his body and his blood, lifted the event to awesome dimensions. Its re-enactment in the Catholic Mass and in the Protestant Communion service partakes of that awesomeness. These are the rites of the Eucharist which have played so central a role in Christianity. Jews, however, could not but find these ideas repellent. The Torah (Leviticus 17:10–12) had specifically for-

[6] Fulton J. Sheen: *This Is the Mass* (New York: Hawthorn Books; 1958), pp. 11, 12, 17.

bidden the drinking of blood: "And if any man of the house of Israel or of the strangers who reside among them partake of any blood, I will set My face against the person who partakes of the blood, and I will cut him off from among his kin. . . . No person among you shall partake of blood, nor shall the stranger who resides among you partake of blood."

Some scholars have indeed questioned whether the events of the Last Supper could really have occurred as described in the Gospels.[7] Since Jesus and his disciples were all Jews, it would have evoked revulsion in them to consider drinking blood, even if this were meant symbolically. Jews were bound to recoil from the suggestion of drinking *any* blood. They were bound to recoil with special horror at the thought that God wanted the messiah to be crucified and that it was incumbent on them to drink his blood.

Writing as a historian, Professor Guignebert declares these rites as clearly a later development, representing the influence of paganism on the growing Church: "Never had any rite of the pagan Mysteries been charged with more significance, nor with more seductive hopes than the Pauline Eucharist, but it belonged to their species, and not in any way to the Jewish spirit; it introduced into the Apostolic Church 'a bit of paganism.' "[8] The same point of view is expressed by Alfred Loisy. He deems the sacramental interpretation of the bread and the wine as a contribution of Paul who acted under the influence of the pagan mysteries.[9]

The New Testament cites a "proof" from the Book of Psalms that the sacrifice of Jesus was divinely ordained, to replace the less perfect sacrifice which had been prescribed in the Pentateuchal law (Hebrews 10:1–10): "For since the law has but a shadow of the good things to come instead of the true form of these realities, it can never, by the same sacrifices which are offered year after year, make perfect those who draw near. Otherwise, would they not have ceased to be offered? If the worshippers had once been

[7] Alan E. Brooke: Commentary on John 6:41–5, in A. S. Peake (ed.): *A Commentary on the Bible*, and cf. Raymond E. Brown: *The Gospel According to John*, pp. 284–94.

[8] Charles Guignebert: *Christianity, Past and Present* (New York: The Macmillan Company; 1927), pp. 105 ff.

[9] Alfred Loisy: "The Christian Mystery," *Hibbert Journal*, X (1911–12); 54–7.

cleansed, they would no longer have any consciousness of sin. But in these sacrifices there is a reminder of sin year after year. For it is impossible that the blood of bulls and goats should take away sins.

"Consequently, when Christ came into the world, he said [Psalms 40:6–8], 'Sacrifices and offerings thou hast not desired, but a body hast thou prepared for me; in burnt offerings and sin offerings thou hast taken no pleasure.' Then I said, 'Lo, I have come to do thy will, O God, as it is written for me in the roll of the book.' When he said above, 'Thou hast neither desired nor taken pleasure in sacrifices and offerings and burnt offerings and sin offerings' (these are offered according to the law), then he added, 'Lo, I have come to do thy will.' He abolished the first in order to establish the second. And by that will we have been sanctified through the offering of the body of Jesus Christ once for all."

We have cited this rather lengthy passage from Hebrews because it embraces so much of the typical Christian argumentation on the subject. The author invokes logic as well as the authority of an Old Testament text to establish his point. The old order of sacrifices could not possibly be efficacious, he points out, because it is continually repeated. Each year on the Day of Atonement the sacrifices are re-enacted by the officiating High Priest. If those sacrifices cleansed a person then, having once been cleansed, there would be no need to repeat the sacrifice another time. The author is, of course, mistaken as to the nature of sin and its atonement as conceived in Judaism. He is undoubtedly thinking of the Christian concept of sin, which is the inherited sin of Adam's disobedience, a one-time sin which might be atoned in a one-time act of cleansing. The misdeeds for which Jews were taught to seek atonement each year on the Day of Atonement were the misdeeds of everyday life, the continued failures to reach our highest spiritual and moral potential. The struggle against such "sins" is constant and the need to seek atonement is equally constant. The quest for atonement was expressed ritualistically through the sacrifices. But Jewish tradition surrounded those sacrifices with an interpretive context which made it clear that the sacrifice in itself could not effect cleansing. Cleansing was to be attained only through penitence, which involved sincere remorse for wrongdoing, the acts of restitution where these were possible, and the resolution to steer clear of such failures in the future. Spiritual cleansing, like physical cleansing, cannot be accomplished "once for all." All too soon we become soiled again, and the act of cleansing must, therefore, be continuous.

The author's citation from Psalms involves both a misquotation as well as a misinterpretation. As quoted in Hebrews, the verses from Psalms are traced back to the authorship of Jesus, and he appears to be declaring "before His entrance into the world, the surrender of his body, not ritual sacrifice, was required by God as the condition of forgiveness. He was to come in accordance with prophecy ('in the roll of the book it is written of me') to give fulfillment to that will of God." [1]

The original Hebrew does not have "a *body* hast thou prepared for me." In place of "body" it has "ear." The author of Hebrews apparently followed the Greek translation of the Septuagint, which, A. F. Kilpatrick suggests, "may have been a free paraphrase," or it "may have originated in ancient corruption of the Greek text." [2]

Apart from the substitution of "body" for "ear," an examination of the original passage will make it clear that the psalmist is speaking about himself, and the imputation of the authorship of the verse cited to Jesus, who lived hundreds of years after the psalmist, is false to the obvious meaning of the text.

We cite the passage in Psalms as rendered in the Revised Standard Version: "Sacrifice and offering thou dost not desire; but thou hast given me an open ear. Burnt offering and sin offering thou hast not required. Then I said, 'Lo, I come; in the roll of the book it is written of me; I delight to do thy will, O my God; thy law is within my heart.' "

These lines are the psalmist's response to God's goodness, which had stirred him to gratitude. "On such an occasion . . . it

[1] E. F. Scott: Commentary on Hebrews, in *A Commentary on the Bible*, A. S. Peake (ed.) (London: Thomas Nelson & Sons; 1919), p. 896.

[2] A. F. Kilpatrick: Commentary, in *The Book of Psalms* (New York: Cambridge University Press; 1933), p. 212.

was customary for an offering to be presented in payment of vows or as a token of gratitude (cf. 66:13–15). But our psalmist declares that sacrifices of such a kind are not sought by God. . . . The psalmist's offering is himself." [3] The line "Thou hast given me an open ear" (literally, "ears hast thou dug for me") is the psalmist's acknowledgment that God had given him a channel for learning God's will. "Lo, I come," is like "Here, I am," a declaration of his readiness to do what God expects of him. The line "in the roll of the book it is written of me," the Reverend Taylor takes as a reference "to the heavenly book where men's deeds are recorded (cf. 56:8, 87:6)." [4] Other commentators offer the simpler explanation that this verse is a reference to the scroll on which God's law was recorded and which the psalmist acknowledged as the source of his obligation. The latter interpretation appears to have guided the translators of Psalms in the Jewish Publication Society version, which renders the line thus: "Then said I, 'Lo, I come with the roll of a book which is prescribed for me.' "

These lines, in other words, declare a doctrine which is often taught by the prophets and in the Book of Psalms, that material sacrifices in themselves are of little worth, that God wants a life astir with the longing for God, to love Him and to serve Him, by being faithful to His will. It is a doctrine which the Rabbis subsequently summed up in the single but all inclusive statement: "The Merciful One desires the heart" (Sanhedrin 106b). To read into these lines the Christian doctrine of the atoning efficacy of the death of Jesus on the cross is to do violence to the psalmist's meaning, and to subvert the moral grandeur of his thought.

Kilpatrick suggests a kinship between these verses in Psalms and the ministry of Jesus, because Jesus fulfilled the concept of faithfulness idealized by the psalmist.[5] The concept of faithfulness idealized by the psalmist is personal in expression but universal in scope, and, therefore, applicable to *all* noble peoples who live lives of utter devotion and faithfulness to God. The author of Hebrews made Jesus the author of those verses, and he applied

[3] William R. Taylor: Exegesis on Psalms, in *The Interpreter's Bible*, IV, 211 ff.

[4] Ibid., p. 213.

[5] Commentary, in *The Book of Psalms*, p. 212.

them to him solely, and he read into those lines a declaration that God wanted Jesus to die on the cross as a means of atonement for the sins of humanity. There is not a trace of these ideas in the original verses of the psalmist. The psalmist's meaning is simple and Kilpatrick himself summarized it correctly when he declared: "The stanza is an answer to the implied question, How should man express his gratitude? It affirms the common prophetic doctrine that sacrifice in itself was of no value apart from the disposition of heart which it was intended to express. The new commandment of the Exodus was not sacrifice but obedience (Ex. 15:26). See Ps. 50:7 ff.; 51:16; I Sam. 15:22; Hosea 6:6; Micah 6:8; Jer. 7:21 ff." [6]

New Testament writers cited miracles to support the claims for the messiahship of Jesus.

There are miracle stories in the Hebrew Bible and in rabbinic literature, but Jewish teachers did not permit the miracle to have a decisive voice in considerations of doctrine or law. Already Deuteronomy 13:14 cautioned against the admittance of miracle as evidence in the realm of doctrine. The Rabbis extended this position. They tried to interpret miracles so as to make them consistent with an orderly working of nature. And they denied the competence of miracle to intervene in favor of one or another position in law, which they held had to be decided by the majority of those authorized to judge, on the basis of free deliberation of the issues involved (Bereshit Rabbah 85:5, Baba Metzia 59b). The writers of the New Testament, however, looked upon the miracles which were said to have attended the career of Jesus as a telling confirmation of his divine character and his role as messiah. The circumstances of his birth, incidents in his life, and especially his death on the cross, were described as having been accompanied by miracles. The recitation of miracle is often reinforced by an allusion to the Hebrew Bible.

We cite the Gospel account of the miracles that occurred in connection with the crucifixion. Mark's report (15:33–39) runs thus: "And when the sixth hour had come, there was darkness over the whole land—until the ninth hour. . . . And Jesus uttered a loud cry, and breathed his last. And the curtain of the

[6] Ibid., p. 210.

Temple was torn in two, from top to bottom. And when the centurion, who stood facing him, saw that he thus breathed his last, he said, 'Truly, this man was a son of God.' " Matthew's account repeats the miraculous darkness for three hours but adds to the miracles which followed immediately upon his death. Here is his version (27:51–54): "And behold the curtain of the Temple was torn in two, from top to bottom; and the earth shook, and the rocks were split; the tombs also were opened, and many bodies also of the saints who had fallen asleep were raised, and coming out of the tombs after his resurrection they went into the holy city and appeared to many. When the centurion, and those who were with him, keeping watch over Jesus, saw the earth quake and what took place, they were filled with awe, and said 'Truly this was the son of God.' "

The three hours of darkness that immediately preceded Jesus' death was clearly meant as a portent, to convey divine disapproval at the miscarriage of justice, and parallels the plague of three days of darkness that preceded the death of Egypt's first born (Exodus 10:22). This darkness may, however, also allude to the prophecy in Amos 8:9: "And on that day, says the Lord, I will make the sun go down at noon, and darken the earth in broad daylight."

There was a curtain in the ancient Tabernacle built in the days of Moses, and one in the Holy of Holies, in the Jerusalem Temple, as prescribed in Exodus 26:31–33 and Leviticus 21:23. The account of the tearing of the curtain in the Temple following the death of Jesus ("behold, the curtain of the Temple was torn in two from top to bottom," cited in Mark and Matthew) is a symbolic statement of what the death of Jesus signified for the future of Judaism with its central shrine in Jerusalem. It is probably meant to foreshadow the destruction of the Temple. The curtain screened the Holy of Holies, which no one was to enter, except the High Priest on the Day of Atonement. When Jerusalem fell to the Romans, Titus entered the Holy of Holies after violating the curtain (Ecclesiastes Rabbah 5:9). Earthquakes and the splitting of rocks are mentioned in the Hebrew Bible as portents of God's judgment (Judges 5:4, II Samuel 22:8, I Kings 19:11, Psalms 68:9).

David Daube has suggested that the tearing of the curtain was a token of mourning analogous to the rite of tearing a garment as a token of mourning over certain sorrowful events. The Talmud includes among such events the death of a parent, a teacher of Torah, the Patriarch or the Chief of the Court, the receipt of some catastrophic news, the hearing of an utterance of blasphemy, the burning of a scroll of the Torah, the destruction of Judean cities, and the destruction of the Temple in Jerusalem (Moed Katan 25b–26a, Mishnah Sanhedrin 7:5).

Daube has further suggested that the construction of this miracle was probably inspired by the account of Elijah's ascent to heaven, as reported in II Kings 2:12: "And Elisha saw it and cried, My father, my father, the chariot of Israel and the horsemen thereof. And he took hold of his clothes and rent them in two pieces." [7]

Some Gospel commentators see in the tearing of the curtain a suggestion that the death of Jesus had removed the barriers that had previously existed between man and God. There appears to be an allusion to this interpretation in Hebrews 10:19–20: "Therefore, brethren, since we have confidence to enter the sanctuary by the blood of Jesus, by the new and living way which he opened to us through the curtain, that is, through his flesh." The centurion's conversion was cited to show that the death of Jesus, when grasped in its fullest impact, gave added power to the claims of the new faith.

The addition by Matthew of an alleged resurrection of "saints who had fallen asleep" was of course inspired by the ancient belief that in the messianic age all the righteous would be raised from the dead. The claim that this general resurrection had indeed occurred was cited as confirmation that Jesus was the messiah.

The alleged conversion of the Roman centurion has also been interpreted as part of the apologetic purposes sought by the Marcan narrative. The fact that Jesus was executed by the Roman authorities for what appears to have been an offense of sedition against the state proved an embarrassment to the Christian community as it endeavored to win followers in the Roman world.

[7] David Daube: *The New Testament and Rabbinic Judaism* (London; 1956), pp. 23–4.

Christian teachers sought to meet this predicament by showing that though Jesus was born a Jew his own people betrayed him while the Romans, beginning with Pilate, sensed his divine character and were readily won to his side.

Pilate's role in the crucifixion was minimized though it could not be explained away altogether. But the conversion of the centurion illustrated a Roman, one who witnessed the crucifixion, and from this act of seeming defeat, glimpsed the truth that Jesus was truly a divine being. In the words of S. G. F. Brandon: "Mark depicts Jesus, though born a Jew, as rejected and in turn rejecting the Jewish leaders, the Jewish people, and his own family. His death is caused by Jewish rancour, which overcomes Roman humanity; in his extremity he is denied by his Jewish disciples. . . . According to Mark, as Jesus died upon the cross to the taunts of the Jewish priests: 'He saved others; himself he cannot save,' the Roman centurion exclaimed: 'Truly this man was the Son of God!' Thus the author of Mark showed his fellow-Christians in Rome that the first human being to recognize the divine nature of Jesus was a Gentile. . . . Hence at this critical time, the Roman Christians were reassured about Jesus' death as a rebel against Rome and also concerning the Jewish origins of their religion. Jesus was shown, essentially detached from his Jewish background, as the divine Saviour, whose true character was first perceived by a Gentile—the Roman centurion on the hill of Calvary." [8]

Jesus himself, when asked for a sign to confirm his messiahship, is quoted in Matthew 12:39–40 as saying: "An evil and adulterous generation asks for a sign, but no sign shall be given to it except the sign of the prophet Jonah. For as Jonah was three days and three nights in the belly of the whale, so will the Son of man be three days and three nights in the heart of the earth." According to Christian belief, Jesus was resurrected on the third day, so that he could not have been in the grave "three days and three nights." The analogy to Jonah is therefore only approximate. By citing the parallel of Jonah, inexact though it is, we are shown

[8] S. G. F. Brandon: *History, Time and Deity* (New York: Barnes and Noble; 1965), pp. 178–9.

that the fate of Jesus re-enacted a drama which apparently expresses the way in which God deals with His emissaries. That the same drama was played in the the life of Jesus was therefore offered as a confirmation of his mission.

Commentators on the Gospels have noted the undependable character of the miracle stories. In some cases, the Gospel writers themselves elaborated on their sources to extend the scope of the miraculous. Matthew, for example, retells stories taken from Mark but expands on the element of miracle. "Examples of this Matthean extension of the miraculous are: Peter's walking on the water (14:28–30), the resurrection of the dead after the resurrection of Jesus (27:52–53) and the earthquake before the women came to the tomb (28:2). In each of these cases, it is almost certain that Matthew had no written source other than Mark, who did not record the particular miracle that Matthew mentions; and that Matthew has, in fact, increased the frequency of miraculous events in his Gospel, without having historical evidence for them." [9]

The assumption that a particular text in the Hebrew Bible constituted a prophecy had far-reaching implications for the portrayal of the events which were cited as their fulfillment. In some cases, Gospel commentators have noted, the event cited did not rest on independent sources such as records or recollections by witnesses. They were *inferred* from the prediction.

The Old Testament prediction was treated as a historical source, and events were reconstructed to conform to the predictions. In the words of Nineham, "If . . . an Old Testament passage referred to the Passion of Christ, the things it predicted must have happened to Jesus, even if there was no other evidence that they had. Old Testament predictions thus became, to a certain extent, a historical source. . . . Accordingly, the account of Jesus' end, on which our Gospel accounts are based, was derived from historical reminiscences and Old Testament predictions in a proportion which cannot now be exactly determined." [1]

[9] Fenton: *St. Matthew*, p. 20.

[1] D. E. Nineham: *The Gospel of St. Mark* (Baltimore: Penguin Books; 1963), p. 367.

The crucifixion of Jesus was a tragedy, and Jews were well aware of it, for they had witnessed thousands of their people suffer a like fate at the hands of the Romans, as the contemporary historian Josephus testifies. The Christian interpretation of the crucifixion of Jesus as a necessary event in God's design for the world, that the death of Jesus was to serve as a vicarious atonement for the sins of humanity and that men had to believe in this to benefit from his sacrifice, could not but seem strange and bewildering to Jewish ears. It must have seemed to them an uncalled-for obfuscation of a historical tragedy. It must have seemed to them also an unwarranted surrender of a basic element in their conception of God, that He desired "mercy" rather than "sacrifices" (Hosea 6:6), that the noblest offerings to Him were "a contrite spirit" (Psalms 51:19). They remembered the eloquent words of the psalmist, who defined the way for a person to gain merit before God (Psalms 24:3–6): "Who shall ascend to the hill of the Lord and who shall stand in his holy place? He who has clean hands and a pure heart, who does not lift up his soul to what is false, and does not swear deceitfully. He will receive blessing from the Lord, and vindication from the God of his salvation." They remembered the lesson of their Scripture, how a divine voice had halted Abraham when he sought to sacrifice his son Isaac (Genesis 22:12): "Do not raise your hand against the boy, or do anything to him."

Christians generally see in the crucifixion of Jesus, interpreted as a divinely ordained sacrifice, the supreme instance of God's love for man. To Jews it has seemed otherwise. A God who wanted Jesus—or anyone else—to die could not be the God of outgoing love for all His creatures. Nor did their conception of God as a loving Father permit them to agree that by not believing in the sacrifice of Jesus one would doom himself to eternal damnation. They were loath to subscribe to the concept of eternal damnation, in any case, no matter how false a person's way of life might be. Their religion had taught them that the earnest desire to bestow love on fellow creatures fulfills God's basic demand for man.

Christian teachers tried hard to reconcile their view of the crucifixion with the Hebrew Bible, but Jews who read the original Hebrew text found this labor of reconciliation unconvincing. Indeed, the Christian conception of the sacrifice of Jesus, as something sought by God, reminded Jews of the cult of human sacrifice, which was deemed abhorrent in their tradition. That for Christians Jesus was more than a man did not lessen the gravity of God's demand for his sacrifice—it heightened it. However these ideas might seem to those raised in a pagan culture, to Jews raised on the prophetic and Pharisaic tradition they appeared strange and unacceptable. Inevitably there came the parting of the ways. Judaism remained faithful to itself, and Christianity turned its back on the Jews, whom it berated for being stubborn and unyielding to the "truth." Christianity turned toward the pagan world, where the ground proved more fertile. It was among the pagans in the larger world of the Roman Empire that the Christian Gospel was to win her greatest conquests.

Rudolf Bultmann has treated the entire salvation event that is at the heart of the New Testament narrative as myth. In the words of Bultmann: "Human beings are subject to death even before they have committed any sin. And to attribute human mortality to the fall of Adam is sheer nonsense, for guilt implies personal responsibility, and the idea of original sin as an inherited infection is sub-ethical, irrational, and absurd.

"The same objections apply to the doctrine of the atonement. How can the guilt of one man be expiated by the death of another who is sinless—if indeed one may speak of a sinless man at all? What primitive notions of guilt and righteousness does this imply? And what primitive idea of God? The rationale of sacrifice in general may of course throw some light on the theory of the atonement, but even so, what a primitive mythology it is, that a divine Being should become incarnate, and atone for the sins of men through his own blood! Or again, one might adopt an analogy from the law courts, and explain the death of Christ as a transaction between God and man through which God's claims on man were satisfied. But that would make sin a juridical matter; it would be no more than an external transgression of a commandment, and it would make nonsense of all our ethical standards.

Moreover, if the Christ who died such a death was the pre-existent Son of God, what could death mean for him? Obviously very little, if he knew that he would rise again in three days!" [2]

Bultmann retains the New Testament account of the salvation event by "demythologizing" it. He sees in the account itself what one must see in all myth, a symbolic interpretation of human existence. The New Testament myth is for him "in essence that of Jewish apocalyptic and Gnostic redemption myths." Its existential significance is in the judgment that "man cannot achieve this redemption by his own efforts; it must come as a gift through divine intervention." [3] The Christian faith, as read by the light of this New Testament myth, Bultmann further declares, "is not the same as religious idealism; the Christian life does not consist in developing the individual personality, in the improvement of society, or in making the world a better place. The Christian life means a turning away from the world, a detachment from it." [4]

The New Testament account of God's design for man's salvation seemed implausible to Jews both in its factual claims, as well as in its interpretation of human existence. Judaism rejected world transcendence. It deemed the turning away from the world an evasion of man's moral responsibility, which is to hallow life, or as the Jewish liturgy expresses it, "to perfect the world under the kingship of the Almighty." Judaism knew that man's redemption cannot be wholly his own achievement but that he remained dependent on *sayata di-shemaya*, "the help of Heaven (God)." Judaism insisted however that man dare not leave it all to God, but that his own effort remains efficacious in helping to redeem himself and his world from the evil forces arrayed against them. Normative Judaism rejected the apocalyptic and Gnostic visionaries as offering an escapist religion that distorted the world affirming faith of the Hebrew Bible.

Christian missionaries have often invoked passages from the Old Testament to prove the messiahship of Jesus. One of their most serious efforts has been to place the crucifixion in the con-

[2] Rudolf Bultmann *et al.*: *Kerygma and Myth*, Hans Werner Bartsch (ed.) (New York: Harper & Row; 1961), pp. 7–8.

[3] Ibid., p. 15.

[4] Ibid., p. 14.

text of the Old Testament prophecies. But these "proofs" presuppose the will to believe. Jews have generally been unimpressed because the "proofs" in themselves lacked cogency, and the Christian doctrine, on its own merits, did not win them to the new faith.

Chapter XIII
The Bible in Christianity

The Christian conception of man and his destiny, as reflected in the writings of the New Testament, differed radically from that of Judaism. Christianity was negatively oriented toward the existential world. Its goal was not to guide man in meeting the claims of concrete existence, but to teach him how to transcend the world of concrete existence. Christianity was set in the dualism of the material and the spiritual. The material—as the realm of concrete existence—was deemed evil, while the soul alone—as the spiritual principle in man—was deemed the realm of the good. Christian effort centered on "saving" man's soul, on withdrawing him from the material world and leading him to union with God. This solution was accessible to all if they believed in Jesus, who was God robed in the form of humanity. The evil from which man needed to be saved was not the evil which is incidental to the predicaments of concrete existence. It was the evil committed in the prehistorical state, through Adam's disobedience in the Garden of Eden, which had entered the stream of human heredity to contaminate all the descendants of Adam. This sin was remitted through the voluntary sacrifice of Jesus on the cross. Whoever believed in Jesus and followed him became the beneficiary of his sacrifice and was thus cleansed from the taint of original (and hereditary) sin.

The hope whose fulfillment Christians anticipated was not the perfection of the existential world but its destruction. The world of material things and material pursuits, of greed and oppression, of sin and death was regarded as due for a catastrophic end through the intervention of God.

The medium through whom this plan was to be carried out was Jesus, the Christ, to use the Greek equivalent for the Hebrew term *messiah*, who was expected to return to earth in glory. Those who believed in him and followed his teachings would then be rewarded with eternal life, while others would be fated to eternal punishment. New Testament writers believed that this ending of history, this abrupt termination of the world of historical existence, was imminent, and that it would occur in their own lifetime.[1]

If early Christianity reveals a disdain for the things of this world it is largely because of the conviction that these things were trivial and were soon due to pass with the ending of the world. In the words of Karl Kundsin: "The certainty of the near approach of the end of the world and of the coming of the Son of man resulted in a definite attitude toward the surrounding world and toward the brethren. . . . In other words, a serious view of the approaching end of the world resulted in a realization of the necessity of complete inner separation from the world, and likewise the most extreme concern for the salvation of the largest possible number of one's own people from the threatened destruction." [2]

Biblical and rabbinic Judaism are generally opposed to world negation. But there were Jewish sects like the Essenes and the Qumran community, among whom such ideas had gained a foothold. There were apocalyptic writers among the Jews of Palestine and the Diaspora who were attracted to the speculations about the

[1] J. C. Fenton: *The Gospel of St. Matthew* (Baltimore: Penguin Books; 1963), p. 21.

[2] Rudolf Bultmann and Karl Kundsin: *Form Criticism* (New Yorker: Harper & Row; 1962), p. 101.

impending doom of the world. Only one work which may be considered as sympathetic to such views, the Book of Daniel, was admitted to the canon of the Hebrew Bible. The extensive collection of apocalyptic writings was kept out of the Bible, which taught a world-affirming faith, as did the rabbinic writings that make up the Oral Torah. Historians have suggested that in addition to Hellenistic influences, with their disdain for material existence, it was the world-negating tendencies, which were suppressed in official Judaism, that found their freer expression in Christianity.[3]

The most dramatic illustration of otherworldliness in the early Christian community is afforded us in Paul's preference for celibacy over the state of marriage. In Judaism, marriage, the life of cohabitation of husband and wife, and the raising of a family as the fruit of their union, meet a fundamental responsibility of man, to which he is summoned by the First Commandment in Scripture. For Paul, however, celibacy is the preferred state, and marriage but a compromise, necessitated by man's sinful nature. As Paul expressed it in his First Epistle to the Corinthians: "It is well for a man not to touch a woman. But because of the temptation to immorality each man should have his own wife and each woman her own husband. . . . The unmarried man is anxious about the affairs of the Lord, how to please the Lord; but the married man is anxious about worldly affairs, how to please his wife, and his interests are divided. And the unmarried woman or girl is anxious about the affairs of the Lord, how to be holy in body and spirit; but the married woman is anxious about worldly affairs, how to please her husband" (7:1–2, 32–34).

The clash between Christian doctrine and the Hebrew Bible was sharpest in their respective attitudes to the law. For the Jews, as we noted, the law charted the way to God. It was the means of hallowing man's life and that of society. For Christianity the law was obsolete and even a hindrance. The necessity of law derives from the predicament of the many claims that press on man in the course of his involvement in the existential world. But for Christian doctrine the existential world was not a primary concern, since this world was essentially evil and soon due to perish. Ac-

[3] Ibid., pp. 1 ff.

cording to Christian doctrine, it was the business of a Christian to rise above it, and center his interests on purely spiritual, that is, otherworldly pursuits.

The law moreover contravened the cult that was developing around Jesus. For "if justification were through the law, then Christ died to no purpose" (Galatians 2:21). If the claims made by Christian doctrine for the sacrifice of Jesus were true, then the law was superfluous. The sharpest polemics between the spokesmen of the two faiths centered on the issue of the Jewish law, whose foundations are charted in the Bible. Jewish spokesmen insisted on its continuing efficacy, while Christians argued that a more efficacious way to God was available through union with Jesus, thereby benefiting from the atoning power of his sacrifice. The Christian view is clearly stated in Acts 13:38–39: "Be it known unto you, therefore, men and brethren, that through this man is preached to you the forgiveness of sins: And by him all that believe are justified from all things, from which you could not be justified by the law of Moses."

If this was the attitude of Christians to the law, how were Christians to continue recognizing a loyalty to the Hebrew Bible? As we have already noted, the reconciliation between Christian doctrine and the Hebrew Bible was to be attempted by the method of interpretation. The Hebrew Bible is declared to have been revealed at the time when the fuller revelation could not yet win the hearts of men. According to Christian teaching, the law prescribed in the Bible was adapted to the necessities of this interim period, when men were still too weak to follow the fuller revelation, as it was finally given in Jesus. But the Hebrew Bible, it was alleged, bears the message of the fuller truth in hints and allegories, and whoever can see through its literal provisions can see the truths of a more momentous nature which were to come later on. The Hebrew Bible therefore represents an inferior religion, one suited to an earlier epoch in the religious maturation of the human race. "The law," said Paul (Galatians 3:24), "was our custodian until Christ came, that we might be justified by faith."

The most zealous adversary of the law was the Apostle Paul. The law was not merely superfluous and ineffectual; it was actually a source of stumbling to anyone who sought to live by it.

Paul returns to this theme often. It is typically stated in Romans 7:5–8: "While we were living in the flesh, our sinful passions, aroused by the law, were at work in our members to bear fruit for death. But now we are discharged from the law, dead to that which held us captive, so that we serve not under the old written code but in the new life of the Spirit. What then shall we say? That the law is sin? By no means! Yet, if it had not been for the law, I should not have known sin. I should not have known what it is to covet if the law had not said, 'You shall not covet.' But sin, finding opportunity in the commandment, wrought in me all kinds of covetousness. Apart from the law sin lies dead."

Paul does not say that the law itself is sin. Indeed, he concedes that in its original setting the law had a certain degree of holiness (v. 12), when no other way of salvation was available. But now that faith in Jesus is open to man, it is most urgent that he embrace it and shed the law, which "not only makes man conscious of sin . . . but also incites to sin." [4]

Paul's psychology is sound, in some respects. There are some rebellious dispositions who are attracted to a given act precisely because it is forbidden, and the very presence of law creates added temptations to transgression. And Paul is certainly sound in the observation that having a code to live by makes a man conscious of his need to follow the code, and of the perils continually lurking on his way to forsake the code or betray it, knowingly or unknowingly. The repudiation of the code and the demand that a man live with an enthusiasm for an inner faith that centers on an event outside the historical order gives one a sense of inner tranquillity. But is it not the test of a moral man that he is perturbed by the ambiguity of his life, that he sees himself as continually under judgment for the things done or undone? It was a Hebrew prophet who once cried out (Amos 6:1): "Woe to those that are at ease in Zion." Is not this one of the moral problems of our age, that too many people are smug and self-righteous, and overly confident of their rectitude? Law cannot exhaust the moral claims on a man; and the law itself may need periodic adjustment to reckon with new visions and new possibilities. But

[4] John Knox: Commentary, in *The Oxford Annotated Bible* (New York: Oxford University Press; 1962), p. 1366.

the total renunciation of law leads to anarchy and moral suicide.

Some Christian scholars have been troubled by Paul's sweeping denunciation of law, which embraced the ethical as well as the ceremonial. One Jesuit scholar expressed it thus: "That is precisely the delicate—I was about to say the weak—point of Paul's moral teaching: after having completely done away with the Mosaic law, he never says clearly with what he replaces it. . . . In seeing Paul intent on destroying the whole edifice of the ancient Law, without appearing to think of reconstructing it, we ask with anxiety where this work of demolition is going to stop, and on what foundation the obligation of the new dispensation is to rest." [5]

Paul declares in Romans 13:10 that "love is the fulfilling of the law," and some Christian commentators point to this as the Pauline replacement of law which he had abrogated.

The imperative of love for God, as well as man, is a prescription of the Hebrew Bible (Deuteronomy 6:5, Leviticus 19:18). But Judaism knew that it was not enough to give a man a general exhortation and depend on the spontaneous prompting of the heart to implement it in all particular situations. It left man a zone of free initiative where love itself was to suggest what is to be done, and however man responds, it was to be deemed acceptable. But there are some areas of life where too much is at stake to leave it to each individual to improvise for himself the meaning of love. Christianity itself refused to depend on the spontaneity of love to direct man how to serve God. It prescribed rites and sacraments that it deems man's duty to follow. Nor can love of man in itself define man's obligation to his fellowman. We do not depend on the spontaneous generosity of industry to provide a stipend for the sick, the unemployed or the aged, or to give a satisfactory wage for those employed. We provide for these as a matter of law. We do not depend on love alone to guarantee the civil rights of our racial minorities. We seek to provide for these as a matter of law. As E. A. Speiser noted: "The pre-eminent place of the law—*torah*—in the Old Testament and post-biblical Judaism is not due merely to a one-sided emphasis on legalism. Rather it is a reflec-

[5] Ferdinand Prat: *The Theology of St. Paul*, John L. Stoddard (trans.) (Westminster, Md.: The Newman Bookshop; 1961), II, 312.

tion of the unshakable belief, which was first tested in Mesopotamia, that law was the framework of civilization. The validity of that tenet has amply been demonstrated in our own times." [6]

In all walks of life we recognize a need to define a minimum zone of performance to which individuals and society at large will be obligated as a matter of law, however they may understand the imperative to love God or man. Indeed, while law at any given stage of enactment cannot exhaust the imperative of love, it is a vital means of its implementation. Experience would seem to indicate quite the contrary. Love is not the fulfillment of law, because it is both more and less than law. Law is the fulfillment of love, a particular fulfillment for a particular time. Jewish law was a particular fulfillment for a particular time. This is why Jewish law was never static. It went through changes so as to remain cogent for changed times. Other societies, at other times, may write another law. We hope they will be guided by the ideal of love, but they will not be able to depend on love alone. They will have to seek a fulfillment of love through the mediating efficacy of law.

The Rabbis believed that in the messianic age, which was to mark the end of historical time, when man will have reached a level of perfection that will make it possible to establish God's kingship on earth, to be manifest by a new world order based on justice, freedom, and peace, there would be a "withering away" of law. Not all, but many, commandments will then become unnecessary and obsolete, for in that state there will be an enlargement of the zone of free spiritual and moral initiative, and a corresponding shrinkage in the zone of outer-directed prescription. The illusion of Paul was the belief that with the coming of Jesus historic time had reached its end, and in his zeal he demanded the end of all law. His illusion has been repeated often in history when men are so impressed with their particular scheme for human amelioration that they invest it with absolute efficacy and envision its enactment as the dawn of utopia. The overzealous partisans of pre-

[6] E. A. Speiser: "The Ancient Near East and Modern Philosophies of History," *Proceedings of the American Philosophical Society*, 95: 6 (December 1951), 586.

mature utopias have always posed a problem for those seeking to guide man on the long and difficult road he continues to face toward the kingdom of his dreams. The travail of the last twenty centuries, the tears and blood that have flowed like one long river from the innocent crushed under the heels of all kinds of predatory men and nations, makes a mockery of any notion that we live in a postredemption age. We know not how long is the road that yet stretches toward that consummation, but to have any kind of meaning it must be envisioned as a future hope rather than as a past realization.

The relationship alleged between the Hebrew Bible and the new faith centering in the ministry of Jesus found its epitome in the concept of the two Testaments, the Old and the New. This concept was based on the passage in Jeremiah 31:30–33: "Behold the days are coming, says the Lord, when I will make a new covenant with the house of Israel and with the house of Judah, not like the covenant that I made with their fathers when I took them by the hand to bring them out of the land of Egypt, my covenant which they broke, though I was their husband, says the Lord. But this is the covenant which I will make with the house of Israel after those days, says the Lord: I will put my law [*torati*, literally, "My teaching"] within them, and I will write it in their hearts; and I will be their God, and they shall be my people."

The prophet envisions here what is the dream of every religious teacher, surely including the teachers of Christianity. Whatever discipline a religion precribes, conformity is often nominal and external. It does not make its way to the core of a person's life. The goal is always for ever-deeper penetration. Jeremiah acknowledges that the covenant of old (the Christian term "testament" is a synonym for "covenant") had not wholly entered the hearts of the people, and this is the reason they were not fully loyal to it. The prophet envisioned the day when the teachings of the Torah will win a total response from the people, giving them not formal or external allegiance but complete and wholehearted devotion. Indeed, does not the Christian faith, too, need to move from formal profession to a total penetration of the person?

It is clear from a careful examination of Jeremiah's words that he does not envision a replacement of the Torah by a new revelation, but rather a change in the people. It is clear, too, that it is the same Jewish people who remain the bearers of the new covenant as they were of the old. Verse 34, with which the Jeremiah passage continues, allows no other interpretation: "And no longer shall each man teach his neighbor and each his brother saying, 'Know the Lord,' for they shall all know me, from the least of them to the greatest, says the Lord; for I will forgive their iniquity, and I will remember their sin no more." Covenant and people are unchanged, but what is changed is the relation between them. The convenant is made new through a conquering potency, through a yielding of the people without reserve to its truths. In the words of Bernhard W. Anderson, professor of biblical theology at the Theological School of Drew University: "The prophet does not speak of a new Torah but of a new covenant relationship which will enable men to obey the covenant stipulations out of inner motivation. . . . The purpose of covenanting, in both instances, is the establishment of relationship between God and people."[7] James Philip Hyatt, professor of the Old Testament, Vanderbilt University Divinity School, expresses the same thought more categorically: "The new covenant does not involve the giving of a new law; that is unnecessary. . . . The covenant is to be new in the sense that it will confer a new, inward motivation and power for fulfilling the law already known."[8]

Christian exegetes (II Corinthians 3:6, 14) appropriated the vision of Jeremiah for their own ends, declaring that the Hebrew Bible and the law it prescribes constitute the "Old Testament," which was now obsolete since the new covenant had been proclaimed. The new covenant was, in truth, Jesus himself, his life and his teachings, which were set forth for us in the books of the New Testament. Thus the prophet Jeremiah was made to declare

[7] B. W. Anderson (ed.): "The New Covenant and the Old," *The Old Testament and Christian Faith* (New York: Harper & Row; 1963), p. 237.

[8] J. A. Hyatt: Commentary on Jeremiah, in *The Interpreter's Bible* (Nashville, Tenn.: Abingdon Press; 1956), V.

the obsolescence of the Hebrew Bible and its replacement by the Christian faith!

The canon of Christian Scripture includes the Hebrew Bible under the name, "Old Testament." But the Old Testament is so interpreted that it becomes an anticipation of the New Testament. The Old Testament is made to confirm the teachings of the Church. But vast, indeed, is the gap between the Hebrew Bible and the world of thought embraced in the teachings of the Church. To bridge this gap Christian teachers developed a radical interpretation of the Old Testament which ignored the simple and obvious meaning of a text, which tore a text out of its context, which allegorized historical events, and which, in some cases, as we have seen, did not hesitate to amend the Hebrew text by alterations, omissions, or interpolations.

As it emerged from this treatment by Christian exegesis, the Old Testament became a Christian work, differing from the New Testament only in this, that the New Testament taught its truth explicitly, while in the Old Testament the same truths were taught by concealment, in hints, and symbolic allusions. Jews who persisted in defending the historical character of the Hebrew Bible against its transmutation into a work of Christian confirmation were berated as obstinate and blind. The disabilities suffered by the Jewish people after Roman power had destroyed the Temple and crushed their freedom were ultimately invoked as proof that God had rejected the Jews, precisely because they persisted in refusing to embrace the light of the Christian truth. As Beryl Smalley of St. Hilda's College, Oxford, reminds us: "The synagogue is always opposed to the church in the allegorical interpretation as darkness to light, and gradually this type becomes identified with the living Jew, increasing, perhaps helping, to create his unpopularity." [9]

Indeed, some Christian polemicists found in the law taught in the Mosaic code a thing of evil which was imposed on the Jews as an act of divine retribution for their obstinacy. The rite of circumcision, Justin Martyr expounded to the Jew Trypho, "was

[9] Beryl Smalley: *The Study of the Bible in the Middle Ages* (New York: Philosophical Library; 1952), p. 25.

given for a sign, that you should be separated from other nations and us, and that you alone should rightly suffer the things you suffer now, and that your lands should be desolate and your cities burned with fire, and that foreigners should eat up the fruits before your face, and none of you go up to Jerusalem. . . ." [1]

The conception of a New Testament was finally paralleled by the conception of a New Israel. The Christian community proclaimed itself the successor to the Old Israel, which had become obsolete and no longer carried the old promises. The Church was the new Israel, the Israel according to the spirit, the heir of the old promises bestowed upon patriarchs and prophets. The twelve disciples of Jesus corresponded to the twelve tribes of the Israel "after the flesh," and served as a reminder of the break as well as the continuity, the end of the old and its rebirth in the new. Paul was one of the main architects of this concept of the New Israel. In the words of W. D. Davies: "In the death of Jesus, the old Israel had come to an end, and yet in the Resurrection it had begun anew, and there was, therefore, a real continuity between the Israel of the Old Testament and the Christian church, and in the latter Paul sees the world-wide growth of the true Israel, an Israel formed of those who had accepted the claims of Jesus as the messiah." [2]

Christians saw themselves as the true Israel, foreshadowed in all prophecies where Israel is vested with the mission to serve as the custodian of divine promises and obligations. But Christianity shrank the vision of the new Israel in the direction of a narrower religious conception. We have noted that the prophets had clearly transcended religious particularism, acknowledging that non-Jews could reach God on their own terms, without utilizing the specific forms of Jewish piety. The Ninevehites did penance and won a reprieve of the judgment God had decreed against them, according to the account in the Book of Jonah. Nineveh was a pagan city and it remained a pagan city. Their penitence consisted in crying to the Lord, and in turning "everyone from his evil way

[1] *Dialogue with Trypho*, ch. 16.

[2] W. D. Davies: *Paul and Rabbinic Judaism* (London: S.P.C.K.; 1962), p. 75.

and from the violence" that was in his hands. This was sufficient, as we are told: "And God saw their work, that they turned from their evil way, and God repented of the evil that He had said He would do to them" (2:8, 10).

The Apostles preached the Gospel readily to men of all races and nations, but they deemed it indispensable that a person become an adherent of Jesus in order to be "saved." They visualized the Christian community as the new Israel, but they defined the chosenness of the new Israel in exclusive terms, insisting that only through the Christian faith and the Christian rites, only through the efficacy of the sacrifice of Jesus, could a person attain salvation. Even a newborn child, if he should die before baptism, is destined for limbo according to the traditional doctrine of the Catholic and many Protestant churches.

One Christian theologian recently declared that terrestial man is not the only one dependent on Jesus for his salvation. Should there be intelligent beings on other planets in the universe—they, too, would have to believe in Jesus to be "saved." [3] Catholics have recently acknowledged that those outside the Church may be eligible for salvation, but the theory underlying this acknowledgment is that the graces flowing from Jesus may reach a person who is not consciously a communicant of the Church. Jesus thus remains the sole dispenser of salvation.

It is ironic that the unwillingness of Judaism to engage in aggressive missionary activities led Christian interpreters to brand Judaism as "particularistic," while the aggressive missionizing of the Church was taken as a mark of its universality. But the desire to conquer the world, whether inspired by a religious or a political ideology, is a kind of imperialism, rather than an indication of a truly universal spirit in action.

A true universalism is expressed not in the attempt to establish religious or political uniformity, but in the respect shown for the particular forms which life assumes in the course of its unfolding, the individualities of persons and of communities, religious no less than political. Each faces the mission to share with others the

[3] John Marsh: "The Finality of Jesus Christ in the Age of Universal History," *The Ecumenical Review*, XV: 1 (October 1962), 6.

unique fruits of spiritual creativity which emerge in its midst, but each must be left free to integrate such truth with its own pattern of life without the threat of absorption or displacement.

Ananda Kentish Coomaraswamy, viewing Christianity as a believing Hindu, put it thus: "The one outstanding, and perhaps the only real heresy of modern Christianity in the eyes of other believers is its claim to exclusive truth. . . . There are many paths that lead to the summit of one and the same mountain; their differences are the more apparent the lower down we are, but they vanish at the peak; each will naturally take the one that starts from the point at which he finds himself; he who goes round about the mountain looking for another (path) is not climbing. Never let us approach another believer to ask him to become 'one of *us*,' but approach him with respect as one who is already 'one of *His*,' who *is*, and from whose invariable beauty all contingent being depends!" [4]

Arnold J. Toynbee has warned: "In any living creature, the worst of all sins is the idolization of itself or of its own handiwork. This sin is the worst of all because it is the greatest moral and intellectual rebellion that a creature can make against its true state of subordination to God the Absolute Reality, and also because it opens the door to all other sins. This arch-sin is committed by the followers of a higher religion when they idolize their own religious institutions." [5] The claim that a particular religion offers the one and only channel through which a person may achieve salvation is, at least from a Jewish point of view, an instance of this arch-sin of self-idolization.

Rabbi Abraham J. Heschel, in his inaugural address as Harry Emerson Fosdick Visiting Professor at the Union Theological Seminary, warned against this sin of religious self-idolization in claiming exclusive truth. In the words of Rabbi Heschel: "Religion is a means, not the end. It becomes idolatrous when regarded as an end in itself. Over and above all being stands the Creator and

[4] A. K. Coomaraswamy: "Am I My Brother's Keeper," *Christianity: Some Non-Christian Appraisals*, David W. McCain (ed.) (New York: McGraw-Hill; 1964), pp. 64, 72.

[5] Arnold J. Toynbee: *An Historian's Approach to Religion* (London: Oxford University Press; 1956), p. 131.

Lord of history, He who transcends all. To equate religion and God is idolatry.

"Does not the all-inclusiveness of God contradict the exclusiveness of any particular religion? . . . Is it not blasphemous to say: I alone have all the truth and grace, and all those who differ live in darkness, and are abandoned by the grace of God?

"Is it really our desire to build a monolithic society: one party, one view, one leader, and no opposition? Is religious uniformity desirable or even possible? Has it really proved to be a blessing for a country when all its citizens belonged to one denomination? Or has any denomination attained a spiritual climax when it had the adherence of the entire population? Does not the task of preparing the kingdom of God require a diversity of talents, a variety of rituals, soul-searching as well as opposition?

"Perhaps it is the will of God that in this aeon there should be diversity in our forms of devotion and commitment to Him. In this aeon diversity of religions is the will of God." [6]

The frustration of Christian hopes to win the Jews to the new faith gradually changed the orientation of Christian polemics. It turned it toward the pagan world, where Christian prospects indeed proved brightest. But here, too, there was need to deal with the paradox of the messiahship of Jesus and his anticlimactic end on the cross. Taking advantage of the growing resentment of Jews in the Roman world in the period following the Jewish-Roman wars of the first century, Christian spokesmen found it expedient to shift the blame for the crucifixion on the Jews. "The experience of the Church, especially after A.D. 70, was that while the Jews increasingly refused to accept Christ's claims, the Romans were sometimes increasingly friendly and Gentiles in general seemed much more inclined to believe. It was therefore natural to lay blame for the crucifixion exclusively on the Jews and to exonerate the Romans completely, and a steadily increasing tendency can be observed in the New Testament and later Christian literature to transfer all guilt in this matter to Jewish shoulders." [7]

[6] Abraham J. Heschel: "No Religion Is an Island," *Union Seminary Quarterly*, XXI:2 (January 1966), 126.

[7] D. E. Nineham: *The Gospel of St. Mark* (Baltimore: Penguin Books; 1963), p. 368.

It is impossible to reconstruct the events surrounding the crucifixion as they really occurred; the accounts given us in the Gospels reflect editorial revision by men who shaped events to conform to the beliefs and passions of their own day. Summing up the results of what is called "form criticism" in New Testament scholarship, Rudolf Bultmann maintains that all indications point to the crucifixion as a Roman execution for what was in their eyes a political offense and that the Jews had little if any part in it. The movement inaugurated by Jesus must have seemed to the Romans "like any of the other messianic movements which in those decades convulsed the Jewish people and finally led to the war with Rome and the destruction of Jerusalem. The Roman procurators suppressed such movements with blood, and Jesus fell a victim to the intervention of the procurator Pilate. As he came up to Jerusalem with his followers his arrival was viewed by the procurator as politically dangerous. Whatever part the Jewish authorities took in the tragedy cannot now be made out, since the Passion Narrative is too thickly overgrown with legend. For the later Christians the real enemies were the Jews; since they were found to be their standing enemies and accusers in the work of Christian mission (note the representation in the Book of Acts), they were also made responsible for the death of Jesus. It is, of course, possible that the Jewish court in Jerusalem, in order to demonstate its own political innocence, had some part in the tragedy; but at all events we are not entitled to assume that Jesus' ethical teaching so roused the Pharisees and Scribes against him that he finally fell victim to their enmity. That the steady opposition of the Pharisees and the Scribes rest upon the artificial and schematic conception of later Christians has already been shown." [8]

Students of the New Testament discern a deliberate anti-Jewish bias in the Passion narrative, in the earliest stratum of the New Testament, even in the Gospel According to Mark (the oldest of the Gospels). But it becomes more pronounced in writings where Hellenistic influences are more dominant. In Matthew, Mark, and Luke, hostility to Jesus is normally expressed by some Jews, "by particular parties, especially Pharisees, Sadducees or

[8] Bultmann and Kundsin: *Form Criticism*, p. 72.

both, but in St. John's Gospel His opponents are 'the Jews,' the term occurring some seventy times, while the Pharisees are mentioned barely twenty times, and the Sadducees not at all." [9] As Frederick C. Grant put it: "John, despite his glowing paragraphs about 'love' in the abstract nevertheless hates 'the Jews'—i.e. the Jewish leaders—with all his heart. Such orthodoxy and spirituality of profession contradicted by actual performance was a bad heritage for the Hellenistic church, and destined to survive for a long time." [1] The Gospel of St. John is the most anti-Jewish book in the New Testament, but even the Book of Revelation, which is generally regarded as the most friendly, denounces non-Christian Jews as the "Synagogue of Satan" (2:9, 3:9).

Even in their anti-Jewish expositions Christian polemicists drew on the Hebrew Bible. Prophetic criticism of the Jewish people as part of their moral exhortations were turned into denunciations of the Jewish people as such. The prophets' tender expressions for the Jewish people were appropriated for the Church, the denunciations were turned into proof that the Jews had always been depraved; the greatest depravity was of course their rejection of Jesus. In John's Gospel the Jews stood condemned by their own Bible, by Moses and the prophets—for not abandoning Judaism in favor of the faith which centered in Jesus. The following is quoted in the name of Jesus, in an address to the Jews (5:45–46): "Do not think that I shall accuse you to the Father; it is Moses who accuses you, on whom you set your hope. If you believed Moses, you would believe me, for he wrote of me."

The shifting of blame for the crucifixion on the Jews continued to proliferate in Christian literature. The Jews were charged with the frightful crime of "deicide," the "murder of God." This crime was laid on the corporate people who lived at the time of the crucifixion (those in Jerusalem, in Palestine, and in the Diaspora), and it was maintained that the guilt was transmitted by heredity to all Jews forever after. The destruction of the Temple

[9] R. H. Lightfoot: *St. John's Gospel* (London: Oxford University Press; 1963), p. 64.

[1] Frederick C. Grant: *The Gospels* (New York: Harper & Brothers; 1957), p. 179.

in Jerusalem and the subsequent sufferings of the Jewish people under various persecuting regimes throughout the world were cited as proof that God had rejected them.

The notion that mortals can "murder God" rests on a primitive conception of the deity, one which regards the god as subject to birth and death, as a physical being, in other words, whose fate may be determined by human action. The term was used in primitive religion to denote the killing of a totem animal or of a priest-king, whether real or symbolic. A universal and eternal God, who is beyond the limitations of the physical, is not subject to "deicide." Christian polemicists ignored the affront to the deity implied in the charge leveled against the Jews that they were guilty of "deicide." The charge was invoked to carry the hostility to Jews to its most formidable climax, without considering the difficulties involved in the notion that mortal hands could bring injury to God.

The doctrine of Jewish guilt contravened the principle of individual responsibility expounded so forcefully in biblical and rabbinic Judaism. For how could the entire Jewish people who lived during the epoch of the crucifixion be held responsible for the fate which befell Jesus? We have noted that, according to historians, the Gospel narratives cannot be admitted as a factual account of the crucifixion; the indications are that the main actors in that tragedy were the Romans rather than the Jews. But even if those narratives are allowed to stand, the numbers of Jews involved could not have been large. By what principle of law or morality may the offense of *some* be turned into an offense of the people as a whole? One thinks of the outcry of Moses (Numbers 16:22): "If one man sin, wilt Thou be angry with the entire community?"

And by what principle can one justify the transmission of guilt to the generations of Jews who were not even in the world at the time of Jesus? We have noted previously the Christian belief in inherited guilt. Man's basic problem, it was taught by New Testament writers, was his sinful nature, inherited from Adam. In the words of Paul: "Sin came into the world through one man, and death through sin; and so death spread to all men because all men sinned" (Romans 5:12). This became a critical doctrine in Christianity. Adam's fall effected a change in man: it made him mortal; it contaminated his seed forever after with the guilt of his disobedience; and the only atonement available to save men from the frightful consequences of this guilt is the atoning power of the blood of Jesus.

The story of Adam's disobedience is, of course, part of the Hebrew Bible, but Judaism never invested it with doctrinal significance. Indeed, according to the Rabbis, Adam's mortality was not a consequence of his disobedience; it was included in the original design of his birth (Genesis Rabbah 30:8). As a finite creature, he could not have been other than a mortal. The story of the "fall" is rather conceived as a parable depicting man's proneness to disobedience, and his need continually to strive for purging from its consequences; but the story is not seen as an account of the *cause* of his condition.

The belief in corporate guilt, as the belief in inherited guilt, represents moral primitivism which the prophet Ezekiel had denounced centuries earlier. In the words of Ezekiel (18:1-4, 20): "The word of the Lord came to me again: What do you mean by repeating this proverb concerning the land of Israel, 'The fathers have eaten sour grapes and the children's teeth are set on edge'? As I live, says the Lord God, this proverb shall no more be used by you in Israel. Behold all souls are mine; the soul of the father as well as the soul of the son is mine. . . . The soul that sins shall die. The son shall not suffer for the iniquity of the father nor the father suffer for the iniquity of the son; the righteousness of the righteous shall be upon himself, and the wickedness of the wicked shall be upon himself."

There was a certain inconsistency, too, in blaming the Jews for the crucifixion if it was maintained that the death of Jesus was a necessary event in the economy of divine providence, that his death was the supreme triumph of his redemptive ministry, that it was a freely willed sacrifice to atone for the sins of humanity. Christian teachers were not inhibited by the primitivism of believing in corporate guilt and inherited guilt, nor were they disturbed by the inconsistency of blaming the Jews for an event which represented for them the very heart of God's plan for man's salvation. The charges were repeated through the centuries and became a Christian amalgam in the blind passions of Anti-Semitism. In the Middle Ages it was invoked to account for Jewish persecutions and expulsions. As Professor Salo W. Baron summarizes it: "The Jewish prople became in Christian eyes more and more the eternal Ahasuerus [a character in the New Testament who refused to give hospitality to Jesus and who was, therefore, doomed to constant wandering and homelessness], the Wandering Jew who cannot and must not find rest. . . . Was not Abel the prototype of Jesus, the innocent son of man, whose offering was accepted by God, but who for this reason was slain by his elder brother? It appeared only just that the New Cain, the Jewish people, should likewise be a 'fugitive and a vagabond . . . in the earth' (Genesis 4:12)." [2] In our own time this accusation with all its emotional overtones helped condition the German people to accept the Nazi program of murder against the Jews of Europe.

The Christian attempt to turn the Jewish Scriptures into a work of polemics against the Jews and Judaism represents a radical use of exegetical hermeneutics. Those beholding the phenomenon with objectivity have found it of extremely questionable proprICty, to say the least. Professor Robert H. Pfeiffer offers us a succinct characterization of this Christian assault on Jews and Judaism: "It was not long before the Christians regarded themselves as the true Israel to whom the divine promises of the Old Testament had been addressed. Consequently, they went so far as to appropriate the Old Testament Scriptures, even forgetting that they belonged to the Synagogue." [3]

Friedrich Nietzsche was no lover of the Jews or of their Scriptures, but he took sharp issue with the Christological interpretation of the Jewish Scriptures. He scoffed at Christianity as the religion "which during the centuries since its foundation performed the philological burlesque around the Old Testament; I

[2] Salo W. Baron: *A Social and Religious History of the Jews* (New York: Columbia University Press; 1937) II, 32.

[3] R. H. Pfeiffer: *Introduction to the Old Testament* (New York: Harper & Brothers; 1948), p. 6.

mean the attempt to pull the Old Testament from under the body of the Jews with the assertion that it contains nothing but Christian doctrine and belongs to the Christians as the true Israel, while the Jews had only usurped it. One indulged in a frenzy of interpretation and supposition which could not possibly have had a good conscience. However much Jewish scholars protested, everywhere the Old Testament was supposed to speak of Christ and nothing but Christ." [4]

It takes subtleties of reason to create a fabric of interpretation in which the simple is seen as pregnant with hidden complexities. The dialectician who lives in the realm of these subtleties and engages in the intellectual refinements of textual analysis may rise above the inherent simplicities of the text itself, but for those who can look objectively, the exposure to the original Hebrew text or to the text even in translation often becomes a shattering experience. The Jesuit scholar Rev. Joseph Bonsirven has admitted the implausibility of many of the New Testament interpretations that cite Old Testament "proofs" for Christian teachings: "In some cases the connection between the supposed prediction and its fulfillment is of the flimsiest character, and when we get into the field of allegorical interpretation and typology, it often seems as if the only limits to what can be done are set by the resources and fertility of invention of the expositor." [5]

We have cited Christian scholars who have in some instances repudiated the reading of Christian doctrine into the Hebrew Bible, but it is pertinent to add that this practice continues, not only among conservatives but also among active followers of Christian ecumenism. Thus a seminar on biblical studies which was part of a Roman Catholic-Protestant colloquium at Harvard in 1964 reached the following consensus: "The New Testament's interpretation of the Old Testament is accepted as valid, but one does not thereby downgrade the meaning of the Old Testament in its own right. The New Testament does not swallow up the meaning of the Old, but the latter as the 'cradle of Christ,' belongs

[4] *Morgenröthe*, Aphorism 84.

[5] Quoted by H. H. Rowley: *The Unity of the Bible* (Philadelphia: Westminster Press; 1953), p. 120, note 1.

to the interpretation of the Christ-event." [6] The Vatican II statement on Revelation reiterates the conviction that the New Testament is "hidden in the Old" and "the Old made manifest in the New."

The reading of the Bible, especially the Old Testament, has often been a problem for the Christian Church. Many a cherished dogma has seemed questionable in the light of the plain meaning of the biblical text. To deal with this problem various strategies were devised, including the attempt to discourage reading the Bible. The Council of Toulouse (1229) made it an offense for a layman even to harbor a Bible in his home. Pope Innocent III ordered the bishops to be strict in enforcing this law. His statement took the form of a homily based on a text in the Hebrew Bible (Exodus 19:12–13): "The Divine Law has wisely decreed that any beast touching the Holy Mountain should be stoned to death; this typifies that the common people may not presume by their intellect to attain to the sublime heights of Revelation and to preach to others. . . . There remains for you, therefore, but one thing, to obey. Do so voluntarily and you will not be compelled by force." The Synod of Tarragona (1234) ordered all vernacular versions of the Bible to be burnt by the bishops. The prohibition to read Scripture was repeated by Pope Pius IV (r. 1559–65) and Pope Clement VIII (r. 1592–1605). Pope Pius IX in his Syllabus of 1864 condemned Bible societies that encouraged the reading of Scripture by laymen, along with socialism, communism, and freemasonry.

Movements of reformation within the Church were invariably associated with a call for the "open Bible." Especially the Old Testament proved a source of ferment, challenging conventional dogmas with the dynamism of the living history of a people wrestling with God and His claims upon their finite natures. One of its most telling illustrations was the rise of Puritanism in eighteenth-century England. The historian Thomas Macaulay tells us that the Puritans "paid to the Hebrew language a respect which they refused to the tongue in which the discourses of Jesus and

[6] *Ecumenical Dialogue at Harvard* (Cambridge, Mass.: Harvard University Press; 1964), p. 304.

the epistles of Paul had come down to us. They baptized their children by the names, not of Christian saints, but of Hebrew patriarchs and warriors. . . . They sought for principles of jurisprudence in the Mosaic law. . . . Morals and manners were subjected to a code resembling that of the synagogue. . . ." [7]

Exposure to the Old Testament, especially in its original Hebrew idiom, has inspired various anti-Trinitarian or "Judaizing" heresies, as they were sometimes called by Church authorities. Some were indeed led to embrace Judaism, in part, if not completely. The Seventh-Day Adventists have remained fundamentalist Christians, but they have embraced the seventh-day Sabbath, and they keep some of the dietary restrictions as do Jews, after the prescription in the Old Testament. Aime Pallière's remarkable pilgrimage from the priesthood of the Roman Catholic Church to Judaism, received its great impetus from reading the Hebrew Bible. An entire village of Italian peasants in San Nicandro Garganico embraced Judaism in 1946 as a result of studying the Old Testament, and most of them left Italy to settle in Israel.

The Protestant Churches have always stressed the importance of Bible study. The Catholic Church, too, has come to acknowledge the importance of Bible study for the religious life. This has coincided with the growing secularism of our culture which has presented the Bible as a great literature that is to be known in its human dimensions for its literary and aesthetic qualities rather than as a denominational document. It is this wider dissemination of the Bible, we have noted, which has contributed to the ferment of change in Christian thought. Conservative churchmen, while giving their blessings to the popularization of Bible study, have however often cautioned against the free interpretation of it.

The Vatican II statement on Revelation declared unequivocally that "the task of authentically interpreting the word of God . . . has been entrusted exclusively to the living teaching office of the Church, whose authority is exercised in the name of Jesus Christ." The interpretation of Scripture, the same Vatican II statement further declared, must remain "subject . . . to the judg-

[7] T. B. Macaulay: *History of England* (New York: Harper & Brothers; 1875), I, 60–1.

ment of the Church, which carries out the divine commission and ministry of guarding and interpreting the word of God."

We have called attention to a preoccupation of the traditional Christian interpretation of the Bible. It is to present the Old Testament as a preface to the New Testament. It is to turn the Hebrew Bible into a work that negates Judaism and affirms Christianity.

Christological interpretation of the Old Testament has suffered a serious challenge at the hand of modern scholarship. The historical study of the Bible, the advances made in the sciences of archeology and linguistics have tended to reveal the books of the Old Testament as historical documents set in a given time and place and addressed to people dealing with concrete, existential situations. It has seemed difficult to take biblical statements that have a perfectly plausible meaning in their context out of this context, to speak allegorically in prediction of events due to transpire many centuries later. On the other hand, the acceptance of the Old Testament on its own terms has posed certain contradictions to the scheme of dogmas represented in the Christian faith.

The Christian Church has a long history of struggle with the problems posed by the Old Testament. In the early Church, as we noted, there was a proposal to eliminate the Old Testament as antithetical to Christian views. It was made by Marcion who fought ardently for his position. Marcion was hostile to the Jews and to Judaism. He saw in Judaism a force affirming existence, while for him the spiritual life consisted in the renunciation of mundane existence. He taught a doctrine of two deities: the God of the Old Testament was the creator of the transient world, while the God of the New Testament redeems men from the transient world, and he redeems them through Jesus. Marcion was branded a heretic and was expelled from the Roman Catholic Church for the persistent advocacy of his views.

The ideas of Marcion, with their hostility to Judaism and their disparagement of the Old Testament, found new advocates in German Christianity. Friedrich Schleiermacher (1768–1834), Protestant theologian and philosopher, and the well-known

Church historian Adolph Harnack (1851–1930) joined in the call to repudiate the Old Testament as a work of Jewish legalism that can have no meaning for the purely "spiritual" faith of a Christian.

Rudolf Bultmann, the noted contemporary German theologian and authority on the early Church, has joined in the movement to reject the Old Testament as an embodiment of Christian revelation. Its only interest for a Christian, according to him, is historical. Its contribution to Christianity is in the exemplification of a type of piety which confronts man with existence *under the Law,* with demands that man merit God's love by fulfilling conditions. It is in struggling with the impossibilities of meeting the claims of the Law, that man enters the state of *existence under grace,* in which he ceases to strive for merit through his own initiative, and submits himself to God as a sinner, assured that God will accept him as he is in his sinful state. God's acceptance is the gift of salvation or eternal life which man possesses through union with Jesus, who was resurrected after dying on the cross.

Bultmann's position bears within it a moral passivity and resignation which rejects man's capacity for moral growth. It encourages a pessimism concerning man's moral endeavor that will leave him and his society in a state of moral paralysis, for it cancels the call to righteousness as a divine imperative and assures man of divine approval no matter how morally depraved he may be. The nullification of the call to righteousness withdraws the existential world from religious concern and establishes in fact two autonomous kingdoms, the kingdom of the world and the kingdom of the spirit. It centers man's gaze toward an eschatological vision, and renounces the viability of the goal stressed in Judaism, to "perfect the world under the kingship of the Almighty."

The Hebrew Bible did not suggest that man could ever fully meet the divine demand pressing on him, but it asked man to strive in a moral direction, taking God's perfection as a model to emulate. Success in such an endeavor must always remain relative, but it is in whatever steps man succeeds in taking on the upward path that he meets his human vocation. The act of his striving makes him truly human and vindicates the purpose for which he was created. And it is in the fact of his striving that he earns God's love, though God's love is in truth unconditional and available to him, regardless of his merit.

What interests us in Bultmann's position, however, is his recognition of the disparity between the two testaments. In the words of Dr. Bultmann: "*The Old Testament ought not to be understood contrary to its original sense*, as this sense is to be established by historical research alone. For if this were changed, then it would no longer be the Old Testament that speaks. . . . Every form of allegory is idle play or nonsense." [8]

There have been proponents of another solution for modern Christianity, the solution of allowing the Old Testament to speak in its own authentic voice, and to adapt the Christian position so as to make it compatible with the Old Testament view of God and man. This solution is advocated by the noted Swiss theologian H. Emil Brunner. The New Testament, he points out, is written under the inspiration of Greek thought which equates spirit—and consequently the true and the good—with the abstract, disparaging the realm of concrete existence as the antithesis of the spiritual and considering it, therefore, as evil. Resting on the New Testament alone, Christianity would, therefore, become a kind of "mystery" religion, divorced from the existential world, and irrelevant to its problems and its needs.

The Old Testament is a vital balance against this, saving Christianity from the excesses of the Greek view of life. In the words of Dr. Brunner: "The movement away from the world, the flight out of the world of finitude into the eternity, nonworldliness, and impersonality of God is the movement of idealistic, mystical or Greek religion: redemption from the world. . . . The Old Testament knows nothing of this world-escaping, world-negatating ascetic tendency. And that is because God is not the impassive idea beyond existence but the Creator of the world who loves and seeks his world. Therefore, the Old Testament is full of world affirmation, indeed one could say full of worldliness. . . .

[8] Rudolf Bultmann: "The Significance of the Old Testament for the Christian Faith," in *The Old Testament and Christian Faith*, pp. 8–36.

"This worldliness of prophetic eschatology is so pronounced . . . that it appears as though the prophets were not concerned with an ultimate end, with *End-Geschichte*, but only with a historical goal. But manifestly it is this 'accursed Jewish optimism,' as Schopenhauer expressed it, and this very eudemonistic worldliness, as he viewed it, that is necessary so that the New Testament idea of the Kingdom of God can be secured against Schopenhauerian and other misunderstandings, according to which the New Testament idea is akin to the Buddhistic-mystical Nirvana. . . .

"That the redemption of the world in the kingdom of heaven does not mean the Platonic Beyond, the idealistic immortality of the soul, but includes the corporeal; that the world is not to be dissolved but to be brought to completion . . . all this we can understand rightly only against the background of the prophetic hope of the Old Testament. . . . Thus the understanding of the Old Testament is the criterion and basis for understanding the new." [9]

The Old Testament can render this or any other service to man's spiritual life if it is permitted to speak in its authenticity, without being forced into the preconceived assumptions of sectarian apologetics. The recent appearance of the Standard Revised Version of the Bible, which has attempted to translate the Hebrew text without reference to Christian apologetics, gives promise of such a development. Prepared under the sponsorship of the National Council of the Churches of Christ in the United States, this version of the Bible indicates that Christian scholars are prepared to accept the Hebrew Bible as it manifestly is and to permit its distinctive voice to be given a hearing. The Confraternity Version of the Old Testament, as we noted previously, represents a like development in Catholicism.

The challenge that faces Christians in dealing with the Old Testament is to respect the canons of literary authenticity. Facts have a stubborn reality and they have a right not to be interpreted out of existence. The Hebrew Bible has a certain meaning. It

[9] H. Emil Brunner: "The Significance of the Old Testament for Our Faith," in *The Old Testament and Christian Faith*, pp. 260, 261, 264.

speaks with its own voice concerning man and his destiny. This voice must not be subverted for the sake of conformity to a doctrinal position.

The refusal of the Church to follow Marcion in rejecting the Hebrew Bible testifies to an intuition that Christianity belongs within the Jewish orbit. The fuller justice which this intuition demands is to acknowledge the Hebrew Bible for its distinctive vision. The inclusion of the Hebrew Bible in the Christian canon of sacred Scripture will then make its full contribution. For the unique treasury of faith represented in the Hebrew Bible will then be given its legitimate place in Christian, as in Jewish, thought, that its own distinctive light may shine on man's way to God.

Chapter XIV

Between Judaism and Christianity

Judaism and Christianity are linked to each other with a kinship that transcends all their differences. Christianity arose in the Jewish household of faith, and its basic teachings clearly reflect the influence of its family origin. The Jewish Scriptures are hallowed in Christendom as part of its own sacred Scriptures; the Jewish heroes of faith, from Abraham through the prophets, are also deemed as the pioneers of the Christian faith; the basic teachings of Judaism concerning God and man were adopted by Christianity into its own doctrinal structure; Jesus was a Jew who lived within the context of Jewish experience, and the incidents of his life are set in the land of Israel and constitute a chapter in the history of the Jewish people.

Christianity is a tributary that has flown from the mainstream of Judaism, and it constitutes one of the major Jewish contributions to civilization. Jews and Christians have sometimes forgotten their true relationship. In our own time the Nazis, in their demonic fury, forced upon them the remembrance of it. Their morbid hate for Judaism overflowed and was extended to Christianity as well;

Christianity was for them only another version of the Jewish idea, against which they had pledged uncompromising warfare.

The kinship between the two traditions exists in the face of all that has divided them. But we have noted the vast differences between them. It will be well to recall the basic differences that separate the two faiths. It will help us to see the problem of a possible reconciliation between them in better perspective.

Most of the reservation which a Jew must feel concerning Christianity stems from the belief in the messiahship of Jesus and its various doctrinal elaborations. The *man* Jesus, who lived and taught and struggled for his ideals and in the end died a martyr's death, is a major figure in Jewish history. But Christianity has invested his being with metaphysical significance. It has made his role as mediator between God and man an indispensable element in the scheme of human salvation.

As defined in Christianity, Jesus is God incarnate in human form. The ministry of Jesus in cleansing man from the taint of guilt due to his Adamic nature is further identified by Christians with the redeeming mission that Jewish tradition had associated with the messiah. In Jesus Christians see the messiah long anticipated in Judaism, whose ministry offers those who believe in him redemption from sin, and its consequences.

The pagan world, as Otto Rank has shown, idealized its heroes by raising them above human stature, by characterizing them as semi-divine or divine beings.[1] Sometimes it speaks of them as born of a virgin through impregnation by a deity. Judaism knew that an impassable gulf existed between God and man. It fought against the over-idealization of its own heroes. It presents them all as *human* figures, whose deeds, great as they were, are only a token of the heights to which a *man* may rise in meeting the claims of the divine imperatives which summon him (Yalkut Shimeoni, Joshua, ch. 2). The deification of human figures so current in the Hellenistic world was for the Rabbis an idolatrous practice which they denounced as inconsistent with the belief in the unity and transcendent majesty of God. The Christian belief in the Incarnation, ascribing divine stature to Jesus, with its various doc-

[1] Otto Rank: *The Myth of the Birth of the Hero*, Philip Freund (ed.) (New York: Alfred A. Knopf; 1959), pp. 1–96.

trinal ramifications, will always prove unacceptable to those schooled in the conception of God as taught in Jewish tradition.

Judaism at one time included the offering of sacrifices in its system of piety, but these, as some Jewish teachers explained, were allowed as a concession to popular habit. The offering of sacrifices was so well established in antiquity that its total abolition would have been too radical a step for an ancient people to accept. The Torah therefore retained the cult of sacrifices, purging it of pagan elements and directing it to the service of the one God. But the blood of the sacrifice was not deemed indispensable in Judaism, and thus when the Temple in Jerusalem was destroyed the Rabbis did not hesitate to declare that a piety based on prayer, the Sabbath and festivals, the study of Torah, and the performance of good deeds was superior to a piety based on sacrifices. The belief that man's salvation can be effected only by God's "self-sacrifice," by the blood of the crucified Jesus, is for the Jew a reversion to the primitive, which he cannot reconcile with his conviction that "clean hands and a pure heart" (Psalms 24:4) is all a man needs to come before his Maker.

Judaism teaches a belief in the messiah, but what is primary in the messianic faith in Judaism is its historical content. The core of this belief is the vision of a new world order of justice, freedom, and peace to replace the present epoch of oppression of man by man and nation by nation. The term *messiah* means the "anointed one"; it alludes to the fact that great leaders in antiquity were anointed with oil. As the belief in the new world order, sometimes called the Kingdom of God, attained its fullest proliferation, it added the element of expectation that its inauguration would be effected through the mediating role of an ideal leader, an "anointed one," who would guide men to the inner moral and spiritual transformations which would in turn be translated into a new order of human interrelations. The belief that the messiah's role is to free men from sin and that this has already been effected by Jesus robs the Jewish belief of its historical content and shrinks seriously man's hope for the future. For if ours is a post-messianic age, if our world, with its gross wrongs and frightful injustices, is a world *after* redemption, then life is a vanity of vanities.

Martin Buber differentiated the Jewish and Christian conceptions of the messiah in these terms: "If we wish to reduce the schism between Jews and Christians, between Israel and the Church, to a formula, we can say: The Church stands on the belief in the 'having come' of Christ as the God-given redemption of man. We, Israel, are incapable of believing this. The Church views our declaration either as a case of not wanting to believe, as a very questionable sort of obduracy, or else as a kind of curse, as a basic limitation on the ability to recognize reality, as the blinding of Israel which prevents it from seeing the light. . . . But we . . . know . . . that the world has not yet been redeemed. We know it as surely as we know that the air which we breathe exists. . . . We apprehend the unredeemedness of the world. . . . For us, the redemption of the world is indivisibly equated with the completion of creation, with the erection of a unity no longer hindered by anything, no longer suffering any contradiction, realized in all the multiplicity of the world, equated, in short, with the fulfillment of the kingdom of God. We are incapable of comprehending anticipation of the *consummate* redemption of the world, in any partial respect, such as the soul's already being redeemed, however much redeeming and becoming redeemed manifest themselves to us too in our mortal hours." [2]

The Christian conception of its mission in the world was rooted, as we noted previously, in the claim that in the Church was the new Israel, the heir to the prerogatives of the Jewish people as expressed in Abraham's call to "be a blessing" to all the families of the earth, and as further confirmed in the covenant formed at Sinai. But as we indicated previously, Judaism, in developing the conception of its mission, raised it to universal dimensions by conceding the legitimacy of diverse paths to God. It defined its task to be a witness to the spiritual and moral truths of the Torah, without requiring that those to whom it spoke step out of their ancestral faiths to express those truths through specifically Jewish rites and symbols. Any religious faith is capable of spiritual and moral progress, and its own rites and symbols can be an efficacious expression of a universal value system. While Judaism was willing

[2] *The Writings of Martin Buber*, Will Herberg (ed.) (New York: Meridian Books; 1956), pp. 179 ff.

to admit proselytes, its primary aim was not to convert men to itself, in a formal sense, but to be a force for moral and spiritual progress among all men, regardless of their formal religious affiliations. Christianity, however, particularized this conception, insisting that men cannot be "saved" except through Jesus, and that they can come to Jesus only by entering the Church.

The role which Christianity assigned to Jesus in the drama of salvation presupposed a conception of human nature which was itself an issue between Judaism and Christianity. Christianity tends to see man as a depraved creature who is trapped by guilt as a condition of his birth and who cannot extricate himself from his condition regardless of what he may do with his life. The transmission of guilt from Adam to all his offspring forever after, occurs, according to Augustine, "through the sexual act, which by virtue of the lust that accompanies it, is inherently sinful." [3]

What is man to do then to save himself? The Christian answer is that God has provided an answer—it is the freely offered gift of grace conferred through the death of Jesus on the cross, who was offered up by God as an atoning sacrifice for the sins of humanity. Those who believe in Jesus become the beneficiaries of his sacrifice and are thus saved from eternal damnation that awaits all other mortals. Gabriel Herbert has put it thus: "Here we have the distinction of actual sin and Original Sin. Actual sin is acts committed by such and such a person at such and such a time, by thought, word, or deed; Original Sin is the *state* of alienation from God which lies behind. . . . The escape from this enmity or alienation (which is Original Sin) cannot be effected by the Self, for then it would have cause to take pride in its own ingenuity in contriving its escape. . . . The one way of escape is that the means of escape should be provided by God himself, and be received by Man as a gift: and such is the Christian Gospel." [4]

The Christian doctrine of original sin introduced into culture a morbid outlook toward all natural life. It introduced guilt feel-

[3] Wilhelm Pauck: Entry on "Original Sin," *An Encyclopedia of Religion*, Vergilius Ferm (ed.) (New York: Philosophical Library; 1945).

[4] Gabriel Herbert: *The Old Testament From Within* (London: Oxford University Press; 1962), pp. 25 f.

ings toward sex. It fostered a quietism and resignation concerning the *real* evils in man and society. It blunted the passion of the Hebrew prophets, who continually challenged their people toward moral activism, to abandon the lowly aspirations and pursuits, to strive to be better and to do better.

The Christian conception of human nature was usually supported by the story of Adam's fall from grace. There were of course other influences behind this Christian conception. The most important of these no doubt was the Greek disparagement of the body, and indeed of all things physical.

Judaism, as reflected in its authoritative writings, refused to follow this condemnation of human nature. As Dr. Robert Gordis points out: "No such idea [as original sin] is expressed anywhere in the Hebrew Bible, nor did it ever develop in normative Judaism. . . . The Book of *Genesis* itself notes the punishment meted out to each of the malefactors involved in the Garden of Eden: Adam, Eve and the serpent. That man remains a free moral agent, capable of victory over evil, is explicitly affirmed in the very next chapter in *Genesis* [4:7], where the Lord says to Cain, 'If you do well, you will be exalted. But if you do not do well, sin is crouching at the door; its desire is for you, but you can master it.' . . . Centuries later, when the massive power of Roman tyranny seemed eternal and immovable, a sense of despair gripped some circles in Palestine. Their sense of hopelessness found theological expression in the idea that Adam's sin gave his descendants an innate propensity to evil. . . . This mood, however, never became dominant in traditional Judaism, which held fast to the faith that each man is master of his destiny, capable of transforming himself and the world through his will for good, in which, to be sure, he may count on God's aid." [5]

The Jewish hero of faith is Job, who even when he is assailed by God's judgments and everything precious is taken from him continues to maintain defiantly that he is innocent. God is pictured as sustaining his defiance, against his friends who protest that no man can deem himself innocent before the Creator. God's

[5] Robert Gordis: *A Faith for Moderns* (New York: Bloch Publishing; 1960), pp. 195–6.

answer is that in the mysterious complexity of divine providence we cannot insist on a perfect correlation between a man's fate and his state of virtue; an element of tragedy is part of life and an innocent man may well suffer without cause. Such suffering must evoke our pity but it may never be taken as a clue to some hidden guilt.

The noted Christian interpreter of Pharisaism R. Travers Herford offers us a succinct summation of the divergence between Judaism and Christianity: "Judaism, as has been stated, is a detailed system of ethical *practices* by which its adherents consecrated their daily lives to the *service* of God. The cornerstone of Judaism was the *deed*, not the *dogma*. The fundamental characteristic of Christianity, as it was preached by the apostles, and as it is embodied today in both the Protestant and the Catholic Churches was, on the other hand, faith in a Person, that person being, of course, the Founder. 'Believe in the Lord Jesus,' says Christianity, 'and thou shalt be saved.' Salvation for professing Christians is not a consequence of duty done in the conscious service of God; it is something mystically received as a gift of divine grace. Christ was regarded as an agent in a mysterious transaction whereby a divine purpose of redemption by love had been accomplished by a personal sacrifice, the benefits of which were open to all those who were willing but to signify their faith in him. Christianity and Judaism appealed to different sides of human nature; the former to the passive side, the latter to the active side. Christianity stressed *faith*, Judaism *right action*. Christianity preached a mystical communion through faith with a divine power by which the evils of life disappear without any effort of the personal will. Judaism insisted on the conscious individual consecration of each single human being by thought and will and act to the service of his God." [6]

Tolerance is shown by the measure of respect one shows toward those with whom one disagrees. The differences between Judaism and Christianity in themselves should not have been a cause of hostility. The two traditions should have been glad to

[6] R. T. Herford: *The Truth About the Pharisees* (New York: The Menorah Press; 1925), pp. 36 f.

cherish what they had in common, and otherwise agree to disagree without a loss of good will. But circumstances conspired to make their disagreement disagreeable.

Christians from their earliest history were an aggressively missionary community. The earliest group they sought to missionize was the very group in whose midst their movement arose, the Jewish people. Hence there arose a fierce polemic between Jews and Christians on the subject of the new faith. And as the Jewish people remained unyielding in rejecting the claims of Christians, the polemic grew sharper and more bitter.

Christian spokesmen attacked the spiritual leaders of the Jewish people, the Pharisees, and the people themselves, who were castigated as blind and unspiritual and as impervious to the light of the new revelation. Exasperated by the resistance of Jews to the new faith, the Gospel of John put these words on the lips of Jesus (8:43–47): "Why do you not understand what I say? It is because you cannot bear to hear my word. You are of your father the devil, and your will is to do your father's desires. . . . He who is of God hears the words of God; the reason why you do not hear them is that you are not of God." John's invective proliferated and gave rise to the myth which was popular in medieval folklore, that the Jews were in league with the devil. The devil was a real personality throughout the pre-modern period (and for many even in the modern period), and the identification of the Jew with the devil invited the obvious inference that by striking at the Jew one was really performing a virtuous act of striking at the devil.

The Christian polemic became more offensive when it turned the Hebrew Scriptures against the Jewish people. The prophetic denunciation of the Jews, because they did not reach the high moral standard set for them by the the prophets, was turned by Christian apologists into the evidence that the Jews had always been obdurate and their old failures were of a piece with their new failure in having rejected Jesus. The prophecies that spoke glowingly of Israel's destiny as God's servant were appropriated by Christians to their own community. Isaiah's fifty-third chapter, which idealizes the Jewish people as the suffering servant of the Lord, the custodian of the Covenant, the source of light by which all mankind would find its way to God, was given a new interpretation, applying it to Jesus. And when Roman power destroyed the last vestiges of Jewish independence and brought the Jerusalem Temple to ruins, Christian spokesmen, forgetting the lesson of Job—that a man may suffer in innocence—took the disaster which befell the Jewish people as sure proof of their guilt. The doctrine was expounded that the Jewish dispersion and persecution were really a merited punishment, visited by a righteous God against the Jews for the frightful crime of "deicide." The Jews were deemed a people under a curse, rejected by God, doomed to wander, and to suffer for having turned their backs on the Savior.

The Christian utilization of the Hebrew Bible in the polemic against Judaism, as we have noted previously, took on another equally grievous form. It became accepted Christian doctrine that the "Old" Testament was a preparation for the New Testament, that the new faith was the completion and perfection of the old. This led to a twofold development. Christians, though they admitted the Hebrew Bible to their canon of Scriptures, nevertheless felt constrained to contrast the two Testaments, always showing the higher spiritual reach of the New as compared with the Old. A common attack was that the God of the Old Testament is a God of justice, while the God of the New Testament is a God of love. Justice without love would indeed be tyranny, even as love without justice is no more than sentimentality. The truth of course is that the writers of the New Testament also knew how to invoke God's wrath on sinners, even as writers of the Hebrew Bible knew how to speak tenderly of God's love. Is there a nobler exposition of God's love than the Book of Hosea, the Book of Jonah, and the greater number of the Psalms?

This phase in the polemic use of the Hebrew Bible also moved in another direction. It was centered in the quest for proof texts from the Old Testament, which allegedly anticipate Christian doctrine or incidents in the career of Jesus. We have analyzed some of these proof texts and have noted the distortions of the Hebrew text involved by them. Innumerable such proof texts have been invoked by missionaries directing their appeal to Jews. Those who do not know the original Hebrew text, and those who forget the boundaries of the centuries that separated the authors of the Hebrew Bible from the events of the New Testament, may sometimes find such proof texts impressive. For those who are familiar with the original, the continued use of these proofs is a clear falsification of truth in the service of sectarian expediency.

This perversion of the Hebrew Bible into a weapon against Jews was well described by Rev. Bernhard E. Olson: "Out of their dire need the church fathers argued for the antiquity and originality of Christianity. In doing so they correctly claimed the Old Testament as the Church's history, yet they were highly selective and invidious in their use of it. They claimed the prophets and heroes for the Church and reserved the villains and their villainy for the synagogue.

"Israel's failures were seen as Jewish failures, but Israel's victories belonged to the Church. The Old Testament promises and blessings were appropriated for Christians while the denunciations and judgments were to fall on Jews alone.

"By means of these selective and provocative arguments 'the Jews' became in Christian thinking a theological abstraction, not a real people. The Jews were fashioned into the image of idolators, evil-doers, and devils; while Christians in their own eyes became true, noble, and angelic. Thus, when St. Chrysostom wrote in the fourth century: 'The synagogue is . . . a place of prostitution, it is a den of thieves and a hiding place of wild animals. . . . God is not worshipped there; it is simply a house of idolatry. . . . The Jews are possessed by demons . . . ,' he was not making judgments about actual synagogues or the actions of Jews whose lives he had observed. Rather, he was exegeting Scripture according to the invidious tradition then being formed. . . .

"The negative definition of the Jews was carried over also into the Christian's treatment of the New Testament. The teachings and acts of Jesus, the apostles, and of the early Church were divorced from their Jewish context. Everything was turned into opposition to Judaism or seen as being opposed by Judaism. In this context the Jew became an enemy who denied the true faith, who rejected and killed the Christ." [7]

[7] Bernhard E. Olson: "Anti-Semitism: A Lively Skeleton," *Christian Advocate* (April 22, 1965), p. 8.

This interpretation of Jewish history gave the cue to Church councils and to secular Christian rulers throughout the medieval period to pass all kinds of discriminatory legislation against the Jews. Raul Hilberg, in his recent work *The Destruction of the European Jews*, has shown that the Nazi program for dealing with the Jewish question followed the guideline of Christian pronouncements against the Jews. The only point where the Nazis became innovaters was in the adoption of the "final solution," the physical destruction of Jewry.[8]

The attacks against Judaism were not confined to the spokesmen of Christian orthodoxy. Representatives of Protestantism contributed their share to it. The father of the Reformation, Martin Luther, began his ministry with a call for improving the status of Jewry, but he was not concerned with enlarging freedom to an underprivileged group. He had the notion that persecutions had solidified Jewish resistance to Christianity, and that an improvement of their lot would make them more receptive to the messages of the Church, especially of his new Church, which he felt was free of the abuses of the old. Toward Judaism he was always uncompromisingly hostile; and when the Jews did not prove receptive to his call, he turned to bitter hostility toward them. Luther's invective against the Jewish people entered the mainstream of German culture to become one of the ingredients of its pronounced anti-Semitism.

It is instructive to compare Luther's words at the inception of his career as a reformer, when he still hoped to convert the Jews, and those which he wrote later on, when he realized that his expectations had not materialized. In 1523 he wrote: "I will therefore show by means of the Bible the causes which induce me to believe that Christ was a Jew born of a virgin. Perhaps I will attract some of the Jews to the Christian faith. For our fools—the popes, bishops, sophists, and monks—the coarse blockheads! have until this time so treated the Jews that to be a good Christian one would have to become a Jew. And if I had been a Jew and had seen such idiots and blockheads ruling and teaching the Christian religion, I would rather have been a sow than a Christian. . . .

[8] Raul Hilberg: *The Destruction of the European Jews* (Chicago: Quadrangle Books; 1961).

"I hope that, if the Jews are treated friendly and are instructed kindly through the Bible, many of them will become real Christians and come back to the ancestral faith of the prophets and patriarchs. [Luther considered the heroes of the Old Testament good Christians.] . . .

"I would advise and beg everybody to deal kindly with the Jews and to instruct them in the Scriptures; in such a case we could expect them to come over to us. If, however, we use brute force and slander them . . . and treat them like dogs, what good can we expect of them?"

In 1543 he used a dramatically different tone: "What then shall we Christians do with this damned, rejected race of Jews? [The Jews were rejected by God, since they refused to accept Jesus as the messiah.] Since they live among us and we know about their lying and blasphemy and cursing, we cannot tolerate them if we do not wish to share in their lies, curses, and blasphemy. In this way we cannot quench the inextinguishable fire of divine rage (as the prophets say) nor convert the Jews. We must prayerfully and reverentially practice a merciful severity. Perhaps we may save a few from the fire and the flames [of hell]. We must not seek vengeance. They are surely being punished a thousand times more than we might wish them. Let me give you my honest advice.

"First, their synagogues or churches should be set on fire, and whatever does not burn up should be covered or spread over with dirt so that no one may ever be able to see a cinder or stone of it. And this ought to be done for the honor of God and of Christianity in order that God may see that we are Christians, and that we have not wittingly tolerated or approved of such public lying, cursing, and blaspheming of His Son and His Christians [Luther and others believed that the Jews cursed the Christians in their daily prayers]. . . .

"Secondly, their homes should likewise be broken down and destroyed. For they perpetrate the same things there that they do in their synagogues. For this reason they ought to be put under one roof or in a stable, like gypsies, in order that they may realize that they are not masters in our land, as they boast, but miserable captives, as they complain of us incessantly before God with bitter wailing.

"Thirdly, they should be deprived of their prayer-books and Talmuds in which such idolatry, lies, cursing, and blasphemy are taught.

"Fourthly, their rabbis must be forbidden under threat of death to teach any more. . . ." [9]

Christian humanists looked on the study of Hebrew as part of the classical heritage which they sought to recover. And many Christian divines and men of letters pursued assiduously Hebrew studies, often from Jewish teachers. But this development, too, did not lead directly to a more sympathetic appreciation of Judaism. These students of Hebrew usually sought a knowledge of the Cabbalah, where they believed were secret doctrines confirming some of the truths of Christianity. They were eager to strengthen their own faith, but they were also concerned with using their knowledge as a weapon in their polemics against Judaism.

Their enthusiasm for Hebrew studies was not disinterested. Its conscious or subconscious goal was to confirm or exalt Christianity, to deride Judaism, and, if possible, to convert the Jews to the Christian faith. Even Sebastian Münster (1489–1552), whose knowledge of Hebrew literature had earned him the epithet "Rabbi Münster," waged an active campaign for the conversion of Jews to Christianity.

In a pamphlet called *De Meschia Disputatio*, which Münster published in Basel in 1529 in Hebrew and Latin, he presents a disputation between a Jew and a Christian. The introduction well characterizes this work: "In this book, the Christian discusses various questions with the brazen Jew concerning the faith of the Jews to show that they are involved in many and grievous errors. For the Lord banished them on account of their sins in refusing to believe in the Messiah who came to this world to redeem from sin everyone who believes in him, and without whom there is no salvation or refuge in heaven and on earth. And it is only those who believe in him who constitute a people holy unto the Lord his

[9] Quoted by Jacob R. Marcus: *The Jew in the Medieval World* (New York: Meridian Books; 1962), pp. 166 ff.

God, selected by Him to be His own chosen people. But since the Jews refused to accept the belief in our Messiah, they were banished to eternal exile and they are fallen into a darkness of heart to this day."

Another Christian Hebraist, Paulus Fagius, published in 1512 a Latin translation of the missionary pamphlet *Sefer Emunah* (A Tractate on Faith), written by an anonymous apostate from Judaism, to prove that "the beliefs of the followers of Jesus the Messiah who conceive the Holy One blessed be He as father, son, and holy ghost . . . are sound and authentic, and are clearly established on the foundation of the Torah, the prophets and the other writings of sacred Scripture." [1]

The Christian missionary propaganda was not confined to tracts and pamphlets. It was at times forced on Jews by more drastic means. During the medieval period, it was not uncommon for public religious disputations to be held at which Jews were forced to select a "champion" to defend their cause. The spectacle was attended by the highest dignitaries of church and state. The Jewish spokesman usually felt inhibited from speaking too openly, as he would be charged with disrespect for the dominant religion. In the sixteenth century, by decrees of Popes Paul IV (r. 1555–9) and Pius V (r. 1566–72), it became mandatory for Jews to listen to Christian missionary sermons several times each year. Jews who yielded to missionary pressure were kept under strict surveilance against relapsing to their old faith. In 1568 Pius V decreed that converted Jews were not to set foot into the Roman ghetto, or to maintain any social relations with their unconverted brethren. The punishment incurred for disobeying this decree was "a three day period of public torture for men, and flailing for women." [2]

Edward A. Synan, professor at the Pontifical Institute of Medieval Studies, University of Toronto, has characterized the atti-

[1] Cf. I. Zinberg: *Die Geschichte fin der Literatur bei Yidn,* IV:6 (1933), 470 f.

[2] Gerhard Bellinger: "The Jews in the Roman Catechism," in Theodore Filthaut (ed.): *Israel in Christian Religious Instruction* (Notre Dame, Ind.: University of Notre Dame Press; 1965), pp. 96–7.

tude of the popes toward the Jews in these words: "Although no pope of any period has thought it permissible to force a Jew to accept baptism, medieval popes did not include in their conception of force the most extreme moral and psychological pressures, nor did they exclude the use of naked force to compel the attendance of Jews at sermons designed to convert them. . . ." A churchman cited by Synan complained that these compulsory preachments did not prove efficacious: "We everywhere see Hebrews obstinate in their disbelief, even though they have many times been present at preaching." [3]

The Christian preoccupation with Jewish guilt over the rejection of Jesus was to have unfortunate consequences for the Christian conscience. The notion that suffering always betokens guilt, as the Book of Job explains, is an invitation to smugness and self-righteousness. It enables a man to see those who suffer without feeling a sense of outrage, because of the ready assumption that the suffering must be somehow deserved. The point of the Book of Job is that men may suffer in innocence, and that to protest against unjust suffering is part of a moral man's response to life. Indeed, if we ever allowed ourselves to regard suffering as a token of guilt, we would have to say that the Christians thrown by the Romans to the lions, the millions tortured and done to death by Hitler and Stalin were all guilty, for otherwise a just providence would have kept them from harm. In an unredeemed world men will often suffer unjustly, and their suffering is meant to arouse in us sympathy and identification, whose true expression is the will to redress their condition.

Instead of sympathy and the will to redress, instead of a sense of outrage, Christians often reacted to Jewish suffering with a certain satisfaction, for here they found evidence for the truth of their faith. We have a good illustration of this in a footnote to a description by Josephus of Jewish suffering under the Romans. As a result of the Jewish rebellion against Rome, the Roman forces unleashed a reign of terror against the Jews. So many Jews were crucified by the Romans that, according to Josephus, "room

[3] Edward A. Synan: *The Popes and the Jews in the Middle Ages* (New York: The Macmillan Company; 1965), p. 120.

was wanting for the crosses, and crosses wanting for the bodies" (*Wars of the Jews* V 11:1). The editor of Josephus, William Whiston, adds a footnote to the above statement, quoting a certain churchman Reland who "notices here how justly this judgment came upon the Jews, since they had brought it on themselves by the crucifixion of their Messiah." Another Christian writer noting the toll of life taken by the Romans in their suppression of the Jewish bid for freedom gloats with even greater excitement. Quoting Josephus he states: "In this siege [of Jerusalem] it was computed that 1,100,000 perished and 97,000 were taken captives, besides 237,490 (according to Josephus) who fell in the wars which preceded it." He then concludes his account thus: "Such was the end of the once famous city of Jerusalem . . . from which time those obstinate and perverse people were no longer a nation but have ever since been dispersed and despised throughout the whole face of the earth." [4] The triumphal arch in honor of Titus's victory over Jerusalem this author describes as commemorating his "noble exploits against the Jews" and as a "monument of the impiety and perverseness of that nation." Christians can certainly be compassionate and they know how to sympathize with the victims of injustice, but dogma made them insensitive when it came to the sufferings of the Jewish people.

Throughout the Middle Ages Jewish expulsions, massacres, and all kinds of discriminatory legislation were common. Church leaders, in most cases, felt no sense of outrage. On the contrary, in many instances they even encouraged these actions. Jewish suffering did not trouble their conscience because they saw it in the light of their obsession with Jewish guilt. Even when they themselves instigated the suffering, they felt at peace with themselves, for in their own eyes they were only aiding a divinely ordained process of retribution to act against its intended victim.

The desensitizing of the Christian conscience enabled some Christians to face even the crimes of Nazism without a sense of outrage. The Protestant Federation of France interpreted the sufferings of the Jews under the Nazis as a divine reminder of

[4] John Kitko: *An Illustrated History of the Holy Bible* (Norwich, Conn.: Henry Bill; 1867), p. 656.

their error, and an "appeal to conversion and to turn from their unfaithfulness." [5] In 1933 while Hitler readied ovens for the "final solution" of the Jewish question, H. Frauenknecht, a leader of Evangelical Christianity in Germany, wrote complacently: "The Messiah came, but His people cried 'Crucify him.' They were angered as much by His sharp rejection of pharisaic self-righteousness as by His human lowliness and they rejected as blasphemy His claim to be the son of God. Thus they called down the judgment of God upon themselves. 'His blood be on us, and on our children.' In this, rather than in political or general human factors, lies the secret of the strange destiny of this people since then, a destiny characterized by blood and tears." [6] The Reichsbruderrat of the Evangelical Church in Germany, meeting at Darmstadt in 1948, declared: "Christ was crucified and rose again, also for the Jews. . . . The fate of the Jews is a silent sermon, reminding us that God will not allow Himself to be mocked. It is a warning to us, and an admonition to the Jews to be converted to him, who is their sole hope of salvation." [7]

This melancholy past continues to cast a shadow on Jewish-Christian relations. The memory of the Christian missionary as a persecutor, as one engaged to trap Jewish souls by fair means or foul, and to rob the Jew of his most precious treasure—his faith—has made some Jews suspicious of every Christian invitation to dialogue. They suspect that the dialogue is only another tactic for an age-old endeavor to subvert Jews from their faith and to turn them toward the Church. It will take time and a demonstration of disinterested goodwill to overcome these suspicions.

What are the possibilities of effecting a reconciliation between Judaism and Christianity? The doctrinal cleavage between Judaism and Christianity remains unresolved but, as our study has indicated, a liberal movement has arisen within the contemporary

[5] *The Relationship of the Church to the Jewish People* (Geneva: World Council of Churches; 1964), p. 5.

[6] Cited by Walter Neidhart in "The Fight Against Anti-Semitism," *The Ecumenical Review*, X:1 (October 1962), pp. 61–2.

[7] *The Relationship of the Church . . .*, p. 50.

Church that has advocated better relations between the Jewish and Christian communities.

There have been tangible actions in the Christian community expressive of the new trend. We have noted that the Revised Standard Version of the Bible has abandoned the reading of Christian doctrines into texts of the Hebrew Bible. The commentary in *The Interpreter's Bible* (a major work of Protestant scholarship) notes and rejects many of the favorite proof texts from the Hebrew Bible usually cited by Christian exegetes in confirmation of Christian doctrine. It rejects them as untenable to sound scholarship. There have been many expressions from various Protestant denominations and from federated church bodies like the National Council of Churches of Christ in the United States of America and the World Council of Churches in denunciation of anti-Semitism and in advocacy of friendly mutual relations between Jews and Christians.

There have been similar developments in Catholicism. We have noted also that the Catholic Confraternity Version of the Bible often ignores Christological interpretations of the Old Testament text in favor of a more authentic interpretation which is demanded by sound scholarship. Under the inspiration of Pope John XXIII, the Catholic liturgy has been purged of various expressions offensive to Jews, including the reference to "perfidious Jews," which was part of the prayers recited on Good Friday. Pope John demonstrated his deep feelings on the subject when the Sistine choir of St. Peter's sang the old version of the Good Friday prayer in his presence. He silenced the choir and demanded that the prayer be sung over again, with the omission of the offending phrase.

The most dramatic illustration of the trend in this direction is the statement adopted by the Ecumenical Council at the Vatican on November 20, 1964. It is part of a declaration on the attitude of the Church toward non-Christian religions, and it states (translation in *The New York Times*):

> As this sacred synod searches into the mystery of the church, it remembers the bond that ties the people of the New Covenant to Abraham's stock.

With a grateful heart, the church of Christ acknowledges that, according to God's saving design, the beginnings of her faith and her election were already among the Patriarchs, Moses and the prophets. She professes that all who believe in Christ—Abraham's sons according to faith—were included in the same Patriarch's call, likewise that her salvation is typically foreshadowed by the chosen people's exodus from the land of bondage.

The church, therefore, cannot forget that she received the revelation of the Old Testament from the people with whom God in His ineffable mercy concluded the former covenant. Nor can she forget that she feeds upon the root of that cultivated olive tree into which the wild shoots of the gentiles have been grafted (cf. Romans ii, 17–24). Indeed, the church believes that by His cross Christ Our Peace reconciled Jews and gentiles, making both one (cf. Ephesians ii, 14–16).

The church keeps ever in mind the words of the Apostle about his kinsmen; theirs is the sonship "and the glory and the covenants and legislation and the worship and the promises; who have their fathers and from whom is the Christ according to the flesh" (Romans ix, 4–5), the Son of Mary the Virgin (Romans ix, 4–5). No less does she recall that the Apostles, the church's mainstay and pillars, as well as most of the early Disciples who proclaimed Christ's gospel to the world, sprang from the Jewish people.

Even though a large part of the Jews did not accept the Gospel, they remain most dear to God for the sake of the Patriarchs. This is the witness of the Apostle, as is the utterance that God's gift and call are irrevocable.

In company with the Prophets and the same Apostle, the church awaits that day, known to God alone, on which all peoples will address the Lord in a single voice and "serve him shoulder to shoulder" (Sophonias iii, 9; Isaias lxvi; Psalms lxv, 45; Romans xi, 11–32).

Since the spiritual patrimony common to Christians and Jews is of such magnitude, this sacred synod wants to support and recommend their mutual knowledge and respect, a knowledge and respect that are the fruit, above all, of Biblical and theological studies as well as of fraternal dialogues.

Moreover, this synod, in her rejection of injustice of whatever kind and wherever inflicted upon men, remains mindful of that common patrimony and so deplores, indeed condemns, hatred and persecution of Jews, whether they arose in former or in our own days.

May, then, all see to it that in their catechetical work or in their preaching of the word of God they do not teach anything that could give rise to hatred or contempt of Jews in the hearts of Christians.

May they never present the Jewish people as one rejected, cursed or guilty of deicide.

All that happened to Christ in His passion cannot be attributed to the whole people then alive, much less to those of today. Besides, the church held and holds that Christ underwent His passion and death freely, because of the sins of all men and out of infinite love.

It is, therefore, the burden of Christian preaching to proclaim the cross of Christ as the sign of God's all-embracing love and as the fountain from which every grace flows.

We cannot truly address God, the Father of all, if we refuse to treat some men or other, in a brotherly way, even though they are created in His image. Man's attitude toward God the Father and his attitude toward his human brethren are so intimately linked, one to the other, that Scripture is able to say: "He who does not love does not know God" (1 John iv, 8; 1 John ii, 9–11; Luke x, 25–37).

Thus, any theory or practice that, so far as their human dignity is concerned, discriminates between man and man or people and people, creating a different set of rights for each of them—any such theory or practice is shown to be without foundation.

All men, therefore, but especially Christians, must refrain from discrimination against, or harassment of, others because of their race, color, creed or walk of life. But this is not enough. Treading the footsteps of the holy Apostles Peter and Paul, this sacred synod ardently implores the faithful that they rather "maintain good conduct among the gentiles" (I Peter ii, 12) and live, if possible that is, so far as it depends on them, in peace with all men (Romans xii, 18) so that they may really be sons of the Father who is in Heaven.

The Vatican statement was revised administratively by the ecclesiastical authorities, and the new draft was confirmed by the Council on October 15, 1965, and finally promulgated on October 28, 1965. The new draft differed in verbiage from the one originally voted, and represented a concession to the conservative forces in the Vatican, as well as to Arab pressure, whose hatred for the state of Israel makes Arabs reluctant to concede any action which would result in diluting hostilities toward the Jewish people. The new draft remains essentially similar in substance.

The text of the final draft, as released by the Documentary Service of the National Catholic Welfare Conference reads thus:

> In our time, when day by day mankind is being drawn closer together, and the ties between different peoples are becoming stronger, the Church examines more closely her relationship to non-Christian religions. In her task of promoting unity and love among men, indeed among nations, she considers above all in this declaration what men have in common and what draws them to fellowship.
>
> One is the community of all peoples, one their origin, for God made the whole human race to live over the face of the earth (cf. Acts 17, 26). One also is their final goal, God. His providence, His manifestations of goodness, His saving design extend to all men (cf. Wis. 8, 1; Acts 14, 17; Rom. 2, 6–7; 1 Tim. 2, 4), until that time when the elect will be united in the Holy City, the city ablaze with the glory of God, where the nations will walk in His light (cf. Apoc. 21, 23 f.).
>
> Men expect from the various religions answers to the unsolved riddles of the human condition, which today, even as in former times, deeply stir the hearts of men: What is man? What is the meaning, the aim of our life? What is moral good, what sin? Whence suffering and what purpose does it serve?

Which is the road to true happiness? What are death, judgment and retribution after death? What, finally, is that ultimate inexpressible mystery which encompasses our existence: whence do we come, and where are we going?

From ancient times down to the present, there is found among various peoples a certain perception of that hidden power which hovers over the course of things and over the events of human history; at times some indeed have come to the recognition of a Supreme Being, or even of a Father. This perception and recognition penetrates their lives with a profound religious sense.

Religions, however, that are bound up with an advanced culture have struggled to answer the same questions by means of more refined concepts and a more developed language. Thus in Hinduism, men contemplate the divine mystery and express it through an inexhaustible abundance of myths and through searching philosophical inquiry. They seek freedom from the anguish of our human condition either through ascetical practices or profound meditation or a flight to God with love and trust. Again, Buddhism, in its various forms, realizes the radical insufficiency of this changeable world; it teaches a way by which men, in a devout and confident spirit, may be able either to acquire the state of perfect liberation, or attain, by their own efforts or through higher help, supreme illumination. Likewise, other religions found everywhere try to counter the restlessness of the human heart, each in its own manner, by proposing "ways," comprising teachings, rules of life, and sacred rites.

The Catholic Church rejects nothing that is true and holy in these religions. She regards with sincere reverence those ways of conduct and of life, those precepts and teachings which, though differing in many aspects from the ones she holds and sets forth, nonetheless often reflect a ray of that Truth which enlightens all men. Indeed, she proclaims, and ever must proclaim Christ, "the way, the truth, and the life" (John 4, 6), in whom men may find the fullness of religious life, in whom God has reconciled all things to Himself (cf. 2 Cor. 5, 18–18).

The Church, therefore, exhorts her sons, that through dialogue and collaboration with the followers of other religions, carried out with prudence and love and in witness to the Christian faith and life, they recognize, preserve and promote the good things, spiritual and moral, as well as the sociocultural values found among these men.

The Church regards with esteem also the Moslems. They adore the one God, living and subsisting in Himself, merciful and all-powerful, the Creator of heaven and earth (cf. St. Gregory VII, Letter XXI to Anzir [Nacir], king of Mauritania [PL 148, col. 450 f.]), who has spoken to men; they take pains to submit wholeheartedly to even His inscrutable decrees, just as Abraham, with whom the faith of Islam takes pleasure in linking itself, submitted to God. Though they do not acknowledge Jesus as God, they revere Him as a prophet. They also honor Mary, His virgin mother; at times they even call on her with devotion. In addition, they await the day of judgment when God will render their desserts to all those who have been raised up from the dead. Finally, they value the moral life and worship God especially through prayer, almsgiving and fasting.

Since in the course of centuries not a few quarrels and hostilities have arisen between Christians and Moslems, this sacred synod urges all to forget the past and to work sincerely for mutual understanding and to preserve as well as to promote together for the benefit of all mankind social justice and moral welfare, as well as peace and freedom.

As the sacred synod searches into the mystery of the Church, it remembers the bond that spiritually ties the people of the New Covenant to Abraham's stock.

Thus the Church of Christ acknowledges that, according to God's saving design, the beginnings of her faith and her election are found already among the Patriarchs, Moses and the prophets. She professes that all who believe in Christ—Abraham's sons according to faith (cf. Gal. 3, 7)—are included in the same Patriarch's call, and likewise that the salvation of the Church is mysteriously foreshadowed by the chosen people's exodus from the land of bondage. The

Church, therefore, cannot forget that she received the revelation of the Old Testament through the people with whom God in His inexpressible mercy concluded the Ancient Covenant. Nor can she forget that she draws sustenance from the root of that well-cultivated olive tree onto which have been grafted the wild shoots, the Gentiles (Cf. Rom. 11, 17–24). Indeed, the Church believes that by His cross Christ Our Peace reconciled Jews and Gentiles, making both one in Himself (Cf. Eph. 2, 14–16).

The Church keeps ever in mind the words of the Apostle about his kinsmen: "Theirs is the sonship and the glory and the covenants and the law and the worship and the promises; theirs are the fathers and from them is the Christ according to the flesh" (Rom. 9, 4–5), the Son of the Virgin Mary. She also recalls that the Apostles, the Church's mainstay and pillars, as well as most of the early disciples who proclaimed Christ's Gospel to the world, sprang from the Jewish people.

As Holy Scripture testifies, Jerusalem did not recognize the time of her visitation (Cf. 19, 44), nor did the Jews, in large number, accept the Gospel; indeed not a few opposed its spreading (Cf. Rom. 11, 28). Nevertheless God holds the Jews most dear for the sake of their Fathers; He does not repent of the gifts He makes or of the calls He issues—such is the witness of the Apostle (Cf. Rom. 11, 28–29; cf. Dogmatic Constitution Lumen Gentium [Light of Nations], AAS, 57 [1965], p. 20). In company with the Prophets and the same Apostle, the Church awaits that day, known to God alone, on which all peoples will address the Lord in a single voice and "serve him shoulder to shoulder" (Soph. 3, 9) (Cf. Is. 66, 23; Ps. 65, 4; Rom. 11, 11–32).

Since the spiritual patrimony common to Christians and Jews is thus so great, this sacred synod wants to foster and recommend that mutual understanding and respect which is the fruit, above all, of biblical and theological studies as well as of fraternal dialogues.

True, the Jewish authorities and those who followed their lead pressed for the death of Christ (Cf. John 19, 6); still, what happened in His passion cannot be charged against all the Jews, without distinction, then alive, nor against the Jews of today. Although the Church is the new people of God, the Jews should not be presented as rejected or accursed by God, as if this followed from the Holy Scriptures. All should see to it, then, that in catechetical work or in the preaching of the word of God they do not teach anything that does not conform to the truth of the Gospel and the spirit of Christ.

Furthermore, in her rejection of every persecution against any man, the Church, mindful of the patrimony she shares with the Jews and moved not by political reasons but by the Gospel's spiritual love, decries hatred, persecutions, displays of anti-Semitism, directed against Jews at any time and by anyone.

Besides, as the Church has always held and holds now, Christ underwent His passion and death freely, because of the sins of men and out of infinite love, in order that all may reach salvation. It is, therefore, the burden of the Church's preaching to proclaim the cross of Christ as the sign of God's all-embracing love and as the fountain from which every grace flows.

We cannot truly call on God, the Father of all, if we refuse to treat in a brotherly way any man, created as he is in the image of God. Man's relation to God the Father and his relation to men his brothers are so linked together that Scripture says: "He who does not love does not know God" (I John 4, 8).

No foundation therefore remains for any theory or practice that leads to discrimination between man and man or people and people, so far as their human dignity and the rights flowing from it are concerned.

The Church reproves, as foreign to the mind of Christ, any discrimination against men or harassment of them because of their race, color, condition of life, or religion. On the contrary, following in the footsteps of the holy Apostles Peter and Paul, this sacred synod ardently implores the Christian faithful to "maintain good fellowship among the nations" (I

Peter 2,12), and, if possible, to live for their part in peace with all men (Cf. Rom. 12,18), so that they may truly be sons of the Father who is in heaven (Cf. Matt. 5, 45).

What is responsible for these developments? The statement of the Vatican regards the quest for mutual knowledge and respect between Jews and Christians as "the fruit, above all, of biblical and theological studies as well as of fraternal dialogues." We have noted some of the biblical and theological studies which have challenged the conventional Christian image of the Jew and Judaism.

There has been the effect of historical scholarship which has sought to sift truth from legend and which has sought an authentic reconstruction of the events involved in the rise of Christianity. Augustin Cardinal Bea, in presenting the statement on the Jews before the recent session of the Ecumenical Council at the Vatican and arguing for its adoption, pointed out that the historical and archeological evidence was against the interpretation which put the blame for the crucifixion on the Jews. It has become clear that Jesus never rejected his people or his religious heritage, that he lived as a Jew, that his ministry was not a rebellion against Judaism but a new affirmation of it. As Professor Guignebert summed it up, Jesus "had neither founded nor desired the church. Perhaps this is the most obvious truth forced upon whoever studies the Gospels without prejudice and, indeed, the contrary position is an absurdity from the historical point of view. . . . Finally do not forget that he was a Jew who was entirely devoted to the religious Law of Israel. When he apparently was opposing it he meant only in reality to extend its scope according to that which he deemed its true spirit." [8] Movements often go beyond the original aims of their founders, and this is obviously what happened with Christianity. But the attacks against the Jews and Judaism thus seemed an attack against the central figure in the Christian design for salvation, and a slur against the source from which his own faith was nourished. At the same time scholars like George Foot Moore, James Parkes, Herbert Danby, and

[8] Charles Guignebert: *Christianity, Past and Present* (New York: The Macmillan Company; 1927), p. 125.

R. Travers Herford showed that rabbinic Judaism was of a high moral and spiritual order and did not conform to the image of it as presented in Christian polemics.

Linguistic studies have made it clear that the Christological interpretation of the Hebrew Bible is forced, and false to the obvious meaning of the original Hebrew text. The new biblical scholarship, too, tends to present the writings of the Hebrew Bible as a great literature which is significant for its own sake, for whatever light it has to shed on man's quest to know himself and to meet the commitments of living. The new scholarship with its quest for authenticity undermined the conventional Christian interpretations, which turned the Hebrew Bible into a work of riddles whose secret goal was to prophesy incidents in the life of Jesus or the teachings of Christian doctrine.

The rise of the state of Israel has also shaken a basic dogma in the conventional Christian stereotype of the Jew. The conventional Christian dogma saw the destruction of the Jewish state and dispersion of the Jews as a merited punishment for their rejection of Christianity. Their fated condition was to be wandering, persecuted strangers everywhere, and by their condition to confirm their guilt for having rejected Jesus. The restoration of the state of Israel, without the prior conversion by the Jews to Christianity, contradicts this dogma and brings into question a basic conventional Christian interpretation of Jewish destiny.

The most shattering event that has given many Christians a sense of urgency in revising the Christian attitude toward the Jew was the Nazi holocaust. Nazism exposed the ghastly possibilities in all anti-Semitism. The painful fact that Christian teaching, instead of preventing this bestiality, was in truth one of the causes that helped precipitate it proved a shattering realization to sensitive Christians. It was this disturbance that challenged the young German poet Rolf Hochhuth to write *The Deputy*, an impassioned protest against the failure of Pope Pius XII to speak out against Nazi atrocities.

Some of the defenders of Pope Pius have maintained that his protest would have been ineffectual, since it would have been in conflict with the overriding loyalties of the German people to their state and nation, but this only defines the full scope of the

Christian predicament. In the words of Claire Huchet Bishop, in her introduction to Jules Isaac's *The Teaching of Contempt:* "It must be shamefully confessed that it took nothing less than destruction of European Jewry to awaken the collective Christian conscience. How could Hitler's Germany have been possible, a country which had been Christian for fifteen hundred years? The terrifying responsibility for this unbelievable cruelty has been underlined by the Protestant scholar, Dr. Bernhard E. Olson: 'Hitler's program was but the crown and pinnacle of a long history of hatred toward the Jew, participated in (if not initiated) by those whose duty it was to teach their children the truths of Christianity.' "[9]

The ethical failure of Christianity, exposed so glaringly by Nazism, seemed especially disturbing to those who had felt the impact of a growing Christian liberalism, with its profound social consciousness. Marxist criticism of religion as an "opiate of the masses" that dulled them to the problems of society and the need for social change had stimulated a shift of emphasis in all religious communities. Doctrinal and ritual issues receded and the ethical loomed larger in importance. Religious and lay leaders in all religious denominations felt that religion had to concern itself with the problems of the social order, that it had to lead men as did the prophets of old toward social justice, racial equality, toward the freedom of the individual and the national community, and toward world peace. The Marxist attack on all religion also tended to emphasize the need of cooperation rather than competitiveness among religious bodies, to meet the challenge of the new adversary.

The growing concern with the problems of the existential world automatically narrowed the rift between Judaism and Christianity. For this was the primary emphasis in Judaism, in contrast to Christianity, which has a strong tendency to otherworldliness. Christian liberals felt a new appreciation for biblical law, which had as one of its main objectives to establish a just order of human relationships. They felt a new reverence for the impassioned writings of the prophets in protest against oppression

[9] (New York: Holt, Rinehart & Winston; 1964), p. 5.

and in affirmation of the ideal of a good society, where men were free of material deprivation, of oppressive government, and the scourge of war. Jews and Judaism were seen in a nobler light, while the Christian acquiescence to hatred and violence against Jews seemed all the more shocking to the more ethically sensitized Christian conscience.

This work of reconciliation was aided by a continuing dialogue which has been going on for some time between Jewish and Christian leaders. In democratic countries which have made religious freedom a part of their democracy, Jews and Christians were often involved in dealing with common problems, as citizens, and they gained new respect for one another. The stereotype of the Jew fell away as Christians and Jews met in their day-to-day endeavors. The reality contradicted the myth, and the myth had to give way.

The quest for better understanding was fostered by a number of organizations who made this a basic goal of their endeavors. Among them have been the American Jewish Committee, the Anti-Defamation League of B'nai B'rith, the Institute for Religious and Social Studies and the Conference on Science, Philosophy and Religion (both sponsored by the Jewish Theological Seminary of America), as well as Institutes on Judaism for the clergy sponsored in various communities by local congregations. The National Conference of Christian and Jews in this country and related bodies in other countries have propagated the conception of Jews and Christians as brothers who share common goals for the betterment of man, and they have denounced bigotry and hatred based on race and creed as inconsistent with the American national ideal, or the ideal of human love which figures so prominently in the Jewish, as well as the Christian tradition.

One of the culminating efforts in this endeavor which initiated the Vatican confrontation of the issue was the work of Jules Isaac. Professor Isaac, who was born in 1877, is a French Jew, a noted historian and humanist, who was at one time Inspector General of Education for all of France. The Nazi atrocities, which took the lives of the greater part of his own family, shocked him to ponder the causes of anti-Semitism.

He was convinced that Christianity had played a major role in fermenting it. But he saw in anti-Semitism a caricature of the teachings of Jesus and a betrayal of his legacy to the Church. He developed his ideas in his volume *Jesus et Isräel* and he began a series of meetings with distinguished churchmen to alert them to the problem. In 1948 he created a French interfaith group called L'Amité Judeo-Chrétienne, whose purpose was to work for better relations between Jews and Christians.

In an audience with Pope Pius XII he complained that the liturgy of the Catholic Church on Good Friday referred to the Jews as *perfidis judaeis*. He was not satisfied with the compromise offered by Pope Pius to translate *perfidis* as "unfaithful" or "unbelieving," instead of the more literal and offensive term "perfidious." The next pope, John XXIII, proved more sensitive to the problem. As we noted previously, Pope John simply struck the word *perfidis* from the prayer.

Jules Isaac met with Pope John XXIII and proposed official action by the Church to condemn the teaching of contempt for Jews and Judaism. The Pope was sympathetic, and it was he who appointed a subcommission of the Secretariat for Promoting of Christian Unity, under the chairmanship of Augustin Cardinal Bea, to prepare a document dealing with this question for the Ecumenical Council which John had convened.

The statement on the Jews finally adopted by the Ecumenical Council and promulgated by Pope Paul VI owed its original impetus to the efforts of Pope John XXIII and was first conceived in that memorable conference between the Pope and Jules Isaac.[1]

The statements on Jewish-Christian relations which have been adopted by various Protestant Church bodies are not as comprehensive as the Vatican document but they are similar in spirit. They express goodwill for Jews and repudiate anti-Semitism. They generally reject the allegation of Jewish guilt in the events of the crucifixion. But their disavowal of Jewish guilt in the crucifixion betrays grave limitations, as does the Vatican docu-

[1] A brief biography of Jules Isaac and an outline of his views are contained in his *The Teaching of Contempt*.

ment. They generally ground their disavowal on the contention that the death of Jesus cannot be blamed merely on the designs of men since his death was—theologically—a necessity in order to effect atonement for the sins of all men. They thus fail to reckon with the results of historical scholarship which has shown that the primary responsibility for the crucifixion was with the Romans, that the Jewish "leaders" who were involved in it were in truth Roman puppets who carried out a Roman rather than a Jewish policy.

The goodwill offered to the Jews by Christian bodies implies a sharp distinction between Jews "according to the flesh," to use a New Testament phrase, and the religious inheritance to which Jews profess their loyalty; the friendly gestures are limited to Jews as an ethnic or racial community; toward Judaism, the predominant Christian attitude remains one of disdain and condescension and often of outright hostility.

The Protestant Commission on the Witness to Israel, speaking on behalf of the Protestant Federation of France, presented a paper entitled "The Approach to Israel" for the First Assembly of the World Council of Churches, held in Amsterdam from August 22 to September 5, 1948. This paper deplored anti-Semitism, but it offered melancholy evidence of deep hostility toward Jews who remain faithful to their religious inheritance. The destiny of the Jew, according to this paper, is to embrace Christianity, and the insistence of Jews on remaining Jews is therefore an act of "unfaithfulness." But despite this "unfaithfulness," the paper declared magnanimously, Christians should not persecute Jews because "persecution of the Jews is always harmful to the Church," since it hardens Jewish resistance to Christianity. "So long as a Jew can suppose that Christians, as a whole, are anti-Semitic," this paper continues with candor, "or that the Church does not fight anti-Semitism in every shape and form, there will inevitably be a movement of repulsion, turning Jewish eyes away from the Gospel which their sincerest friends in the Church want to lay before them. It follows that unless we are to be at cross purposes, a clear distinction should be drawn between anti-Semitism and anti-Judaism which is involved in every summons to conversion. . . . The aim of general conversion cannot be anything less than the spiritual destruction of Judaism." [2]

A similar spirit informs the pronouncements on the Jewish question adopted by the First Assembly of the World Council of Churches held in 1948; by the consultation held at the Ecumenical Institute in Bossey, Switzerland in 1956; and by the Third Assembly of the World Council of Churches in New Delhi, India, in 1961. These statements repudiate anti-Semitism, but this is not their primary directive. The repudiation of anti-Semitism is part of the introduction to these pronouncements, whose primary objective is the call to create a favorable climate for their main concern, which is to win Jews for the Church. Directly or indirectly they breathe hostility to Judaism.

A recent Catholic work in denunciation of anti-Semitism, *The Anguish of the Jews*, by Edward H. Flannery, from which we have quoted earlier, maintains the same position, that Christianity can be expected to shun anti-Semitism but not anti-Judaism. In the words of the Reverend Flannery: "A distinction—difficult to draw—must be recognized, however, between the ambiguous phenomenon of 'Christian anti-Semitism' and anti-Judaism which legitimately and essentially constitutes a part of Christian teaching and apologetics. The latter is purely theological; it rejects Judaism as a way of salvation but not the Jews as a people." [3] The Reverend Flannery acknowledges the difficulty of distinguishing between the two hostilities. For we live in a world of persons rather than of abstract ideas, and contempt for an idea invariably spills over to a contempt for the persons professing it. It is indeed noteworthy that the Reverend Flannery deems the Jews themselves as "co-responsible" for anti-Semitism. Their responsibility stems from their persistence in remaining Jews.

The very pronouncements against anti-Semitism which are issued by proponents of Christian goodwill for Jews sometimes express the grossest distortions of Judaism and reflect contempt for its adherents. This is well illustrated in Walter Neidhart's paper "The Fight Against Anti-Semitism in Christian Education,"

[2] *The Relationship of the Church . . .*, pp. 150 ff.
[3] *The Anguish of the Jews*, p. 60.

which appeared in a recent issue of *The Ecumenical Review*.[4] Directly or indirectly he speaks of Jewish piety as "ridiculous," "illogical," and "unreasonable." Speaking of the Orthodox Jew of today he states: "His zeal in the observance of the individual laws falls under the suspicion of being basically hypocrisy and a cloak for corruption within." The author urges the Christian teacher to suppress his feelings toward Jewish piety and to foster friendly feelings toward the Jewish person, for "our attitude toward our Jewish fellows must not depend on whether we think his religiosity admirable or absurd." The great hope which he holds out for the Jewish people is their eventual conversion to Christianity, and this Christian hope is cited to mitigate the antipathy felt for Jews in their present state of resistance to Christianity.[5] The author's unfamiliarity with Judaism is graphically illustrated by his startling statement that the Jewish observance of the Law "has remained unchanged since the days of Ezra and Nehemiah." [6] Walter Neidhart's statements are especially saddening because they appeared in the leading journal of the Ecumenical movement, which has embraced as one of its goals the fight against anti-Semitism.

The great hope with which many Christians look upon the Jew is his disappearance as a Jew. Here is how one Christian theologian puts it: "The Christian church labors with a burdensome sense of guilt because of the shocking demonstrations of anti-Semitism in lands supposedly controlled by the Christian principle of love. This sense of guilt urges many in the church to make approaches to the Jews in the hope that a clear understanding of present-day Judaism and a winsome presentation of the gospel will in some measure rectify past evils and establish Israel within the Church." [7]

Catholic spokesmen have voiced the same hope. We cite the statement by Theodor Filthaut in a paper which seeks to establish guidelines for the Catholic educator in interpreting the Jew in

[4] XV:1 (October 1962).
[5] Ibid., pp. 59, 61, 63, 64, 66.
[6] Ibid., p. 59.
[7] *The Reformed Review*, II (December 1965), 37.

the Religious School classroom: "The history of the relations between Church and Synagogue will last until the second coming of Christ. Until then it is the task of the Church to wait for the Jews and to win them over, not for reasons of human desire to rule, but for the sake of their Salvation. . . . A most gratifying result of such instruction will be the eradication from the Christian consciousness of that erroneous concept of the eternal damnation of the Jews—and thus no more reason for the so-called superiority over Israel." [8]

Indeed one Catholic periodical [9] refers to an apostate from Judaism as a "Jewish-Christian." If the term is intended to refer to the Jewish amalgam which persists as a vital element in Christianity, then every Christian is a "Jewish-Christian." Its exclusive use in describing apostates from Judaism suggests that for this periodical the term Jew suggests only ethnic origin, and is devoid of allusion to a religious dimension, which—for Jews—is the most significant aspect of their Jewish identity. There is no more legitimacy in describing a Jew who left his faith to become a Christian as a "Jewish-Christian" than there would be in describing a Christian who left his faith to become a Jew as a "Christian-Jew." The same periodical employs as an illustration in the same article an eight branch candelabrum with a cross superimposed on it. Does it not suggest, symbolically, the Christian claim that the Church has superseded Judaism?

The halting and feeble voices with which Christian statesmanship has dealt with the inequities committed against Jews and Judaism in Christian tradition, confirms the grim but challenging words penned by the noted New Testament scholar Frederick C. Grant: "The anti-Jewish dogma was deeply fixed in Christian thought and devotion. . . . This terrible inheritance of hatred and bigotry the early church passed on to the medieval, and the medieval to the Reformation and post-Reformation churches. . . . This is our situation today. We have inherited the bitter prejudices and the narrow fanatical ideology cultivated through many centuries in both eastern and western Europe. So deeply in-

[8] T. Filthaut (ed.): *The Jew in Christian Religious Education*, pp. 21, 23.

[9] *The United States Catholic* (February 1966), pp. 21–9.

grained is this prejudice that many of us, for whom religion means chiefly theology, doctrines, or even philosophical views, can scarcely think of Judaism as religion. . . . Thus prejudice always rebounds upon those who share it. Our own sacred book is distorted, and our own religious life deformed, in the interests of maintaining a theological principle, namely, the 'rejection' of the Jews and the divine condemnation of 'moralism' and 'legalism.' "[1]

The declaration on the Jews adopted by the Ecumenical Council and promulgated by Pope Paul, even though it represents a dilution of the earlier draft which had been adopted by the Council, is truly historic. It recognizes elements that are "true and holy" in all religions. Its most important provision in the section dealing with the Jews is the statement that "what happened to His [Jesus'] passion cannot be charged against all Jews, without distinction, then alive, nor against the Jews of today," and that "the Jews should not be presented as rejected or accursed by God, as if this followed from the Holy Scriptures." It also affirms that the Church "decries hatred, persecutions, displays of anti-Semitism directed at Jews at any time and by anyone." If faithfully implemented these statements alone would work a vast change for the better in the Christian attitude toward the Jews. If all the implications of these statements should be fully explicated, a major cause for Christian anti-Semitism would disappear.

Nevertheless, we must view this declaration with serious reservations. In its references to the Old Testament this declaration reaffirms the belief that the Hebrew Bible was a foreshadowing of Jesus, and a veiled anticipation of Christian doctrines. This ignores the distinctiveness and authenticity of the Hebrew Bible, in its own terms. It quotes Paul's characterization of Jesus as a Jew "according to the flesh" (Romans 9:4–5). This ignores the findings of modern scholarship which portrays Jesus as a Jew in spirit, and not only "in the flesh." The Pauline view tends to suggest that Jesus had broken with his religion, because presumably he found —as Paul indeed insisted—that it was sterile and unspiritual, and that his ministry consisted in proclaiming a new faith that was free of the abuses of the old. This is part of the Christian dispar-

[1] F. C. Grant: *Ancient Judaism and the New Testament* (New York: The Macmillan Company; 1959), pp. 14–15.

agement of Judaism, which is based on a misreading of history.

The declaration finds Jews at fault because "Jerusalem did not recognize the time of her visitation." This is a Christian point of view—that Jesus fulfilled all Jewish hopes for a glorious future. But Jerusalem at the time when Jesus appeared was under the heel of the Romans, and the heel continued to press ever harder on the Jewish people until Jerusalem was finally destroyed. It is difficult for one who knows the historical realities by which Jerusalem was so sorely pressed to accept this statement, which judges the Jews harshly for not abandoning historical criteria in evaluating the state of their country.

The declaration alleges that "the Jewish authorities and those who followed their lead pressed for the death of Christ." This statement, too, shows a singular disregard for the historical realities of life in Palestine under the Roman occupation. The impression one gets from this characterization is that the responsible and representative elements of the Jewish people were involved in the crucifixion, and that their involvement was primary as the initiators of the action, who bore pressure on Pilate to perform the act. We have noted that this was not the case.

The "Jewish authorities," the "chief priests" and their associates, had never been chosen by the Jewish people, nor were they responsible to them; they were part of the Roman apparatus of keeping the subject Judeans under their control. When the Jews finally rebelled against Rome in 66 C.E., the chief priests and their associates did all they could to sabotage the revolution. The reigning High Priest and his brother went into hiding for fear of reprisals; they were finally caught and executed by the Jewish loyalists as traitors to their people and collaborators of the Romans. It is no more equitable to speak of these men as "Jewish leaders" than it would have been equitable to speak of Quisling and his small coterie of Norwegian Nazis who ruled Norway under the Nazi occupation as "leaders" of the Norwegian people. The primary responsibility for the crucifixion of Jesus lay with those who were the masters of the order he threatened, with the Roman occupation. Any other version of the facts is a perversion of history, as we have seen in the detailed study of the trial of Jesus and the crucifixion following it.

The declaration makes the claim that "the Church is the new people of God." This is of course an appropriation of a concept by which the Hebrew Bible characterized the people of Israel. In making this claim the Church is here only reiterating its larger claim that it is the new Israel, that Christianity has superseded Judaism and has come into possession of all the prerogatives once pertaining to the Jewish people. It is noteworthy, however, that as interpreted by the Church this concept is reduced to its most primitive level and fails to reach the universalism which this concept attained in Judaism.

As used by the Church, the concept of "the people of God" is exclusive in scope. There is only one people of God. In antiquity, prior to the coming of Jesus, the Jews were "the people of God." Now that Jesus has come, the Church has taken over this role. The Church makes this claim as a corollary to its other claim, that it alone possesses the full truth, that it alone is the custodian of the complete and perfect revelation of God.

There were undoubtedly some in Judaism for whom this concept had a like meaning. But Jewish teachers labored to free this concept of its parochial connotations. The prophet Isaiah, speaking in the name of God, declared (19:24–25) that there will come a time when Israel shall "be the third with Egypt and Assyria, a blessing in the midst of the earth, for the Lord of hosts has blessed him saying: 'Blessed be Egypt My people and Assyria the work of My hands, and Israel, Mine inheritance.' "

Rabbi Saadia Gaon gave this doctrine its maturest formulation. "All creatures," he declared, "are His creatures and we may not say that He has taken to Himself one, to the exclusion of another, or to a greater degree than another." The truth is that the acknowledgment of being God's chosen only testifies to the maturity of a people that has become aware of its divine Benefactor and thereby seeks to extoll Him and to praise Him. "Thus when the Psalmist exclaims (Psalms 16:5), 'The Lord is the portion of Mine inheritance and My cup,' did He alone want to possess the Master of the worlds?" [2]

From this perspective, all people whom God has given breath

[2] Israel Davidson: *Saadia's Polemic Against Hivi Al-Balkhi* (New York: Jewish Theological Seminary; 1915), pp. 59, 60.

are His people. God is close to them to the measure that they seek His closeness and open their hearts to His presence. He is close to them to the measure that they are, in Martin Buber's definition, a *goy zaddik*, people of righteousness. Conformity to a creed or a rite or technical affiliation with one religious community or another does not, in itself, establish closeness to God. For Jews it cannot but seem ironic to encounter in the Church's conception of itself an old concept of Judaism, but turned toward parochialism, so as to place them (and presumably all non-Catholics) outside the category of "God's people."

The most serious reservation one must feel is toward the statement: "May all see to it then that in catechetical work or in preaching the word of God they do not teach anything that is inconsistent with the truth of the Gospel and with the spirit of Christ." This compares with the statement in the earlier draft: "May, then, all see to it that in their catechetical work or in their preaching the word of God they do not teach anything that could give rise to hatred or contempt of Jews in the heart of Christians." The revised statement is ominously vague. Christians who taught a doctrine that has fostered hatred for the Jews surely believed that they were not "inconsistent with the truth of the Gospel and the spirit of Christ." Father Tiso, a Roman Catholic priest who was Hitler's *gauleiter* in Slovakia undoubtedly believed he was consistent "with the truth of the Gospel and the spirit of Christ." So did Father Coughlin, the Detroit priest whose magazine *Social Justice* served as a vehicle for Nazi anti-Semitism in this country. Indeed, as Rev. Dominic M. Crossan observed in his article in the Jesuit periodical *Theological Studies*,[3] the Gospels themselves, particularly the Gospel According to Luke and the Gospel According to John, lend themselves to anti-Semitic interpretations. Frederick C. Grant has expressed this more categorically: "The New Testament itself contains anti-Semitism. This fact should be frankly acknowledged. . . ."[4] The Vatican decla-

[3] "Anti-Semitism and the Gospel," *Theological Studies*, XXVI:2 (June 1965), pp. 189–215.

[4] Frederick C. Grant: "Vatican Council: The Ninth Inning," *The Episcopalian* (September 1965), p. 27.

ration has thus left the door open for the bigot to persist in his bigotry without running counter to guidelines laid down by the Church. The weight of the revised statement, as compared with the parallel one in the original draft, is clearly a dilution and a disappointing retreat into what will surely prove an ineffectual vagueness.

One must find it disappointing, too, that the revised draft fails to condemn hatred of the Jews; it employs the term "decry" (the earlier translation of the same Latin word was "deplore") instead of the stronger term "condemn." If hatred of the Jews when based on Christian teaching is immoral and a perversion of Christian doctrine, then any attempt to attack it with less than the maximum force reflects less concern than the issue warrants.

The Vatican declaration affirms that Jesus has reconciled Jews and Gentiles, "making both one in Himself." It states that God's election of the Jewish people remains in effect; for God "does not repent of the gifts He makes or the calls He issues." The latter statement is followed by the affirmation of faith in the eventual unity of all men in the common service of God. The authority cited in support of these statements is the apostle Paul, in Ephesians 2:14–16 and Romans 11–32. An examination of these passages indicates that they are based on the expectation that the Jews will eventually embrace Christianity. The unity was to be accomplished "through the cross" (Ephesians 2:16). For Paul, too, God has not revoked the election of the Jewish people because of the ultimate hope of their conversion to Christianity. The day awaited by the Church when "all peoples will address the Lord in a single voice," as defined in the passage cited from the apostle Paul, is the day when Jews will join the Gentiles in a common acknowledgment of Jesus as the Savior. Paul makes it clear that the final inclusion of the Jews among those "saved" depends on their entrance into the Church: "And even the others [the Jews], if they do not persist in their unbelief, will be grafted in, for God has the power to graft them in again" (Romans 11:23). The Vatican declaration acknowledges aspects of truth in non-Christian religions, but it maintains that "the fullness of religious life" is to be found only in Christianity. The Vatican document, in short, sets its friendly expressions toward those outside the Church on the expectation that sooner or later (on a day "known to God alone"), they will enter the Church.

Official Catholic commentaries on this document indicate clearly that our reservations about its efficacy are indeed well founded. One Catholic theologian explains the omission of the reference to "deicide" in the revised document thus: "It is an historical fact that *some* Jews who lived in Jerusalem at the time of our Lord did contribute toward bringing about His death. Since then we believe He is true God, we must logically conclude that objectively these Jews committed deicide. However, these Jews were only a small portion of the Jews then living throughout the world. Moreover, the deed perpetrated by this small number of Jews, mostly Pharisees, was only a material, not a formal sin of deicide. In other words, they did not realize that the man whose death they were bringing about was truly a divine person. . . . From all this it is evident how unjust it is to brand the Jewish people indiscriminately with the charge of deicide." [5]

It is for Christians to ponder how a mortal can be efficacious in slaying God, if God is really what we mean by God. But it is melancholy to note the historical distortions which continue to be perpetrated in repeating the malignity against the Pharisees. The death of Jesus is treated as though it occurred in a historical vacuum, without reference to the power struggle waged by the Romans to defend their occupation of Judea against Jewish dissidents, especially those who dreamt of a new kingdom that was to replace the kingdom of Caesar. It continues to be perpetrated in the face of all the evidence which shows that the action against Jesus was taken by the Roman authorities and their collaborators, and that the Pharisees who remained aloof from the pro-Roman oligarchy were not the culpable agents in that tragedy.

The harsh judgment against Jews and Judaism, which was once more reiterated by the Roman Catholic Bishop Carli, illustrates glaringly that the Vatican pronouncement on the Jewish question has not put an end to bigotry. In an extended article that appeared in the clerical review *Palestro del Clero* Bishop Luigi

[5] Francis J. Connell: "Answers to Questions," *The American Ecclesiastical Review*, XLIV: 3 (March 1966), pp. 205–6.

Carli of Segni, Italy, was quoted as having declared: "Judaism, that is the religious institution, although radically changed [after the destruction of Jerusalem in 70 C.E.] from that of the Old Testament by the disappearance of the Temple and the priesthood, continued, in fact, to survive, but illegally with respect to God. It carries in fact always with it, one would say by its very nature, the judgment of condemnation by God because, refusing Christ . . . it puts itself against the will of God. . . . It is for this reason that, whoever, knowing Christ, consciously and freely adheres to Judaism participates in conscience in that judgment of condemnation." Bishop Carli even reiterates the charge of deicide against the Jews. The term "deicide," he declared, "is theologically unexceptionable; even the only fitting one." [6]

A more recent commentary on this document by Augustin Cardinal Bea,[7] who was the primary force in Roman Catholic hierarchy to steer its passage through the Ecumenical Council, reinforces all the reservations we have expressed concerning it. He maintains that the sanhedrin which was involved in the incidents preparatory to the crucifixion was a legitimate and representative authority of the Jewish people, without reckoning with the fact that these men functioned under a Roman rather than Jewish sovereignty. He excludes the charge of deicide from the Jews because the original guilt was borne by the people of Jerusalem solely, and because they did not know that the man they destroyed was a deity, and finally because Jesus forgave their treachery. He regards Judaism as obsolete since its only function was to prepare for the coming of Jesus. He denies that the Jews have been rejected or are under a curse, since they are still open to Christian illumination, and he sees the Vatican document as resting on the hope that the Jews will ultimately join the Church. He denies Christian culpability in anti-Semitism. He explains the issuance of the Vatican document as having been necessitated by the notion of Jews (an erroneous notion he believes) that the guilt commonly attributed to the Jewish people for the crucifixion has stimulated anti-Semitism, and by the contingency that

[6] *The New York Times*, April 20, 1966, p. 16.

[7] *The Church and the Jewish People* (New York: Harper & Row; 1966), pp. 69, 87, 88, 96, 100 f., 157, 160 ff.

Nazi propaganda might indeed have bred hostility toward Jews among some Catholics. One may only wonder to what extent these positions reflect Cardinal Bea's own thought and to what extent he may have bent his thought to accommodate the more conservative Council fathers whose consent was necessary for any softening of the Church's attitude toward the Jews.

It is clear that the ideological cleavage between Judaism and Christianity remains unresolved. The conventional Christian concept of the Jew and Judaism is intertwined with basic Christian doctrine whose revision cannot be expected merely for the sake of facilitating better relations with Jews. Such revision can come about only through the compulsion of truth, if the Church becomes convinced that this is indeed what the truth calls for. The test of progress in this direction will be the extent to which Christianity comes to acknowledge the legitimacy of diverse paths to God.

The pronouncements on the Jews which have emerged from various Christian bodies have not met the full test of Jewish-Christian understanding, but they represent a development which remains significant. For this is the first time in the span of long centuries that Christianity has felt itself challenged to deal with the question. Official pronouncements from ecclesiastical bodies are generally in the nature of a compromise between the advocates of reform and the defenders of the status quo. These pronouncements, therefore, do not reflect the total Christian conviction on the subject. There are conservatives for whom these pronouncements go too far. There are, on the other hand, liberals in each denomination who sense the issue in broader terms and they will continue to bear witness to their concern.

The forces which released the ferment that placed the issue before Christendom will, no doubt, continue to act, and we may expect the subject to come up on the agenda of Christian concern again and again. The most important factor which will work toward this end will undoubtedly remain the work of biblical scholarship. Modern studies of the Bible, the works of leading Catholic as well as Protestant scholars, have cast doubt on the authenticity of the New Testament as a historical record. They tend to look on the New Testament portrayal of Jews and Judaism as a distortion of the facts inspired by animosity toward Jews and Judaism.

As W. D. Davies testifies: "The study of the New Testament has had repercussions for me outside Protestantism. These came primarily from an attempt to understand the interaction between Christianity and its mother faith, Judaism. Here certainly criticism has played a reconciling role and has issued not only in a deeper appreciation of Judaism, but in the conviction that the renewal of Christendom is tied up with the rediscovery of its roots in Judaism. If I may be allowed to say so, we only hope that a cry may go forth from Rome and elsewhere, not only that Christians may be one, but to remind the churches everywhere of their specifically Jewish inheritance. This would not only help to atone for the guilt of Christendom but help it to rediscover its own soul." [8]

Jewish scholars will contribute toward this endeavor by expounding the teachings of their own faith and by reacting to the claims of Christianity especially where they distort or falsify the meaning of Jewish destiny. But the work of scholarship is essentially nonsectarian and Christian theologians and scholars will continue in the future as in the past to seek the truth behind the biblical and historical origins of Christianity. Jewish-Christian tensions derive from a mythical conception of the Jew and from a distorted conception of Judaism. All who will seek to expose the myth, to correct distortion and to vindicate truth will contribute to a lessening of those tensions.

The work of Jewish scholars in clarifying the historical and doctrinal aspects of their faith is itself a contribution to the Jewish-Christian dialogue. Ideas, in whatever context they are expressed, have their own cogency and they enter into the ferment of thought in which truth finds its continued refinement.

What of the direct confrontation of Jewish and Christian spokesmen probing areas of agreement in their respective faiths? Here we tread a zone of great delicacy. For Christians the interfaith dialogue is often but another tactic in a missionary endeavor. As Rev. Dr. Martin-Achard, professor of the Old Testament and dean of the theological faculty of the University of Geneva, expressed it in the opening lecture of the thirteenth session of the

[8] *Ecumenical Dialogue at Harvard*, pp. 112–13.

Graduate School of Ecumenical Studies in Bossey, Switzerland: "The Gospel cannot be proclaimed in one and the same way to the masses of Asia or Africa—or of Europe!—and also to the people of Moses, the prophets and the apostles, and even of Jesus himself. The proselytism which has only made victims and aroused so much bitterness and mistrust must give way to dialogue. . . ." [9] To the extent that a Christian seeks to use the dialogue as a tactic in missionizing for his faith, fruitful conversation with him on aspects of religious doctrine is of little efficacy. The dialogue, to be efficacious, must be a disinterested seeking for truth. Where it is but a mask for ulterior missionary motives it is bound to prove irritating. Such "dialogue" may in some instances even intensify Jewish-Christian tensions, rather than diminish them.

The interfaith dialogue, even when free of missionary impediments, remains an endeavor that calls for great wisdom and prudence on the part of those who engage in it. It can be pursued only by people who are thoroughly knowledgeable in the doctrinal and historical aspects of their faith, who themselves cherish the beliefs and sanctities of their religious heritage. Such men should likewise have a basic understanding and appreciation of their neighbors' faith. They should also be endowed with tact and moderation and know how to bear witness to the truth as they see it without being disrespectful toward those who see the truth in another light and from another perspective. The desire to promote intergroup understanding does not in itself qualify a person to meet the spokesman of another faith in dialogical confrontation.

The most efficacious scope of the interfaith dialogue will concern itself with the problems of the social order. It will center in the effort to explore and utilize the common moral insights of Judaism and Christianity toward the amelioration of the condition of man in a world that seeks to debase him and to dehumanize him. In the common endeavor to enlarge the scope of justice, to repel the irrationality that spills over into violence between man and man and nation and nation, the bonds of Jewish-Christian

[9] *Bulletin:* X:2 (Geneva: World Council of Churches; 1964), p. 29.

brotherhood will be deepened. The greatest incentive toward ideological revision is the perception that one's ideology is the nurturing ground for hostility toward those whom we have learnt to accept as our brothers, and contempt for their way of life.

Judaism entertains no ambition to displace the other religions. It sees every religion as potentially capable of rising to the dimension of universality and thus adequate to meet the spiritual needs of its adherents. The goal of Judaism is to serve the cause of such a development. It is to act, when necessary, as a leaven stimulating the religion with which it enters into a dialogical relationship "toward higher development and the elimination of their baser elements," in the words of Rabbi Kook, whom we have quoted earlier.

It is this conception of the Jewish mission which informs the Jewish attitude toward Christianity. Jews will cherish the common ground of tradition and conviction which link Judaism and Christianity to each other. They will join with Christians in a shared endeavor to ameliorate social abuses which deny their common vision of human dignity. But where Judaism finds itself in divergence from Christianity, Judaism will be itself, expressing the divergence respectfully but unequivocally. It will thereby serve the cause of its own integrity and, at the same time, render Christianity its greatest service. For the greatest service we render each other is to bear witness to the truth as we see it, that its light may shine on the dark areas of life. It is to offer one another a ministry of criticism and stimulation, through which a greater truth is born.

The conventional idiom by which Christianity has described its conception of the Jews and Judaism remains in the official language of all Christian denominations, thanks to the weight of tradition and inertia. But there are many Christians for whom this idiom no longer describes reality as they see it, and this is part of the Christian predicament in the presence of Judaism. A call to face up to the challenge which this situation involves was recently sounded by J. Coert Rylaarsdam, of the University of Chicago Divinity School. Writing in the December 1965 issue of *New City* he declared: "This mystery of an eternal Israel epitomized in our century by the Warsaw Ghetto and by the Return [the restoration of Israel] embarrasses the Christian. He resents it. As a human being it fills him with awe, pity and admiration; but it contradicts his faith. His tradition tells him that this agony of the Jew has been superfluous for two millenia. It is only a mark of Jewish pride and stubbornness; it illustrates the Jew's rejection and punishment by God. The promise is fulfilled, the sin of man has been expiated, redemption has come. The Old Covenant has been summed up in the New and those who stand in the Old without participating in the New have been tossed on the scrap pile of *Heilsgeschichte*. With respect to God's purpose they are functionally obsolete. Stripped of her commission Israel stands as a reminder of what happens to those who disobey God. The stubborn tenacity of the Jew is not a mark of his faithfulness but of his blindness.

"But Christians have begun to sense that this age-old rationale about the fate and meaning of Israel makes antisemitism inevitable. They seldom spell it out aloud today, for they are deeply troubled and penitent about the horrible human results it helped to produce. They tone it down when it comes to the surface liturgically: the ancient prayers of the Church are pruned; slurring implications are culled from curricula; and on Passion Sunday the priest, preaching on the Messianic claims of Jesus, makes a point of saying that it might have been anybody who rejected these claims, not just the Jews.

"This is all very well, as far as it goes. But it fails to come to grips with the very real fact of Judaism as a living faith today: the mystery of Israel and the embarrassment of the Warsaw Ghetto and of the Return remain. The Christian is confronted by the challenge: What think you of the Jew? Can you acknowledge the enduring validity of his claim to a divine vocation, not in your covenant, but in his? Is the faith and witness of the Jew today a mark of God's judgment, or of his faithfulness? Can you recognize the super-natural Jew and converse with him as with a peer or a brother?" [1]

Martin Buber offers us an eloquent statement as to the way Judaism and Christianity may live with one another in this

[1] "Common Ground and Difference," *New City* (December 1965), pp. 10 ff.

interim period, between the now and the time of true reconciliation which is to be part of a future consummation. Speaking before a Christian audience he said: "Your expectation is directed toward a second coming, ours to a coming which has not been anticipated by a first. To you the phrasing of world history is determined by one absolute midpoint, the year one; to us, it is an unbroken flow of tones following each other without a pause from their origin to their consummation. But we can wait for the advent of the One together, and there are moments when we may prepare the way before him together.

"Pre-messianically, our destinies are divided. Now to the Christian, the Jew is the incomprehensibly obdurate man, who declines to see what has happened; and to the Jew, the Christian is the incomprehensibly daring man, who affirms in an unredeemed world that its redemption has been accomplished. This is a gulf which no human power can bridge. But it does not prevent the common watch for a unity to come to us from God, which, soaring above all of your imagination and all of ours, affirms and denies, denies and affirms, what you hold and we hold, and which replaces all the creedal truths of earth by the ontological truth of heaven which is one.

"It behooves both you and us to hold inviolably fast to our own true faith, that is to our own deepest relationship to truth. It behooves both of us to show a religious respect for the true faith of the other. This is not what is called 'tolerance'; our task is not to tolerate each other's waywardness, but to acknowledge the real relationship in which both stand to the truth. Whenever we both, Christian and Jew, care more for God himself than for our images of God, we are united in the feeling that our Father's house is differently constructed than all our human models take it to be." [2]

[2] M. Buber: *Writings of Martin Buber*, pp. 275, 276.

Bibliography

The field of Jewish-Christian relations as conceived in the present study is broad in scope and embraces the interaction of the two communities on the sociological as well as the theological plane. A vast literature, most of it highly technical and recorded in many languages, ancient as well as modern, tells the varied aspects of this relationship. The bibliography here suggested is meant for the lay reader rather than the scholar, and it is limited to works available in English.

The basic source from which Judaism, as well as Christianity, unfolded is the Hebrew Bible. The Jewish Publication Society issued a translation of the Hebrew Bible in 1917, which was free of various mistranslations and misinterpretations that were found in the Old Testament translations used by the Protestant and Catholic churches. A new translation of the Five Books of Moses was issued by the Jewish Publication Society in 1962, under the title *The Torah*. The Five Books of Moses, including the Hebrew text and the older Jewish Publication Society translation, with an extended commentary by Dr. Joseph H. Hertz, the late Chief Rabbi of the British Empire, was issued by the Soncino Press in England in 1936. The Soncino Press has also issued (in 1950) the individual books of the Bible with commentaries and introductions, under the general editorship of A. Cohen. All these Soncino books will be helpful to the general reader.

The best edition of the Bible—both the Old and the New Testaments—under Protestant auspices is the Revised Standard Version (New York, Toronto, and Edinburgh: Thomas Nelson & Sons; 1952) and the best edition under Catholic auspices is the Confraternity Version (New York: Guild Press; 1964). These translations generally reckon with the results of Biblical scholarship, which has repudiated many older translations where Christian sectarian polemics were read into the Hebrew text. *The Interpreter's Bible* (Nashville, Tenn.: Abingdon Press; 1956), a Protestant work in twelve volumes, adds a valuable commentary and introduction to each biblical book. The *Oxford Annotated Bible* (New York: Oxford University Press; 1962) offers the Revised Standard Version of both Testaments, with succinct commentaries to each biblical book, and with brief introductions to each Testament as well as to each individual book in the two Testaments, all in one volume. The Confraternity Version is also available with introduction and commentary, offering similar aid to the Catholic community.

The *Anchor Bible* (Garden City: Doubleday & Company) is a nonsectarian work, and those books of the Bible which have already appeared show good translations, and helpful commentary and introduction. *The Book of Genesis* by E. A. Speiser (1964) is especially to be commended as a notable achievement. U. Cassuto's *From Adam to Noah*, translated from the Hebrew by Israel Abrahams (Jerusalem: Magnes Press; 1961), is a good illustration of the historic-philologic method of interpretation which have made this scholar's contribution to Bible study noteworthy. Robert Gordis is the author of a fine new translation of Ecclesiastes under the title *Kohelet, The Man and His World* (New York: Jewish Theological Seminary; 1951), and a translation of Job entitled *The Book of God and Man* (Chicago: University of Chicago Press; 1966). Both these volumes are accompanied by valuable introduction and commentary.

The Penguin Books edition of the synoptic Gospels, offering the Revised Standard Version text with the Pelican Gospel commentaries and introductory essays, are splendid achievements, which bring to bear the fruits of modern Bible scholarship on the historical aspects of the Gospel narrative, and they help bring to light the sectarian bias that guided the Gospel writers especially in dealing with the Jewish involvement in the events of the crucifixion. *Saint Matthew* is edited by J. C. Fenton, *Saint Mark* by D. E. Nineham, and *Saint Luke* by G. B. Caird (Baltimore: Penguin Books; 1963).

For the general treatment of the biblical period, the following works will be found especially helpful: John Bright's *A History of Israel* (Philadelphia: Westminster Press; 1959), W. F. Albright's *The Biblical Period from Abraham to Ezra* (New York: Harper & Row; 1963), Yehezkel Kaufmann's *The Religion of Israel,* translated and condensed from the Hebrew by Moshe Greenberg (Chicago: University of Chicago Press; 1960), H. M. Orlinsky's *Ancient Israel* (Ithaca: Cornell University Press; 1960).

Robert H. Pfeiffer's *Introduction to the Old Testament* (New York: Harper & Brothers; 1948) is an important and very readable study of the historical background, thought, and style of the Hebrew Bible. Frederick C. Grant offers us a valuable guide to the study of the New Testament in his *Ancient Judaism and the New Testament* (New York: The Macmillan Company; 1959). Gaalyahu Cornfield's *From Adam to Daniel* and *From Daniel to Paul* (New York: The Macmillan Company; 1961, 1962) are helpful companions to the study of both Testaments. One of the pioneers in reconstructing the substratum of history behind the Gospel stories was the German theologian Rudolf Bultmann. A succinct and highly readable summation of his views is available in English in his essay "The Study of the Synoptic Gospels." It is published, together with an essay by Karl Kundsin on "Primitive Christianity in the Light of Gospel Research," both translated by Frederick Grant, in a Harper Torchbook entitled *Form Criticism* (New York: Harper & Row; 1962).

There are many studies of Jesus and the rise of the early Church. Among those which reckon with the results of historical scholarship are Maurice Goguel's *Jesus and the Origins of Christianity* (New York: Harper & Row; 1962), Charles Guignebert's *The Early History of Christianity* (New York: Twayne Publishers; 1962), S. G. F. Brandon's *The Fall of Jerusalem and the Christian Church* (London: S.P.C.K.; 1957), Albert Schweitzer's *The Quest of the Historical Jesus* (New York: The Macmillan Company; 1910, 1948). A valuable contribution to this study is made by S. G. F. Brandon in the sixth chapter of his *History, Time and Deity* (New York: Barnes & Noble; 1965). Solomon Zeitlin's *Who Crucified Jesus?* (New York: Harper & Brothers; 1947) and Paul Winter's *On the Trial of Jesus* (Berlin: Walter DeGruyter & Co.; 1961) are valuable studies of the events leading up to the crucifixion. Joseph Klausner's *Jesus of Nazareth*, translated by Herbert Danby (New York: The Macmillan Company; 1953), and *From Jesus to Paul* (New York: The Macmillan Company; 1943) cite valuable material, especially from rabbinic sources, but his work does not reflect the more recent conclusions of biblical scholarship.

Bernhard W. Anderson edited a volume of essays summing up contemporary Christian thinking about the Old Testament; some of these essays are extremely valuable. The volume is entitled *The Old Testament and the Christian Faith* (New York: Harper & Row; 1963). Samuel Sandmel's *We Jews and Jesus* (New York: Oxford University Press; 1965) is a brief treatment of the life and teaching of Jesus as seen from the point of view of a leading scholar in Reform Judaism. A popular reaction to Christianity by a scholar of more traditional Jewish orientation is Trude Weiss Rosemaren's *Judaism and Christianity: The differences* (New York: Jonathan David Co.; 1943).

The state of Judaism during the formative centuries of Christianity is presented with great competence by George Foote Moore in his three-volume work, *Judaism in the First Century of the Christian Era* (Cambridge, Mass.: Harvard University Press; 1927–30). R. Travers Herford has written a lucid interpretation of Pharisaism in his *The Pharisees* (New York: The Macmillan Company; 1924). Herford is also the author of a work that explores the references to Christianity in rabbinic literature under the title *Christianity in Talmud and Midrash* (London: William & Norgate; 1903).

Dr. Louis Finkelstein, Chancellor of The Jewish Theological Seminary, who has made vital contributions to the Jewish-Christian understanding by his initiative in the sponsorship of the Institute for Religious and Social Studies and the Conference on Science, Philosophy and Religion, is also the author of several works that help to elucidate the classic epoch in Judaism: *The Pharisees*, a two-volume work published by the Jewish Publication Society in 1938 and reissued in revised form in 1962; and *Akiba: Scholar, Saint and Martyr*, published by Covici-Friede in 1936. He also edited a two-volume work, *The Jews: Their History, Culture and Religion.* This consists of forty-two essays by leading scholars on the historical as well as contemporary aspects of Judaism. It was published by Harper & Row, and the third edition was issued in 1960.

Professor Salo W. Baron, under whom I was privileged to study Jewish history at Columbia University, is the author of the most important modern history of the Jews and Judaism, *A Social and Religious History of the Jews* (New York: Columbia University Press; 1957). Of the second revised edition of this work ten volumes have appeared thus far, the first two of which offer the most comprehensive treatment of the Jewish-Christian encounter. The first volume begins the Jewish odyssey and carries it to the beginning of the Christian era, and the second is devoted to the first five centuries of the Christian era.

The relations between Judaism and Christianity are explored in Leo Baeck's *Judaism and Christianity*, translated from the German by W. Kaufmann (Philadelphia: Jewish Publication Society; 1958), Martin Buber's *Two Types of Faith* (New York: Harper & Row; 1961), James Parkes's *Foundations of Judaism and Christianity* (Chicago: Quadrangle Books; 1960) and Abba Hillel Silver's *Where Judaism Differed* (Philadelphia: Jewish Publication Society; 1957). Two works by James Parkes, *Anti-Semitism—A Concise World History* (Chicago: Quadrangle Books; 1964) and *The Conflict of the Church and the Synagogue* (New York: Meridian Books; 1961), are helpful studies of Jewish-Christian tensions, with due recognition of the role played by Christian teaching in the formation of anti-Jewish prejudice. *The Teaching of Contempt* by Jules Isaac, translated from French by H. Weaver (New York: Holt, Rinehart & Winston; 1964) played an important role in challenging Christian statesmanship to re-examine—and correct—the role of conventional Christian doctrine in fostering anti-Semitism. Bernhard E. Olson's *Faith and Prejudice* (New Haven, Conn.: Yale University Press; 1963) explores the roots of prejudice in the conventional teachings of religion. A more recent study of contemporary anti-Semitism as affected by Christian teaching is *Christian Beliefs and Anti-Semitism* by Charles Y. Glock and Rodney Stark (New York: Harper & Row; 1966). This is the first volume in a series based on the University of California Five-Year Study of Anti-Semitism in the United States being conducted by the Survey Research Center under a grant from the Anti-Defamation League of B'nai B'rith.

Index

A Note About the Author

BEN ZION BOKSER was ordained as Rabbi by the Jewish Theological Seminary in 1931. He received his general education at the College of the City of New York where he took his B.A. in 1928, and at Columbia University where he took his M.A. in 1930 and his Ph.D. in 1933. In 1964 the Seminary awarded him an honorary degree of Doctor of Divinity. He held pulpits in the Bronx, New York, and in Vancouver, British Columbia, and has been Rabbi of the Forest Hills Jewish Center since 1933. During World War II he served as a chaplain in the United States Army for a period of two years. In addition to his service in the active rabbinate, Dr. Bokser also serves as a member of the faculty of the Rabbinical School of the Jewish Theological Seminary and as program editor of the Seminary's "Eternal Light" radio program. Rabbi Bokser is the author of eight other books; one, *Judaism: Profile of a Faith*, also published by Alfred A. Knopf, was awarded a citation by the Jewish Book Council of America as the most significant work in Jewish thought to appear in 1963. Rabbi and Mrs. Bokser have a son and a daughter and they make their home in Forest Hills, New York.

A Note on the Type

The text of this book was set on the Linotype in Janson, a recutting made direct from type cast from matrices long thought to have been made by the Dutchman Anton Janson, who was a practicing type founder in Leipzig during the years 1668-87. However, it has been conclusively demonstrated that these types are actually the work of Nicholas Kis (1650-1702), a Hungarian, who most probably learned his trade from the master Dutch type founder Kirk Voskens. The type is an excellent example of the influential and sturdy Dutch types that prevailed in England up to the time William Caslon developed his own incomparable designs from these Dutch faces. This book was composed, printed, and bound by H. Wolff Book Manufacturing Co., New York.